THE MATERIAL, THE REAL, AND THE FRACTURED SELF:
SUBJECTIVITY AND REPRESENTATION
FROM RIMBAUD TO RÉDA

The Material, the Real, and the Fractured Self

Subjectivity and Representation from Rimbaud to Réda

Susan Harrow

UNIVERSITY OF TORONTO PRESS
Toronto Buffalo London

© University of Toronto Press Incorporated 2004
Toronto Buffalo London
Printed in Canada

ISBN 0-8020-8722-1

University of Toronto Romance series

Printed on acid-free paper

National Library of Canada Cataloguing in Publication

Harrow, Susan
    The material, the real, and the fractured self : subjectivity and
representation from Rimbaud to Réda / Susan Harrow.

    (University of Toronto romance series)
    Includes bibliographical references and index.
    ISBN 0-8020-8722-1 (bound)

    1. French poetry – 20th century – History and criticism.   2. French
poetry – 19th century – History and criticism.   3. Modernism
(Literature) – France.   I. Title.   II. Series.

    PQ441.H37 2004   841'.9109   C2004-900890-0

University of Toronto Press acknowledges the financial assistance to
its publishing program of the Canada Council for the Arts and the
Ontario Arts Council.

University of Toronto Press acknowledges the financial support for
its publishing activities of the Government of Canada through the
Book Publishing Industry Development Program (BPIDP).

Contents

Acknowledgments   vii

Introduction   3

1 Debris, Mess, and the Modernist Self:
   Rimbaud from *Poésies* to the *Illuminations*   11

2 Material Fragments, Autobiographical Fantasy:
   Reading Apollinaire's *Calligrammes*   62

3 From Culture Critique to Poetic Capital:
   Ponge's Things-in-Language   113

4 Sweeping the (Sub)urban Savannah:
   Everyday Culture and the Rédean Sublime   164

Summations, Speculations   217

Notes   225
Bibliography   257
Index   263

Acknowledgments

The writing of this book was completed during a period of research leave granted by the University of Wales Swansea, and extended by the Arts and Humanities Research Board of Great Britain. I am grateful for their invaluable support.

Part of chapter 2, which appeared in article form, is reprinted by kind permission of the editors of *Modern Language Review*.

Monsieur Jacques Réda responded generously to my questions, and I thank him most warmly.

I am indebted to Jean Duffy, André Guyon, and Andrew Rothwell for their active support. Francis Clarke found elegant solutions to textual and technical problems. For her many kindnesses, I thank Margaret Gray in Bloomington. For suggestions and expressions of encouragement, I am grateful to Michael Sheringham, Edward Hughes, and Johnnie Gratton. It is a pleasure to acknowledge those who made it possible for me to present earlier versions of this work at conferences held in Philadelphia, Urbana-Champaign, Glasgow, and Tallahassee: Lawrence Schehr, Keith Reader, and Pamela Genova. Research grants from the British Academy and the Department of French at Swansea are gratefully acknowledged.

Jill McConkey was a receptive, responsive editor; it was my great fortune to work with her.

My parents, Ann and Alex Harrow, have been hugely supportive, always; special thanks go to them. Finally, Francis – for sharing your magical mappings (Pralognan with Ponge, rue Didot with Réda) – this book is for you.

THE MATERIAL, THE REAL, AND THE FRACTURED SELF

Introduction

Research in the humanities continues to probe modern and postmodern subjectivity from a variety of perspectives – postcolonial, feminist, psychoanalytical, sociological, new historical. Where the purer forms of deconstructionist thinking plotted to abolish the human subject, new approaches – in history, ethnography, autobiography theory, psychoanalysis, and gender studies – have worked to recover fictions of experience and retrieve dispersed narratives of the self. The emergence of a self constituted in language, at once shaped by and straining against material, historical, cultural, and linguistic containments, has revealed the fertile relation of contemporary theory to literary narrative in particular. Certainly, in French studies, theoretical approaches to subjectivity have been guided almost exclusively towards the novel, where their impact has, in some areas, been discipline-defining: I am thinking of the contribution of visual theory and psychoanalysis to Proust studies, of feminist theory to Duras, and of the influence of autobiography theory across the spectrum of first-person narrative. These are some of the signal beneficiaries of theory's migrations. Poetry, however, as a genre, has been singularly marginalized in applications of contemporary theory. This book addresses that marginalization, putting contemporary theory to work on modern and modernist poetry. In pragmatic ways, I aim to show how new approaches to subjectivity – deriving primarily from autobiography theory, gender studies, cultural history, and visual theory – can open fresh critical perspectives on the writing of four major French poets of the modernist tradition.

My purpose in writing this book is to explore the intriguing interrelation of subjectivity and materiality in the post-Baudelairean lyric, specifically in the poetry and related writings of Arthur Rimbaud, Guillaume

Apollinaire, Francis Ponge, and Jacques Réda. I was drawn to these poets specifically because their writing combines a problematic (and problematizing) exploration of subjectivity with a resolute commitment to outwardness, a passion for what Rimbaud called 'rugged reality.' On the face of it, Réda's embrace of *l'impersonnel* and Rimbaud's demand for *poésie objective*, Ponge's immersion in a world of 'natural' things, and Apollinaire's hailing of modernism as a sublimely objective *art de dissection*, energetically deny – or, at least, displace – the concept of pre-formed subjecthood. Yet, as humanistic models of subjecthood are dismantled or displaced in the writing of these poets, so subjectivity as a process – pliant and permeable – is drawn into material frames of reference and representation. It is this crossover or coincidence of materiality and subjectivity that is the focus of my study.

The material frames that connect Rimbaud, Apollinaire, Ponge, and Réda are themselves multifarious and overlapping: they take in culture and commodity, physical objects and everyday practices, the city and the natural environment, beauty and colour, debris and mess, sensation and perception. Material frames are shaped by human actions and transformative desire (transitive desire, for Ponge); in turn they shape affect in the form of pleasure and pressure, anxiety and elation. Wherever materiality and subjectivity are deeply, reciprocally imbricated, the body emerges as an exquisitely receptive interface between self and world. The tendency of the body to make its presence felt acutely, urgently, in the writing of the four poets has led me to pay particular attention to the body's expressivity, to its narrative possibilities. I see my insistence on the body's insistence as contributing to righting a wrong, for the body has been accorded too little attention in poetry studies, its fluctuating, fractured fate viewed as the natural preoccupation, preserve even, of narrative fiction.

My study is driven by key questions concerning the correspondence between subjectivity and the 'real,' the cluster of signs – hard objects, language, culture, contingency, individuality, desire, art, ideology – by which the self comes into being. I will be asking how this relation is represented in the poetry of Rimbaud, Apollinaire, Ponge, and Réda. Is it feasible to talk about 'fictions of a self-in-the-world' or a 'self-in-things'? If so, how does self-formative activity, with its drive to recovery, narrative integrity, and representation, resist the processes of dislocation and fragmentation at the heart of modernism's structural and formal experiment? Any study of modernism has to be equally alert to the coincidence or the collision of thematic content and formal structure. In the work of each poet, I will pay particular attention to how the language of materiality rolls into the materiality of language. By the 'materiality of language,' I mean the performative aspects of poetic language, poetry's sense of itself as productively disruptive both of external formations – taste, normative beauty, readerly assumptions – and of its own internal structures. In this respect, the writing of the four poets takes forth modernism's urge to contest and to fracture stable formations, to destabilize pre-formed meanings, to embrace provisionality as the proper structural or stylistic response to the variable relief map of human consciousness contoured by the alternately alienating and exhilarating experience of material modernity.

Rimbaud, Apollinaire, and Ponge are canonical figures on university French poetry programs.[1] Canonical foundations, however, are notoriously prone to shift and redefinition. In recent years, Rimbaud's star, at least in English-language criticism and in the conference forum, has been eclipsed by that of Mallarmé, who is perhaps judged, paradoxically given his difficulty, a poet more in touch with our dispassionate, commitedly apolitical, textually absorbed era. Yet, lately, Rimbaud's critical fortunes have begun to change: insightful studies by Steve Murphy and Kristin Ross, and, more recently, Graham Robb's marvellous, textually informed biography of the poet have revealed Rimbaud for a new generation. It is to Rimbaud as a radical appraiser of culture and nature, sexuality and writing, mess and modernity, that I devote my opening chapter. In making an integral reading of Rimbaud from *Poésies* through *Une Saison en enfer* to the *Illuminations*, I have taken a middle way, in contradistinction to the tendency of Rimbaud critics (particularly in France) to favour either the weighty single-author monograph or short articles devoted to the elucidation of obscurities or influences, or to the tracking of a particular motif.

Canonical constructions tend to rise, precipitately, from a narrow baseline. Apollinaire's reputation is founded on *Alcools* (1913), yet scant critical attention is paid to the fertile crossover from *Alcools* to the poet's most intense experimentalist period of 1912–14, represented in the *Ondes* sequence of *Calligrammes* (1918). The opening-up of the war poetry of *Calligrammes* to a broader readership is overdue: in its hybridity, its mixing of the real and the phantasmatic, the personal and the collective, autobiography and history, technology and memory, Apollinaire's war poetry offers rich possibilities for today's readers alert to the negotiation of identity and the imbrication of violence and desire.

Ponge seems forever cast in the mould of a 'poet of things,' his work before or after the seminal *Le Parti pris des choses* (1942) dimly known beyond the world of specialists. My study builds on current interest in Ponge studies, but focuses on the underexplored territory of subjectivity, offering an integrated discussion of the writer's poetry, art criticism, and related writings. In my broad reading of Ponge, I want to factor in the poet's engagement with culture, and build textual bridges between Ponge the satirist and Ponge the searcher for perceptual and poetic beauty.

To date, Jacques Réda, one of France's foremost contemporary poets, stands independent of the academic canon. His work, particularly since *Les Ruines de Paris* (1977), has attracted intense critical interest in France, but English-language studies of Réda, with the exception of a series of illuminating essays by Michael Sheringham, are scarce.[2] Réda's remapping of the tradition of urban poetics makes his work an inviting, underexplored terrain.

In broad terms, the poets studied here represent major *étapes* in the definition and generation of poetic modernity since Baudelaire, and for that reason I have chosen to read across the century's (indeed centuries') divide, a crossing that critics are strangely reluctant to make, as if to do so were at once to pay too much attention and not enough to historical change.[3] While my choice of the corpus of four poets is too restrictive, indeed too subjective, to provide a broad diachronic reading of the development of modern and modernist poetry in French, my aim in examining the textual practices of these four poets is to nourish a sense of the variety of modernist responses to problems of subjectivity and the representation of materiality. The conclusions from this study have to be situated relative to the structural and substantive developments in modern aesthetics occurring since 1870; that wide-angled contextual reading would demand another book. The scope of the present book is more narrowly defined: a series of independent, though interrelated readings, each of which is devoted to a specific corpus of texts. To this end, I will indicate retrospective and prospective connections, identifying shared critical preoccupations and convergent tropes: the culture critique that relates Rimbaud to Ponge, the representation of material practices that connects Apollinaire and Réda, and the link back from Réda to Rimbaud in the form of debris-sifting and the sublimity of colour-work.

Chapter 1 proposes an integrated reading of Rimbaud's poetry from *Poésies* to *Une Saison en enfer* and the *Illuminations*. In the tortured metaphysical autobiography *Une Saison en enfer*, the rush to embrace 'la réalité rugueuse' is usually read as a consequence of the retreat from the visionary project. Taking issue with this view, I argue here that the embrace of material asperity is integral to Rimbaud's poetry from the outset. I begin by mapping the relations between subjectivities and the socio-cultural and ideological structures informing aesthetics, politics, social class, love, memory, religion, and the body. I show how the material and the particular – a wall besmirched, a patina smudged, a fragment of torn fabric – provide an index of individual crisis or cultural breakdown. Signalled by sudden colour saturation, the deep graining of texture, or a strident auditory signal, consciousness – anxious, exasperated, or exhilarated – is revealed at work on the surface of things. Even as the visionary poetry aspires to the sublime point at which writing would rip free of its material moorings ('Le Bateau ivre'), the exasperation of metaphysical longing forces the splintered self to confront the material in its most acutely embodied forms: in scenarios of flayed corporeality and physical dereliction, and in the urgent – ecstatic or anxious – activity of self-recovery amid the debris of history and fantasy, culture and consciousness. Throughout this chapter I consider the forward momentum of Rimbaud's project, and its implications for the poetry of Apollinaire, Ponge, and Réda. Prospective links from Rimbaud to the writing of the other poets are provided by the critique of the ideology of modernity (Apollinaire, Ponge, Réda), phantasmatic work on the body (Apollinaire, Ponge), material saturation and perceptual alteration (Ponge, Réda), and self as fictional or autobiographical construct (Apollinaire, Réda).

Apollinaire's poetry is a striking example of modernist writing engaging with the material world – in peacetime and in war – and exploring its representability in the flux of subjectivity. *Calligrammes*, Apollinaire's second major volume of poetry, illustrates most urgently the tension between the material and the subjective as the modernist consciousness grapples to make sense of a technologically challenging new world, both in its exhilarating potential and in the pressures it exerts across the range of human experience and activity. In chapter 2, I focus initially on the tensions that criss-cross Apollinaire's writing from *Alcools* (1913) to *Calligrammes* (1918), before embarking on a close reading of the paradoxical modernism of the opening *Ondes* sequence of *Calligrammes*. With its glittering tropes of technology, communications, travel, and commodities, relayed through fractured structures, Apollinaire's poetry makes its most pressing claim to 'objectivity.' And yet, even as the 'objective' brilliance of these texts works to obscure subjectivity, the process seems to reverse itself and shower their material outwardness with sparks of self-expressivity. The surge towards the contemporary and empirical is rivalled by an acute awareness of social dislocation, loss of familiarity, and the dispersal of self. Thus Apollinaire's poetry reveals a characteristically modernist tendency to dialogize contrastive assessments of the material world. The fracturing scepticism and self-questioning of Apollinaire's writing are closer to the rich, uncertain fluctuations of Eliot than to the flat-line fervour of Marinetti. Drawing on perspectives offered by Barthes and by cultural theory, I show how the persistence of the ordinary and the marginal asserts the compelling hybridity of everyday life, and intimates the hopes and desires, the habits and practices enfolded in familiar objects.

The historical dislocation caused by the First World War challenges the ahistoricity of modernist writing. The dazzling deployment of experimentalist values of spatiality, synchronicity, and self-reflexivity in the pre-war *Ondes* series is now confronted by demands for the moral absolutes ('History,' 'Truth') to which modernism is reputedly resistant. I argue that Apollinaire's war poetry negotiates these competing pressures via an autobiographical project that situates the fiction of the writing-written self in the nexus of a subjective, provisional 'histoire.' This self-writing project both confirms and challenges the key assumptions of contemporary autobiography theory (Eakin, Lejeune). I focus on the relationship of the writing-written self to the signs (hard objects, language, male homosocial culture, individuality, ideology, desire, and dream-work) by which that self comes into being.

In Ponge's world of texts brimming with 'things,' the dreaming, desiring, undecidable self of modern sensibility has seemed singularly absent. In chapter 3, I address this blind spot in Ponge criticism. My study begins with Ponge's bleak reflection on the human situation under conditions of enforced modernity in *Douze petits écrits* (1926). Here, deep dysphoria induced by ossified language and atrophying routine extends Rimbaud's vision of a levelled metropolis, and anticipates Henri Lefebvre's fractured 'subcultures.' I argue that the culture critique emerging in these texts has profound connections with Ponge's subsequent writing, for it exposes, through the standardizing structures of economic and social modernity, a crisis of subjectivity that seeks its corrective in the particularity of material things and in the folds of language. I go on to show how Ponge's poetry and his other writing – art criticism, literary essays, (auto)biography – rally the constituents of a richer subjectivity against a world where the clamour of discourses stifles the 'voix du plus précieux' ('Pas et le saut,' *Proêmes*). Ponge's writing proposes a remedy for diminished subjectivity in voluptuous receptivity to material forms of knowledge. Ordinary objects, in their affecting singularity, call forth extraordinary acts of retrieval and discovery; they urge us to retrospective action – to recover what has been depleted – and they move us prospectively to open up fresh perceptual and lexical seams. The fuller perceptual attention turned on the habitually overlooked object finds its reward in beauty, surprise, joy, learning, and recognition – forms of subjective regeneration that unfold in the deep texture of analogy. The desire to capture in language the rush of consciousness at the point of material contact with the world generates analogy and allegory. As the poem affirms the impossibility of ever definitively possessing its object, materially or linguistically, it begins to unfold its fantasy of overcoming that incapacity through the generative activity of description. Analogies mime the movement of consciousness in a rush of brilliant leaps or in the patient, persistent effort of approximation.

Ranging widely across Réda's urban and suburban poetry from *Les Ruines de Paris* (1977) to *Accidents de la circulation* (2001), chapter 4 examines the passionate materiality of a poet who holds up to view the multifarious fabric of everyday life: human exchanges, economic rituals and cultural practices, and the physical objects shaping and shaped by these practices. My reading of Réda's artisans of the everyday is informed by post-*Annales* theories of cultural history. I move on to trace the resolute outwardness of Réda's project to its source in excursive desire, and focus on the body as a seam of contact between self and world. The relationality between sentient self and non-sentient world is revealed in moments of intense contact with things, contact that takes the form of empathy, irony, surprise, and humour. I pay particular attention to the body's kinetic modes (jumping, leaping, walking, travelling, Solex-riding) and to the coincidence of patterns of physical and textual pliancy in a discussion that draws on Certeau's description of 'rhétoriques cheminatoires.' I extend these considerations to the practice of gleaning, an intensely subjective form of contact with material things that plays across the divide between material recuperation and poetic recycling. Réda's narratives of gleaning are illuminated in the comparative discussion of issues raised in Agnès Varda's documentary film *Les Glaneurs et la glaneuse* (2000). Material things offer pockets of subjective and cultural resistance, and bring regeneration in writing where tensions are not resolved but constantly reactivated through structuring oxymoron (luxuriant dereliction; obsolescent opulence;

everyday exoticism; bourgeois ascendancy as a phenomenon of flattening). Taking forward this model of creative tension and textual pliancy,
I look at how Réda works his taut magic between the material and the
sublime, as the action of delving deep into the minutiae of the human
and the material is transposed into a reach for the rarefied. I explore
Réda's colourist expressivity in terms of depersonalized subjectivity
captured in moments of mesmerizing, violating intensity. Visual rarefaction in Réda is related to a tradition, traced throughout this book,
that connects Rimbaud's visionary writing, Apollinaire's *surnaturalisme*
and writerly fantasy, and Ponge's strange beauty in things.

1 Debris, Mess, and the Modernist Self: Rimbaud from *Poésies* to the *Illuminations*

Brimming and brilliant, Rimbaud's poetry is breathtaking in its expansiveness and mesmerizing in its intensity. Passionately outward-looking, his poetry encompasses history, society, nature, art, geography, aesthetics, the body, religion, revolution, politics, myth, mess, and urban modernity. At the same time, the teeming vividness and raw energy of Rimbaud's writing bear an affective charge that is revealed in energized descriptions of colour, light, surface, and texture. In Rimbaud's dazzling mix of thematic capaciousness and verbal concentration, the self emerges at once fractured and extendible, fissiparous and boundless, quivering and blasting: this radically uncentred subjectivity, formed in the pressured and pleasurable displacements of language, reminds us why 'JE est un autre' has become a rallying cry for modernism and a tenet of postmodern poetics and identity politics.[1]

I begin by situating the concept of subjectivity in terms of Rimbaud's theoretical positions, and relative to the questions of materiality that underpin this study.[2] The proposition 'JE est un autre' announces the poet's rejection of the stable, coherent subject of humanistic assumption, and asserts his challenge to Cartesian recuperations of cognitive agency. The disjunctive syntax of the proposition calls urgent attention to the constitution of self in language, a process spectacularly dramatized in Rimbaud's modernist autobiographical narrative *Une Saison en enfer*.[3] In the second of the iconic *voyant* letters of May 1871, addressed to Paul Demeny, Rimbaud elucidates his enigmatic proposition by envisioning the act of consciousness as a performance materializing in sensations of sight and sound: 'Je est un autre. Si le cuivre s'éveille clairon, il n'y a rien de sa faute. Cela m'est évident: j'assiste à l'éclosion de ma pensée: je la regarde, je l'écoute: je lance un coup d'archet: la symphonie fait son remuement dans les profondeurs, ou vient d'un bond sur la scène.'[4] Rimbaud stresses analytical self-detachment as formative of a modernist, visionary project in which thought erupts and is instantly transposed into visual and acoustic perceptions. There is here a sense of self, first as other, formed in the perpetual displacements of language, and subsequently as a mental process materialized. While the possessive instance stresses cognitive authority ('ma pensée'), the construction of thought as a perceptual event experienced from the outside performs syntactically the self-objectification to which 'JE est un autre' alludes, and which comes forth in Rimbaud's poetry in representations of the body, sensation, colour, atmosphere, nature, objects, and debris. *Une Saison en enfer* offers an illustration of this when the narrator recalls his childhood admiration for the irredeemable prisoner, defiant and mentally unbounded: 'je voyais *avec son idée* le ciel bleu et le travail fleuri de la campagne; je flairais sa fatalité dans les villes' ('Mauvais sang'). Every subjectivity is permeable and intersubjective, formed in the migration between perceptual work and interpretative activity: 'voir avec une idée'; 'flairer une fatalité.'

The disintegration of the unitary ideal of a retrievable crystalline self induces a yearning for what cannot be grasped or set down, and is rendered by the slippage between pronouns ('je' / 'il'), or by the brusque displacement of one voice or vision by another in the *Illuminations*. When thought materializes as a sensation or perception ('je la regarde, je l'écoute'), the body emerges as the interface between self and world, consciousness and its objects, the mind and its socio-cultural configurations. States of consciousness, both euphoric and disenchanted, are corporealized in the rush of sensations across the skin, the quickening of the flesh, the eruption of colour or sound, or the 'wounding' of fabric. Bringing to language perceptual experience at its meliorative and aversive extremes is integral, I would argue, to the goal of 'poésie objective,' which Rimbaud outlines in his first *lettre du voyant*, to Georges Izambard, on 13 May 1871.[5] How, though, do we reconcile the implications of 'poésie objective' with Rimbaud's tumultuous lyricism, for his passionate, exasperated poetry is the antithesis of impersonal expression and 'objectivity'?

Perplexingly, in his letter to Izambard, Rimbaud offers no definition or description of 'poésie objective,' but implicitly he contrasts its vigour and viability with Izambard's wan sentimentalist efforts, scornfully dismissing the latter as 'poésie subjective [...] fadasse.' Rimbaud's 'poésie objective,' far from being a call to neutrality or impersonality, can be understood as an attempt to seize self in the migration between material and mental worlds. Plunging into the deep texture of things, capturing the glimmer of chromatic reflection, relishing mud and muck, or reconstructing verbal fragments in anticipation of cubism, Rimbaud's poetry is formed at the confluence of the language of materiality and the materiality of language. Through the intense, uneven experience of material things and their verbal representation, Rimbaud charts the trajectory of the mind as it veers between exhilaration and despair.

My aim in this chapter is to explore the conjunction of materiality and subjectivity in Rimbaud's principal verse and prose poetry. Taking forward, together, those defining qualities of expansiveness and intensity, I begin with the early poems (*Poésies*), move through *Une Saison en enfer*, and conclude with the *Illuminations* and related visionary poems.[6] I want to map – in broad terms – the trajectory of Rimbaud's poetry as it evolves from the language of materiality (*Poésies*) to the materiality of language (the *Illuminations*). First, it is necessary to mark out the three main phases of Rimbaud's poetic adventure.

1. *Poésies*   The early poetry is full of the litter of perceptual experience: clothes, furniture, architecture, food, human actions and gestures, body and skin, weather, wounds, plants and flowers, sounds and smells, artefacts, colours, mess and stains. The material is a site of human affect, attracting and generating appraisal, love, revolt, pathos, disgust, defiance, bitterness, passion, loathing, empathy, and irony.

Rimbaud's critical exploration of social realities and cultural structures reveals a self pressured and stimulated, at once contained and straining against containment. Materializing in the form of arresting colour sensation, the intense gleam of a patina, a nauseating smell, an arousing breeze, or an acute acoustic signal, consciousness – in its scathing or exhilarated eruptions – is captured at work on the surface of things or deep within their substance. James Lawler's assertion that 'Le Bateau ivre' 'flaunts the body and colour of sensation' can be applied to the range of the early poetry, for it is here that Rimbaud brings to language the lushness of visual sensation or the visceral intensity of smell.[7] Enthralled attention to the material and the particular is, as Yves Bonnefoy affirms, a feature of the earlier poems that carries over into the visionary phase: 'Depuis longtemps [Rimbaud] avait recherché dans le regard quotidien, les phosphènes du fantastique. Le poète de sept ans, pour obtenir la Vision, écrasait son oeil darne; et le goût exprimé dans "Sensation" et ailleurs pour les boissons tiédies, l'odeur des prés mouillés, la puanteur des ruelles révélait la plus ardente attention, déjà, à tout ce qui trahit dans la figure des choses le travail d'une obscure intériorité.'[8]

The material *prégnance* of the early Rimbaud evokes an intense relationship between subjectivity and the world, between the experience of
things and the struggle to bring that experience to language. The quickening of a consciousness keenly receptive to cultural, aesthetic, corporeal, erotic, religious, or political formations is brought forth in vivid,
vitalizing representations of perceptual material. Rimbaud captures
the acuity of perception in the eruptive and the fractured: in splinters
of colour ('les crachats rouges de la mitraille'), in darting sensation ('le
soleil [...] / Lui darde une migraine'), in indiscriminate clutter ('fouillis
de vieilles vieilleries'), in dry crackling sounds ('leurs doigts électriques
et doux / Font crépiter [...] / Sous leurs ongles royaux la mort des
petits poux').[9]

2. *Une Saison en enfer* is an extended metaphor for the agony of self-
examination. It is the narrative of the tortured confrontation of the
speaker (and the reader) with the constituents of a subjectivity dispersed across the planes of human thought and action. Rimbaud's
poetic autobiography is radically unsettling because its tortured self-
scrutiny ('me connais-je?') gnaws at the reader's precarious sense of
self. Where, in *Poésies*, the poet had placed, under the magnifying glass,
social class, sexuality, the family, nature, catholicism, art, aesthetics, and
poetry itself, in *Une Saison* he turns to examine the ripped fabric of
subjectivity. Withdrawing – or, at least, appearing to withdraw – from
contemporary social and cultural structures, the poet retreats into symbolic material in a narrative impelled by self-writing desire. The self-
sequestering principle of *Une Saison* marks a signal departure from
Poésies in that the material of identity-formation is less physical and
perceptual than psychic and phantasmatic. In the hellish hall of mirrors, the material frames that shaped *Poésies* – religion, family, sexuality,
the city, work, poetry, love, society, science, culture, history – disintegrate into a mass – or a mess – of haphazardly gathered memory
fragments. *Une Saison* stages the failure of subjectivity to coalesce,
anticipating the processes of scattering and re-forming that will emerge
in the proto-cubist compositions of the *Illuminations*. What interests me
here is that, at its symbolic extreme, the psychic drama of *Une Saison en
enfer* tends to re-materialize in visions of flesh: scrofulous, spurned,
writhing, and abject. Hell is a metaphor for the crisis of self-recognition.

3. *Illuminations*   Their breathtaking virtuosity notwithstanding, the abstract visionary quality of the *Illuminations* (and of the verse poems

'Voyelles' and 'Le Bateau ivre,' which anticipate them) invites a more disinterested, cooler interpretative activity than *Une Saison en enfer*. The work of bringing the material world to language in the early poetry would appear to be reversed in the *Illuminations* by the drive to materialize consciousness, to track visionary creativity in the sublime metaphors of construction and devastation, inauguration and chaos. If the unbounded visionary poetry appears to abolish empirical referentiality, Rimbaud's passion for the particular surges in his extraordinary attention to colour, surface, texture, and process. The fate of the real in the visionary Rimbaud is to be absorbed and refracted in the glimmers of material detail illuminating non-coalescent structures. This is the context in which I consider how the visionary poetry takes forward the socio-cultural critique of *Poésies* in the proto-cubist representation of urban space.

For all its abstractive purity and uncanny beauty, there is no anaesthetizing detachment in the *Illuminations*: rather there is a desire to represent perceptual and oneiric experience in opulent image-streams, in eruptions of violence-saturated colour, or in descriptions of movement fractured by desire and uncertainty. My argument is that subjectivity is not absent in the *Illuminations*; rather it is submerged and resurfaces in sporadic, discontinuous visions, illuminating the conscious preoccupations of a constantly re-forming self. My reading acknowledges Leo Bersani's contention that the *Illuminations* are Rimbaud's attempt to move beyond Western values of depth and complexity by subverting the concept of a settled, coalescent subjectivity. However, Bersani's emphasis on the semiotic emptiness of the prose poetry ('[the mind has] broken up its contents into meaningless pieces. At the very most those pieces are merely available for new relations') would appear to be challenged by eruptions of subjective affect.[10] I consider how these eruptions shape reader formations in poetry that reflects on the making and the reading of poetry. I focus on how narrator and reader positions coincide at material sites of anxiety or exhilaration as visionary language at once stimulates and resists attempts to fashion verbal debris into meaningful complexes.

Poésies: Material Encounters

In the tortured metaphysical autobiography *Une Saison en enfer*, the rush to 'rugged reality' ('la réalité rugueuse') is usually read as signalling the retreat from the visionary project and announcing a precipitate new departure. In fact it marks a return, for the real and the material, in their unevenness and eruptive quality, are a passionate concern of Rimbaud from the outset. Rimbaud's embrace of physical asperity in *Une Saison* reminds us of the stubborn, messy qualities of the real, and of the capacity of dirt and debris to disrupt every effort to smooth and reify the world. In the early poetry (*Poésies*), the material and the particular – a wall besmirched, a smudge of colour, a fragment of torn fabric – signal a fresh alertness to the coincidence of subjectivity and the world.

In 'Le Forgeron,' a poetic critique of autocracy and inequality written at the declaration of the Franco-Prussian war, which morphs Napoleon III into Louis XVI, the physical world bears the soiled and soiling traces of the political desire to make a mark, a desire materialized in the 'veste sale' of the poor that is dragged along the gilded furnishings of the Tuileries, or, in the words of the blacksmith, in the spewing, foaming fury of the people: '"C'est la Crapule, / Sire. Ça bave aux murs, ça monte, ça pullule."'[11] The Bastille's 'murs lépreux qui [...] racontaient tout' underscore the semiotic charge of material surfaces, while the diatribe (against the king, against the emperor) culminates with the hurling of the Phrygian bonnet from the same blacksmith's hand, described as 'large et superbe de crasse.' Repeatedly, the metonymics of mess becomes a metaphor for the disruption of class boundaries by the political underclass; it is a sign of the positive reclaiming of dirt that drives the project of cultural, subjective, and poetic renewal, and surfaces in 'Les Poètes de sept ans' and 'Vénus Anadyomène,' and later in *Une Saison en enfer*.[12]

Throughout the early poetry, the process of rubbing up against the world, marking it, and carrying away its imprint is linked to the making and the relishing of mess. This is most vivid in the 'bohemian' narratives, the poetic *robinsonnades* ('Roman') inspired by Rimbaud's travels in Belgium in the summer of 1870. Propelled by excursive desire, the worn boots of the bouncing bohemian reveal the traces of a productive friction between self and the world. The used and the worn are signs of the wearing of self against material surfaces, a process whose desirability is reaffirmed in 'Bannières de mai' (*Vers nouveaux*): 'Je veux bien que les saisons *m'usent* / A toi, Nature, je me rends; / Et ma faim et toute ma soif / Et, s'il te plaît, nourris, abreuve' (my emphasis). The active, even hyperactive outwardness of Rimbaud's project has its origin in the desire to put down the burden of solipsis and, through pleasurable corporeal risk-taking ('Si un rayon me blesse / Je succomberai sur la mousse'), to find affective fulfilment ('[être] moins seul et moins nul').

Like his shoelaces and his creative urge, the roving poet of 'Ma bohème' is incredibly sprung, his boundless yearning captured in exclamation and impassioned repetition ('Oh! là! là!'). His tattered clothes betoken freedom and the pleasure of unbinding. Holes and tears, patches and mismatches, disrupt the smooth fabric of things; they are signs of the 'injuring' of human perfectibility, the wounding of social convention. The young poet's sartorial dereliction ('poches crevées,' 'culotte [à] large trou,' 'souliers blessés') signals affirmative mess-making as he actively engages with material things, and lets the world in. As he rummages and dreams, relishes and writes, so the world etches itself upon him, leaves its imprint on worn fabric. This reciprocal wearing and tearing maps metaphorically to a readiness to strip away layers of selfhood in order to achieve a state of optimal receptivity to the exterior world. Graham Robb reminds us that Rimbaud's Belgium travels are consciously formative, a method for learning and expanding awareness, a deliberate project rather than a spontaneous flight.[13] Robb's touching portrait of the poet's tenderness for his feet reaffirms the body as an exasperatingly uneven, but invariably productive, seam of contact between self and world: 'in his rancorous relationship with his own body, his [...] feet had always been the favoured exception: a means of escape and contact with a solid earth – almost little Arthurs in their own right, deserving of comfort and respect.'[14] 'Ma bohème' captures the quickening of the relation between the material world and the wanderer's poetic and peripatetic idea(l) in complementary figures: the hushed swishing of stars is the cosmic materialization of human passage through the world, while the young bohemian's overcoat de-materializes in the sublimity of his desire ('Mon paletot aussi devenait idéal').

The act of wearing out shoes on the stony road hastens arrival at the Green Inn ('J'avais déchiré mes bottines sur les cailloux de la route,' 'Au Cabaret-Vert'), and brings fresh material engagement in the lusty appreciation of succulent ham sandwiches and a foaming tankard of ale. Alimentary pleasure is boosted libidinally in the perceptual traffic between delicious food and delectable flesh: 'Et ce fut adorable, / Quand la fille aux tétons énormes, aux yeux vifs, / [...] / Rieuse, m'apporta des tartines de beurre, / Du jambon tiède, dans un plat colorié.'[15] The experience of gorging on visual sensations brings gustatory, erotic, and writerly appetites to a climax in the luminous description of the beer ('[q]ue dorait un rayon de soleil arriéré'). The poet's enraptured attention to the lustre and lushness of material things absorbs the entire scene, and ultimately the poem itself, in a surge of visual pleasure. A poetic itinerary whose source in sartorial decrepitude and affective *disponibilité* has its outflow in perceptual and sensual plenitude.[16]

Rimbaud's early poetry, as 'Ma bohème,' 'Au Cabaret-Vert,' and 'Sensation' reveal, brims with the material signs of perceptual acuity, brought forth in vivid representations of taste, sight, touch, sound, and smell. The heightened contact of self and world often takes an exquisitely acute form in epidermal arousal.[17] In 'Les Reparties de Nina,' for example, the sensual coincidence of self and nature, self and other, is figured as an eroticized quickening of the flesh:

Quand tout le bois frissonnant saigne
    Muet d'amour

De chaque branche, gouttes vertes,
    Des bourgeons clairs,
On sent dans les choses ouvertes
    Frémir des chairs

'Sensation' envisions an exquisite prickling of the skin, part pleasurable, part painful, a stimulating mingling of sensations of smooth liquidity ('sentir la fraîcheur à mes pieds'; the wind 'bathes' his bare head) and spiky aridity ('fouler l'herbe menue'; 'picoté par les blés'). The cascade of visual and haptic sensations is captured in the successive future tenses that generate the poem's forward momentum, imparting the sense that everything is still to experience and to write. In 'Sensation,' material pleasure is linked, not to the state of being, but to the fantasy of *becoming* (he is 'comme un bohémien' therefore not one); repeated simile articulates the yearning to possess, rather than actual possession (he is 'heureux comme avec une femme,' therefore not with one). The pliant, intensely pleasurable experience of the senses triggers the fantasizing of the moment of satisfaction, while its repeated deferral ('j'irai,' '[je] sentirai,' 'je laisserai') generates more desire and more text. The sensual and verbal energy deployed in 'Sensation' makes this brief poem, in Robb's words, 'an unusual escape from the thud of rhetorical machinery' typical of the poetry of the period.[18] It is succeeded in *Poésies* by 'Soleil et chair' which, as it extends the theme of perceptual quickening, exposes and challenges the constraints on writing poetry in the sludgy wake of decorative (and decorous) Parnassianism.

Eschewing the airy brevity and the verbal spontaneity of 'Sensation,' Rimbaud immerses himself now in the dense discourse of neo-paganist poetics. With memories of his own schoolboy translation of a passage from Lucretius's *De rerum natura* guiding his pen, he produces what begins as a pastiche vision of a nubile earth, its breast heavy with sap.[19] This Orphic hymn to body–earth union goes on to set pagan idealism against material modernity in a world where the gods (and God), banished, are replaced by dulled, self-regarding man, enslaved to the harsh rhythms of industrialization. The poem flouts the limitations of pastiche, taking forward the generative, aspirational desire of 'Sensation.' Rimbaud exposes the wretchedness of the modern individual who, mired in ignorance, is resistant to perceptual experience ('les yeux fermés et les oreilles closes') and, consequently, to material and writerly sources of self-transforming, world-altering potential.

Rimbaud asserts, in his letter to Demeny of 15 May 1871, that '[l]a poésie ne rythmera plus l'action; elle *sera en avant.'*[20] The desire to act in and upon the world has to be preceded by the desire to radicalize poetry. Rimbaud's urge to savage the sleek surfaces of lyric convention erupts in his 'tainting' of the Parnassian ideal with the discourse of sexual taboo. In a text that mimics Parnassian style in order to repudiate it, the vision of the advent of modern man – a parody of man – falling from the maternal vulva recalls the startling gynaecological frankness of Courbet's 'L'Origine du monde' (1866), but Rimbaud's perspective is pessimistic: 'Singes d'hommes tombés de la vulve des mères.'[21]

The dystopic (and prescient) image of cloned humanity is dispelled by the earthy voluptuousness of 'Les Éffarés' and its depiction of 'ce trou chaud [qui] souffle la vie,' the bakery oven. Ripples of synaesthetic pleasure radiate from this life-giving orifice as a gaggle of hungry children *hear* the bread bake and listen to the 'singing scents' of the crusts. The poet's delight in language-work that mixes the innocent, the alimentary, and the libidinal finds its ironic analogue in the quasi-erotic action of the baker's 'fort bras blanc qui tourne / La pâte grise, et qui l'enfourne / Dans un trou clair.'[22] 'Les Effarés' is a poem formed in perceptual and lexical pliancy, whose attention to the verbal texturing of physical sensation anticipates Ponge's 'Le Pain.' To agree with Yves Bonnefoy that 'Les Effarés' is about the discovery of transparency in things is, however, to rush over the latent eroticism of the text which, for all its easy poignancy and chubby-bottomed tweeness, delivers a smarting dose of irony in the coincidence of alimentary and erotic economies of lack.[23]

Rimbaud's early poetry oscillates between expressions of ecstatic self-becoming and narratives of disillusionment and failure. Subjectivity is bodied forth as an intense visual or haptic sensation, or as an arresting acoustic or olfactory signal: the *stink* of hypocrisy rises from the shoes of the priest; the oleaginous *texture* of ecclesiastical cant surfaces in the priest's uvular intonings ('grasseyant les divins babillages'). These material metaphors compound the notion of sullying and besmirching represented by the 'quinze laids marmots encrassant les piliers' of village churches, described in the opening stanza of 'Les Premières communions.' In 'Les Pauvres à l'église,' a diatribe against stultifying belief in a patently uncaring God, the *colour* of devotional self-interest epitomized by 'les Dames des quartiers distingués' migrates from fabric ('plis de soie / Banals') to flesh ('sourires verts'). The social parade and the ritualistic performance of religion conjure up a human bestiary ('Parqués entre des bancs de chêne [...] les Pauvres,' 'vingt gueules gueulant les cantiques pieux,' 'humiliés comme des chiens battus,' 'Tous bavant la foi'). Multiple embodiments of dirt and degradation produce a hybrid cast of 'effarés,' 'épileptiques,' 'aveugles,' and, perhaps most disturbingly, the subhuman species indicated by 'des *espèces* d'enfants.' The catalogue of sickening smells, itself an index of social-class differences ('senteurs de viande et d'étoffes moisies'), is exacerbated by the muffled sounds of the wheezing gerontocracy ('geint, nasille, chuchote / Une collection de vieilles à fanons'). Language strains to represent the horror via a material 'thickening' of the notional relations between social and verbal structures: obtrusive neologisms ('puamment,' 'mauvaisement') draw attention to the physical deformation of words, and to their discrepancy relative to the accepted term, such that poetic expression begins to mime the forms of material awkwardness bodied forth in disease, poverty, and misery. Rimbaud's adverbial 'mess-making' is a lexical riposte to the moral fetidness of the congregation, and compounds the aversive thematics of the text.

The filth poetics that shapes 'Les Pauvres à l'église' needs to be placed in the context of Rimbaud's letter of 2 November 1870 to Georges Izambard: 'Je meurs, je me décompose dans la platitude, dans la mauvaiseté, dans la grisaille.'[24] Here, the exasperated young poet evokes his predicament in suffocating Charleville, but the entropic experience, expressed in metaphors of miasma, decay, mediocrity, and opaqueness, reveals itself, paradoxically, to be a wellspring of poetic energy. In his letter of 13 May 1871 to his former teacher, he proclaims the sheer necessity of making oneself abject (non-conformist, radical, insurgent) as a preparation for his visionary vocation: 'Maintenant, je m'encrapule le plus possible. Pourquoi? Je veux être poète et, je travaille à me rendre *Voyant*: vous ne comprendrez pas du tout, et je ne saurais presque vous expliquer. Il s'agit d'arriver à l'inconnu par le dérèglement de *tous les sens*.'[25] In order to free himself for the visionary project launched in 'Voyelles' and 'Le Bateau ivre,' the poet must first confront the quotidian forms of alienation (hypocrisy, repetitiveness, apathy, boredom). To this end, indistinctness, filth, and obfuscation will quickly become the raw matter of his poetic strategy and his culture critique, unleashing allegories that burst with loathing for complacency and inertia. Poems such as 'Les Assis' and 'Vénus Anadyomène,' which I shall explore later, put exasperation to work in explosive expressivity and sublime grotesqueness.

In 'À la musique,' the fetishized fabric of bourgeois social life is revealed by clothes and the bodies that they clad. The burghers of Charleville, and the text they generate, are swamped by the hypertrophia of voluminous clothing and accessory objects. Saturated in signs of commodity fetishism, and covered in ridicule by the poet, they parade their acquisitiveness ('chiffres,' 'breloques'); sartorially and mentally, they epitomize empty excess. Wearing (and bearing forth) their egotistic pettiness, the bourgeois citizens parade ('portent') values and assumptions that, in turn, seem to flow back into the poem's material correlatives; thus the 'place de la Gare' is described as 'taillée en mesquines pelouses.' The satirical portrait cedes, unexpectedly, to erotic reverie as the poet imagines viewing and stroking the local girls under their clothes: 'Je suis, sous le corsage et les frêles atours, / Le dos divin après la courbe des épaules.' The metaphors and metonymies of acquisitive desire are the screen on to which the poet projects his own temptations and learned behaviour as he declines his voyeuristic practices in a succession of predictable part-objects ('J'ai bientôt déniché la bottine, le bas... / — Je reconstruis les corps, brûlé de belles fièvres'). The focus on his own activity as a voyeur-appraiser, one who knowingly duplicates the bourgeois master-gaze, precipitates self-deflation, spurred by the girls' mockery. Veering from overt socio-political critique to implicit self-critique, the two phases of the poem converge in the dismantling of masculine (visual) authority.[26] I shall return to the debunking of the master-gaze, and to the work of Rimbaud as an 'ironic anthropologist'[27] (and, one might add, 'self-ironizing'), when I consider his refiguring – or disfiguring – of the Venus trope and his savage critique of viewing practices in 'Vénus Anadyomène.' For the moment, though, I want to consider more fully the representation of the body beyond the satirical.

The body, dressed or undressed, free or constrained, pleasure-taking or pressured, bears traces of the encounter between self and other, self and the structures of repressed desire. The puffy eyelids and the laboured breathing of the children in 'Les Étrennes des orphelins' somatize their experience of maternal privation.[28] Here the body's insistent expressivity is mimed in the repeated 'point de' in part IV ('Il n'est point de parents, de foyers, de clefs prises / Partant, point de baisers, point de douces surprises!'), while the children's arrhythmic breathing makes its syntactic imprint in the fracturing of tenses ('c'était si charmant [...] Mais comme il est changé, le logis d'autrefois'). Temporal disjunctions point up the contrast between the acuteness of lack and the memory of material richness and emotional plenitude. The description of a dream vision crammed with the remembered objects of parental (maternal) generosity and family celebration materializes that lack and the uncertainty of its ultimate satisfaction in the *fort–da* of fantasy:

> Chacun, pendant la nuit, avait rêvé de [...] [ses étrennes]
> Dans quelque songe étrange où l'on voyait joujoux,
> Bonbons habillés d'or, étincelants bijoux,
> Tourbillonner, danser une danse sonore,
> Puis fuir sous les rideaux, puis reparaître encore!

Corporeal unevenness ('Tant leurs yeux sont gonflés et leur souffle pénible') signals the reality principle that surges against the scintillating smoothness and polished surfaces captured in the repetition of liquid sounds and in the mesmerizing circulation of rubescent light across glittering baubles, brightly wrapped sweets, and cherished patinas: 'Et les reflets *ver*meils, *sortis* du grand foyer, / *Sur* les meubles *vernis* aimaient à tournoyer ...' (my emphasis).

As the children somatize their lack, they confirm the unfailing tendency for what is on the inside (desire, anxiety, exasperation) to resurface on the exterior. Throughout *Poésies*, Rimbaud alerts us to the legibility of bodily signs, in tones that veer from pathos to caustic derision and self-mockery, in anticipation of *Une Saison en enfer*. Figuring himself as a fallen angel in 'Oraison du soir,' the poet affirms the propensity of psychic material to somatize ('[m]ille Rêves en moi font de douces brûlures'), producing a sensation that may only be relieved when, as a micturating Christ-figure, he can release his shame and his unquenched urges (and some thirty glasses of beer) in an appeasing torrent of urine.

The body is at times startlingly legible or semiotic, as 'Les Premières communions' reveals, first in the portrait of the repressed desire of a village priest, and subsequently, and at length, in the psychosomatic drama of the female first communicant. The signs of a crisis whose origin is more acutely sexual than spiritual erupt on (and in) the young girl's body, and surface in fractured rhythms and disjunctive sense-groupings: 'Et l'enfant ne peut plus. Elle s'agite, cambre / Les reins et d'une main ouvre le rideau bleu / Pour amener un peu la fraîcheur de la chambre / Sous le drap, vers son ventre et sa poitrine en feu...'[29] Erotic yearnings surge uncontainably in the pubescent girl, but natural sexual expressivity is challenged by the demands of spiritual continence. The desiring self struggles, hopelessly, against the obscurantist control of those who would repress and distort desire, figured as flesh withered and consumed: 'Qui dira ces langueurs et ces pitiés immondes, / Et ce qu'il lui viendra de haine, ô sales fous / Dont le travail divin déforme encor les mondes, / Quand la lèpre à la fin mangera ce corps doux?'

In narratives of frustrated desire, the representation of colour assumes a powerful affective or ideological charge. In 'Les Premières communions,' the village priest is the 'noir grotesque' whose solid fingers press relentlessly upon children's vulnerable flesh, in a metonymic close-up of repressed desire surfacing in the form of abuse: 'Ils sortent, oubliant que la peau leur fourmille / Où le Prêtre du Christ plaqua ses doigts puissants.'[30] The priest is stalked by erotic urges that traverse his body, quickening sensation in his lower body: 'dans son clos, les vêpres dites, quand / L'air s'emplit du lointain nasillement des danses, / Il se sent, en dépit des célestes défenses, / Les doigts de pied ravis et le mollet marquant; / — La Nuit vient, noir pirate aux cieux d'or débarquant.' Psycho-sexual conflict materializes in the chromatic clash: whilst the village priest represents the obscurantism of hypocrisy and self-deception, the young girl aspires to the sublimity of whiteness but fantasizes in the colour of violent desire ('Elle avait rêvé rouge'). Deep colour saturation absorbs the distinctions between the tropes of menstruation, defloration, and sacramental symbolism.

'Les Premières communions' is a text of desire unsuccessfully repressed and resurfacing in the hysteric narrative inscribed on female flesh. The body in *Poésies* – and throughout Rimbaud's writing – is repeatedly signing the subject's deepest longing and uncertainty. An index of the perpetually unresolved relationship between self and other (whether object or surface, physical environment, social structure, or cultural formation), the body stages the surge against abstract, generalized forces (those of ideology, religion, social class, art). This surge comes through in productive forms of revolt and resistance or, as here, in one of their pathological variants, hysteria. The corporeal resistance of the pubescent communicant contrasts with those irretrievably dysfunctional instances where the body appears deeply complicit with the external agencies that seek to constrain and suppress individuality. In the biting social fantasy 'Les Assis,' Rimbaud maps the alienated petit-bourgeois mindset in an aversive corporeal narrative that exposes the extremes of material and mental atrophy.

The placing of colour adjectives in singularly stressed positions (at the start of the poem's first two lines) affirms the affective freight of colour. 'Noirs de loupes' ushers in the opaque horror of the office workers through tropes of viscous impenetrability and light-defying inwardness. The sense of ocular hideousness, heightened by the radical enjambement ('les yeux cerclés de bagues / Vertes'), is aggravated by the visualization of contagion and erosion ('Le sinciput plaqué de hargnosités vagues / Comme les floraisons lépreuses des vieux murs'), and compounded by the arid anatomical discourse and by the evocation of dryly rasping clusters of tonsils ('des grappes d'amygdales / [...] s'agitent à crever'). A nauseating seamlessness between the seated and their seats brings the (sub)human and the material together in one fused mass: their bodies leave a skeletal imprint in the office chairs, while the scrawny wooden bars of the desks ('rachitiques') emerge formed in the enfeebled image of the office workers. The poet dissects the grotesque pathologies of the bureaucrats, their monstrous corporeal extensions and protuberances, in language redolent of Baudelairean spleen: 'cognant leurs têtes chauves.' As in *Les Fleurs du mal*, loathing has its flip side in ironic fascination: the office workers' coat buttons 'accrochent l'oeil,' a reprise of the trope of ironic fascination at the centre of Baudelaire's 'Les Sept Vieillards.' Rimbaud's extraordinary portrait of the dehumanizing horror of modernity seems to overwhelm critics like Yves Bonnefoy who, referring to Rimbaud's 'expressionnisme brutal, dangereux,' conflates pathology and the ironic pathologist, the object of criticism and the language of the culture critic.[31] 'Les Assis' anticipates a Célinean or Kafkaesque dystopia, and the nightmarish surrealist visions of Max Ernst. And, as we shall see later in this study, Rimbaud's alienated bureaucrats prefigure Ponge's sclerotic office workers in 'R.C. Seine n°.'

As a social autopsy and a graphic evisceration of cultural and readerly assumptions, 'Les Assis' has an aesthetic analogue in 'Vénus Anadyomène.' Rimbaud's scandalous sonnet deploys the anatomical lexicon to dissect academic art and the sugary neo-classical nudes that characterized the style of contemporary establishment painters like Bouguereau and Cabanel.[32] Here, the poet attacks the commodification of visual culture in an allegory that stages simultaneously art's debasement and the necessary purging of clichéd forms in anticipation of the radical beauty of the *Illuminations* and the difficult pleasure of twentieth-century art.[33] Through the systematic violation of the trope of ideal beauty, Rimbaud brings about the disfigurement of Venus, and hastens the re-figuring of the aesthetic ideal. In 'Vénus Anadyomène' the sacrosanct body-object of masculine appraisal (and aesthetic perfection) has been toppled from its plinth and, rising (literally) in its place, from a foul enamel bathtub, is modernism's anti-ideal. Techniques of dissection and distortion are mobilized in a perverse refashioning of the figure of Venus rising. Crudeness and 'mess' distort the allegorical frame and, as in 'Les Assis,' the horror is vivid and pervasive. The repudiation of art's expired representations entails a savagely remodelling of the subject as Beauty is pathologized, turned into a cadaver. But a more implicit, but no less intent, critique is made of visual mastery: the narrator's gaze, angled through the jostling lenses of voyeurism, commodity fetishism, and medical diagnosis, travels down the body from top to bottom, fracturing female flesh into so many part-objects ('omoplates'). Suspended between Life and Death, the female figure hovers sickeningly, the verb 'remuer' imparting a sense of monstrous slowness. The graphic impact of extremes of sickness and morbidity is exacerbated by viewing modes where leering fascination mingles with disturbing equanimity ('un peu') – an ironically modest means of describing what is immoderately repulsive. The vision culminates with the sublime abjectness ('Belle hideusement d'un ulcère à l'anus'), the oxymoron a defiant assertion of Rimbaud's project to reclaim horror, to relish baseness and dirt, to elevate desecration to a strategy, and, in the process, abolish Beauty as a stabilized, immutable reification. In short, to reinvent Venus, with a sting in her tail.

The sclerosing of the body, whether in representations of the automata of the modern metropolis (a feature that will recur in certain of the *Illuminations*) or in visions of the degraded female body, materializes the bourgeois mindset as a living death. The poet contests the authority of mainstream culture through its representative discourses, particularly those of modern capitalist bureaucracy and of contemporary aesthetic taste. The pervasiveness of signs of sterility and morbidness in these allegorical representations is synonymous with aesthetic redundancy and paralysis; conversely, the production of mess (in the form of the wilfully indiscriminate desecration of tropes, and in the purposive mixing of rhetorical styles) takes forward the urge to disrupt and displace what is culturally smoothed and levelled. The material is the index of a social or cultural crisis that spills out in signs of mess (contamination, pollution, disfigurement, waste, entropy) and that, in turn, generates a mess of signs (iconoclasm, stylistic clashes, infringements of taste, and tonal conflicts).[34]

As the most conspicuous manifestation of Rimbaud's challenge to 'la vieillerie poétique,' the early 'mess' aesthetics has important implications for the post-*Poésies* phase: *Une Saison en enfer* will sift the autobiographical debris of a self fractured and scattered; the *Illuminations* will reveal the outflow of purposive mess-making as readerly expectations are dismantled, and the structures of meaning collapse and re-form in mesmerically jagged visions. Rimbaud is extraordinarily prescient, anticipating the generative 'mess art' that will be at the centre of twentieth-century literary and artistic preoccupations.[35]

It is useful at this point to draw some provisional conclusions about *Poésies*. The outwardness of the early poems brings ecstatic contact with nature and energizing sentient experience, while the exasperated confrontation with contemporary cultural structures is productive in exposing the forces of coercion and alienation. The representation of the body, formed in the discourses of religion, art, social life, work, and sexuality, is central to the capacious narrative of *Poésies*. The body is the site of the 'éclosion de [s]a pensée' into sensation and perception, and into material metaphors that register the quickening of consciousness as it veers from euphoria (in bohemian and excursive narratives like 'Sensation') to bitter disenchantment and disgust. The rush of consciousness made visible in material things and on the body's surface takes forward a desire to challenge what diminishes and to seek fresh connections between self and other, self and world. It is in this light that I turn to consider 'Les Poètes de sept ans,' where, through the nexus of the body and materiality, more urgent connections emerge between childhood and creative freedom, between sexuality and art, between social constraint and visionary aspiration. In this *poème d'apprentissage*, materiality and its most obtrusive topos, mess, are key to the quickening of consciousness.

The portrait of the exasperated child-poet brings to language an acute sense of the body's legibility, its tendency to somatize affect: 'des tics noirs, quelques traits / Semblaient prouver en lui d'âcres hypocrisies.'[36] The child's obscure ticks signal his rejection of parental authority; the asperity of his ironic detachment ('âcres hypocrisies') challenges the atrophying culture of the bourgeois home metonymized in its mildewed drapes.

Here the body tells the story of its constraint and its liberation. The child's sweating obedience ('suer') imparts the physical strain of keeping up appearances, whilst the 'éminences' that form the relief map of his forehead are at once bodily signs of a clash between self and the world (in the form of a punitive parent, perhaps) and an assertion of the obstinate superiority of the child who defies the smooth containments of class and upbringing, and corporealizes that disruptive potential in the noble bumps that he presents to the world. The body's nervous ticks, sweating, and sticking-out tongue connect with the messier and, paradoxically, more salutary output implied by the child's retreat to 'la fraîcheur des latrines.' The oxymoron of productive mess comes through in a latrinal stench that is synonymous with coolness and clear-mindedness, while the 'odeurs du jour' pervading bourgeois private space are rank. Creative (visionary) freedom is stimulated by material filth, a metaphor for the limit point at which body and consciousness coincide in temporary bliss: 'Il pensait là, tranquille et livrant ses narines.'

The mustiness of the public rooms is banished in favour of the liberating stench of authenticity. Mess, specifically excremental mess, is purposive: it has to do with truth-seeking and desire-forming. 'Les Poètes de sept ans' may be usefully compared with 'Honte' (*Vers nouveaux*), where the *carpe diem* conclusion to a fantasy self-autopsy leads to the assertion that 'l'enfant gêneur' must 'empuantir toutes sphères' – the child-poet must cause a stink, turn flowers into tonsils, and swap the flora of poetic inspiration for enemas and potato blight ('Ce qu'on dit au poète à propos de fleurs').[37]

The desire for contact with what is usually repressed or proscribed, brings into focus other forms of 'mess': sexual transgression, political revolt, blaspheming, and the blurring of social-class boundaries. The young poet's enjoyment of the company of stinking children with muddy fingers and runny eyes; the erotico-gustatory pleasure of sinking his teeth into the fleshy buttocks of a village girl, and emerging bruised by her revenge: these instances fulfil his desire to leave his imprint on the world, to puncture the smooth surface of things, and connect again with the bliss-filled holes and tears of the bohemian narratives.[38] Likewise, his masturbatory urge and his deposing of God in favour of factory heroes are signs of his relishing rawness and delighting in forms of sexual, social, political, and material 'contamination': pleasurable, productive minglings.[39] Signs of mess and the mess of signs proliferate as Rimbaud explores analogies between sexual self-understanding and creativity, between the stirring of a radical political consciousness and the repudiation of a bourgeois upbringing with its ideological prescriptions and prohibitions.[40]

The process of reclaiming dirt and debris puts to work the poet's expressed objective 'je m'encrapule le plus possible,' offering an outlet in metaphor for the urge to challenge and dismantle. The strategy of 'encrassement' is positive, rather than perverse as Robb contends, for a freshly invigorated aesthetic experience springs from contact with the raw and with filth.[41] The seven-year-old poet is moved and inspired by the physical abjection of children, spurred to 'pitiés immondes'; the material experience of dirt, debris, and dereliction is endlessly generative. The creative stimulation to be found in muck and mess, in the mixing of the metaphorical and the material, the unformed and the transgressive, brings the young poet to the brink of the visionary project:

> – Il rêvait la prairie amoureuse, où des houles
> Lumineuses, parfums sains, pubescences d'or
> Font leur remuement calme et prennent leur essor!

Dreaming of savannahs and torrents, anticipating brilliant, violent horizons, the poet and the reader plunge into quickening pools of reverberating light and saturated colours, while neighbourhood noises burst out as a reminder of the material and the quotidian. The lurching of poetry between the prosaic and the sublime, between mess and the mesmeric, ushers in the visionary episode.

There is, then, a compelling need for mess, for not only does it coincide with fresh thinking, it appears to stimulate it. Inhaling latrinal odours makes thoughts and poetry flow, and in this respect 'Les Poètes de sept ans' bears comparison with 'Accroupissements,' a contemporaneous text where mess-poetics is at its most active. Here, the symptoms – migraine, pilosity, hiccuping, filth, quaking intestines, insomnia, mental hyperactivity – afflicting Milotus the monk proliferate, colonizing the material world, such that the whole text becomes engorged with signs of torrid filth. The depiction of intense nausea brings forth truth and illumination, quite literally in the proto-Proustian painterly instance: '[le] clair soleil [...] plaque / Des jaunes de brioche aux vitres de papier.' The oxymoron of latrinal freshness identifies sublime contact with forms of mess as a route to visionary intensity and to the radical beauty of the *Illuminations*. To become a visionary poet, as Rimbaud asserts in his letter to Paul Demeny, one needs to know oneself at one's most aversive: 'il s'agit de faire l'âme monstrueuse: à l'instar des comprachicos, quoi! Imaginez un homme s'implantant et se cultivant des verrues sur le visage. Je dis qu'il faut être *voyant*, se faire *voyant*.'[42] To that end, poems like 'Les Poètes de sept ans' and 'Accroupissements,' with their embrace of the material in its singularly obtrusive manifestations, appear not so much to contradict, as to present an analogue to, the cool voluptuousness of 'Sensation.'

In *Poésies*, the exploration of material extremes, whether aversive or meliorative, makes possible the unburdening and the regeneration of self. Whether savouring miasmic stench, delighting in sartorial abandon, or gorging on lush sensuality, the young poet embraces 'rugged reality' passionately, like the future traveller through hell, or the narrator of 'Ce qu'on dit au poète à propos de fleurs,' who trades the Orphic lyre for telegraph poles.[43] 'Les Poètes de sept ans' and 'Accroupissements' open the way to 'Comédie de la soif' (probably 1872), where the enraptured plunge into the abject (drinking dry every urn, drowning in barbarous seas, spurning purity, immersing self in 'l'affreuse crème' of the pool) rewrites an 'art poétique' as an aesthetics of 'messing.' Rimbaud's early poetry is about the intense, ceaselessly stimulating encounter of self and world; it charts the opening of self to the possibilities of the world; it is about subjective permeability and *disponibilité*. Those gaps and holes, the cool draught of the latrines, ensure that the world enters, that the wind arouses a sentient, responsive body surface. It is here that thinking is radically refreshed and poetry oxygenated.

The Debris of Autobiography

The material narrative of the early poetry carries over into the spectacular physicality of the agonizing self in *Une Saison en enfer*. Where the dismantling of aesthetic assumptions and cultural structures in *Poésies* takes the form of bodily aggression or corporeal sclerosis suffered by an external agency (the iconic Venus or grotesque bureaucrats), hypercritical energy is now turned against the autobiographical self (and its alter egos and surrogates). The narrative of *Une Saison en enfer*, particularly in the earlier sections, which are my primary focus, overflows with signs of torture, disease, scourge, suffocation, thirst, drunkenness, filth, bastardy, misery, pestilence, and madness. Tropes of alienation and abomination, of ostracism and fracturing, signal material that is autobiographical and symbolic, for representing the body's physical agony is an acutely expressive means of self-authoring at the point where words fail: 'Connais-je encore la nature? me connais-je? — *Plus de mots*' ('Mauvais sang'). Where verbal structures are perceived as inadequate, body language is a way of writing oneself from the outside and of giving oneself to be read. Obsessively inscribed, repeatedly storied, the body is autobiography's material surface and its source.

Fragilized flesh is an analogue to the irretrievably fractured sense of identity confronted in *Une Saison en enfer*. Its eight 'chapters' narrate the speaker's repeated attempts to come to self-knowledge by examining the debris of history, science, war, paganism, art, Christianity, democracy, and visionary poetry. As the self-recriminating narrator sifts the dross of his soured fantasies and failed projects, the metaphorics of identity-formation resurfaces in a series of physical metonymies, the messy extrusions of an abject self: waste matter, dried blood, mud, thirst, spilled wine, sores and boils, tears, dust, shattered pottery, leprosy, crumbling walls, and shrivelled skin.

The first sequence, 'Mauvais sang,' conjures up a wasteland where the narrator sits, impotent and outcast, amid the vestiges of human abandonment and futile endeavour:

> Je suis assis, lépreux, sur les pots cassés et les orties, au pied d'un mur rongé par le soleil.

The broken pottery is a figure for the shattering of the ideal unity of self and language; it is a proleptic metaphor for the fragmented discourses strewn across *Une Saison en enfer*: those of modernity, economy, love, ethnicity, patrilinearity, work, democracy, poetic creativity, action, and health. The mental disarray of a self struggling to process the chaos of ideas, instincts, pressures, sensations, and conflicts has its outflow in a tortured (and expressively tortuous) autobiography.

In *Une Saison en enfer*, material debris and its corporeal correlative, abject flesh, express the exasperation and self-loathing of a first-person narrator who seeks forms of action or assuagement in revolt, nostalgia, or the desire for self-transformation. Debris is the sign of the psychic overflow that occurs as the narrator confronts the litter of his past, and fails to make sense of it. Sifting psychic debris inevitably generates more narrative material and more material mess: this is Rimbaud's hell.

There is a strong consonance between the metaphorics of mess and modernist autobiography. Composite, chaotic, and incomplete, mess narratives and modernist autobiographical narratives solicit readerly acts of retrieval and recycling, only to subvert those acts by exposing the instability of language and the ontologically free-floating self that is a product of the fluctuations of discourse. As Nathaniel Wing has shown in his groundbreaking reading, Rimbaud's text mimes the procedures for expressing selfhood (the 'rhetoric of autobiography') and, in the process, reveals the self to be the pure construction of language (the 'autobiography of rhetoric').[44] *Une Saison en enfer* hovers between the urge to construct (a meaningful narrative of self) and the desire to dismantle (the myth that the unitary self is retrievable through language).

The processing of litter and the production of autobiography presuppose a desire to turn chaos into order. This is reflected in the material presentation of *Une Saison en enfer*, particularly in its conspicuous framing of paratextual and intertextual features. The reproduction of the cover page of the original 1873 edition stresses the status of *Une Saison en enfer* as a material, indeed iconic, artefact. But straightaway the sense of completeness is challenged by the narrator's explicitly restricted proffering to the demon of 'quelques hideux feuillets' that define the text before us as an extract – presumably the most salient or representative – from a longer, withheld 'carnet.' At the same time, the verb 'détacher' suggests a more pondered action than the precipitous abruptness that 'arracher' would have implied; it is a clue to Rimbaud's constructivist approach to autobiography.[45] The episodic construction of the text, like the splicing of prose poetry with reworked verse material from Rimbaud's existing corpus, points to a careful textual archaeology founded on the self-critical analysis of fragments. André Guyaux situates *Une Saison en enfer* as 'un cas unique dans l'histoire littéraire, d'autocritique agrémentée ou argumentée d'autocitations.'[46] *Une Saison en enfer* would appear to be closer to a purposively constructed cubist *papiers collés*, or collage, than to an art of the random and fortuitous.[47] Debris may be the material outcome of contingency (accidents of birth, natural catastrophes), but the processing of debris is an intentional, meaning-giving act. And yet, modernist autobiography, like mess, remains resistant to ordering; it is indeterminate, hybrid, non-coalescent, and endlessly extendible, like cubist collage. Debris and autobiography have in common a double lack: that of a determinable beginning and a conceivable end. Thus, the narrator's proffering of selected pages prompts us to ask if the beginning is really the beginning, and the end indeed the end. The inconclusiveness of *Une Saison en enfer*, this unresolved narrative that sets up premises and positions only to demolish and subsequently reinstate them, reminds us that the components of mess and of autobiography can be infinitely reordered, transformed, restored, developed, and elided. Modern autobiography and mess are incomplete and multifarious, constantly in process; in this respect they present compelling analogues to the provisionality and hybridity of self-identity.

The prologue of *Une Saison en enfer* opens with the remembrance of an intensely meliorative experience, the chiastic structure of the incipit recovering memories of physical and affective plenitude: 'Jadis, si je me souviens bien, ma vie était un festin où s'ouvraient tous les coeurs, où tous les vins coulaient.' This banquet of the senses and of sensibility recalls a halcyon era brimming with moments of candour, energy, and euphoria: then, self and other formed an ideal unity. The prologue thus recalls the capacious, world-altering desire first expressed by the quixotic dreamer of 'Ma bohème,' 'Roman,' 'Au Cabaret-Vert' and 'Sensation,' reprised in the verse poem 'Chanson de la plus haute tour' ('les coeurs s'éprennent'), and embedded in 'Alchimie du verbe.' But nostalgia is suddenly dispelled by the more recent memory of the violent rejection of Beauty ('je l'ai trouvée amère'), the disjunction between the lost ideal and the resurgent real reflected in the rupture of imperfective duration by a series of perfective tenses.[48] The frantic crushing of affirmative values triggers the exasperated abandonment of self to mess and to mud. Aversive values surge as the narrator recalls how, when his experience of material and emotional fulfilment turned literally sour, he vented his exasperation through masochistic desire and the appeal to harsh correctives: 'J'ai appelé les bourreaux [...] J'ai appelé les fléaux [...] Le malheur a été mon dieu. Je me suis allongé dans la boue. Je me suis séché à l'air du crime. Et j'ai joué de bons tours à la folie' (prologue). The accumulation of reflexive and active instances inscribes the enthusiastic capitulation to abjection, and the spurning of hope, beauty, peace, charity, and creativity, ideals that the narrator presumed – and again presumes – false or failed.

Self-punitive desire bursts forth in tropes of torture and tyranny, but the holocaust does not lead to purifying lucidity and the salutary loss of illusion; instead it propels him to the threshold of madness: 'Et le printemps m'a apporté l'affreux rire de l'idiot' (prologue). Recognizing the limit point beyond which cathartic desire would veer towards self-destruction, he reverts nostalgically to the ideal of a blissful unity between self and world:

> Or, tout dernièrement m'étant trouvé sur le point de faire le dernier *couac*! j'ai songé à rechercher la clef du festin ancien, où je reprendrais peut-être l'appétit.   (prologue)

Now, as the narrator presents the selected sheets from his infernal 'carnet,' he is seeking (vainly) to recover that discarded ideal and invest it once more with fragile hope. There is a fracture here between the past (narrated) self, who cast out joy, goodness, and generosity, and the present (narrating) self, who seeks a route back to the pre-repudiation time. Anticipation of the body's ultimate crisis stirs the desire to retrieve what had previously been consigned to the dross-heap of cultural memory, namely, those meliorative values of beauty and taste. But regressive hope is thwarted when taste is (again) radically redefined as corrosive asperity in 'Alchimie du verbe,' in the intercalated poem 'Faim': 'Si j'ai du goût, ce n'est guère / Que pour la terre et les pierres. / Je déjeune toujours d'air, / De roc, de charbons, de fer.' This latest definition of taste, formed in an elemental, industrial dystopia, prefigures the explicit conversion to 'réalité rugueuse' ('Adieu'), as creativity and beauty are ultimately refigured as harsh and sublime in remembered anticipation of the visionary *Illuminations*. The nostalgic desire to negate the earlier, iconoclastic rejection of Beauty, and thus salvage the lost ideal, is opposed by the urgency of confronting new subjective pressures with no hope of triumph, for self is irredeemably damned. To be damned is to be modern; it is a metaphor for the exasperated acceptance of an unstable relation of self to discourse, for the fracturing of the unitary ideal, and for the materializing of that fracture in agonizing self-examination:

> J'ai avalé une fameuse gorgée de poison. [...] Les entrailles me brûlent. La violence du venin tord mes membres, me rend difforme, me terrasse. Je meurs de soif, j'étouffe, je ne puis crier. C'est l'enfer, l'éternelle peine! Voyez comme le feu se relève! Je brûle comme il faut!   ('Nuit de l'enfer')

The prologue recalls the temptation of abjection that was embraced and then rejected, only to be found to be intractable and, paradoxically, generative (at least in textual terms). Obsessive negation, already a feature of the prologue, is a structuring principle of *Une Saison en enfer*, identified by Leo Bersani as signalling Rimbaud's rejection of whatever he risks becoming ('repudiat[ing] his own repudiations').[49] This circular structure (of negations triggering their negation) emerges clearly in 'Adieu,' where the capitulation to contingency is recalled ('Je me revois la peau rongée par la boue et la peste, des vers plein les cheveux et les aisselles et encore de plus gros vers dans le coeur') and promptly repudiated ('J'exècre la misère'), only for the meliorative corollary of that repudiation to be instantly rejected ('Et je redoute l'hiver parce que c'est la saison du comfort!'). Thus, positions are continually proposed and rejected, while temporary alleviation from the wearing alternance of opposites is sought in geopolitical fantasy ('Quelquefois je vois au ciel des plages sans fin couvertes de blanches nations en joie,' 'Adieu'). But, dream-work and the visionary project will be ultimately spurned when the narrator is drawn to 'rough reality,' only to cast doubt upon that choice ('Suis-je trompé?,' 'Adieu').

Examining the wreckage of one's past – cultural, patrilinear, linguistic, personal – presupposes an activity of recovery and a desire for self-retrieval. Yet repeated attempts, in the opening sequences of *Une Saison en enfer*, to shore up the fragments of his past only confirm the narrator's deeply unresolved relations to lineage, language, nationality, race, sexuality, poetry, work, belief, metaphysical desire, aesthetics, and – most acutely – to his own body. Hell is a metaphor for the tortured project of self-knowing and the body is both the vehicle of that project and its constantly available object of appraisal. Viewed as a cultural entity, an ethnic legacy, and a semiotic surface (tattooed, telling its own story), the body emerges most spectacularly in the first section of *Une Saison en enfer*, 'Mauvais sang.'

The body is identified straightaway as the site of inherited guilt and of mental and physical debility ('J'ai de mes ancêtres gaulois l'oeil bleu blanc, la cervelle étroite, et la maladresse dans la lutte.') By staging his body's torture (at times endeavouring to stand apart from it as narrator and witness, but always furiously trapped in his agonizing flesh), the traveller through hell struggles to confront the burden of his tainted heredity and his thwarted relation to European civilization. As a self-declared descendent of the Gauls, he is the inheritor of sloth and savagery, idolatry and deceit ('mensonge et paresse'), while his actively parasitic relation to the families of Europe (whom he claims to leave exhausted both in terms of unproductive familiarity and of the sapping of their resources) makes him the very embodiment of inertia ('Sans me servir pour vivre même de mon corps, et plus oisif que le crapaud, j'ai vécu partout.') Work – physical and intellectual – offers no corrective: his spurning of the activity of 'hands' ('J'ai horreur de tous les métiers. Maîtres et ouvriers, tous paysans, ignobles') is both a denial of socio-economic reality and a rejection of efforts to alter the world, whether materially or through language ('La main à plume vaut la main à charrue. [...] Je n'aurai jamais ma main'). The ethos of mental and physical application, defiantly rejected here as a means of self-constitution, is restored towards the end of 'Mauvais sang,' when the narrator seeks to remedy his lack of ontological substance ('ma vie n'est pas assez pesante, elle s'envole et flotte loin au-dessus de l'action, ce cher point du monde'). He may have put down his load temporarily by committing it to language ('L'ennui n'est plus mon amour. Les rages, les débauches, la folie, dont je sais tous les élans et les désastres, — tout mon fardeau est déposé'), but material weightlessness presents an intolerable new burden. The reversibility of propositions emerges here as the value appraised and rejected ('le travail') is reinstated ('La vie fleurit par le travail'), only for that reinstatement (the negation of the negation) itself to be negated at a later stage, where action is equated with the slide into entropy and with the dispersal of self in meaningless, repeated gestures: 'l'action n'est pas la vie, mais une façon de gâcher quelque force, un énervement. La morale est la faiblesse de la cervelle' ('Délires: Alchimie du verbe').

In a further reversal, the potential of work erupts clamorously in 'L'Éclair': 'Le travail humain! C'est l'explosion qui éclaire mon abîme de temps en temps.' But human labour is denounced once more as the prime instrument of the false religion of modernity that replaces salvation with alienation. Work slows or accelerates time unbearably for one who declares his life 'usée' and seeks solace in escapist illusion and self-indulgence: 'feignons, fainéantons, ô pitié. Et nous existerons en nous amusant, en rêvant monstres et univers fantastiques, en nous plaignant et en querellant les apparences du monde.' If work is judged an ineffective container for the resurfacing hubris of the narrator ('Non! Non! à présent je me révolte contre la mort! Le travail paraît trop léger à mon orgueil,' 'L'Éclair'), in 'Matin' the work ethic is resurrected in the yearning for fresh, rational forms of knowledge, and in the rejection of regressive beliefs: 'Quand irons-nous [...] saluer la naissance du travail nouveau, la sagesse nouvelle, la fuite des tyrans et des démons, la fin de la superstition, adorer – les premiers! – Noël sur la terre!'

This fractured meditation on the relation of embodied consciousness to work filters the debris of memory, desire, and instincts, and reveals the resistance of the disparate fragments of the narrator's past to forming meaningful structures. Identity is exasperatingly unfixable, consciousness resists teleological ordering, and the autobiographical self amounts to no more than a continual turning-over of shattered perspectives, worn beliefs, faltering convictions, and expired values. (The series of reversals that structures the text anticipates the alternating cursive/recursive patterning of such seminal modernist texts as *Ulysses* and *The Wasteland*.)[50] In *Une Saison en enfer* the value or perspective initially rejected is reinstated only for that reinstatement to be subsequently cancelled. Thus, moving on involves turning back: this imposes a circular structure on a (presumably) linear reading. The narrator continues, implicitly, to challenge the teleological premise of autobiography in the same way that he had explicitly questioned the linear and progressive organization of culture and society ('Le monde marche. Pourquoi ne tournerait-il pas?', 'Mauvais sang'). At every stage of the traveller's crossing of hell, the indeterminacies of self contradict occasional expressions of naive hope in autobiography as a solution to fractured identity ('Qu'étais-je au siècle dernier: je ne me retrouve qu'aujourd'hui'). From the beginning, assertions trigger their cancellation: the celebration of entropic inclinations ('paresse') prompts their castigation; languishing in vice provokes a new repudiation of the regressive instincts of his own 'race inférieure'; recognition of his pariah status ('Si j'avais des antécédents à un point quelconque de l'histoire de France! Mais non, rien') provokes him to compensate his lack of patrilinear attachment through speculative fantasies ('j'aurais fait, manant, le voyage de terre sainte'; 'Plus tard, reître, j'aurais bivaqué sous les nuits d'Allemagne'). Rummaging in the debris of memories brings the stark realization that self-analytical desire is inexhaustible, and that identity, built on the shifting sands of language, is only ever provisional: 'Je n'en finirais pas de me revoir dans ce passé. Mais toujours seul; sans famille; même, quelle langue parlais-je?' Self is constituted in the unceasing flow of imaginary permutations and fluctuating fictions; thus an exotic fantasy of bodily and mental invigoration is briefly envisioned –

Me voici sur la plage armoricaine. [...] je quitte l'Europe. L'air marin brûlera mes poumons; les climats perdus me tanneront. Nager, broyer l'herbe, chasser, fumer surtout; boire des liqueurs fortes comme du métal bouillant, — comme faisaient ces chers ancêtres autour des feux. Je reviendrai, avec des membres de fer, la peau sombre, l'oeil furieux: sur mon masque on me jugera d'une race forte.   ('Mauvais sang')

– before the potential for self-fulfilment is tersely negated ('On ne part pas').

The fantasized journey of perceptual and affective stimulation, with its echoes of 'Le Bateau ivre,' is displaced by the reality of a long, forced march with sin and guilt as a crushing burden: 'Reprenons les chemins d'ici, chargé de mon vice, le vice qui a poussé ses racines de souffrance à mon côté, dès l'âge de raison – qui monte au ciel, me bat, me renverse, me traîne' ('Mauvais sang'). Here, the representation of suffering as a fractured (and fracturing) experience intensifies the sense of subjective and corporeal dislocation whose causes are enumerated ('la marche, le fardeau, le désert, l'ennui et la colère'). Self-punitive desire is legitimated, formalized, in a scenario of summary execution, with the body as the object of collective retribution: 'Je me voyais devant une foule exaspérée, en face du peloton d'exécution, pleurant du malheur qu'ils n'aient pas pu comprendre, et pardonnant!'

As visions are constructed and quickly cancelled, the possibility of a Christian conversion is, almost simultaneously, envisaged ('Dieu fait ma force, et je loue Dieu,' 'Mauvais sang') and denied ('Je ne me crois pas embarqué pour une noce avec Jésus-Christ pour beau-père') in the rapid alternation between veneration and blasphemy. One who belongs to a 'race inférieure' split against itself is subject to atrocious conflicts: at once spurred on and disgusted by his inherited inferiority, he alternately craves and castigates God. Every assertion provokes its negation. Similarly, the plunge into the phosphorescent sublime of the visionary project is recalled and, in the very process, relegated to the now remote bliss of self-delusion: 'je dus voyager, distraire les enchantements assemblés sur mon cerveau. Sur la mer, que j'aimais comme si elle eût dû me laver d'une souillure, je voyais se lever la croix consolatrice' ('Délires: Alchimie du verbe'). As he sifts the debris of false and failed solutions, the narrator's urge to ransack memory and plunder fantasy generates more instability and produces deeper cracks in his self-writing project.

'Vite! est-il d'autres vies?' ('Mauvais sang') calls into question the possibility, the desirability even, of ever stabilizing self-identity. Thus, from the outset, the criteria for traditional autobiography are challenged as provisionality displaces certainty and dispersion prevails over any sense of wholeness. In 'Nuit de l'enfer,' the narrator's acute awareness of subjectivity as irretrievably fractured provokes the desire for multiple hells ('Je devrais avoir un enfer pour la colère, mon enfer pour l'orgueil, – et l'enfer de la caresse'), until the language of self-reasoning itself breaks down at the prospect of an undifferentiated cacophony of sounds ('un concert d'enfers'). Autobiographical desire is now rerouted away from hopes of self-sameness and towards a series of performances involving assumed personae, alter egos, and surrogates of self.

Right from the start, the expectation of a narrative reconstruction of events is rivalled by a sense of verbal spontaneity and unpredictability, for the mood of the first-person narrator alternates between resignation ('je suis tellement délaissé,' 'Mauvais sang') and eruptive rawness ('Faim, soif, cris, danse, danse, danse, danse!'); the tone is alternately shrill and subdued, vituperative ('Non! Non! à présent je me révolte contre la mort!', 'Eclair'), and vacillating ('Par quel crime, par quelle erreur, ai-je mérité ma faiblesse actuelle?', 'Matin'). Language is improvised by a ventriloquizing narrator who projects multiple personae. Thus, in 'Nuit de l'enfer,' the voice of an everyday trick-performer, a master of fair-ground phantasmagoria, announces what may be read as a strategic trivialization of the visionary project as the disguised narrator opens a Pandora's box of paltry tricks: 'J'ai tous les talents! – Il n'y a personne ici et il y a quelqu'un [...] Veut-on des chants nègres, des danses de houris? Veut-on que je disparaisse, que je plonge à la recherche de l'*anneau*? Veut-on? Je ferai de l'or, des remèdes.' Conscious self-devaluation is sustained as the persona of the tawdry trickster segues into a debased Christ figure: 'Fiez-vous donc à moi, la foi soulage, guide, guérit. Tous, venez, – même les petits enfants, – que je vous console, qu'on répande pour vous son coeur' ('Nuit de l'enfer').

   The re-channelling of self-inventive desire into the search for parallel subjectivities conjures into life and into language the figure of the Foolish Virgin and her sadistic partner in 'Délires I: Vierge folle,' as performative desire shifts from first-person narrator to another third-person surrogate. A gender-transposed version of the narrator, the virgin duplicates his masochistic desire. The Virgin's entrance is announced by 'Écoutons,' reproducing the oral context that launches *Une Saison en enfer* and the narrator's (presumed) recitation from his 'carnet de damné.' Likewise, the Virgin's exit from the specular hell prompts the summative utterance 'À moi, l'histoire d'une de mes folies' (at the beginning of the second 'Délires' episode, 'Alchimie du verbe'), an utterance that binds the re-emerging narrator, retrospectively, to the Foolish Virgin just as urgently as it signals, prospectively, the failure of the narrator's visionary project.

The Virgin is the narrator's alter ego or 'companion' in hell, a conflation of self and other and, in biographical terms, a composite of the identities of Rimbaud, his mother, his lover Verlaine, and Mathilde, Verlaine's wife. The narrator's enduring struggle with language ('puis-je décrire la vision!', 'Nuit de l'enfer') passes inevitably to her ('Comment vous le décrire! Je ne sais même plus parler,' 'Délires: Vierge folle'). Language exposes repeatedly the breakdown between self and other, for experience that cannot be described cannot be shared. So, verbal breakdown is troped in the domestic violence inflicted by the Époux as an exasperated way of making bodies speak (and one not unfamiliar to Rimbaud from his closeness to the antagonistic relations between Verlaine and Mathilde).[51]

Powerlessness to bring experience to language both frustrates the self-writing project and takes it forward (the prologue launches the autobiographical narrative in the acknowledged absence of 'facultés descriptives ou instructives'). The fragmentation of subjectivity and the disintegration of language, already materialized in the fragilized body, are duplicated in the thematic fractures that recur across this episode as the narrator's thoughts lurch between the banality of marital discord and the sublimity of metaphysical longing; between empathy with the Virgin and exasperation at what she represents; between the direct speech of the Virgin and the reported speech of her spouse; between the crass reactiveness of a hypercritical Husband and the critique of economically driven marital arrangements (articulated by the same Husband, desperate, like Rimbaud, to reinvent love beyond the constraints of marriage and modern capitalism).

The dispositions of the Husband coincide with the narrator's assumptions: the Husband, too, is 'de race lointaine,' cannibalistic and self-mutilating; like the narrator, he laughs 'affreusement' ('Délires: Vierge folle'). He shares the narrator's desire for self-invention and feels the same urge to make the body speak: 'Je me ferai des entailles partout le corps, je me tatouerai, je veux devenir hideux comme un Mongol.' The Husband's urge to self-mutilate as a means to authentic (hellish) self-confrontation echoes the (relative) conviction of the narrator in 'Nuit de l'enfer': 'Un homme qui veut se mutiler est bien damné, n'est-ce pas? Je me crois en enfer, donc j'y suis.' Just as the poison that courses through the narrator's veins in 'Nuit de l'enfer' ('la violence du venin tord mes membres') is the ink that inscribes the writhings of his autobiography, so the Husband's projected self-scarifying envisages for the body a more vivid language than mere words can produce. The duplication of the narrating self in the specular persona of the Husband is a further mut(il)ation in the series that originates in the prologue with the demon's threatened morphing of the narrator into a hyena.

The Virgin's attempt to analyse her spouse transposes and extends the narrator's self-analysing project. She denounces her Husband's attempt at self-enlightenment as a sham, but each assertion of the Virgin inevitably forces us to assess the reliability of the word of one presented as *folle*. This linguistic indeterminacy merely underscores the impossibility of stabilizing interpretations that has shaped readerly experience from the outset. Indeed, there is more equivocation than alienation here, for their mutual antipathy is offset by empathy, tenderness, camaraderie, and the desire of each to make sense of the other's actions. Even when the Husband affirms his lack of love for women, his assertion is categorial and abstract rather than particular and individualizing. The relations between the Virgin and her Husband (and their respective positions relative to the narrator) present, as intersecting planes, a kind of collage in which surfaces and perspectives overlap, but without any differentiated or stabilized positions emerging; rather, they perform the indeterminacies of self.

At this point it is useful to review the discussion before considering, in more consolidated terms, the remaining sequences of the text. *Une Saison en enfer* calls into question the assumptions of traditional self-writing, specifically the illusory unity of writing self and written self. Rimbaud's modernist autobiography challenges the settled subject of humanistic assumption, exploding the relationship between self and history, self and the real (inheritance, love, work, origins, fantasy, the body, language), and exposing a self, in the words of Nathaniel Wing, 'deprived of any ontological ground.'[52] *Une Saison en enfer* is the narrative of the agonizing discovery that self, with no original or stable relation to language, is formed in the discursive drift.

Rimbaud makes a similar point with his anti-Cartesian, proto-Sartrean claim to Izambard, 'c'est faux de dire: Je pense: on devrait dire on me pense.'[53] Challenging the humanistic assumption of unitary subjecthood means externalizing, objectifying the self, as Rimbaud illustrates with the materialization of his thoughts as sensations and perceptions formed at the corporeal interface of consciousness and the world. Rimbaud's repudiation of the myth of the joined-up self in his 'voyant' letters of May 1871 is taken forward by the self-objectifying momentum of *Une Saison en enfer*, and dramatized in the exasperation of every attempt to shore up self's fractured relations to family, personal memory, ethnicity, work, European civilization, poetry, and love. Thus, in 'Alchimie du verbe,' 'je devins un opéra fabuleux' resurrects the fantasy of conjuring visual, gestural, and acoustic signs into a coherent subjectivity, while the literal and etymological meaning of 'opera' (a work or text) reaffirms language, its artifice and arbitrariness, as the origin of subjectivity.

Une Saison en enfer chronicles the realization that the crisis of subjectivity is, at root, a crisis of language. The desire for self-knowledge is always in excess of the potential of language to deliver it. Yet the very realization that language is inadequate ('me connais-je? — *Plus de mots,*' 'Mauvais sang') produces, paradoxically, not fewer or no words, but many more, confirming that there is no self outside of language. The scattered fragments of an irretrievable self disperse the possibilities for meaning across *Une Saison en enfer*: material and affective debris washes up as words; self is eternally rolling around in language.

Subjectivity in *Une Saison en enfer* experiences its limbo. This causes anxiety for the narrator and the reader alike as they struggle to 'centre' an uncentrable subjectivity in the dizzying reversibilities of language. Retrospective assessments are conditional ('si je me souviens bien,' prologue), while judgments and assertions formed in the present of narration are frustratingly aporetic. Self-absence is equivalent to self-presence; visibility is interchangeable with obscurity: 'Il n'y a personne ici et il y a quelqu'un,' 'je suis caché et je ne le suis pas' ('Nuit de l'enfer'). The conditions for meaning are radically undercut where affirmation and negation amount to no more than a grammatical transformation. The endless substitution of visions postpones the prospect of resolution. Distinctions collapse as part of a difference-neutralizing strategy that renders everything the same. 'Chacun a sa raison, mépris et charité' ('Mauvais sang') elevates indifference to an ethics. The rejection of the unitary self of humanist construction is coextensive with the repudiation of the ideals of beauty, justice, and legitimacy, for the outcome of the narrator's attempts to stabilize his relation to history, language, nationality, desire, poetry, work, and violence is as unstable as the orthodoxies themselves.

The structuring of *Une Saison en enfer* as a series of assertions and cancellations confirms Wing's view that Rimbaud rejects the telos of conventional autobiography (progress through hell towards light and truth) and, instead, forces our attention onto language, its making and its breaking, by repeatedly thwarting the reader's expectation of thematic and tonal consistency. And yet, as questions are posed, orthodoxies reviewed, solutions envisaged and (usually) rejected, the text sets up a logic that is discernible, if chaotic. Thus, in 'L'Impossible' the narrator begins by rejecting the (false) self-sufficiency that defined his youth:

> Ah! cette vie de mon enfance, la grande route par tous les temps, sobre naturellement, plus désintéressé que le meilleur des mendiants, fier de n'avoir ni pays, ni amis, quelle sottise c'était. — Et je m'en aperçois seulement!

He goes on to factor in context (European, Western) as the formative basis of his thought. The mind, as a (temporary) guarantor of lucidity and the antithesis of instinctual reactiveness, is the object of accumulated regret and uncertain hope:

> Si [mon esprit] était bien éveillé toujours à partir de ce moment, nous serions bientôt à la vérité [...] S'il avait été éveillé jusqu'à ce moment-ci, c'est que je n'aurais pas cédé aux instincts délétères, à une époque immémoriale!... — S'il avait toujours été bien éveillé, je voguerais en pleine sagesse!

Even in those moments when capacious desire seems to rally the constituents of human endeavour and action, language works to reveal the hollowness behind it. Perhaps, here, it is no more than a repository of exhausted verbal fragments, like a grammar drill (conditional clauses and their tense variations) interminably rehearsed by the school pupil.[54]

Certainly, in the next section, 'L'Éclair,' reason and its applications are violently repudiated by one who blasts the damaging discipline of work and bourgeois education (or upbringing): 'Je connais le travail; et la science est trop lente'; 'Je reconnais là ma sale éducation d'enfance.' The narrator envisages capitulating to atavistic aggression, but once again the mood is speculative and action is deferred:

> Non! Non! à présent je me révolte contre la mort! Le travail paraît trop léger à mon orgueil: ma trahison au monde serait un supplice trop court. Au dernier moment, j'attaquerais à droite, à gauche...

Spurred by this tentative mapping of the future, the reader's anticipation of a teleological scheme leads into the trap of reading as definitive the most recent assertion. The textual subversion of that expectation thrusts us into fresh uncertainty with the narrator's claim that language has deserted him –

> Moi, je ne puis pas plus m'expliquer que le mendiant avec ses continuels *Pater* et *Ave Maria. Je ne sais plus parler!*   ('Matin')

– only for that statement to be instantly contradicted by the narrator's summative utterances and his evident defeat of aphasia. What, then, of the conclusion?

In 'Adieu,' the prospect of stability materializes with the return to the quotidian world and the embrace of rugged reality ('je suis rendu au sol, avec un devoir à chercher, et la réalité rugueuse à étreindre!'). The idolatrous savage of 'Mauvais sang,' who morphed into the persona of the mad virgin, is transformed into the peasant who gravitates to the territory of modernity: the heaving metropolis with its compelling mix of action and boredom, enchantment and anomie, eclecticism and sameness. The distressingly absent 'main amie' emblematizes his longing for reconciliation and solidarity, and contrasts with the spurned hand of the ploughman or writer in 'Mauvais sang.' Debris-shifting has produced a provisional solution evident in the meliorative values embraced by one who, it would appear, has finally rejected scepticism and indifference. Bonnefoy relates the 'heure nouvelle' and the anticipation of historical modernity to the confident embrace of a reality without miracle, a world without metaphysical absolute.[55]

Yet where the unity of mind and body, self and world, is envisioned in the conclusion, the narrator's arrival at that point is ultimately deferred in a move that connects recursively with the 'jadis' of the prologue, and cursively with the resurrection of the ideal that was initially rejected: the unity of mind and body, of consciousness and the real ('il me sera loisible de *posséder la vérité dans une âme et un corps*,' 'Adieu').[56] Desire, never exhausted and never relinquished, is ceaselessly deferred.

The ultimate deferral of desire and the denial of autobiographical closure remind us that the subject has no fixable position. Self is no more than the constant turnover of competing values that was acknowledged at the outset: 'À qui me louer? Quelle bête faut-il adorer? Quelle sainte image attaque-t-on? Quels coeurs briserai-je? Quel mensonge dois-je

tenir? – Dans quel sang marcher?' ('Mauvais sang'). Rallying, indis-
criminately, to one or other cause points up the dual impossibility of
being out of discourse and of stabilizing any position within discourse:
'j'offre à n'importe quelle divine image des élans vers la perfection.' At
the same time, autobiographical desire cannot be contained by language, for the narrator's self-awareness is always in excess of his power
to represent it verbally: 'Ma vie serait toujours trop immense' ('Délires:
Alchimie du verbe'). Self is the uncontainable sum of conflicts and
pressures, straining the limits of language and generating an affective
overload that can only be discharged through the oscillations of
expressivity: ecstasy, vituperation, resignation, indifference, nostalgia,
and cancellation. All that is settled in *Une Saison en enfer* is the principle
of instability.

The narrative of *Une Saison en enfer* sets up the conditions for meaning and repeatedly undercuts those conditions: discrete utterances deliver (generally) coherent meaning but, read consecutively, as a series of
potentially relatable instances, they resist our attempts at continuous,
linear interpretation; disjunctive structures have a self-cancelling effect.
The reader aspires to reach some potentially stable meaning, but is
repeatedly plunged back into uncertainty. Like the narrator, the reader
sifts disparate subjective instances, unable to determine the relative
validity of one instance compared to another; narrator and reader alike
are caught in the discursive drift (positivist, anti-Christian, solipsistic,
progressive, visionary, or democratic). As one assertion melts into or is
swept away by another, the two appear usually mutually exclusive; yet
they exist relationally because for one to come forward, another must
recede or be negated. This disjunctive structuring is, as we shall see, at
the centre of the reading problematics exposed in the *Illuminations*.[57]

The text of *Une Saison en enfer*, anticipating the prose poetry, presents
some analogies with cubist practice, where the subject or object of
representation is not available to view as a unitary entity (or identity),
but materializes sporadically as fracture or fragment, as in Picasso's
portrait 'L'Homme à la pipe' (1911). The fractured self emerges as a
construct in language, a self assembled, dismantled, and recomposed
on the broken stones of meaning that litter *Une Saison*. The process of
dismantling subjecthood and exposing its basis in the displacements of
language presages cubism's shattered perspectives and the reconstruction of the object in non-linear, non-naturalistic ways such that continuity cedes to simultaneity, and content is subordinated to process. As in
analytical cubism, the visualization of the process of composition pre-

vails over the visibility of the represented subject or object. Nathaniel Wing stresses that *histoire* and *discours* are in conflict, but that the act of narrating prevails over the content of narrative: '[the narrator] performs a reading which deflects interest from the (pseudo-)referential content of the text and towards the operations of language.'[58] *Une Saison* prefigures texts like 'Ville' and 'Les Ponts' with their decentred or ungrounded subject matter, their 'rugged reality' of disparate planes and surfaces. In *Une Saison en enfer*, the volatile array of assertions and cancellations constantly shifts the reader on in the exasperating search for meaning. In the *Illuminations*, the near impossibility of stabilizing any perspective plunges the reader deeper into the narrator's mental vortex.

The Visionary Project: Disturbing Beauty, Disrupting Reading

The *Illuminations* envision the process of the liberated consciousness as it encounters and transfigures the real, producing descriptions of bewildering beauty. The rush of consciousness emerges in mesmerizing visual work that directs attention less to the interpretation-resisting images per se than to the writerly production of those images and to the response they solicit from a reader plunged into the uncertain hope that the swirl of signifiers will spiral into meaning. Through cascading visions powered and fragilized by the forces of transformation and abolition, Rimbaud's prose poetry reveals its creative momentum and its visionary aspiration. In his innovative study of Rimbaud's prose poetry, Leo Bersani points up the conflicting demands of linguistic order and of unbounded visionary desire that cause successive image series to surge and tumble, shatter and reform:

> [L]anguage [as] a structured system [...] is inherently antagonistic to mental life as discontinuous, hallucinated and random identifications with the external world. The poetic illumination must pass through or 'cross' language, but it must also dismiss a medium which both serves it and subverts its value. It should therefore 'stay' in language as briefly as possible.[59]

I would argue that, rather than visionary desire investing language for the briefest possible time, desire is constituted in language for there *is* only language. Reading the *Illuminations* together with the related *Poésies* texts 'Voyelles' and 'Le Bateau ivre' reveals, not a disjunction between

the material (language) and the visionary, but an urgent desire to materialize the visionary project in exquisite, affect-bearing descriptions of
colour, texture, form, sound, and surface. With its voluptuous wounding of the body's intactness, 'Being Beauteous' proffers an allegory of
reading that is lavish and fractured, sumptuous and splintered –

> Devant une neige un Être de Beauté de haute taille. Des sifflements de
> mort et des cercles de musique sourde font monter, s'élargir et trembler
> comme un spectre ce corps adoré: des blessures écarlates et noires éclatent
> dans les chairs superbes.

– and subject to transfiguration in dervish-like swirls of colour:

> Les couleurs propres de la vie se foncent, dansent, et se dégagent autour
> de la Vision, sur le chantier.

The visual and acoustic impetus of the prose poetry is ecstatically
anticipated in the verse poems 'Voyelles' and 'Le Bateau ivre,' which
invest sound and colour sensation with anxiety, elation, and awe.[60]
'Voyelles' ushers in Rimbaud's visionary project and makes visible the
fluctuations of affect as subjectivity disperses and re-forms in instances
of mesmeric beauty. Thus, the arbitrary correspondence between the
letter 'A' and 'noir' causes erotic desire and morbid horror to mingle,
before dispersing in the silent expanses of the 'golfes d'ombre.' This
dispersal precipitates the next correspondence, where the chaos of discrete figures releases a brief vision of the diffused awe and remote
majesty of white ('E, candeurs des vapeurs et des tentes, / Lances des
glaciers fiers, rois blancs, frissons d'ombelles'). Here we touch on the
paradox of visionary revelation that, for all its abstraction and rarefaction, is intensely subjectivized: colour description reverberates with
intimations of pride, disgust, attraction, violence, confidence, uncertainty, and exhilaration. Where the incipit of 'Voyelles' proclaims a
radical anti-mimetic program, and the conspicuously arbitrary association of vowels and colours undercuts the interpretative act, the poem
immediately challenges its own premises as the narrator promises (and
defers) the release of meaning ('Je dirai quelque jour vos naissances
latentes'). Meanwhile, the reader is invited to occupy that space with
her or his necessarily speculative reading.[61]

Like 'Voyelles,' 'Le Bateau ivre' aspires to the blissful point at which
writing would rip free of its material moorings and achieve sublimity,

but, once more, affect surges in descriptions of movement and mael-strom, acute sensation and expansive kinesthesia. The fate of the boat's haulers signals the immobilization of the old order ('cloués') and the restoration of mental freedom that is bodied forth in a certain lightness of being ('Plus léger qu'un bouchon j'ai dansé sur les flots'). 'Le Bateau ivre' is the chronicle of a consciousness rushed by rival perceptions and uncoupled energies. To chart the visionary waters is to become im-mersed in atmosphere, flesh, smell, space, surface, texture, and mess; it is to submit to a cascade of colour signifiers: 'Peaux-Rouges,' 'poteaux de couleurs,' 'eau verte,' 'taches de vins bleus,' 'lactescent,' 'rousseurs,' 'violets,' 'nuit verte,' 'neiges éblouies,' 'éveil jaune et bleu des phosphores chanteurs,' 'arcs-en-ciel,' 'soleils d'argent,' 'flots nacreux,' 'golfes bruns,' 'noirs parfums,' 'flot bleu,' 'poissons d'or,' 'ventouses jaunes,' 'yeux blonds,' 'brumes violettes,' 'morves d'azur,' 'hippocampes noires,' 'cieux ultramarins.' The chaos of colours captures at once the embrace of risk and the enthralled discovery of visionary beauty: shattered, abstractive, and beguiling. The quickened consciousness bobs and plunges, gushes and trembles, only to surge again in the evocation of arrested sublimities ('azurs verts,' 'immobilités bleues'), or alternatively, in the capitulation to processes of staining or washing ('l'eau verte pénétra ma coque de sapin,' '[l'eau verte me lava] des taches de vins bleus et des vomissures,' 'teignant tout à coup les bleuités / [...] Fermentent les rousseurs amères de l'amour!,' 'le ciel rougeoyant').

Exposure to the hyperactive consciousness of the first-person narra-tor has a quickening effect on the reader, who, borne along on the visual-verbal torrent, is caught up in the expansions and the hesitations of 'je.' The first-person instances lash together the narrator and the reader through the tumultuous displacements of visionary desire ('J'ai rêvé,' 'J'ai heurté'). The creative impetus of Rimbaud's visionary project propels the narrator and the reader in a dazzling precipitation that barely allows attention to register each discrete image. It is as if to seek to fix and interpret a visual instance, to try to hold it down, might be to damage its precarious beauty. 'Le Bateau ivre' reveals visionary mo-mentum as volatile and fragile, like the uncanny beauty that it brings forth, and prone to fracture when doubt invades the poem, depleting energy and willpower. The visionary urge contracts in the yearning for the modest and the familiar, and nostalgia materializes, in the penulti-mate stanza, through the Ardennes dialectal variation on 'flaque': 'Si je désire une eau d'Europe, c'est la flache / Noire et froide où vers le crépuscule embaumé / Un enfant accroupi plein de tristesses, lâche /

Un bateau frêle comme un papillon de mai.' The monochrome certainty of the ocean-displacing puddle and the banality of the white-winged moth represent the negation of visionary virtuosity and the exasperated recognition of impotence:

> Je ne puis plus, baigné de vos langueurs, ô lames,
> Enlever leur sillage aux porteurs de cotons,
> Ni traverser l'orgueil des drapeaux et des flammes,
> Ni nager sous les yeux horribles des pontons.[62]

Visionary poetry constantly tests its possibilities and its limits, and reflects on its equivocation. The irresistibility and the impossibility of bringing such liminal experience to language connect 'Le Bateau ivre' (and *Une Saison en enfer*) to the *Illuminations*. In 'Le Bateau ivre' and *Une Saison*, the exasperation of creative or metaphysical longing forces the self to confront scenarios of physical fracture and dereliction ('O que ma quille éclate!'), and to begin the anxious activity of self-recovery amid the debris of cultural memory and private fantasy. In the *Illuminations*, language shatters on the threshold of inexpressibility (the liminal point identified as atrociousness): 'Rouler aux blessures, par l'air lassant et la mer; aux supplices, par le silence des eaux et de l'air meurtriers; aux tortures qui rient, dans leur silence atrocement houleux' ('Angoisse').

When language does not run out in silence, it runs away, accelerating through expressions of self-mocking irony:

> À vendre les Corps sans prix [...] À vendre l'anarchie pour les masses [...] À vendre les habitations et les migrations [...] À vendre les applications de calcul et les sauts d'harmonie inouïs. [...] À vendre les Corps, les voix, l'immense opulence inquestionable, ce qu'on ne vendra jamais. Les vendeurs ne sont pas à bout de solde! Les voyageurs n'ont pas à rendre leur commission de si tôt!   ('Solde')

In 'Le Bateau ivre,' the dissolution of creative desire in debilitating self-doubt affirms the structure of reversibility that is a constant of Rimbaud's writing from *Une Saison en enfer* onwards. While the conclusion of 'Le Bateau ivre' anticipates the abandonment of the visionary project in *Une Saison en enfer*, we read with a sense that the efforts of a hyperactive consciousness are merely suspended, not concluded, and that desire, undiminished, will resurge in the *Illuminations*. The juxtaposition of the triptych 'Vies' and 'Départ' mirrors this: across these two texts the poet's nostalgic immersion is converted into a new visionary initiative that surges to cancel self-doubt. In 'Vies,' there persists only a flurry of memories of refreshing discovery and affective fulfilment: 'je me souviens des heures d'argent et de soleil vers les fleuves, la main de la campagne sur mon épaule, et de nos caresses debout dans les plaines poivrées. — Un envol de pigeons écarlates tonne autour de ma pensée.' The consolation of remembrance soon gives way to sour concentration as the lessons of negativity are acknowledged and the corrosive self-examination of *Une Saison en enfer* is briefly resumed: 'l'air sobre de cette aigre campagne alimente fort activement mon atroce scepticisme.' Rising to counter the lapse into sardonic indifference ('Je suis réellement d'outretombe, et pas de commissions'), the succeeding poem 'Départ' confronts instances of existential exhaustion anaphorically, and pro-poses a corrective in fresh surges of mental and physical energy:

> Assez vu. La vision s'est rencontrée à tous les airs.
> Assez eu. Rumeurs des villes, le soir, et au soleil, et toujours.
> Assez connu. Les arrêts de la vie. — Ô Rumeurs et Visions!
> Départ dans l'affection et le bruit neufs!

The texts of the *Illuminations* expose the uneven trajectory of the creative consciousness. Charged with its own alternately exhilarated and tremulous intentionality, visionary momentum is always suscepti-ble to disruption by scepticism, irony, or nostalgia. This tension be-tween boundless confidence and resurfacing anxiety heightens, rather than diminishes, the tantalizing quality of Rimbaud's prose poetry. The deep uncertainty pervading the visionary narrative is duplicated in the readerly response to descriptions of sublime beauty; I will return to questions of equivocation and unresolve in discussing the reading para-dox posed in the *Illuminations*. I want first, however, to consider those instances where the pure visionary urge falters and cedes to the real, reconnecting with society and with the fate of subjectivity in modern culture through representations of work, architecture, the built space, performance, art, and objects. This is particularly striking in the urban visions emerging in certain of the *Illuminations*.

Re-figuring the Real: Envisioning the City

The representation of the city in the *Illuminations* takes forward the culture critique of the *Poésies* in the ironic coincidence of the material and the abstract, the sublime and the everyday. Metropolitan modernity is visualized in the baroque fantasy of 'Villes II,' which constructs an extortionate, fetish-crammed folly ('candélabres géants,' 'diligence de diamants,' 'divans de velours rouge').[63] The visionary city is, in every sense, unfathomable – to the narrator, and to the reader drawn into the complex play of perspectives:

> Sur quelques points des passerelles de cuivre, des plates-formes, des escaliers qui contournent les halles et les piliers, j'ai cru pouvoir juger la profondeur de la ville! C'est le prodige dont je n'ai pu me rendre compte: quels sont les niveaux des autres quartiers sur ou sous l'acropole? Pour l'étranger de notre temps la reconnaissance est impossible.

'Villes II' narrates the impossibility of stabilizing perceptual experience, spatially or representationally, in the modern city. Epistemological doubt compounds the psychic instability ('des drames assez sombres') that threatens to disrupt the shimmering flow of fetish-objects. Returning to the language of materiality, the poet takes forward, now in a more lapidary way, the critique of aesthetic taste central to 'Vénus Anadyomène' and 'Ce qu'on dit au poète à propos de fleurs.' Unfolding an *avant la lettre* critique of postmodern architecture, Rimbaud exposes the city as a vast recuperation of earlier architectural styles: 'On a reproduit dans un goût d'énormité singulier toutes les merveilles classiques de l'architecture.' The textual abstraction of 'quelques cents âmes' into 'l'élément démocratique' mimes the alienation of the individual and the erosion of subjecthood in ways that presage the literature and visual culture of twentieth- and twenty-first-century dystopias. Predicting, perhaps most directly, the dehumanized cityscapes of De Chirico and Céline, 'Villes II' issues an ironic riposte to the call, uttered at the end of *Une Saison en enfer*, to enter 'les splendides villes.'

Anticipating the proliferation of cityscapes in the *Illuminations*, 'Ville' launches the critique of metropolitan modernity through a disenchanted or dismally indifferent citizen-narrator who affirms that all known taste has been levelled in the conceptualization of the city. The reduction of depth and mystery is duplicated in the language of erasure and sameness ('tout goût connu a été éludé'; 'vous ne signaleriez les traces d'aucun monument de superstition').[64] As the narrator confronts and flees the crushing predictabilities of urban living – unmourned Death, desperate Love and an enticing Crime – allegory intimates the diminishment of subjectivity in the city.[65]

Where 'Villes II' and 'Ville' reveal a thematic link back to the social critique of certain texts of *Poésies*, the critique of modernist ideology assumes an abstract form in 'Les Ponts,' where the flattening (and multiplication) of perspectives is integral to the structuring of the text.[66] The bewildering geometry of 'Les Ponts,' prefigures the abstraction and anti-representationalism of cubist painting (as well as its restricted colour palette), while at the same time intimating the modern city's unfathomable qualities. Alienation is mapped as a chaos of lines and planes:

> Des ciels gris de cristal. Un bizarre dessin de ponts, ceux-ci droits, ceux-là bombés, d'autres descendant ou obliquant en angles sur les premiers, et ces figures se renouvelant dans les autres circuits éclairés du canal, mais tous tellement longs et légers que les rives, chargées de dômes s'abaissent et s'amoindrissent.

If the heaping of image fragments announces a proto-cubist concern with formal features, affective instances ('bizarres,' 'tous tellement longs') import elements of culture critique into an outwardly 'objective' tableau. This would appear to contradict Bersani's contention that Rimbaud's prose poetry is characterized by 'floating a-sociability.'[67] Rather, the subjective colouring of material line and surface would lead more directly to Apollinaire's vision of the dehumanized city in '1909' and 'Le Voyageur,' texts whose dislocated structures articulate a consciousness alternately in thrall to, or in retreat from, the pressures of modernity. Speculative identifications of sounds, colours, and shapes underline the indeterminacy of interpreting positions: 'On distingue une veste rouge, peut-être d'autres costumes et des instruments de musique' ('Les Ponts'). The poem's represented objects elude the narrator's (and the reader's) attempt to stabilize them, as flattened perspectives ('les rives [...] s'abaissent et s'amoindrissent') are increasingly rivalled by acoustic eruptions ('Sont-ce des airs populaires, des bouts de concerts seigneuriaux, des restants de hymnes publics?'). Paradoxically, the material traces of human presence precipitate the erasure of the subject of representation in a prospective intimation of cubist abstraction: 'Un rayon blanc, tombant du haut du ciel, anéantit cette comédie.' The destructive shaft of light is paradoxically generative, for, in abolishing its own construction of the real, it hastens the revelation of the pure(r) visionary sublime.

Sublime Beauty and the Reading Paradox

Visionary poetry is, by definition, unprecedented, for poet and for reader alike: 'Hourra pour l'oeuvre inouïe et pour le corps merveilleux, pour la première fois!' ('Matinée d'ivresse'). Language captures the experience of coming to sublime beauty and of returning to it with impassioned urgency: 'Je ris au wasserfall blond qui s'échevela à travers les sapins: à la cime argentée je reconnus la déesse. Alors je levai un à un les voiles' ('Aube'). Such episodes reveal poetry reflecting on its writerly production and its readerly reception through a 'je' that is undecidably self and other, creator and recipient of the visionary gift. A sense of perpetual inauguration is sustained as images of startling beauty surge, dissolve, and re-form in vertiginous cascades. The visual lavishness of Rimbaud's prose poetry is awesome, alienating even, in its de-realization of the quotidian and familiar. The *Illuminations* prefigure in crucial ways the convulsive beauty prophesied in the epilogue to *Nadja*: 'la beauté sera convulsive ou ne sera pas.'[68] In the prose poetry, uncanny beauty erupts in the chaotic, shattered forms that will define the twentieth-century modernist aesthetic as disturbing and stimulating, a wellspring of anxiety and exhilaration. Beauty will be at once elemental and ornamental, as in this prefigurement of Max Ernst's 'The Robing of the Bride' (1940): 'Sur la pente du talus les anges tournent leurs robes de laine dans les herbages d'acier et d'émeraude' ('Mystique'). Already in *Poésies*, 'Vénus Anadyomène' had severed beauty from its traditional location in representations of the feminine. The depersonalized voluptuousness of 'L'Étoile a pleuré rose...' had intimated a radical new beauty as Rimbaud reversed the process of bringing the material world to language and sought, instead, to duplicate the coruscating discoveries of the visionary consciousness in metaphors of materiality.[69] This fragmentary *blason* of the eroticized body unfolds an allegory of modernist beauty that suffuses the sublime with voluptuousness and violence:

> L'étoile a pleuré rose au coeur de tes oreilles,
> L'infini roulé blanc de ta nuque à tes reins
> La mer a perlé rousse à tes mammes vermeilles
> Et l'Homme saigné noir à ton flanc souverain

The mesmeric colour-work of 'Voyelles' gives rise to the exploded prisms of 'Marine,' 'Nocturne vulgaire,' and 'Fleurs,' with their descriptions of beauty that is at once opulent and disturbing:

> D'un gradin d'or, — parmi les cordons de soie, les gazes grises, les velours verts et les disques de cristal qui noircissent comme du bronze au soleil, — je vois la digitale s'ouvrir sur un tapis de filigranes d'argent, d'yeux et de chevelures. ('Fleurs')

Poetry reveals itself as a hallucinatory spillage of fabric, flesh, events, histories, and desires. In 'Après le déluge,' the clash of the prosaic and the polar, the sordid and the sublime, captures the momentous experience of visionary invention and reception. The initial rush of consciousness reverses the paralysis of the hare; the succession of past historic tenses imparts processes of abolition and substitution, as the postdiluvian torrent powers a tumultuous narrative. Language strains to render something of the pulse and the density of things, and to track the unceasing displacement of creative desire. Verbal momentum surges through images of acoustic energy (banging doors) and kinaesthetic activity (the lugging of boats and the building of market-stalls, the gushing of blood and milk; the violation of bodies). In this bursting paean to visual-verbal creativity, readerly attention is directed to extraordinary acts of physical construction and dismantling, to processes of moving and transforming materials: such events are metaphors for the successive displacements (of logic, of narrative assumptions) demanded of the writer and the reader of visionary description. Mourning children, in thrall to 'les merveilleuses images,' behold the visual means of compensating their lack. Poetry reflects both on its own process and on the experience of the reader astonished and enthralled, an unformed viewer seeing expansively, authentically, for the first time. The flow of material and affective debris through landscapes of beauty and barbarity, is swept into a glittering construction, monumental and precarious, suspended on a homophonic quiver ('autels'-'hôtel'):

> Madame *** établit un piano dans les Alpes. La messe et les premières communions se célébrèrent aux cent mille autels de la cathédrale.

> Les caravanes partirent. Et le Splendide-Hôtel fut bâti dans le chaos de glaces et de nuit du pôle.

The exhilarating stream of language debris that forms the poem (metaphorized by the uncanny construction of the hotel) illustrates the concept of a generative *débâcle* outlined by Michel Leiris in *Brisées*.[70] The fracturing and dissolution of the ice floes ('le chaos de glaces et de nuit du pôle') releases the transformative potential of visionary desire that will surge in torrents and tides ('Écume, roule sur le pont et par-dessus les bois,' 'Eaux et tristesses, montez et relevez les Déluges,' 'Après le déluge').

Rimbaud's poetry aspires to the visionary absoluteness represented by polar oceans and alpine spaces that are reminiscent of the privileged territory of the Kantian sublime, only to lapse in expressions of inaction and exasperation. In the deflection or the fall from sublimity, writerly angst resurfaces and coincides with reader anxiety over the break-up and unbearable drift of meaning, as the extremes of visionary possibility – its fulfilment and its curtailment – are confronted:

> Car depuis qu[e les Déluges] sont dissipés, — oh les pierres précieuses s'enfouissant, et les fleurs ouvertes! — c'est un ennui! Et la Reine, la Sorcière qui allume sa braise dans le pot de terre, ne voudra jamais nous raconter ce qu'elle sait, et que nous ignorons.   ('Après le déluge')

Promethean passion is a means of remedying mental torpor and transforming the failures of action (exposed in 'Conte,' 'Départ,' 'Royauté'), but language in full visionary spate is always subject to undercurrents of apprehension and distress.[71] Moments of equivocation and faltering signal a return to subjectivity-in-things (in material detail and datum), as expressions of longing surface like the warm tears on the ocean of 'Enfance': 'des fleurs magiques bourdonnaient. [...] Des bêtes d'une élégance fabuleuse circulaient. Les nuées s'amassaient sur la haute mer faite d'une éternité de chaudes larmes.'[72]

Rimbaud's prose poetry stirs the reader intellectually and imaginatively, inducing both cool exhilaration and bewildered uncertainty. Yet, in poetry that foregrounds the dereliction of meaning over its desirable coalescence, we are destined always to read at a distance. The seductive lavishness of the prose poetry, and the visual-verbal saturation of texts are constantly rivalled by the sparseness of the interpretative ground: this is the reading paradox at the centre of the *Illuminations*. The teeming visuality of the poems at once spurs repeated efforts of interpretation and forecloses every attempt to stabilize the flow of images. This indeterminacy is, then, a source of readerly anxiety and a trigger for readerly activity.

The *Illuminations* force the reader to engage in the making of meaning, rather than in the reception of pre-formed meaning. The prose poetry constantly problematizes interpretative practice, stimulating reflection on the available choices: whether to focus on the particular, and risk breaking the visionary momentum, or to attempt to integrate the randomness of all those verbal shards into a larger structure (which would imply embracing the concept of destructuring, and, by seeking to transcend non-coalescence, denying it).

The prose poems elevate the random and the provisional to a structuring principle as the reader senses that any discrete visual instance or figure could be substituted by another; the text's synthetic 'meaning' would be virtually undisturbed. The dynamic of substitution is inscribed in texts that read as if they are constantly improvising their own material: in 'Veillées,' the poem's visual fabric is the product of the acoustic reverberations of the sounds 't,' 'i,' and 'd': 'Les tapisseries, jusqu'à mi-hauteur, des taillis de dentelle, teinte d'émeraude, où se jettent des tourterelles de la veillée.' Yet, this is no maelstrom of meaningless signifiers, for interpretative possibilities crystallize around recurrent formations of image or suggestion, or, as Bersani himself affirms, 'the mere fact of repetition points to an obsessive affective pattern.'[73] The reader abdicates interpretative authority and submits instead to the precarious (and pleasure-giving) oscillation whereby meaning surges in the particular and sporadic, as it recedes in the general and continuous (or vice versa). This comes through in the apparently disjunctive identifications of 'Veillées,' whose affective relationality is implied anaphorically, and is then called into (unanswerable) question before the uncertainties of the rational mind evaporate in the vivifying power of dream:

C'est le repos éclairé, ni fièvre, ni langueur, sur le lit ou sur le pré.
C'est l'ami ni ardent ni faible. L'ami.
C'est l'aimée ni tourmentante ni tourmentée. L'aimée.
L'air et le monde point cherchés. La vie.
— Était-ce donc ceci?
— Et le rêve fraîchit.

Immersed in the ravishing, reason-defying logic of visionary poetry, the reader finds her or his subjective positions repeatedly dissolving and re-forming. The constant unsettling of the interpretative ground has its source in the overturning of normative expectations of linearity, sequence, logic, temporal coherence, and verisimilitude: this is figured in 'Enfance' in the description of the cathedral's steep verticality and the reversal of that *plunging* perspective in the image of the lake *rising*. As the texts problematize their own premises and positions, they resist any critical frames that we seek to apply. Ahearn, for example, endeavours to stabilize 'Matinée d'ivresse' as a poem that obeys the 'convention of post-ecstatic speech concerning near-ecstatic experience.'[74] However, 'Matinée d'ivresse' reverses its recapitulative inclination as it anticipates the resurgence of visionary bliss: 'Cela commença sous les rires des enfants, cela finira par eux.' The visionary experience, while inclining to the recursive urge that Ahearn discerns, is primarily forward-pressing, predicting futures at once harsh and beguiling:

> Cela commença par quelques dégoûts et cela finit, — ne pouvant nous saisir sur-le-champ de cette éternité, — cela finit par une débandade de parfums.
>
> Rire des enfants, discrétion des esclaves, austérité des vierges, horreur des figures et des objets d'ici, sacrés soyez-vous par le souvenir de cette veille. Cela commençait par toute la rustrerie, voici que cela finit par des anges de flamme et de glace.

Attempts to read integrally, to read for consistency, are frustrated by the abstractive momentum of the writing, by the tendency for the particular to dissolve. For example, in 'Nocturne vulgaire,' the implied material object is obscured by prismatic abstraction ('Un vert et un bleu très foncés envahissent l'image'); the process is reversed in 'Jeunesse,' where the abstract and notional are materialized ('Reprenons l'étude au bruit de l'oeuvre dévorante qui se rassemble et remonte dans les masses'). To read, then, is to confront the tension between particularity and abstraction, between detail (whose very meaning connotes a fixed focus) and dissolution (or process, rapidity, instability, negation, neutralization). Linearity and connectedness cede to dream or visionary logic as images melt together and spill over in tonal mixings of vacillation and irony, contradiction and assertion. The extreme straining of the poem's visual syntax subverts readerly expectations by means of a dissociative viewpoint that gathers thematically unconnected (but grammatically coherent) instances into a bewildering narrative logic: 'Un cheval détale sur le turf suburbain, et le long des cultures et des boisements, percé par la peste carbonique. Une misérable femme de drame, quelque part dans le monde, soupire après des abandons improbables' ('Jeunesse'). Texts foreground the semantic splitting of subject and verb ('le sang chante,' 'Parade'; 'Sur les versants des moissons de fleurs grandes comme nos armes et nos coupes, mugissent,' 'Villes I'). Thus, in the *Illuminations*, things-in-themselves are displaced by things-in-process (as in 'Fleurs') or by the formation of unprecedented contiguities and reason-defying conflations ('le pavillon en viande saignante' of 'Barbare'). Particularly destabilizing are those moments when the transformative process is itself obscured. We don't see things becoming other things; simply and bafflingly, they already *are*, like the polar flowers in 'Barbare' before their textual cancellation: 'des fleurs arctiques; (elles n'existent pas.)' Visionary poetry draws attention to the invisible processes that constitute its particular logic: abolition, substitution, shifting, melting, transformation, fracture, collapse, dispersion. But perhaps the signal feature of Rimbaud's poetry is the verbal cramming that produces the simultanist intensity of 'Promontoire':

> Des fanums qu'éclaire la rentrée des théories; d'immenses vues de la défense des côtes modernes; des dunes illustrées de chaudes fleurs et de bacchanales; de grands canaux de Carthage et des Embankments d'une Venise louche, de molles éruptions d'Etnas et des crevasses de fleurs et d'eaux des glaciers, des lavoirs entourés de peupliers d'Allemagne; des talus de parcs singuliers penchant des têtes d'Arbre du Japon; et les façades circulaires des 'Royal' ou des 'Grand' de Scarbro' ou de Brooklyn, et leurs railways flanquent, creusent, surplombent les dispositions dans cet Hôtel.

Any image or image series leads not to closure but to the prospect of new beginnings, for the series is transformable at any point along its trajectory, and infinitely extendible. The course of the *Illuminations* is space-filling, rather than time-charting. Progress and linearity are suspended; we read with a sense of the poem taking us back or sending us forwards, but we cannot say with precision in which direction we are moving. In poems that purport to explore memory, history, or childhood, time frames collapse ('leur raillerie ou leur terreur dure une minute, ou des mois entiers,' 'Parade').

Interpretation is an active and exasperating process, for the texts propose continuities and, at the same time, radically undermine those continuities. The poet eschews narrative values of duration and continuity (as he had in *Une Saison en enfer*) in favour of discontinuous visualizations that simultaneously invite and inhibit attempts to form empathetic readings, as in the aborted syntax of 'Veillées,' which simultaneously brings forth and breaks up the affective freight: 'La mer de la veillée, telle que les seins d'Amélie.'

The resistance of images to forming determinable structures generates the epistemological equivocation at the centre of the reading experience. The reader is baffled by concatenations of splintered images and fractured visions, and persists in struggling to sort and sift them. The reader's approach is, unavoidably, anti-Rimbaldian in seeking to impose cohesive meaning on what resists and subverts structuring desire. Denied the possibility of discerning larger narrative structures and patterns, our particularizing attention moves instinctively towards those visual-verbal fragments – as the leper of *Une Saison en enfer* surrounds himself with the tesserae of his memories and fantasies – even at the risk of overdetermining them. The desire for contraction and consolidation, the turning from the sublime to the definable and the nameable, is articulated in 'Phrases': 'Quand le monde sera réduit en un seul bois noir pour nos quatre yeux étonnés, — en une plage pour deux enfants fidèles, — en une maison musicale pour notre claire sympathie, je vous trouverai.'

Anxiety is temporarily assuaged (but ultimately aggravated) by the simulacra of formal containment. Rimbaud exploits framing devices and, in particular, references to theatricality that reaffirm the threshold between the real and the fictional. This nourishes the illusion that narrating space is somehow less imagined and more real than narrated space (both are equally invented). Framing is invoked (or applied) in multifarious references to painting ('Mystique'), to staging ('Parade'), to artifice ('Scènes'), and to forms of illumination. The sense of a frame, whether painterly or theatrical, poetic or generic ('Conte,' 'Soir historique'), signals the desirability of giving form and boundaries to the improvised and the inchoate. This relates to Rimbaud's overtly cautious qualifying of his visionary project ('raisonné') in the second of his *voyant* letters: 'Le poète se fait voyant par un long, immense et raisonné *dérèglement* de tous les sens.' In the *Illuminations*, explicit ekphrastic indications militate against the impression of an unstoppable, overwhelming flow. In 'Mystique,' our reading is guided compositionally across the *tableau* by a series of prepositional markers: 'À gauche le terreau de l'arête est piétiné par tous les homicides'; 'Derrière l'arête de droite la ligne des orients, des progrès'; 'la bande en haut du tableau est formée de la rumeur tournante.' In 'Royauté,' the consistency of the past historic and imperfect tenses provides the frame that transforms the narrative of a couple's regal aspiration into fable, thus reinstating the boundary between fantasy and the real, between illusion and its verbal production. In 'Parade,' the narrator ('je') declares that he holds the key as the one who directs and delivers meaning. In 'Aube,' the shift from the first-person to third-person voice effects a sudden, ironic distancing from the dream experience, and the adoption of the past historic tense performs a disjunction between the oneiric experience and its (presumed) real-time narration. Such devices provide the illusion of containment and stabilization, reaffirming the distinction between visionary content ('histoire') and the *discours* that invents it and brings its forth. Formed by the irresistibility of interpretation, the readerly desire to stabilize meaning works to turn dissociative images into visual structures. As tropes of theatricality come forward in the *Illuminations*, any lingering sense of a unitary subject recedes. Affect is dispersed across a huge cast of personae appropriated from literature (from Shakespeare to Flaubert), from folklore and mythology, and from the ethnography of the everyday. Multiple personae and fractured subjectivities emerge in multifarious performances. We encounter, *inter alia*, an unnamed, homicidal, interchangeable, and ultimately self-obliterating Prince-Genie ('Conte'); a hyperactive classical actor or theatre director ('J'ai eu une scène où jouer les chefs-d'oeuvres dramatiques de toutes les littératures,' 'Vies'); an inventor and illustrator of the *Comédie humaine* ('Vies'); the 'toi' of 'À une raison'; a working-class couple composed of the narrator and Henrika with her anachronistic taste in clothes ('Ouvriers'); a complacent metropolitan man dully aware of his own insignificance ('Ville'); the disembodied 'on' of 'Les Ponts'; the eponymous Bottom from *A Midsummer's Night Dream*; and metropolitan crowds who, siphoned into 'l'élément démocratique' ('Villes II'), underscore the starkly desubjectivized vision of the everyday.[75] These *dramatis personae* comprise a hybrid cast, everyday and exotic, contemporary and timeless, desiring and disabused. The *Illuminations* extends the performative aspects of the autobiographical narrative of *Une Saison en enfer* through the multiple displacements of identity. It is, then, in the *Illuminations* that 'JE est un autre' is most thoroughly actualized.

Rimbaud's reputation as a modern poet is built on the luminous intensity of his visionary poetry, on the searing self-analysis of *Une Saison en enfer*, and on the transformative engagement of his early poetry with art, taste, politics, landscape, history, the body, work, religion, social class, and the family. From *Poésies* to *Une Saison en enfer* and the *Illuminations*,

Rimbaud's startling mix of the material and the sublime, the mundane and the metaphysical, reveals a prophet for modernity who alternately – or simultaneously – blasts and yearns, ironizes and agonizes.

The unceasing visualization of affect is the connective tissue linking the three crucial phases of Rimbaud's writing career. In the early poetry, ecstatic contact with the external world is duplicated in the perceptual lavishness of poems like 'Sensation' and in the exuberance of the bohemian travelogues. Hypercritical exasperation with social rigidities and ideological containments – with all that diminishes human potential – is channelled, through the generative embrace of crudeness, scatology, blaspheming, dirt, and debris, into the iconoclastic expressivity of texts such as 'Vénus Anadyomène' and 'Les Assis.' The radical assault on the other (the bourgeoisie, Parnassianism, establishment art, the Church, social institutions) precipitates a reverse attack on self as the external objects of loathing and mockery cede to the self-torturing pressures of acrimony, guilt, and unresolve in *Une Saison en enfer*. The distinctions between outward and inward, between society and self, disperse in the tumultuous beauty of the *Illuminations*, but the sublimity of the visionary poetry is disrupted by the return of affect in sporadic expressions of longing or anguish. Whether in the verbal self-lacerations of *Une Saison en enfer* or in the quivering exhilaration of the *Illuminations*, poetic expression brings forth a sense of what language cannot contain: irrepressible, unquenchable desire.

At the start of this chapter, I outlined the transition in Rimbaud's poetry from the language of materiality (*Poésies*) to the materiality of language (*Illuminations*). My reading confirms and complicates this opposition. In the early poetry and in *Une Saison en enfer*, the representation of material things and abstract structures is 'thickened' in startling descriptions of mess and matter, colour, and texture. As the language of materiality unfolds, so the materiality of language is revealed: to contest aesthetic frames or critique processes of identity-formation is to challenge the integrity and the stability of language. As poetic expressivity is stretched and reinvented, the clash and collapse of discourses duplicates the hybridness or the messiness of things. Hence, Rimbaud's teeming style, with its tonal conflicts, its scattering of neologism, archaism, and regionalism, its interspersing of idiomatic speech with technical terminology, its mixing of literary discourse with taboo slang. The exasperated engagement with socio-cultural rigidities in *Poésies* exploits the language of materiality and, in the process, draws into focus the materiality of language. This prepares the ground for *Une*

Saison en enfer, where de(con)structive energy is turned directly on a self trapped in the mesh of discourses. The autobiography of a smouldering, uncontainable 'je' who veers between longing and self-loathing, between corrosive fulmination and sterile exasperation, puts language itself on trial. The challenge to reinvent poetic idiom, taken up in *Poésies* and extended through the discursive rifts and shifts of *Une Saison en enfer*, is radically redefined in the *Illuminations*, where the conditions for reading are themselves problematized. The disrupted structures and vertiginous shifts of the visionary poetry foreground the interpretative act, its possibilities and its limitations. Poetry's reflection on its processes (construction, fracturing, transformation, abolition) directs readerly attention once more to the materiality of language – to the convulsive opulence of the visionary imagination. Confronting the desirability and the impossibility of arresting the cascades of sublime beauty, the reader is mesmerically drawn to those moments where anxiety or longing materialize, momentarily, in visions of flesh and fabric, in pools of saturated colour and patches of luminosity. In the beguiling remoteness of the Rimbaldian sublime, affect returns formed in the language of the material world.

2 Material Fragments, Autobiographical Fantasy: Reading Apollinaire's *Calligrammes*

Of the poets explored in this book, Apollinaire illustrates most urgently the tension between materiality and subjectivity as the modernist consciousness grapples to make sense of a technologically challenging new world, both in its exhilarating potential and in the pressures it exerts across the range of human experience and activity.[1] The preface-text of *Calligrammes*, Apollinaire's second major collection of poetry, exposes a paradoxical, irremediably fractured self, a self at once in thrall to material modernity and tempted by regressive introspection:

J'écris seulement pour vous exalter
Ô sens ô sens chéris
Ennemis du souvenir
Ennemis du désir

Ennemis du regret
Ennemis des larmes
Ennemis de tout ce que j'aime encore   ('Liens')

The acute aporia probed in this opening poem demands to be set in the wider context of the tensions that criss-cross Apollinaire's writing from *Alcools* (1913) to *Calligrammes* (1918). Throughout the earlier collection, an enduring attachment to Romantic and Symbolist expression is increasingly rivalled by irony and self-scepticism: in *Alcools*, the gentle, even lyricism of 'Rhénanes' is disrupted by the frame-shattering innovation of 'Le Voyageur' and 'Zone.' The elegiac tradition is aggressively challenged by the pressures of global immediacy and the insistent 'objectivism' of cubist-inspired textual practices. But where the siren-song of the past is drowned out by galloping gramophones ('Tu chantes avec les autres tandis que les phonographes galopent,' 'Arbre'), a closer reading of Apollinaire's post-*Alcools* poetry reveals a more hesitant, unresolved sensibility struggling with the rival demands of self-nourishing inwardness and the Futurist-prescribed embrace of the new. For Apollinaire, composing his poetic testament in 1918 – a crystalline moment of personal definition and aesthetic self-evaluation – the appeal of permanency and the thrill of experimentalism reaffirm the productive tensions that work their taut magic across his poetry:

Je sais d'ancien et de nouveau autant qu'un homme seul
   pourrait des deux savoir
Et sans m'inquiéter aujourd'hui de cette guerre
Entre nous et pour nous mes amis
Je juge cette longue querelle de la tradition et de l'invention
         De l'Ordre et de l'Aventure   ('La Jolie Rousse')

Not only in retrospective self-assessment, but consciously and lucidly at every point along his creative trajectory, Apollinaire stages the competing pressures that shape his strain of receptive and yet passionately independent poetic modernism in the first two decades of the twentieth century. Those pressures are summed up powerfully in the transformative opening vision of 'La Chanson du mal-aimé,' where the distinctions between urban violence and human vulnerability, biblical persecution and personal guilt, myth and the everyday collapse together in a searing expression of anxiety and desire:

Je suivis ce mauvais garçon
Qui sifflotait mains dans les poches
Nous semblions entre les maisons
Onde ouverte de la mer Rouge
Lui les Hébreux moi Pharaon

Que tombent ces vagues de briques
Si tu ne fus pas bien aimée
Je suis le souverain d'Égypte
Sa soeur-épouse son armée
Si tu n'es pas l'amour unique

The focus of this chapter is the richly textured poetry of *Calligrammes:*

Poèmes de la paix et de la guerre, Apollinaire's major collection of the post-1912 period. Composed in two phases – the pre-war experimentalist series (*Ondes*) and the autobiographical war poetry – *Calligrammes* confronts the relations between materiality and subjectivity in urgent new ways. Apollinaire sources his material in everyday culture and in the exceptional contingency of world conflict; he sets the palpable pleasure experienced in the real against the anxiety induced by a deep sense of historical dislocation; he probes the fractured experience of subjectivity shaped by quotidian events and by the desire to wrest free of the real through fantasy and dream-work. While the image-texts (*idéogrammes lyriques*) explode the differences between the visual and the verbal, signified and signifier, in more sporadic ways, the creative instabilities sustained across *Calligrammes* articulate an exquisitely contradictory subjectivity, one deeply immersed in the physical and material.

For all its significance in the canon of European twentieth-century modernist poetry, *Calligrammes* continues, with several signal exceptions, to suffer a lack of critical exposure compared with *Alcools*. The opening *Ondes* series has been brilliantly illumined by Marjorie Perloff in comparative readings, and has sparked an adventurous, more sustained analysis by Timothy Mathews; the war poetry has benefited from an authoritative contextual study and a fine critical edition by Claude Debon.[2] Yet, with the unsurpassed exception of Anne Hyde Greet and S.I. Lockerbie's bilingual edition, there have been very few integral readings of the complete volume.[3] While this chapter goes some way to addressing that lacuna, my primary aim is to track the coincidence of subjectivity and the material across the span of Apollinaire's major post-*Alcools* output.

I focus first on the poetry of 1912–14, the most radically modernist phase. Here, subjectivity confronts the rival pressures of material saturation and sublime abstraction as poetry strives to capture in words the visual expressivity of Robert Delaunay's pure colour harmonies.[4] With its glittering tropes of technology, communications, travel, commodities, leisure, sensory data, transport, new media, sociability, habitat, clothing, and leisure, this is the poetry for which the most pressing claim to 'objectivity' can be made in terms of hard empirical content, the textual fracturing of colour and light sensations, and the materialization of the shock of the new in structural discontinuity, radical juxtapositions, and elliptical syntax. And yet, even as the 'objective' brilliance of these texts works to obscure subjectivity, the process seems to reverse itself and shower the conspicuous outwardness of Apollinaire's 1912–14 poetry with sparks of self-expressivity.[5]

The fate of subjectivity comes powerfully and poignantly into focus in the war poetry of *Calligrammes*, presented chronologically in five sections from *Étendards* to *La Tête étoilée*. The second, longer part of this chapter is devoted to this substantial final phase of Apollinaire's output. The autobiographical probing of the extreme pressures of physical survival and psychic self-preservation makes the war poetry a compelling case study of subjective–material interrelations.

Calligrammes presents us, then, with two very different writing contexts defined retrospectively by the historical dislocation of 1914 ('poèmes de la paix' / 'poèmes de la guerre'). Linking these two phases is the urgency of negotiating subjectivity in radically altered material situations defined, in *Ondes*, by the modern urban context and, in the subsequent sections of the book, by front-line experience of the First World War. I treat the 'poèmes de la paix' and the 'poèmes de la guerre' for the most part independently, focusing on the outward 'objectivity' and the dispersed 'je' of *Ondes* and tracking the fluctuations of autobiographical writing in the war poems.[6]

Material Limits – The Experimental Poetry 1912–1914

Apollinaire's experimental poetry is dazzling evidence of modernism's embrace of what we might call, after Pound, a language of concrete things.[7] As *Ondes* unfolds the compelling, colour-saturated fabric of contemporary life, the materiality of the poems of 1912–14 finds concrete form in the ideogrammatic texts, but achieves a more pervasive expression in a seam of references to events, exchanges, sensations, perceptions, physical entities, and objects both simple and complex, organic and mechanical. Apollinaire's texts capture the sheer diversity of material experience from the mesmerizing pleasure of paring an orange to the natural cacophony of the tropical rain forest; they impart the thrill of transcontinental train journeys and register simple, timeless acts like that of an old man bathing his feet.

The preoccupation with material modernity first erupts in the major city poems of Apollinaire's celebrated *Alcools* collection. Frenzied trams blazing along their tracks reverberate with the anguish of the inwardly broken subject of 'La Chanson du mal-aimé': 'Flambant de l'électricité / Les tramways feux verts sur l'échine / Musiquent au long des portées / De rails leur folie de machines.' The energized, resolutely outward vision of 'Zone,' the iconically modernist overture to *Alcools*, encompasses the Eiffel Tower and the mass marketing of popular fiction, the harsh reality of community ghettoes and high culture's colonization of 'primitive' art. Yet, even as 'Zone' celebrates receptivity and activity, movement and exchange, its fractured narrative and splintering simultanism tell of an irremediable loss of centredness. This is variously expressed in the language of religious scepticism, individual displacement, nostalgia, violence, self-doubt, ethnic isolation, and the meagre aspirations of emigrants. In the city poems of *Alcools* modernity emerges as an unsettlingly hybrid experience, alternately stimulating and desolating, thrilling and corrosive ('Ta vie que tu bois comme une eau-de-vie').

Apollinaire catches the variability of modern experience in poetry that is vitally capacious and deeply fragmentary; his 'simultanism' combines global unboundedness and intense compression as if the whole of life – its epic, technology-mapped expanses and its tiny human-filled instances – were momentarily held together in the sudden ample dilation of consciousness.[8] The texts of 1912–14 take forward the simultaneous desire to plunge into the infinitely small and to embrace the large-scale and structurally complex that is manifest in certain pre-1913 texts like 'Le Voyageur,' 'Zone,' and 'La Chanson du mal-aimé,' and theorized by Apollinaire in his 1917 lecture *L'Esprit nouveau et les poètes*:

[L'esprit du poète] poursuit la découverte aussi bien dans les synthèses les plus vastes et les plus insaisissables: foules, nébuleuses, océans, nations, que dans les faits en apparence les plus simples: une main qui fouille une poche, une allumette qui s'allume par le frottement, des cris d'animaux, l'odeur des jardins après la pluie, une flamme qui naît dans un foyer.[9]

The urge to synthesize the epic and the banal, the exotic and the ordinary, envisages a new, optimal equality between material things as part of the broader aim of democratizing the relations between poetry and the contemporary media:

Dans le domaine de l'inspiration, [la] liberté [des poètes modernes] ne peut pas être moins grande que celle d'un journal quotidien qui traite dans une seule feuille des matières les plus diverses, parcourt les pays les plus éloignés. On se demande pourquoi le poète n'aurait pas une liberté au moins égale et serait tenu, à une époque de téléphone, de télégraphie sans fil et d'aviation, à plus de circonspection vis-à-vis des espaces.[10]

In the 1912–14 texts, the desire to achieve a new synergy and symmetry between poetry and the modern world drives the expansion of thematic horizons and accelerates the simultanist dynamic. These changes bring a new acuity and a harder edge to the mythopoeic modernism that had produced, in *Alcools*, the vision of London terraced houses crashing into the Red Sea, and the aerial fantasy of assorted prophets and philosophers swirling around the allegorical trophy of the new century, the punningly secular aeroplane ('changé en oiseau ce siècle comme Jésus monte dans l'air,' 'Zone').

The profusion of references to scientific and technological materiality in *Ondes* imparts the heroic current of modern sensibility in more fractured but no less intense visions. 'Les Collines' presents a series of modernist epiphanies where a car driver sounds his horn as he rounds each bend in anticipation of a revelation, and where a resplendent twentieth-century muse ascends in a lift, hailing discovery, literally at every level.[11] In its deployment of images of mechanicity and movement, desire and transfiguration, 'Les Collines' anticipates the far horizon of the new century's experimentalism and, more imminently, the birth of surrealism:

L'esclave tient une épée nue
Semblable aux sources et aux fleuves
Et chaque fois qu'elle s'abaisse
Un univers est éventré
Dont il sort des mondes nouveaux

The poems of *Ondes* take forward the heroic current through a chain of references linking 'train,' 'tramway,' 'câbles sous-marins,' 'téléphone,' 'avion,' 'biplan,' 'cablegramme,' 'hydroplan,' 'ascenseur,' 'trolley,' 'transsibérien,' 'autobus,' and 'vaisseaux.' The abundance of these linked signifiers injects poetry with actuality, forming tropes of travel, speed, discovery, surprise, exchange, functionalism, progress, production, and communication that combine to evoke the prodigious expansion of relations between the individual citizen and the physical world. Apollinaire's investment, in his poetry and his critical texts alike, in the key referents of material modernity affirms the penetrating impact of technology on the contemporary consciousness.

Exploring the semantics of objectivity in literary texts, Roland Barthes identifies a writerly obsession with the use-value of material things, their place in everyday praxis, and their enabling and enhancing functions.[12] The poems of *Ondes* register this obsession in the vision of a night-train rushing through a wintry Canadian landscape ('Les Fenêtres'), in a jokey allusion to the usefulness of telephones for communicating poetry ('Les Fenêtres'), and most overtly in the calligrammatic representations of a 'cigar-as-it-burns' ('Paysage') and a radio beacon emitting sound waves ('Lettre-Océan'). The poetic capturing of material things in *motion* or as *process* confirms Barthes's insistence on the transitive relation between objects and their users for there exist no objects without intentions being directed towards those objects, and, conversely, no human action is possible without the mediation of things.[13] Through subject–matter transitivity, the significance of objects quickly exceeds their instrumentality or functional value: objects become the bearers of social and cultural information – both affirmative and depreciative – in a nexus of symbolic meanings that spans power, pleasure, alienation, globalization, social exchange, receptivity, and standardization. What Barthes identifies as 'une sorte d'échappée de l'objet [...] vers l'infiniment social' expands in Apollinaire's poetic inventory to include the infinitely cultural, technical, geographical, economic, and ethnographical.[14] Like a sociologist or cultural commentator, the poet surveys the urban terrain, observing modes of production and consumption, noting evidence of spiritual belief-systems, employment practices, professional protocols, sartorial customs, the creative use of time and space, the incidence of illness and deviance, leisure activities, and food consumption. Like a fly-on-the-wall documentary-maker in 'Lundi rue Christine,' he inserts himself in the space of sociability, and registers linguistic mores and cultural practices in the raw as he records everything from overheard plans for criminal activity to friendship rituals, intimations of sexual transgression, and codes of social snobbery.

At the same time, the splicing of 'objective' instances with humorous or self-debunking interjections ('comme l'on s'amuse si bien') or proto-surrealist fantasies ('Cette dame a le nez comme un ver solitaire') cancels any claim to narratorial neutrality, and affirms subjectivity as the force sifting the multicoloured tesserae of quotidian experience and poetic invention.[15]

In 'Les Fenêtres,' the globalization of communications remaps the quotidian, and extends the boundaries of experience and knowability into the (formerly) exotic reaches of the northern and southern hemispheres: from the tropics ('Quand chantent les aras dans les forêts natales') to the vast silent spaces of North America ('Vancouver / Où le train blanc de neige et de feux nocturnes fuit l'hiver'). The internationalization of exchanges is underlined in 'Arbre' by the textual circulation of consumer goods, from the bulk cargo of 'deux vaisseaux norvégiens amarrés à Rouen' to the more modest stock of the 'voyageur en bijouterie' with its clear echo of Cendrars's *Prose du Transsibérien et de la petite Jeanne de France.*[16] Whether in the form of a carton of Russian cigarettes ('À travers l'Europe') or a coveted fur coat ('Lundi rue Christine') intertextually fashioned from the Canadian raccoon skins evoked in 'Les Fenêtres' – the lure of luxury, the appeal of the exotic, the technological colonization of space, and the sheer desirability of other things and other places trigger a surge of euphoria whose source lies, not in individualized self-presence, but in decentred subjectivity that attaches intermittently to material things.

The vividness of concrete language, the vitality imparted by numerous indications of travel and transit ('Paris Vancouver Hyères Maintenon New-York et les Antilles' in 'Les Fenêtres'), and the accumulation of chaotic fragments of everyday existence reveal an intensely active engagement with the real:

> Entre les pierres
> Entre les vêtements multicolores de la vitrine
> Entre les charbons ardents du marchand de marrons
> Entre deux vaisseaux norvégiens amarrés à Rouen
> Il y a ton image   ('Arbre')

It is precisely in those most outwardly 'objective' descriptions that the subject – alternately sceptical and elated, permeable and resistant – makes its return, a movement that Barthes calls 'une sorte d'échappée de l'objet vers l'infiniment *subjectif*' (my emphasis).[17]

The focus on a particular quality of an object or surface beheld – colour, movement, and refracted light – brings forth stunningly visual images: there is the cool brilliance of the 'étincelant diamant' recovered in 'Les Fenêtres,' the dizzying dance of the 'petits feux multicolores' glimpsed in 'À travers l'Europe.' Such fractured instances of perception are expansive in their momentum and synthetic in their potential: they are the sign of poetry surpassing the limitations of physical objectivity in order to articulate an subjectively energized experience of the material world. Here metonymy falls away to reveal metaphors of beauty and iridescence: 'Ispahan s'est fait un ciel de carreaux émaillés de bleu' ('Arbre'). This synthesis of fragmentation and expansiveness has important implications for visual–verbal relations: the rush of colour and light sensations generates a euphoric synergy between poetry and painting, exemplified by the collaboration of Apollinaire and the painter Robert Delaunay. The coloured rhythms of Delaunay's *cubisme orphique*[18] capture modernity's most stunning visualizations: advertising, sport, the Eiffel Tower, the automobile, and, most compellingly and prospectively, aviation.[19] The colour and vitality flashing through *Ondes* find a pictorial analogue in Delaunay's 'L'Équipe de Cardiff' (1913), where the athletic energy of the rugby players and the locomotion of plane and Ferris wheel create a prismatic harmony. 'Les Fenêtres' is a poetic complement to Delaunay's homonymic series of abstract paintings in its polychromatic purity ('Du rouge au vert tout le jaune se meurt') and its explosive colour and luminosity ('La fenêtre s'ouvre comme une orange / Le beau fruit de la lumière').

Visual and verbal media form the touchstone of a modern sensibility alive to the dazzling creativity inhering in the organic and technological. At the same time, Apollinaire's modernist poetry diverges from the unequivocally confident assumptions of Orphist painting in bringing forward competing perspectives on material modernity. Euphoria is sapped by disenchantment as the sublime concord glimpsed in 'Liens' is cancelled by the polyglottal jangle erupting on the radio waves that radiate across the textual space of 'Lettre-Océan.' Already in *Alcools*, signs of acoustic discord resonate across the city-texts, intimating an exasperated, even brutalized consciousness: in 'Le Voyageur,' raucous 'sonneries électriques' are placed in ironic juxtaposition to idyllic 'chants des moissonneuses.' The dystopic vision of the age of mechanical reproduction originating in '1909' (*Alcools*) is relayed through 'Arbre' (*Calligrammes*), where mass production is envisioned as an inhuman birthing process, prefiguring anxieties over human cloning in our own era: 'L'univers se plaint par ta voix / Et des êtres nouveaux surgissent / Trois par trois.' City experience from *Alcools* through to *Calligrammes* is outwardly energizing but irreversibly entropic when animation veers towards anomie and desire descends into dementia ('Les villes que j'ai vues vivaient comme des folles,' 'Le Voyageur'). Poetry pathologizes subjective disarray in hallucinatory visions of a fevered metropolis: 'Te souviens-tu du long orphelinat des gares / Nous traversâmes des villes qui tout le jour tournaient / Et vomissaient la nuit le soleil des journées' ('Le Voyageur'). The vision of the fragilized, failing body of the city is taken forward in *Ondes* by the proliferation of individualized signs of illness and morbidity, from the wheezing of 'la patronne poitrinaire' ('Lundi rue Christine'), through the poignant reminder of 'certaines jeunes filles fraîches mais près de la mort' ('Un fantôme de nuées'), to the spasms of the solitary epileptic in the first-class railway waiting room ('Arbre').

If these particularized instances of depression and debility puncture the confident expressivity of *Ondes* in sporadic ways, the entire 1912–14 series is darkened from the outset by the violent dystopia unleashed in the visual and sound assault of 'Liens': 'Cordes faites de cris / Sons de cloches à travers l'Europe / Siècles pendus.' This premonitory intimation of conflict and extreme suffering echoes through the image of 'hung centuries,' a figure for the historical dislocation of 1914 and its world-shaping human impact. Thus, the opening poem of *Ondes* provides a prospective, even prophetic, link to 'La Petite Auto,' and the vast psychic trauma that unfolds in this introductory poem of the war poetry of *Calligrammes*.[20] The unremitting bleakness of the opening lines of 'Liens' is refigured as a phenomenology of hardness and constraint ('Rails qui ligotez les nations'), but what is most striking is the poem's exposure of its conscious indeterminacy: the oscillation between deep pessimism and catastrophe prophecy, on the one hand, and, on the other, the luminous transformation of unfathomable human suffering in a dream of sublime harmony ('D'autres liens plus ténus / Blancs rayons de lumière / Cordes et Concorde'). 'Liens' illustrates modernism's tendency to expose, through its disrupted structures and non-coalescent images, the tensions at its centre, most urgently those between perceptual acuity and inner seams of consoling affectivity.

The poems of 1912–14 articulate alternately the euphoric engagement with the material world – its natural and cultural richness, its luxury and its lush luminosity – and the tenacious resistance of self to its aversive effects: standardization, automation, and the unbearable acceleration of the rhythms of everyday life. The variability of subjective responses to modernity brought forth in *Ondes* reflects the intractability of self–world relations: the desire for closure and resolution is resisted and, instead, the ideology of modernity is problematized through its signal objects, the constraining as well as the affirmatively captivating. With the surge towards the contemporary and the real rivalled by an acute awareness of social dislocation, loss of familiarity, and the dispersal of self, Apollinaire's poetry, from the great city poems of *Alcools* to *Ondes* and beyond, reveals a characteristically modernist tendency to dialogize contrastive assessments of the material world. Apollinaire's consciously unresolved response to the contemporary world and his probing of the competing pressures on subjectivity subscribe to a current of European literary modernism that responds to the avant-garde's more solid enthusiasms with fracturing scepticism and destabilizing self-questioning. Apollinaire is closer to the rich, uncertain fluctuations of Eliot than to the flat-line fervour of Marinetti.

My reading has focused thus far on the subjective coloration of the dominant tropes of technology, commerce, and travel in the cosmopolitan space of these texts. I want now to turn to the corpora of small, insignificant things whose obtrusion throughout these poems is striking although largely eclipsed, in critical analyses, by the seductively complex configurations of marine engineering or railway construction. Banal things are presented in the 'raw,' directly incorporated in spare, precise language. While the dull familiarity of old shoes, a pocket watch, a white tie, half a dozen mirrors, sawdust, hashish, a barrel organ, a malachite ring, gas burners, a postcard, a pile of plates, a railway waiting room, and grubby floor rugs provides something of a reality effect, the persistence of trivial objects exceeds the narrow scope of local colour. Their spare, minimally particularized presentation draws attention both to the facticity of such objects and to language in its material, stripped-down aspect. The remarkable aggregate of unremarkable things in the texts of 1912–14 alludes to acts of comfort and consolation, to individual gestures of alteration and transformation. The fascinated gaze that Apollinaire directs at the small-scale objects of everyday consumption, via concise notations, reveals a profoundly human-informed reality and a material counterweight to the overwhelming technological entities that are the epic expression of the modern age. The embrace of the real, at its most unspectacular in whittled-down language, confirms the permeability of poetry, while the sheer proliferation of palpable things – via their signifiers – imparts the desirability of 'thickening' and reclaiming the real as a stand against the levelling effects of a mechanized, streamlined world. Poetry celebrates the persistence of the ordinary, the clichéd, the anachronistic, and the discarded: thus, it brings forth the compelling hybridity of everyday life and intimates the hopes and the habits enfolded in familiar objects. The subjective engagement with accessible, alterable objects generates acts of transformation – real and imaginary – as the everyday is reworked. Transformative practice is purposefully incorporated into the poetry-making process: 'La seule feuille que j'aie cueillie s'est changée en plusieurs mirages' ('Arbre'); 'Tours / Les tours ce sont les rues / Puits / Puits ce sont les places' ('Les Fenêtres'). The transformability of the real, intimately connected to the desire for self-expression and creative invention, links *Ondes* to the war poetry of *Calligrammes*. In my reading of Apollinaire's war poetry, I will return to practices of transformation both in their literal effects (shrapnel turned into rings and whistles, railway sleepers made into a human shelter) and in their metaphorical forms in fantasy and dream-work.

Banal Things and Raw Language

The remarkable openness of Apollinaire's poetry to banal objects and to their analogues in everyday lexical items and speech fragments extends the simultanist urge to communicate the immediacy of contemporary socio-cultural experience in the very language of that experience. This radical remapping of the lexical boundaries of poetry occurs as part of the broader diachronic shift from romantico-symbolist valorizations of literariness, immateriality, and ideality to fresh, 'hard' language more *transparently* communicative of external reality.[21] Poetry seeks to optimize its receptivity to life, and so demands highly readable language that gives the appearance of translating directly the perceived thing or object. Apollinaire practises the kind of poetic permeability that would have a lasting impact on the modernist sensibility, from Cendrars, who implicitly recognized this in 1919 when he claimed 'Les fenêtres de ma poésie sont grand'ouvertes sur les boulevards,' through surrealism, the beat poets, and punk lyrics.[22] By maximizing discursive simplicity and directness, Apollinaire challenges the arbitrary separation of poetic lyricism and lived language, and the absolute separation of language and its material object. This produces 'Lundi rue Christine,' a linguistically hybrid text composed of snatches of conversation ('Si tu es un homme tu m'accompagneras ce soir'), social and professional protocols ('Cher Monsieur,' 'Voici monsieur'), innuendoes, clichés, pleonasms ('C'est complètement impossible'), and exclamations. In this conversational collage, narratorial interventions jostle with foreign-language borrowings, while commercial insignia ('Compagnie de navigation mixte') and phatic interjections compete with self-referential and self-reflexive instances. The dialogical splintering of this text, and related works like 'Les Fenêtres' and 'Arbre,' anticipates the fractured, everyday polyphony of *The Wasteland* ('HURRY UP PLEASE IT'S TIME').

In 'Les Fenêtres,' the onomatopoeia '[l]'oie oua-oua' is both playful and instructive in revealing the mimetic capacity of language to rematerialize perception. The acoustic adventure of these texts extends from human language via animal communication to sound more gener-

ally ('Pim pam pim' captures the behind-the-bar activity of 'Lundi rue
Christine,' and 'les glouglous les couacs' of the street organ reverberate
through 'Un fantôme de nuées'). The logical – or wilfully illogical –
extreme of no-holds-barred sound-play is the noisist endgame of 'La
Victoire' (1917). In this penultimate poem of *Calligrammes*, Apollinaire
reflects on the scope and the limits of experimentalism, when language
is reduced to raw, meaning-free sound:

> On veut de nouveaux sons de nouveaux sons de nouveaux sons
> On veut des consonnes sans voyelles
> Des consonnes qui pètent sourdement
>   Imitez le son de la toupie
> Laissez pétiller un son nasal et continu
> Faites claquer votre langue
> Servez-vous du bruit sourd de celui qui mange sans civilité
> Le raclement aspiré du crachement ferait aussi une belle consonne
>
> Les divers pets labiaux rendraient aussi vos discours claironnants
> Habituez-vous à roter à volonté

If the radical agenda prescribed in this proto-Dadaist manifesto trans-
gresses normative linguistic, literary, and social codes in ways unantici-
pated in the poems of *Ondes*, Apollinaire hovers between musing
playfulness and an ironic alertness to the dangers of linguistic disintegration. Placed under the sign of blind fliers and obsessive figures of
failed audacity ('Icare le faux'), the text exposes the deep anxiety of a
modernist poet who, at the brink of art's dehumanization, retreats to a
more purposive, integrative vision of the contemporary world, and
reasserts the inseparability of the material from affirmative receptivity:

> Nous n'aimons pas assez la joie
> De voir les belles choses neuves
> O mon amie hâte-toi
> Crains qu'un jour un train ne t'émeuve
>   Plus
> Regarde-le plus vite pour toi
> Ces chemins de fer qui circulent
> Sortiront bientôt de la vie
> Ils seront beaux et ridicules

The passion for the contemporary proclaimed in 'La Victoire,' not abstracted or de-realized, but materially present and impinging on consciousness, is a signal feature of *Ondes*, and anticipates a twentieth-century philosophical and aesthetic tradition that runs from surrealism through situationism to the *Annales* school, and reaches all the way to installation art. Apollinaire's dual preoccupation, in the texts of 1912–14, with material things and with the matter of everyday language extends into cultural practices whose diversity and generative potential are celebrated in ways that anticipate the work of the French philosopher Michel de Certeau.[23] This is further evidence of a democratic undertow in poetry, and a sign of the modern lyric turning outward to embrace real life and community-based forms of resistance to the aversive effects of material modernity, that is, to the imposition of a rationalized city-space in which difference and ambiguity – what Certeau calls 'les opacités de l'histoire' – have been factored out.[24] Apollinaire's purview extends from the surreptitious plotting of criminal practices overheard in 'Lundi rue Christine' –

La mère de la concierge et la concierge laisseront tout passer
Si tu es un homme tu m'accompagneras ce soir
Il suffirait qu'un type maintînt la porte cochère
Pendant que l'autre monterait

– to the rights of superstition and fortune-telling celebrated in 'Sur les prophéties':

J'ai connu quelques prophétesses
Madame Salmajour avait appris en Océanie à tirer les cartes
[...]
En ce qui concerne l'avenir elle ne se trompait jamais
[...]

Tout ce qu[e] [Madame Deroy] m'a dit du passé était vrai et tout ce qu'elle
M'a annoncé s'est vérifié dans le temps qu'elle indiquait
[...]
Miroir brisé sel renversé ou pain qui tombe
Puissent ces dieux sans figure m'épargner toujours
[...]

Tout le monde est prophète mon cher André Billy
Mais il y a si longtemps qu'on fait croire aux gens
Qu'ils n'ont aucun avenir qu'ils sont ignorants à jamais
                          Et idiots de naissance
Qu'on en a pris son parti et que nul n'a même l'idée
De se demander s'il connaît l'avenir ou non

Such practices – and 'Sur les prophéties' is unambiguous in this respect – develop as forms of resistance to official recuperations and sanctioned histories. As such they generate imaginative narratives populated by self-selecting protagonists who plot their moves and work patiently and passionately against the flow of rationality and formal prescription, and, in the process, construct alternative visions of the world. The persistence in the modern metropolis of traditional popular entertainments is offered as an arresting example of the creativity of the marginal:

Ces gens qui font des tours en plein air
Commencent à être rares à Paris
Dans ma jeunesse on en voyait beaucoup plus qu'aujourd'hui
Ils s'en sont allés presque tous en province   ('Un fantôme de nuées')

Introducing his subject in direct, prosaic tones, the autobiographical poet-narrator identifies in a tawdry acrobatic performance a salient example of the potential of the everyday to oppose normal space and time contingencies. The performance unfolds to reveal a (symbolically) transformative activity as the pliancy of the smallest acrobat, 'l'enfant miraculeux,' momentarily restores the magical and irrational and all that such a restoration represents in the sublimely *unflat* terms of incident, wonderment, and desire:

Une jambe en arrière prête à la génuflexion
Il salua ainsi aux quatre points cardinaux
Et quand il marcha sur une boule
Son corps mince devint une musique si délicate que nul parmi les
    spectateurs n'y fut insensible
Un petit esprit sans aucune humanité
Pensa chacun
Et cette musique des formes
Détruisit celle de l'orgue mécanique
[...]

Musique angélique des arbres
Disparition de l'enfant
Les saltimbanques soulevèrent les gros haltères à bout de bras
Ils jonglèrent avec les poids

Mais chaque spectateur cherchait en soi l'enfant miraculeux
Siècle ô siècle des nuages

The kinetic creativity of the acrobat brings forth the sublime in a performance that connects subject and surface, performer and audience, consciousness and its object, world and text in mutually illuminating interaction. The spectators discern in the acrobat's sinuous movement a metaphor for their own desire to escape finitude. As the marvellous – what Apollinaire calls *surnaturalisme* – floods the everyday, contingency is overruled, and a rarefied moment is captured as mythopoeic memory.

Subjective desire and the urge to creative and narrative transformation are provisionally unbounded in manifold acts of moving, prophesying, plotting, desiring, myth-making, and dreaming. Such deviation from the (model) modern citizen's linear progress along the well-paved routes of rationality and utility involve acts of boundary-crossing (the boundaries being those of space and time, regulation, and habit); such acts represent a symbolic seizing of freedom. A parallel text to 'Un fantôme de nuées,' in this respect, is 'Le Musicien de Saint-Merry.' Here the *surnaturaliste* consciousness originates in the mythically refigured time-space of externality, and develops actively in the dream-work of the first-person poet-narrator. Excursive freedom ('Je chante la joie d'errer et le plaisir d'en mourir') gives rise to a modernist revision of the Pied Piper legend, and to a poetic vision that elides the boundaries between desire and anxiety, walking and dreaming, past and present, self and other, body and consciousness:[25]

Le 21 du mois de mai 1913
Passeur des morts et les mordonnantes mériennes
Des millions de mouches éventaient une splendeur
Quand un homme sans yeux sans nez et sans oreilles
Quittant le Sébasto entra dans la rue Aubry-le-Boucher
Jeune l'homme était brun et ce couleur de fraise sur les joues
Homme Ah! Ariane
Il jouait de la flûte et la musique dirigeait ses pas
Il s'arrêta au coin de la rue Saint-Martin
Jouant l'air que je chante et que j'ai inventé

Where 'Un fantôme de nuées' develops as an *account* of the *surnaturaliste* potential of the everyday, 'Le Musicien de Saint-Merry' is performative in its active incorporation of transformation as a textual strategy. Here, the everyday that is disjunctively present in simultanist eruptions ('Ailleurs / Elle traverse un pont qui relie Bonn à Beuel et disparaît à travers Pützchen'; 'Tu pleurais assise près de moi au fond d'un fiacre') provides the material for a fantastic figuration of the anxious desire of the solipsistic narrator:

> Les femmes le suivirent dans la maison abandonnée
> Et toutes y entrèrent confondues en bande
> Toutes toutes y entrèrent sans regarder derrière elles
> Sans regretter le jour la vie et la mémoire

Visualizing the Everyday

Ondes brings forth the creative potential of practices as diverse as fortune-telling and street acrobatics, criminal plotting, and individual acts of fantasizing. As they generate narratives of subjectivity momentarily transfigured, such practices surge against the standardizing ideologies of material modernity – rationalism, uniformity, productivity, and utility. They transform, temporarily, the prosaic and the constrained into events of restorative self-expressivity. As *Ondes* celebrates the mythic reserves of the everyday, it reveals poetry's capacious embrace of the quotidian as a model for its creativity. Already in 'Zone,' Apollinaire had proclaimed this signal aesthetic reorientation when he turned his gaze on advertising tracts and cheap detective novels, and announced 'voilà la poésie ce matin.' Now, in *Ondes*, the call to merge materiality and poetry, high art and commodity culture becomes more insistent: 'Rivalise donc poète avec les étiquettes des parfumeurs' ('Le Musicien de Saint-Merry').

The inspiriting coincidence of word and image has its most conspicuous impact in the concrete poems of *Ondes*, but the *calligrammes* are only one manifestation of the creative energy invested in forms of visual–verbal relationality sourced in the everyday. The joyous interplay of colour, shape, and language in advertisements, the mythic potential of familiar cultural practices, and the paradoxical magic of banal things, reveal – throughout the experimental series – an acute consciousness of the aesthetic possibilities of quotidian reality. *Ondes* translates the perceptual intensity generated by ordinary things into poetic visions of mesmerizing beauty. In 'Les Fenêtres,' the evocation of an array of fish and shellfish calls up the range of visual and haptic qualities – from the seductively smooth to the intriguingly rough – to create the verbal analogue of a luminous Chardinesque still life, but teeming with the cosmopolitan life that is relayed by the exoticism of the names 'Bigorneaux Lotte multiples Soleils et l'Oursin du couchant.' The dual perception of the autonomy of discrete objects and of the contingent relations between objects affirms their plasticity, and produces in 'Lundi rue Christine' a still-life composition with three objects: 'Des piles de soucoupes des fleurs un calendrier.' With its tropes of consumption, nature, and transience, this 'objective' construction recalls contemporary cubist *papiers collés*, material syntheses that embrace everyday reality (typically that of the café counter) and bear physically composite title descriptions like Braque's famous 'Verre, carafe et journaux' (1913).[26]

The concept of a pictorial object constructed from diverse everyday materials is something Apollinaire seeks to approximate at two related levels – the local, or micro-textual, and the global, or macro-textual. The 'local' level pertains to the material referents of discrete lexical structures and fragments, the thematic components of the text. At 'global' level, the text works to transcend its material content in order to become an object in its own right – to out-sum the sum of its parts. This is most vividly instanced in 'Les Fenêtres,' where the global objective (what we might call experimentalist 'textuality') is promoted by the composition of a textual surface from autonomous, discontinuous structures and by the suspension of narrative linearity in favour of self-referential circularity. The framing of the poem by the non-objective interplay of pure colour ('Du rouge au vert tout le jaune se meurt') is an abstract expression of the writerly urge to situate the text beyond the materiality of its thematic content in the space of non-representationality.

Yet, it is precisely at the point where modernist poetry, in its push to formalist autonomy, achieves a materiality of its own that it turns back to reaffirm its empathy with the empirical and the real. The production of a composite, simultanist textuality is coextensive with the actualization and 'objectification' of poetry's themes, for empirical referentiality demands textual structures that are hard and dense, fractured and reconstructable. The more compacted form of 'Les Fenêtres' (marked by the absence of blank spaces between lines) signals the harder consistency of the object-poem, consonant with its material thematics. (It is the typographical antithesis of the more aerated, open forms deployed by Pierre Reverdy in *Les Ardoises du toit*.)[27] Where the proliferation of nouns, proper and common, the high incidence of metonymies, and the structural fracturing of the poem combine to produce a static textual surface in 'Les Fenêtres,' this is challenged from below by themes of dynamism, movement, light, and rhythmic colour. The direction of the flow reverses again, for the transparency of discrete lexical or syntactic units is vigorously contested by the opaqueness of the poem's global 'message,' by its non-delivery of a continuous narrative seam. This is where the resolutely ironic value of Apollinaire's windows-text relativizes its opening on to the world in a *fort-da* game; now revealing, now obscuring its summative meaning. The experimental poem thus activates a problematics of reading: if the open structures of the poem invite readerly creativity, they deny the interpreting reader access to a stable defined speaker, and thwart our attempts to impose hierarchical order on instances that appear to claim equal weight. The traces of a traditionally stable – falsely reliable – narrating voice are rarely audible except in occasional ironic intrusions like 'Ça a l'air de rimer,' where patently nothing rhymes ('Lundi rue Christine'), or in playful instances when he speaks of the poem to be hatched and dispatched ('Nous l'enverrons en message téléphonique,' ibid.). By maximizing lacunae, abridging some structures and extending others, creating slippages between present, past, and future time/tense, the text multiplies its possibilities for meaning, maximizes the fluidity of its verbal instances in the absence of punctuation, and affirms the resistance of experimental writing to monological recuperation. There is, in this respect, a strong correlation between the material status of Apollinaire's most experimental poetry and his reflections on contemporary painting's rejection of the figurative and representational:

> Beaucoup de peintres nouveaux ne peignent que des tableaux où il n'y a pas de sujet véritable. [...] La vraisemblance n'a plus aucune importance, car tout est sacrifié par l'artiste aux vérités, aux nécessités d'une nature supérieure qu'il suppose sans la découvrir. Le sujet ne compte plus ou s'il compte c'est à peine. (*Les Peintres cubistes*, 58)

At the same time, Apollinaire retreats from the limit position of object-free, subject-free abstractionism to which the formalist experiment leads. Even the most elliptical poetic syntax, in the friction of contiguous surfaces, becomes flooded with subjectivity. In 'Arbre' the juxtaposition of dissonant objectivities produces a vision of vulnerability and violence in the very absence of connective syntax:

Un enfant
Un veau dépouillé pendu à l'étal
Un enfant

The productive unevenness of the textual surface brings forth deep affective associations that resist the frame of a pure textual object. The pull to the material is, then, always a pull to the subjective, and this is arguably what Apollinaire has in mind when he refers to the constitution of the literary text in words 'faits d'avance,' distinct from the 'admirable' objectivizing language of cubist painting.[28] So, even as Apollinaire tests the transposability to poetry of the art of analytical dissection that he championed in *Les Peintres cubistes*, his texts expose the limitations of objective impersonality and the irresistible surge of subjectivity.

Apollinaire's probing of the intractably uneven experience of material modernity generates poetry that is capacious and disjunctive, sublimely permeable and inherently complex.[29] The splintered surfaces and hybrid structures of the *Ondes* poems articulate competing visions of physical modernity. In the constant fluctuation of euphoric and dystopic instances, subjectivity returns dispersed across the seductive debris of everyday culture. Surfacing through destabilized syntax and simultaneous displacements, the processes of gathering, relaying, and transforming material things sustain the shoring of fragments of enduring human experience against the threats of subjective dissolution and cultural levelling. Regeneration comes in the production of visually charged moments that rip free of contingency, and fill with colour and luminosity.

Apollinaire's war poetry takes forward the complex engagement of the self with materiality at the point where the exceptional conditions of front-line war experience pose a severe challenge to the physical and psychic preservation of self. Whereas in *Ondes* subjectivity is enfolded into the material and breaks forth in world-transfiguring instances, the war poetry forms subjectivity in a more sustained autobiographical consciousness that is shaped by and strains against extraordinary contingencies.

Autobiographical Fantasy: The War Poetry

Controversial in its content, tantalizingly elusive in its response to an exceptional moment in history, Apollinaire's war poetry met with a hostile reaction from apologists of the moral purpose of the genre. Many contemporary readers, most vociferously the surrealists, felt that poetry directly inspired by a soldier's experience at the front should be driven by an ethical mission to condemn war and a public responsibility to reflect its horror. The reaction of André Breton was not untypical:

> [Dans les poèmes d'Apollinaire] passait toujours la même flamme mais rien n'y marquait une prise de conscience appréciable des événements. Tout se résolvait par un enthousiasme à coup sûr sincère, mais qui rejoignait alors l'enthousiasme de commande, et, en dépit de l'expression toujours très neuve du sentiment, ne laissait pas pour moi de verser dans le conformisme. Les pires réalités de la guerre étaient éludées ici, les plus légitimes inquiétudes détournées au bénéfice d'une activité de jeu qui se donne toute licence dans les Calligrammes proprement dits, tandis que l'esprit s'obstine on ne peut plus déraisonnablement à vouloir trouver son bien dans le 'décor' de la guerre.[30]

Breton's remarks raise crucial questions over the representation of war in poetry. They engage, prescriptively, with the representability of the real and material, and with the relation of the writer to ethics, history, ideology, military culture, language, and creativity. In light of Breton's reading of Calligrammes, I want first to probe the most urgent of these issues: ethics and the soldier-poet's relation to history.[31]

The surrealists' frustrated search for historical 'fact,' in the form of a 'truthful' depiction of human suffering and an unambiguous indictment of militarism, condemns as inadequate, even cynical, Apollinaire's approach to 'writing the war.' For Breton, the war poetry of Calligrammes is doubly discrepant: not only does it fail to condemn war outright, it neglects (presumed) historical truth in order to stage the illusion of an aestheticized war (what Aragon refers to scathingly as the representation of war's 'beaux côtés' – and what a less partisan and more attentive textual reading might describe as the visual and phantasmatic dimension of Apollinaire's writing).

The surrealist critique presupposes an ethically committed subject, hardwired to History and able to supply an authoritative, monological representation of the bitter reality of combative experience. Breton's ideal narrator-subject would act as a conduit of the extratextual, ensuring the kind of relational transparency between signifier and signified that Breton comes to allegorize some years later in the prologue to his poetic autobiography Nadja: 'je continuerai à habiter ma maison de verre, où l'on peut voir à toute heure qui vient me rendre visite... où je repose la nuit sur un lit de verre aux draps de verre, où *qui je suis* m'apparaîtra tôt ou tard gravé au diamant.'[32] Breton's assessment of Apollinaire's war poetry asserts the desirability of a self-mastering narrator, supremely able to filter out the variability of subjective experience, and give voice to a single, unchanging ideological position. But these assumptions are at variance with modernist poetic practice, founded on affective indeterminacy, self-reflexivity, scepticism, fantasy, and dream-work. War in *Calligrammes* is a complex, lived experience – uneven and contradictory – an experience that, however susceptible to public and collective recuperation, is perceived subjectively, in flashes of recollection, glimmers of recognition, and surges of desire. The discrepancy between the drive to monological recuperation and the demands of experimentalist practice opens a dilemma that is revisited with every world-altering conflict and every attempt to represent it, most stunningly in our own multimedia age by Baudrillard's provocative theorizing of the Gulf War: the representability of war, the intractable relation between lived experience and the narrative transformation of that experience as History.

The restrictive focus of contemporary readers on Apollinaire's alleged moral indifference denies the rights of the individual consciousness, promoting instead a predetermined ethical response; this is radically at odds with the specifically modernist, autobiographical project of *Calligrammes*.[33] My purpose is not to debate the relative legitimacy of competing sets of values (moral versus subjective, mimetic versus experimental, diachronic versus simultanist), but to explore the interactive processes implied as the soldier-poet resists the pressure to 'write History' and opts instead to write the self in ways that privilege consciousness over conscience, private self over public persona.

History, Modernism, Autobiography

The historical dislocation produced by the outbreak of war in 1914 poses a strong challenge to the ahistoricity assumed in modernist writing.[34] As the harsh critical reception of Apollinaire's war poetry makes clear, the sense of a sudden break in the *experiential* narrative of human lives seeks consolation in *textual* narratives that are unbroken, unequivocal, and chronology-bound. Still, such narratives mark a retreat from experimentalist values of spatiality, synchronicity, inwardness, and self-reflexivity, values so pervasively deployed in the pre-war series *Ondes* and in the major poems of *Alcools* from 'La Chanson du mal-aimé' to 'Le Voyageur' and 'Zone.'

The representation of history presents particular difficulties for the modernist poet who is a direct participant in the world-shaping event; specifically, how to reconcile art and actuality, writing and memory, creative experiment and human experience. Apollinaire's commitment to structural pliancy, to semantic openness, and to cubist-informed simultanism, dazzlingly evident in *Ondes*, is suddenly rivalled by demands for moral absolutes and the very abstractions ('History' and 'Truth') to which modernism is passionately resistant. How does Apollinaire negotiate these competing pressures?

The desire to explore the lived reality of war, to probe a shared masculine experience of soldiering – with its drama and its banality, its contradictions and its repetitions, its crushing boredom and its snatched pleasures – brings urgently into focus the desire to know – to know self, to know the multifarious, indefinable Other (comrade, enemy, absent lover), to know the material world. The crucial questions of how self comes into being in these texts and how poetry articulates the variable relations between self and external event, self and the collective real, throw into relief the desirability of narrating the story of the individual, 'his story,' as against the abstract representational prerogative of History. Writerly desire takes the form of an autobiographical project that tracks, through the fluctuations of consciousness, the struggle to make sense of the real; in the process, it exposes soldierly experience as fractured, provisional, and overwhelmingly subjective. The autobiographical project of *Calligrammes* originates with 'La Petite Auto,' where an acute sense of historical dislocation is figured as an apocalyptic birth or rebirth; it concludes with the testamentary text 'La Jolie Rousse.' These poems establish birth and death as the liminal points of the writing project, and invite us to read the intervening texts as the poetico-autobiographical reconstruction of the soldierly experience of war.

The alignment I am proposing between modern poetry and autobiography has first to be set in the context of current theoretical positions. Contemporary autobiography theory has generally excluded poetry on the grounds of the assumed universality and non-specificity of the lyrical 'I.'[35] It is clear that Apollinaire's war poetry substitutes, for that universal self, a strong, referential identity between the extratextual writer and a writing-written self textually present in the specificity of a historically and materially located 'je.' The autobiographical narrative of the war poetry mixes remembrance with fantasy, realism with allegory, humour with deep empathy, whilst references to companions and locations, to events and exchanges – variously verifiable in terms of the real-life experience of the writer – support Apollinaire's claim that 'chacun de mes poèmes est la commémoration d'un événement de ma vie.'[36] Textual and paratextual features commemorate individual participation in the events of a specific historical moment. The subtitle 'Poèmes de la paix et de la guerre, 1913–1916,' and the prefatory references to the context and the methods of reproduction of the *Case d'armons* series affirm a strong relation between textual and extratextual, and, by extension, between the experience of the poet in war and the narrating-narrated 'je.' This is the basis of the autobiographical contract between Apollinaire and his reader.

Before I begin to explore the autobiographical project of *Calligrammes*, I want to consider the particular stylistic appeal of autobiographical writing to the modernist poet.

Autobiographical writing stages a fractured self, doubly represented by the narrating 'je' of the present and the narrated 'je,' the latter fissured along the multiple fault lines of a past variously archived, recalled, reconstructed, fantasized, and allegorized. This fractured self intersects with collective instances ('nous') that signal the absorption of subjectivity in the structures of male homosociality. The self merges more intriguingly with phantomatic second persons, movements captured in the dialogical shifts ('je'/'tu') of poetry that resists implacably fixed third-person positions.[37] This discontinuous, perpetually self-displacing 'je' forms the precarious site where autobiographical pliancy and unresolved modern subjectivity (launched by Rimbaud's fractured 'JE est un autre') coincide.

The fissuring of the autobiographical self into multiple narrative instances has its structural analogue in the processes of destabilization, pluralization, and frame-breaking that derive from cubism and inform the seminal texts of *Alcools*, where the search for self is refracted through the splintering of surfaces, the mixing of fantasy and the prosaic, the compressing of myth and the everyday.[38] The materials of autobiographical writing, like those of modernism, are eclectic: document, dream, art, memory, imagination, desire, allegory, abstraction, the epic, fantasy and phantasm, irony, pathos.[39] The autobiographical impulse shares a characteristically modernist resistance to presenting subjectivity in a single, predetermined way. Subjectivity in autobiographical and modernist writing is protean and paradoxical. Autobiographical writing is coextensive with the experimentalist search for style: the creative, self-generating impulses of autobiography and modernism produce texts that are heterogeneous, permeable, and susceptible to accumulation and to fissure.

Autobiographical writing and modernist writing are characterized by their complex, equivocal engagement with perceptions of external reality. The illusion that autobiography, by recovering the 'real,' will establish 'truth' raises urgent questions – just as modernism does – about the relationship of the self to the material world, hard objects, the body, events, myth, language, history, writing – the very signs by which the self comes into being. The tendency of autobiographical and modernist writing to privilege memory and desire negates the expectation of historical reconstruction, importing in its place indeterminacy and plurality. The coming-into-being of the self gives rise to epistemological uncertainty that is repeatedly figured in these texts in the refusal of visions to coalesce, in disruptive surges of tender or erotic memory, and in the pervasiveness of dream. Fantasies and visionary episodes, however indistinct, represent a deep structuring of desire and anxiety. The soldier-self is an uncertain subject, as unresolved as the structures that contain him; he veers between alienation and a sense of empowerment. The competing discourses – euphoric and dystopic, realist and fantastic, mythic and prosaic, epic and erotic, humorous and poignant, allegorical and colloquial – give voice to permanent uncertainty that is amplified through the structural (and expressive) indeterminacy of the writing. A sense of detachment, masking deep-running alienation and inducing moments of intense introspection, rivals with feelings of exhilarated participation and comradely belonging. The discrepant experience of soldiering exposes subjectivity as intractably anxious and deeply unresolved, caught between the pressures of the real and the pleasures of sublime fantasy.

The Autobiographical Project

In the 'Poèmes de la guerre' of *Calligrammes*, the pressures to account for the historical and to reconstruct soldierly experience are confronted in an autobiographical project that situates the fiction of the writing-written self in the nexus of history viewed, not as objective, transparent, and absolute, but as subjective and provisional.

Classic autobiographical writing presupposes a consistently strong identity between the extratextual writer and the writing-written self. This identity-equation surfaces in instances of explicit self-signature (the naming of 'Gui,' 'Guillaume Apollinaire') and extends through references to known friends, close comrades, and distant lovers.[40] But identity textualized is identity enacted and problematized in writing that de-naturalizes, fragments, and spatializes its subject. Thus, 'Merveille de la guerre' offers a consciously performative instance in which the writing self ('je') signs the narrative of a third-person other constructed in memory and the imagination. The illusory autobiographical 'oneness' of narrator and narratee is thus fractured:

Je lègue à l'avenir l'histoire de Guillaume Apollinaire
Qui fut à la guerre et sut être partout

This transparent and consciously fractured affirmation of a self-life-writing project raises key issues in current autobiography theory: it affirms the process of turning the collective narrative (Histoire) into a personal fiction ('l'histoire de Guillaume Apollinaire'); it alludes to (succumbs to?) the irresistibility of self-fetishization. Crucially, the disjunction between narrating self ('je') and narrated self ('lui, Guillaume Apollinaire') reminds us that, in autobiographical writing, as in modernism, identity focuses not on the holistic, autonomous, stable subject of humanistic interpretation, but on a self constituted in language, a self 'in process,' at once shaped by and straining against material, historical, cultural, linguistic, and narrative containments. As 'Merveille de la guerre' makes explicit, the narrator works to constitute a legendary identity: this struggle has its biographical source in the onomastic fluctuations between 'Wilhelm Apollinaris de Kostrowitzky' (the poet's civil identity; 'Wilhelm' to his mother and his brother) and 'Guillaume Apollinaire' (the pseudonym he chose in 1899 as he embarked on his writing career).

Initiation and Self-Invention

The mobilization of 'l'intrépide bleusaille' ('À Nîmes') offers exceptional conditions for the self coming into being, but for the 'birth' of the autobiographical self we have to look to the opening poem of the war poetry of *Calligrammes*, 'La Petite Auto.' Here, the soldier-narrator aligns his personal anticipation of war (on the eve of mobilization) with a surge in the collective consciousness, with the admixture of euphoria and dread that floods perceptions of social and political upheaval.

Here, a fiction of origins, intertwining personal and collective fates, unfolds through apocalyptic visions of the unknowability of war, its extreme otherness. Unnatural stirrings across the human, animal, and mythical worlds shudder into visions of cataclysm and dystopia. But the same traumatic awakenings and quickening life forms break through scenarios of subjugation to intimate a new era of epic human potential:

Nous dîmes adieu à toute une époque
Des géants furieux se dressaient sur l'Europe
Les aigles quittaient leur aire attendant le soleil
Les poissons voraces montaient des abîmes
Les peuples accouraient pour se connaître à fond
Les morts tremblaient de peur dans leurs sombres demeures

Les chiens aboyaient vers là-bas où étaient les frontières
Je m'en allais portant en moi toutes ces armées qui se battaient
Je les sentais monter en moi et s'étaler les contrées où elles serpentaient

[...]

Océans profonds où remuaient les monstres
Dans les vieilles carcasses naufragées
Hauteurs inimaginables où l'homme combat
Plus haut que l'aigle ne plane
L'homme y combat contre l'homme
Et descend tout à coup comme une étoile filante   ·
Je sentais en moi des êtres neufs pleins de dextérité
Bâtir et aussi agencer un univers nouveau

The Unanimist-inspired vision of multiplied powers subsides and the mythic 'je' is displaced by the discourse of an ordinary human subject whose destiny will be shaped by the forces of history:

Nous arrivâmes à Paris
Au moment où l'on affichait la mobilisation
Nous comprîmes mon camarade et moi
Que la petite auto nous avait conduits dans une époque Nouvelle
Et bien qu'étant déjà tous deux des hommes mûrs
Nous venions cependant de naître   ·

This opening text engages directly with the coming-into-being of the self, illuminating the crucial relationship of individual to collectivity in radically altered ideological and material conditions. Their impact is registered in the destabilizing play of competing styles. The discursive shifting between personal and collective narratives, between mythic agents and a human subject, has implications for what Michael Levenson, with reference to Anglo-American modernist writing, has called the 'fate of individuality.'[41] Here, subjective fate is viewed, retrospectively, as determined by the perception of time as radically discontinuous, by the experience of the historical moment as life-engendering ('bien qu'étant déjà tous deux des hommes mûrs / Nous venions cependant de naître').

The oneirico-mythic vision of mobilization as a traumatic and energizing moment of self-birthing is the inaugural moment of the autobiographical project that concludes, some fifty-seven poems later, with the testamentary text 'La Jolie Rousse' ('Ayant vu la guerre dans l'Artillerie et l'Infanterie / Blessé à la tête trépané sous le chloroforme / Ayant perdu ses meilleurs amis dans l'effroyable lutte / Je sais d'ancien et de nouveau autant qu'un homme seul pourrait des deux savoir'). 'La Jolie Rousse' unfolds as a valedictory affirmation of the narrator's creative and human achievement, as a self-portrait and the summative assessment of a life. It stages the moment at which the writing self and written self coincide most completely – in the plenitude of the testamentary present. The fixing of the narrator's symbolic rebirth and his anticipation of his own death as the liminal points of the self-writing project invites us to reconstruct the intervening texts as a poetic narrative lived *in* and *through* war in which subjectivity is shaped by and actively shapes the representation of history: put simply, I am in history and history is in me.[42]

The broadly chronological ordering of the war poetry in terms of the successive phases of the soldier-narrator's real-time experience responds to the need to impose diachronic structure on the unordered flow of experience, to map that experience developmentally as a 'history of self,' from initiation and the raising of the standard in *Étendards*, through participation in artillery action and the vicissitudes of soldierly experience in *Case d'armons*, to increasing interiorization, fantasizing, and dream-work, processes that coincide with Apollinaire's transfer from artillery duty to front-line infantry service in November 1915. These processes are marked by the consciously poetic titles of the later sections (*Lueurs des tirs, Obus couleur de lune, La Tête étoilée*).

Objects and the Real

Apollinaire's war poetry raises compelling questions about the relationship of the writing-written self to history and, by extension, to the real – the signs (hard objects, language, male homosocial culture, individuality, ideology, desire and dream-work) by which that self comes into being. Referential grounding is key to the authentication of autobiographical writing, a function assumed here by the initiated soldier-poet.[43] Combining the roles of participant, ethnographer, and memorialist of war, he enjoys epistemological authority over the uninitiated reader; and this, despite the various technical inaccuracies and misrepresentations recorded by commentators.[44] Still, as Philippe Hamon argues, the creation of a pervasive reality effect relies not on the reader's ability to confirm a particular sign as accurate, but rather on a broader, vaguer recognition of the generic function of the sign.[45] It does not detract from the referential intention that, occasionally, the soldier-poet mis-remembers or mis-represents the actual or the factual, for the test lies not in his aptitude for local and technical accuracy, but in his power to communicate a sense of the real and create the aura of authenticity.

This aura or sense of the real translates in Apollinaire's war poetry as a kind of 'thickening' of the textual world.[46] Thickening involves importing and re-presenting the extra-textual, and emerges most strikingly in pictorial form in the postal franking marks and the handwritten message reproduced in 'Carte postale':[47]

The textualizing of sensory experience, lived and remembered fragmentally, demands the random material texturing of writing that only
a conspicuously eruptive use of the *calligramme* can produce. Thus, in
'Du Coton dans les oreilles,' the graphic eruption of (mainly) auditory
signals is an attempt to 'materialize' experience in writing that simulates
the shuddering impact of exploding shells, the instantaneous burst of
sound and light, and the ghostly diminuendo of the loud-hailer:

These visible, visualized instances of textual thickening consolidate the
more generalized experimentalist techniques that fracture the representation of memory and desire across the war poetry. The discontinuous
structures of the texts allow the real to surface sporadically in discrete
linguistic and lexical instances.

The relation of the writing-written self to the world of war materializes in multiple references to military structures and functions, to ranks
and hierarchies,[48] to the sectorization of space,[49] to equipment, accom-
modation, food, pastimes, camaraderie, and the soldierly sociolect
(songs, puns, jokes). These references are the building blocks out of
which the narrator – and the reader – will construct the illusion of an
ordered world where men have their roles, places their strategic value,
and objects their functions. Let us stay for the moment with objects.

An extensive, entirely predictable inventory of weapons and munitions can be reconstructed from isolated references to 'obus,' 'fusants,' 'marmites,' 'grenades,' 'mitrailleuses,' 'pièces contre avions,' 'revolver,' 'porteur,' 'canons,' 'gaz asphyxiant,' and 'fils de fer.' The writing focuses less on the actual deployment of munitions (the weapons themselves are only partially described and are rarely contextualized) than on the cultural and linguistic processes of differentiating and discriminating between the components of the military arsenal. Soldierly experience throws up a pell-mell assortment of materials; war poetry reproduces this by filling up with discrete linguistic objects. The discourse of technical differentiation defers the crystallization of explicative meaning, producing in its place a series of discontinuous descriptions that impart something of the fractured nature of soldierly experience – a textual rendering of alienation inscribed on the disparate objects of everyday soldiering. The obsessive naming of parts is, at the same time, a lexical diversion from the unrepresentability of the abstract truth of war, and an intimation of the intractable resistance of front-line experience to representation. The effect of this is to displace autobiographical and readerly focus from the large-scale, technologically complex to the personal 'inventory' of a soldier's life (kit bags, photographs, button cases, rings, letters, newspapers, writing paper, pipes, tobacco, wine). It is here in these private, accessory objects and subsidiary substances ('Bouche ouverte sur un harmonium,' 'une chemise qui sèche' in 'Souvenirs') that the relation of the soldier-self to the real is most visibly imprinted.

The narratorial fixation with the small-scale, the trivial, and unspectacular details speaks of the need to interiorize experience, to invest material things with private meaning: there is the finely engraved ring that Gui makes out of shrapnel as a love-token for Lou and the '[p]etit sifflet à deux trous' that affords endless enjoyment, both objects recovered in 'Oracles.' Glimpses of ordinary existence reveal a strong sense of the pleasure to be found in the most prosaic objects, like 'la trousse à boutons' ('Échelon') with its comforting ethos of repair and restoration. The shared, comradely enjoyment of treats like 'tacot,' 'pinard,' 'gros,' which figure repeatedly in the poems, express the same longing for things – objects and substances – that the soldier can possess, relish, and transform.

The proliferation of small objects and everyday substances in the war poems speaks urgently of a need to imprint the world with private desire and longing, to alter its surface. Material signs reveal the struggle of the soldier-self to affirm individuality under conditions of extreme pressure.[50] Objects may be already present (owned and cherished); objects may be created (the postcard is written, the slogan is framed and hung, graffiti is produced on a blank wall); objects may be transformed or recycled (recovered aluminium is turned into rings and whistles). Materials are shaped, carried, contemplated, consumed, preserved by the soldier who, in turn, seeks in the 'friendly' object a reflection of his own passage through the world; the empathy between human subject and the material world is poignantly articulated in Apollinaire's war poetry. Through things, poetry reveals the presence and the performance of self *in* the world and *upon* the world. The circulation of physical things in the textual economy reflects thus a therapeutic commodification of war, where the transformation of materials is an analogue to writerly activity and speaks of the same desire to compensate for the unknowability of war. By salvaging familiar fragments, the soldier-self can begin to assuage feelings of powerlessness. Recreation is then properly re-creative, leading not only to new objects but also to a reaffirmed sense of individuality.

This pleasurable immersion in small things implies a contraction of the soldier's world as human experience is naturalized or domesticated; this produces fragmentary references to 'Des allumettes qui ne prenaient pas' in 'Mutation' and to details of meal times in 'À Nîmes.'[51] The processes of domestication and contraction extend into the representation of working places and living spaces, and take forward the desire to construct a site of material and linguistic resistance within the zone of hostilities.

External space is partially, temporarily reclaimed in the natural world of wood or field, in places where war seems barely to intrude, where the soldier-self, assigned to some inessential look-out post, passes the time in private recollection. The places of unbreached physical passivity and personal sanctuary favour the most intense imaginative activity as uninterrupted solitariness invites day-dreaming, meditation, remembering, and fantasizing ('Fête'). Unconstructed but notionally circumscribed spaces, like the forest clearing, are retreats where the soldier-poet can override contingencies of space and time, and indulge in activities that resist rational construction and collective appropriation: private contemplation and consolatory self-regeneration through fantasy-work. This is a site of representation intimately linked to the privatization of space.

Indoor space is represented textually in descriptions that emphasize the construction, maintenance, use, and decoration of a collectively defined habitat. The soldier's home-away-from-home is the dugout ('le cagnat,' 'le palais du tonnerre,' 'l'abri-caverne'), a materially hybrid construction that is linguistically refashioned from an inventive mixing of prosaicism, humour, or sardonic fantasy. The obsession with interior space, with its patient construction from precious debris, is coextensive with the retreat into objects – each articulates the desire to limit experience to the familiar and the small-scale, and to value materials that protect and enhance living. Just as the individual object is a thing of fascination, of pleasure taken in its making and appreciation, so the domesticated space of the dugout offers retreat and relaxation, and bears the consoling signs of trace-making activities. Constructing a habitat, or fashioning rings and whistles, demands improvisation, the recycling of non-congruent materials sourced from diverse contexts (barbed wire for bedsprings, packaging materials to provide a door). Particularly striking in the representation of these activities is the slippage from metonymy to metaphor ('débris de craie'/'morceaux de vieillesse'; 'crochets'/'mémoire'). The poem entitled 'Le Palais du tonnerre' offers a particularly salient illustration:

> Le plafond est fait de traverses de chemin de fer
> Entre lesquelles il y a des morceaux de craie et des touffes d'aiguilles de
>   sapin
> Et de temps en temps des débris de craie tombent comme des morceaux
>   de vieillesse
> A côté de l'issue que ferme un tissu lâche d'une espèce qui sert
>   généralement aux emballages
> [...]
> Les fils de fer se tendent partout servant de sommier supportant des
>   planches
> Ils forment aussi des crochets et l'on y suspend mille choses
> Comme on fait à la mémoire

Allusions to the instability of materials and their susceptibility to erosion are spurred by the passage of time and overwhelming feelings of vulnerability. As the soldier-narrator draws attention to the precarious seam of contact between self and the outside world, to the fragile resistance of the materials preserving that seam, simile bears the freight of affectivity. Anxiety over the loss of certainties, the dreaded collapse of structures, and the unpredictability of survival surfaces in repeated descriptions of the uncontainable alterability of the physical world. In

'Dans l'abri-caverne' the soldier-self reveals the material deterioration of his troglodyte dwelling and, in the process, exposes a sense of inner vacancy and self-dissolution:

En face de moi la paroi de craie s'effrite
Il y a des cassures
De longues traces d'outils traces lisses et qui semblent être faites dans de
   la stéarine
Des coins de cassures sont arrachés par le passage des types de ma pièce
Moi j'ai ce soir une âme qui s'est creusée qui est vide

Contrasting with the more poignant instances of space-subjectivization, metaphor invests the physical terrain in ways that rationalize or 'naturalize' the business of war by playing on analogical incongruities – a shell hole is described as 'propre comme une salle de bain' ('Saillant'). Humour, subtended by corrosive irony, has the therapeutic effect of denouncing war in the very process of 'naturalizing' it.

It may be tempting to construct the withdrawal into the materials and minutiae of everyday living as a retreat from History, a diversion from the wholesale public horror of war. But this is to lose sight of autobiographical purpose and a self-writing project whose preoccupation with micro-history (that of individual experience) is a means of reaffirming, actively, the personal and the subjective against the totalizing claims of History.[52] The sustained poetic focus on the material and the everyday presents an implicit counter to the bombast and the abstractions purveyed in the patriotic poetry and journalism of the time ('ces milliers de blessures ne font qu'un article de journal,' the soldier-poet reflects ironically in 'Ombre'). Whether in the fashioning of rings from metal fragments, in the building of 'le palais du tonnerre' from salvage, or indeed in the making of text out of the compelling materials of dream and remembrance, the soldier-self seeks to leave his traces on the world.[53]

The Real of Language

As autobiographical war poetry re-enacts the coming-into-being of the self through material things, 'hard' objects, and sensations, it recovers – salvages – the linguistic components of everyday soldierly experience sourced both in personal discourse and in the warrior sociolect.

The lexical flotsam of comradely exchange, filtered through consciousness and memory, resurfaces in fractured, strikingly eclectic forms, creating the illusion of unmediated contact with the real:

- **snippets of song** (in the refrain 'As-tu connu Guy au galop' in 'Les Saisons')
- **fragments of conversation or personal correspondence** ('N'est-ce pas rigolo' in 'Échelon'; 'On ne peut rien dire / Rien de ce qui se passe / Mais on change de secteur' in '14 juin 1915'; 'On est bien plus serré que dans les autobus' in 'Les Saisons'; 'Et vous savez pourquoi' in 'Loin du pigeonnier')
- **pleas, prayers, cries of distress** ('Priez pour moi Bon Dieu je suis le pauvre Pierre' in 'Chant de l'horizon en Champagne')
- **nicknames** ('Guy [...] l'artiflot' in 'Les Saisons'), **code-names** ('Allô la truie' in 'Du Coton dans les oreilles')
- **robust rallying cries** ('VIVE LE CAPISTON,' reproduced in slogan form in 'Saillant')
- **energetic oaths and insults** ('SACRÉ NOM DE DIEU, QUELLE ALLURE NOM DE DIEU,' reproduced in the form of a spurred boot in '2ème canonnier conducteur')
- **official instructions, technical descriptions, commands and orders** ('Allongez le tir' in 'Fusée'; 'rameau central de combat,' 'des bruits entendus' in 'Guerre'; 'Halte là / Qui vive ... Avance au ralliement' in 'Venu de Dieuze,'; 'Aux créneaux Aux créneaux Laissez là les pioches' in 'La Nuit d'avril 1915,'; and 'Pour lutter contre les vapeurs / les lunettes pour protéger les yeux / au moyen d'un masque nocivité gaz / un tissu trempé mouchoir des nez' in 'SP')
- **sounds and onomatopoeia** ('Pan pan perruque' in 'SP'; 'Pif,' the sound of a shell exploding in 'Saillant'; 'Ca ta clac des coups qui meurent en s'éloignant' in 'Désir')
- **superstitions** ('Le riz a brûlé dans la marmite de campement / Ça signifie qu'il faut prendre garde à bien des choses' in 'Fusée')

The alternative, informal lexicon of comradeship, although coextensive with official military discourse, revels in its own distinct naming systems. The soldier's delight in the transformational potential of language presents deep analogies with the pleasures afforded by ring-making or the turning of discarded materials into a provisional habitat. To reclaim linguistic power is to delineate a discursive space separate from that of the army establishment: practices of selecting and transforming the linguistic objects of the everyday world of war generate graffiti, notices, ditties, mottoes, whether framed as in the graphically punning instance 'LES CÉNOBITES TRANQUILLES' or more fragmentally exposed in isolated vocabulary items.

The figurative, often humorous reworking of language is a bid for relative freedom, a reassertion of creativity that occurs within a rigid ideological frame, but does not fundamentally oppose that frame. Puns, nicknames, and humorous renamings of military ranks and equipment take forward the desire to develop a comradely subculture distinct from, but implicitly supportive of, the hierarchical culture of the army establishment.

The soldiers' linguistic inventiveness surfaces at times in bleak, sardonic humour that allows men to confront their fears through repeated language work. Thus, the recurring visceral reference to 'boyau' is a rawer alternative to the standard 'tranchée.' More often the traffic goes in the other (meliorative) direction, when life-affirming desire erupts in whimsical, lighthearted instances that transform the official nomenclature, investing the iteration of ideological rigidity with instinctive creativity and deflecting (temporarily) the seriousness of war. The comrades substitute 'capiston' for 'capitaine,' 'artiflot' for 'artilleur' ('Les Saisons'), 'bobosses' for 'fantassins à bosses' ('Les Soupirs du servant de Dakar').[54] Their lexical materials extend from the vocabulary of oral consumption ('du singe en boîtes carrées' = bully beef) to technical slang whose unexpected poetic or intensely visual qualities delimit a cultural space accessible to those initiated into its mysteries and secrets ('Crapauds et crapoussins' in 'Échelon' refer to German bombs; 'chevaux de frise' is the metaphorical equivalent of 'fils de fer barbelé').[55] The soldierly idiolect stages its own metaphoric possibilities, sometimes straining the criteria of lexical 'accessibility' and 'transparency,' but revealing in the process a deeper poetic purpose: 'les bouteilles crémantes' and 'la bouteille champenoise,' references to French aerial torpedoes, speak of a need to transform, to humanize, a technologically alienating world.

As the war poetry reveals the metaphorical work of ordinary soldiers on the standard lexicon of war, it affirms transformative activity as a means of shoring up collective self-identity in a situation where individual freedom is severely constrained.[56] Men at war make sense of their experience, they constitute their own real, through their creative, unexpectedly poetic inflections of language and, in the process, forge a homosocial identity that supports, but is not reducible to, the official military culture. By integrating the soldierly idiom so comprehensively, Apollinaire underlines that the real is not per se transparent, stable, and predictable, but pliant and subjectively filtered. The war poetry of *Calligrammes* reveals a remarkable coincidence between modernist literary practices and demotic soldierly discourse in its inventive mixing of metaphor and metonymy, its splicing of the prosaic and the fantastic, and its promotion of ironic humour and playful hybridity.

Autobiographical and modernist imperatives coincide, visibly, in the recycling of the language and sounds of war. The process of shoring up the text with fragments of the discursive real satisfies autobiography's demand for referential grounding, while the *papiers collés* technique integral to that process stresses the materiality of language, lending contour and density to representation.

The modernist autobiographical project encompasses and, at the same time, radically exceeds the representational, for it exposes actively the role of language in shaping the individual consciousness in the male homosocial culture of war. There is, thus, a strong ethnographical impulse at work here: the dialogical play of linguistic material reveals the official and the unofficial lexicons as mutually supporting codes that by preserving distinctions between officers and men, between the externally imposed and the playfully created, reaffirm the binary divide and the hierarchical structuring of military life. The comradely sociolect shapes the notions of power, courage, ruse, local loyalty, and patriotism from which the soldier-self configures his image within the group.[57]

The participatory ethos of war comes through in 'À l'Italie,' where the use of the colloquial register, punctuated by the repeated, cohesive 'nous,' insists on an untroubled, even euphoric, identification of the individual with the homosocial group. The survivalist acumen of the group is sustained by the heroic ideal and the collective enjoyment of material pleasures:

> Nous avons le sourire nous devinons ce qu'on ne nous dit pas nous
>   sommes démerdards et même ceux qui se dégonflent sauraient à
>   l'occasion faire preuve de l'esprit de sacrifice qu'on appelle la bravoure
> Et nous fumons du gros avec volupté

The language of the soldierly 'nous' unwraps its ideological content, revealing the encoding of predictable responses of hubris and hostility towards the enemy, and foregrounding the role of camaraderie in mobilizing concepts of courage and national pride. The participatory discourse articulates a sharpened perception of the pure difference represented by the enemy, the other, which is conveyed in the robust threat 'on les aura' ('Carte postale'). The language of soldierly interaction constructs an unnegotiable, dualistic world view, and exposes the limited range of ideological positions available as the self confronts the structures of the collective real.

What emerges through soldierly investments in material things, physical space, and language codes is an undiminished desire to extend and enhance the range of available subjective positions. Turning to larger blocks of language, we see how certain forms of semiotic activity, particularly fiction-making, influence the construction of male subjective identity. In a situation where political, material, and subjective possibilities are severely diminished, the soldier seeks to harness the transformative, meliorative potential of narrative as a means of self-idealization and a way of ennobling or abstracting the here-and-now of his predicament. The soldier-self's explicit recourse to *chansons de geste* and to the *images d'Épinal* of popular tradition affirms identity as an intertextual construct and autobiographical writing as a self-authoring process.

The fictions produced by the soldier-subject turn around the desire to align himself with the 'glorious tradition' of the male warrior and assimilate its ideals of companionship, action, valour, passion in adventure, and collective faith. 'Me voici libre et fier parmi mes compagnons' ('2ème canonnier conducteur') announces the purportedly happy absorption of self into male homosocial structures. Such fragmentary instances support the pervasive strategy of literary affiliation that promises an enhanced sense of self, the possibility of mentally transcending the actual and the contingent, and the restoration of historical coherence at the point where history seems irremediably fractured and the self hopelessly adrift.[58] The desire for affiliation corresponds to what Anthony Cascardi identifies as the compensatory tendency of the subject 'to look in art for the authentication of an experience that has otherwise been degraded, divided or rendered corrupt.'[59] Inventing self encourages the appropriation of traditional models consecrated in chivalric literature or perpetuated in popular culture, and surfacing in fragmentary instances of metaphor and allegory ('le nord glorieux,' 'l'Espoir,' 'Perdre / La vie pour trouver la Victoire'). In '2ème canonnier conducteur' the repeated mythification of the officer figure is an attempt to imbue the military adventure with metaphysical and cosmic significance: 'Le bras de l'officier est mon étoile polaire'; 'Un officier passe au galop / Comme un ange bleu dans la pluie grise.' These discrete instances serve to valorize the soldier-hero as a figure of election and sublimity.

The assimilation of quest exemplars offers a means of affirming subjective agency in the here-and-now, and extending that agency historically and textually; they offer the possibility of writing oneself into history, of inscribing one's fate in the diachronic scheme of things. Quest fictions, however partially integrated, would seem, on the face of it, to lend the cultural authority indispensable to a project of self-idealization. However, this is to ignore the collusion of autobiography and modernism in problematizing inherited models (and, by extension, problematizing the self-idealizing project that strives to assimilate them). The tendency to critique, parody, or otherwise relativize intertextual material through variations in voice, subject position, or metaphorical inflection, is a signal feature of autobiography and of modernism.

'À Nîmes,' with its explicit recourse to Le Charroi de Nîmes, is a key instance of the relativization of repositories of nostalgia in modernist writing.[60] In the first half of the poem, the subject identifies himself as 'le charretier du neuf charroi de Nîmes,' situating himself as a continuer of the epic tradition through an implicit transfer to the artillery driver of the ethos consecrated in the late-twelfth-century chanson de geste. Values of legitimacy, courage, self-sacrifice, allegiance, and passion are pointed up by euphoric appeals to 'l'intrépide bleusaille' and 'Nice la Marine au nom victorieux.' If the assimilation of a traditional model seems at first unproblematic, the second half of the poem (lines 15–28) disrupts the heroic identification as the sheer ordinariness of experience reasserts itself. Here, a sense of poignancy surfaces in the portrait of the territorial soldier munching anchovy salad and sharing his worries about his sick wife back home, and again later, in the vision of the narrator's aimless, solitary wandering after supper (lines 16–17; 25–6). The failure to internalize idealized representations of soldierly masculinity confirms the modernist engagement with traditional material as critical and ironic, and the autobiographical desire for enhanced self-identity as hopelessly blocked. The symbolically charged representation of joyous signing-up is increasingly rivalled in the text by the flatter, more matter-of-fact presentation of ordinary poignancy, almost as if the stylistically 'depressed' discourse were registering the soldier-speaker's surfacing disenchantment. This conflation of competing representations of war experience (heroic and prosaic, euphoric and disconsolate, noble and mundane) precludes any possible stabilization of the relationship between self and the homosocial world of war. The individual's sense of his place in the historical scheme of things is subject to downwards revision. Nostalgia for lost narratives surges in isolated fragments of intertextual remembrance, but is swiftly neutralized in an autobiographical project that shares modernism's drive to integrate traditional material on its own implacable terms. Forced to rival with the multifarious pressures – cultural, social, ideological, geographical, physical – that shape the construction of the soldier-self in war, the coherence of traditional narratives breaks down, and the desirability of anachronistic appropriations is overruled by the demands of material contingency.

'C'est Lou qu'on la nommait' articulates a more explicit critique of self-idealization that relies on the appropriation of cultural material sourced in the *images d'Épinal* of popular tradition. The speaker views his desire to identify with the chivalric heroes of the folk genre as anachronistic, unsustainable, and utterly compelling: 'Où sont-ils ces beaux militaires / Soldats passés Où sont les guerres d'autrefois.' With the failure to appropriate agency, self-certainty dissolves into wistful recognition and prompts an anaphoric reworking of Villon's celebrated refrain ('Où sont les neiges d'antan?'). Poetry exposes the competing pressures on the self-idealizing project: the persistence of heroic representations in cultural memory, and their failure to signify for the individual grappling to make sense of the here-and-now. Writing stages the impossibility of constructing the present on the model of the past; its sublime images survive in the collective memory, nourished by art and negated by experience, just as Villon's refrain haunts the poet. The unsustainability of quest fiction undermines belief in the coherence of inherited narrative and the continuity of history, and fills the subject with anxiety born of an acute sense of cultural dislocation.

If cultural models are perceived – initially and innocently – as a way of containing and transforming anxiety in a situation of extreme pressure, it is clear that they end up producing more anxiety when time-consecrated exemplars are revealed as inadequate to the pressures of the here-and-now. The desire to appropriate traditional material works paradoxically (inevitably?) to aggravate self-doubt where nostalgia for lost narratives is exasperated by their shrivelled relevance. The failure of fiction and personal experience to coalesce is figured as a void filling with anxiety for a subject disenchanted and precariously unfixed:

Moi j'ai ce soir une âme qui s'est creusée qui est vide
On dirait qu'on y tombe sans cesse et sans trouver de fond
Et qu'il n'y a rien pour se raccrocher   ('Dans l'abri-caverne')

What motivates the assimilation of quest fiction is the desire to
'se raccrocher,' to inscribe one's fate in a known, transmittable literary
history. The failure of this idealizing project of self-authorship makes
Apollinaire's war poetry the site of an anxious narrative that erupts in
fractured textual structures, in the shifts from epic to prosaic, realist to
fantastic, allegorical to idiomatic, and in the volatility of highly imaged
writing.

If anxiety is to begin to be transformed, it must first be confronted.
The nightmare of material dissolution, a constant of the war poems,
evokes a descent into dark, phenomenological chaos as physical and
ontological structures give way. Here, the human body becomes indistinguishable from the palpitating monstrosity of sea creatures:

> J'ai bâti une maison au milieu de l'Océan
> Ses fenêtres sont les fleuves qui s'écoulent de mes yeux
> Des poulpes grouillent partout où se tiennent les murailles
> Entendez battre leur triple coeur et leur bec cogner aux vitres
> [...]
> Pâles poulpes des vagues crayeuses ô poulpes aux becs pâles
>
> ('Océan de terre')

Anxiety is staged as a collapse of corporeal integrity in phantasmagoric
immersions that betoken a terrifying loss of self-consistency. Here, the
tropes of liquefaction, viscerality, miasma, and human bodiliness merge
in a disturbing vision of self-dissolution mixed with anal fascination:

> [...] j'ai coulé dans la douceur de cette guerre avec toute ma compagnie
>   au long des longs boyaux
> [...]
> J'ai creusé le lit où je coule en me ramifiant en mille petits fleuves qui
>   vont partout   ('Merveille de la guerre')

The oneiric representation of trench experience is characterized by perverse bodiliness and volatilized by scatological, cannibalistic, and sadistic desire. In 'Merveille de la guerre,' the erotic and the morbid are
conflated with sardonic humour in a nauseating variation on the twinned
themes of bodily dissolution and compelling orality: 'C'est un banquet
que s'offre la terre / Elle a faim et ouvre de longues bouches pâles / [...]
/ Qui aurait dit qu'on pût être à ce point anthropophage / Et qu'il fallût
tant de feu pour rôtir le corps humain / C'est pourquoi l'air a un petit

goût empyreumatique qui n'est ma foi pas désagréable.' Here, as in several other texts, the trench is obsessively figured as the embodiment of scandalous femininity, treacherous and alluring, a site of pleasurable infiltration and primal terror. The Trench-Woman as Orifice-Grave plies fatal seduction and proffers kisses from a castrating mouth:[61]

LA TRANCHÉE

O jeunes gens je m'offre à vous comme une épouse
Mon amour est puissant j'aime jusqu'à la mort
Tapie au fond du sol je vous guette jalouse
Et mon corps n'est en tout qu'un long baiser qui mord

('Chant de l'honneur')

Fantasized union turns swiftly into a death-sealing lure. The mesmerizing merging of death and femininity, desire and morbidity, fascination and monstrosity produces arresting phantasmatic representations. Real horror at the real barbarity of war is simultaneously recognized and abstracted as the displacements of metaphor bring forward universal scenarios of powerless anxiety and trauma. It is here, at the extreme of symbolic representation, that the surrealists' claims of 'trivialization' by Apollinaire can be appreciated at their most breathtakingly naïve.

At the limit of poetic representation, individual and collective bodies dissolve into a single abstraction ('le Corps'). With the lapse into miasmic indistinctness, the earth represents the loss of the body as an inexorable process of decoloration: 'les tranchées blanchissaient' ('Mutation'); 'Je suis la tranchée blanche' ('Chant de l'horizon en Champagne'). In the utter abolition of distinctness, engulfing whiteness comes to figure the erasure of selfhood and the contemplation of abstract horror: 'Là-bas plus blanche est la blessure' ('Échelon'). Unarguably, Apollinaire does not default on the moral imperative to confront the horror of war. He chooses to represent horror in fantasies of dissolution that bring powerfully into focus the dehumanizing, *self*-obliterating process of war.

As anxiety over the fate of the body is absorbed into the symbolic representation of landscape, the pathos of war is avoided in figured theorizations that confront death by abstracting it.[62] The compulsive twinning of tropes of death and femininity is part of a broader representational project in which Woman, war's eternal absentee, is annexed – at times literally incorporated – in the performance of male subjectivity. The negotiation of self with the remembered, obsessively fantasized feminine Other is a particularly compelling, and critically neglected, dimension of Apollinaire's war poetry.

Assuaging soldierly anxiety demands sustained, effective strategies of self-enhancement. For this purpose the everyday culture of soldierly masculinity provides abundant semiotic material in the unspeaking female object of a desiring male subject. Physically and corporeally absent from the war zone, Woman is endlessly available for representation as the warrior's trophy, the 'wife back home,' the sepia image of the longed-for sweetheart, the prostitute and source both of sexual comfort and contempt, and the ideal or allegorical figure ('la France,' 'la Victoire,' and in the unstable gendering of 'la Patrie').[63]

The urgency of compensating for the inaccessibility of real women gives rise to idealizations of the feminine that sustain the collective values of men at war. Woman, commodified, figures among the spoils of war, a prize to be possessed in the utopian vision of post-war colonization and hubristic world conquest unfolding in 'Guerre':

Ne pleurez donc pas sur les horreurs de la guerre
Avant elle nous n'avions que la surface
De la terre et des mers
Après elle nous aurons les abîmes
Le sous-sol et l'espace aviatique
Maîtres du timon
Après après
Nous prendrons toutes les joies
Des vainqueurs qui se délassent
Femmes Jeux Usines Commerce
Industrie Agriculture Métal
Feu Cristal Vitesse

Woman is here linked to a futurist, imperialist vision of modernity that affirms the collective purpose and the destiny of the warring male.[64] Yet the value of idealized femininity is not exclusively prospective, nor is it so unproblematically affirmative. 'La femme' is conflated with 'la patrie' in allegorical representations of France where a heroicized and eroticized representation of sacrifice fills the void left by the unrepresentability of death:

Nous sommes ton collier France
[...]

Rivière d'hommes forts et d'obus dont l'orient chatoie
Diamants qui éclosent la nuit
                    O Roses ô France
Nous nous pâmons de volupté
A ton cou penché vers l'Est   ('De la batterie de tir')

The voluptuous geography of war idealizes the active male body in the service of nationhood figured as Woman, an alluring cipher betokening the seductiveness of notions of self-sacrifice. The idea(l) of incorruptible nationhood is brought forth, here, in allegorical embodiment and mineral adornment.

Allegories of femininity, whether identified with national integrity or with pervasive perversity, compete with representations of women grounded in the real and the everyday. Cutting across such radical shifts in register and stylistic mode, the masculinist discourse of the comrades revisits, constantly, the interrelation of sex and death; this informs gossip, cliché, and everyday fable, as much as it does mythical and allegorical visions. Woman perceived as too close, too physical, too fleshly, risks debilitating the soldierly body. Thus, 'la putain de Nancy' threatens the integrity – physical and moral – of the male collectivity by her sexual proximity, and is 'denounced' in the calligrammatic representation of the rifle in '2ème canonnier conducteur':

The prostitute joins the ranks of the bogey 'Boches,' held at a therapeutic distance through storytelling, humour, oaths, and jokes. Delight in puns and polysemous play reveals sexual abstinence as inevitable or desirable, as in the ironic, homophonic conflation of concepts of monastic chastity and military continence that produces 'Les Cénobites Tranquilles' ('Du coton dans les oreilles').[65] Woman threatening, or in some way threatened, raises the spectre of the uncontainable that will disrupt soldierly activity and destabilize idealized, consolatory representations of femininity: Lou, in 'C'est Lou qu'on la nommait,' is the vulpine figure preying on the warrior (when the military adventure demands 'l'oeil chaste,' not an eroticized gaze); the sick wife back home, poignantly evoked in 'À Nîmes,' represents emotional distraction from the pursuit of military objectives ('Le territorial se mange une salade / À l'anchois en parlant de sa femme malade').[66]

Whether outwardly meliorative (in the 'ennobling' instances of allegory) or depreciative, the soldiers' discourse on Woman is made to bolster normative representations of military masculinity. The discourse of feminine objectification anticipates and legitimates a solipsistic concern with masculine military potential and performance, evident here in the repeated fusing of masculine desire and soldierly violence:

> Mon désir est la région qui est devant moi
> Derrière les lignes boches
> Mon désir est aussi derrière moi
> Après la zone des armées
>
> Mon désir c'est la butte du Mesnil
> Mon désir est là sur quoi je tire   ('Désir')

Imaginary phallic violence inheres in the construction of warrior identity. Thus, 'À Nîmes' allegorizes the displacement of erotic energy from the private sphere to the war zone where exploding shells perform the relentless thrust of soldierly ardour ('L'Amour dit Reste ici Mais là-bas les obus / Épousent ardemment et sans cesse les buts'). At times, the relation between military violence and priapic desire exceeds the confines of analogy: in 'Fusées' the entire soldierly adventure is staged as an erotics of combat where canons are '[v]irilités du siècle où nous sommes.' Here, Woman is 'captured' in a series of corporeal instances overwritten by the signifiers of war: 'Tes seins sont les seuls obus que j'aime' ('Fusés'). The erotics of combat exposes a scopophilic dynamic that works to affirm the masculine (visual) prerogative in a situation of diminished individual authority. The effect of this is to displace deep anxieties over the fracturing of the male body onto an already fractured, imaginary female body. The repeated conjuring of feminine body-objects offers sublimated pleasure and fictive power at the point where masculine physical agency, represented by the soldierly body, is under greatest pressure. As the gaze approaches, seizes, then veers away from the represented feminine body, this process of deferral and displacement mimes the 'highs and lows' of desire in a series of fetishistic attachments to discrete part-objects (breasts, hips).[67] By fragilizing and fracturing its object, this atomistic viewing practice ensures that the feminine other, denied corporeal integrity, can never impede the view-ing subject's project of self-enhancement.[68] Any sense of a living woman evaporates into the symbolic Woman – the mute Other against whom representational violence is turned, with the double purpose of shoring up masculinist self-perception and blocking the urgency of more pro-found self-scrutiny.

The scopophilic gaze, by means of unremittingly fetishistic investment in the feminine imaginary body, enacts the kind of transformation (appropriation, fragilization) of its object necessary to reaffirm mascu-line symbolic agency. The fragmentary representation of the feminine other is mirrored in the fractured textuality of the war poetry of *Calligrammes*. It is tempting to read this specular identity between sub-stance and form as betokening a deeper complicity between masculinist (ideological) and modernist (writerly) preoccupations. Indeed, such a reading would not be at odds with the silencing of the feminine voice by mainstream modernism; likewise it would not contradict the defin-ing tendency of aesthetic experimentalism to promote surface over subject, whether in Picasso's dislocations of the female nude in his century-defining 'Les Demoiselles d'Avignon' or in André Breton's neu-tralization of the eruptive creativity of the disturbed, disturbing Nadja.[69] However, where modernist textual practices appear to repeat masculinist ways of viewing, they expose and implicitly critique the morsellization of the Other as part of the broader strategy of male self-affirmation. Apollinaire's autobiographical writing actively problematizes mascu-line appropriations of the feminine and, in its fluctuations (structural, stylistic, perspectival), resists readerly attempts to stabilize any single interpretative position.

Desire and Dream-work

If scopophilic mastery appears to support the ideological frames of war, or at least not explicitly to dissent from those frames, it leaves radically unsatisfied the hungering for richer possibilities of inwardness. In Apollinaire's poetry, there are numerous instances where the autobio-graphical project runs against the ideological grain, where the self resists the real as constructed by the prevailing military culture. The lines of that resistance emerge in writerly and phantasmatic desire.

Such forms of desire bring forth mesmerizing minglings of the sen-sual and the scriptural. This is performative desire as opposed to the

reactive scopophilic urge that perpetuates phallic authority and en-
forces alienating distance between self and Other, viewer and viewed.
Where scopophilia is fetishistic, writerly desire is at once eruptive and
holistic, opposing the dis-figuring effects of the phallic gaze with new
re-figuring potential.

Desire, unfulfilled in the repetitions of scopophilic viewing, finds
consolation in actual or sublimated self-pleasuring ('Je flatte de la main
le petit canon gris / Gris comme l'eau de Seine et je songe à Paris,' 'À
Nîmes'). More often, however, it is to forms of mental self-pleasuring –
dreaming, fantasizing, imagining – that the soldier-self turns to assuage
frustration and anxiety. 'Dans l'abri-caverne' narrates the experience of
an inner void filling with apprehension, and the contrastively therapeutic activity of the imagination:

> Moi j'ai ce soir une âme qui s'est creusée qui est vide
> On dirait qu'on y tombe sans cesse et sans trouver de fond
> Et qu'il n'y a rien pour se raccrocher
> Ce qui y tombe et qui y vit c'est une sorte d'êtres laids qui me font mal
>   et qui viennent de je ne sais où
> [...]
> Dans ce grand vide de mon âme il manque un soleil il manque ce qui
>   éclaire
> [...]
> Les autres jours je me rattache à toi
> Les autres jours je me console de la solitude et de toutes les horreurs
> En imaginant ta beauté

Dreaming the body is quite distinct from the predictable duplications of
scopophilic viewing; indeed, such phantasmatic work actively counters
the containments of male military culture. It is tempting to read the
unbinding of self through fantasy as a flight from history and a lapse
into self-absorption. Precisely such a reading produces the accusations
of 'reality-denying' levelled at Apollinaire by his detractors. Where the
surrealists view fantasy and inwardness as profoundly incompatible
with the poet's duty to engage ethically with history, in fact the reverse
is true: fantasy and history work *together* to reclaim the body for pleasure as a means of restoring psychic wholeness. Dreaming is, in
Apollinaire's war poetry, a transformative and profoundly re-humaniz-
ing process, a means of overcoming the dualism of self and Other, art
and its object, memory and the real. Bringing the phantasmatic body to
language is a model for achieving a richer sense of being.[70]

In the unresolved structures of the war poems, individuality – subjective and creative – regenerates itself through dream-work that has its origin in rarefied sensory experience. The short text 'Fumées' traces the filtering of the exterior world, the unbinding of physical sensation, and the dissolution of identity in the sublimely sensual space of desire:

Et tandis que la guerre
Ensanglante la terre
Je hausse les odeurs
Près des couleurs-saveurs

   Et je fu
       m
        e
       du
       ta
       bac
      de **NE**
      Zo

Des fleurs à ras du sol regardent par bouffées
Les boucles des odeurs par tes mains décoiffées
Mais je connais aussi les grottes parfumées
Où gravite l'azur unique des fumées
Où plus doux que la nuit et plus pur que le jour
Tu t'étends comme un dieu fatigué par l'amour
      Tu fascines les flammes
      Elles rampent à tes pieds
      Ces nonchalantes femmes
      Tes feuilles de papier

As swirls of smoke and licking flame trace patterns of desire, the real of collective experience dissolves into the symbolic of individual phantasmatic creation to re-form as dream fragments and dream narratives; and the *je-tu* fluctuations signal the unfixing of identity as a sensually playful other merges with the pleasured writerly self.

Like the metal that is recycled into the love-token ring, the personal symbolic is material too (of a de-materialized kind) for the self-writerly consciousness as it works to generate new texts of desire and dreaming. The same process is at work in 'Les Feux du bivouac,' here linked to an exclusively visual experience:

Les feux mouvants du bivouac
Éclairent des formes de rêve
Et le songe dans l'entrelacs
Des branches lentement s'élève

In 'L'Inscription anglaise,' the soldier-self conjures up the memory of his beloved 'apparition' in terms that imply the potential for semiotic production in the interior space of longing. Desire is inextricable from memory and writing, it informs structure and substance, flooding signified and signifier:

Sur un petit bois de la Champagne [...] un soldat s'efforce
Devant le feu d'un bivouac d'évoquer cette apparition
A travers la fumée d'écorce de bouleau
[...]
Tandis que les volutes bleuâtres qui montent
D'un cigare écrivent le plus tendre des noms
Mais les noeuds de couleuvres en se dénouant
Écrivent aussi le nom émouvant
Dont chaque lettre se love en belle anglaise

Et le soldat n'ose point achever
Le jeu de mots bilingue que ne manque point de susciter
Cette calligraphie sylvestre et vernale

If many of the war poems evoke the desirability of inwardness, and explore sites of phantasmatic resistance to the collective culture of war, any sense of passive self-recuperation is displaced by the *active* regeneration of the self–world relationship through texts of desire intended to transform, or at least alleviate, extreme disenchantment and alienation.

Loving and dreaming, desiring and writing are the generous, luminous actions of a subject impelled by the will to rethink the relation of self to the real and, by interweaving physical sensation and psychic material, to begin to heal the rift between exterior and inner worlds. And so, in those very instances of phantasmatic creation where resistance to contingency would seem, on the face of it, to imply an anguished retreat from history and material pressures, the production of fictions of desire provides a means of reconnecting self and the world – urgently and expansively.

In Apollinaire's war poetry, the autobiographical self emerges now less as a construct than as a process in writing – complex, often contradictory, boundlessly mobile. It is a process that engages sometimes affirmatively, sometimes more critically with 'culturally sanctioned models of identity';[71] but it is also a process that solicits other forms of self-production in private fantasy. The disrupted, endlessly open structures of modernist writing take forward this process of self-situating, registering the play of self-writerly desire in ways that are typically autobiographical, typically Apollinaire.

Francis Ponge, in his essay on human suffering and Fautrier's 'Otages' series, evokes Apollinaire's war poetry and its power to bring forth the world in its inspiriting beauty and its unbearable brokenness:

> La plainte d'Apollinaire est certainement plus touchante d'avoir été long-temps retenue, masquée par un enthousiasme, par une volonté de ravisse-ment, par un ravissement sincère, par une cécité, un aveuglement passionnés devant les horreurs de la guerre et de la condition humaine, par une bonté, une indulgence poussées jusqu'à l'héroïsme, à quel hé-roïsme modeste et souriant. Quand elle perce [...] elle est alors déchirante. Elle teinte alors le ravissement lui-même. Elle oblige à le considérer à sa valeur, comme une sublime indulgence envers la nature, la guerre et la condition humaine.[72]

Ponge captures, in the exquisite fluctuations of his own writing, the affective complexity of Apollinaire's war poetry: its self-revising momentum, its deep texturing, and its lyric generosity. The sheer expansiveness of Apollinaire's project is illumined in the concluding text of *Calligrammes*, 'La Jolie Rousse.' This retrospective on the war poetry and on everything that precedes it, and proceeds from it, opens with an apologia of judgment, common sense, and order, and what might be construed as the negation of modernist equivocation by a trenchant subject-witness. But the claim to personal poetic authority quickly gives way to the more characteristic oscillation between confidence and doubt. It is here that the resolutely unresolved modern poet, like those ancient and modern Icarian fliers, at once audacious and anxious, commits himself to the materialization of myths present and future:

> Nous voulons vous donner de vastes et d'étranges domaines
> Où le mystère en fleurs s'offre à qui veut le cueillir

Il y a là des feux nouveaux des couleurs jamais vues
Mille phantasmes impondérables
Auxquels il faut donner de la réalité

[...]
Pitié pour nous qui combattons toujours aux frontières
De l'illimité et de l'avenir
Pitié pour nos erreurs pitié pour nos péchés

As the uncertain Janus-narrator of 'La Jolie Rousse' looks forward, simultaneously he looks back and urges that we do likewise in order to arrive at a precarious summum of our own.

The richly seamed poetry of *Calligrammes* is a striking example of modernist writing engaging with the material world – in peacetime and in war – and exploring its representability in the flux of subjectivity. The capacious materiality of *Ondes* contracts to an acute focus on the everyday objects that make up the social and personal worlds of the soldier, but sustained across *Calligrammes* is the expansive modernist consciousness at once straining against and working with contingency, keenly receptive to myriad sensations and supremely able to transform quotidian material through deeply affecting acts of visual inventiveness and phantasmatic creativity.

3 From Culture Critique to Poetic Capital: Ponge's Things-in-Language

Reading subjectivity in Ponge is an inherently problematical exercise, not least because Ponge's abundant output – poetry, art criticism, critical essays, and interviews – seems to foreclose such a reading. Ponge impresses upon the reader his resistance to writing the subjective, his inclination towards *self*-denying Protestantism, his admiration for the rigour and self-restraint of Malherbe; most of all, he impresses us with the resolute outwardness of his poetry, his probing of the material world, and his excursions into rich, unexplored seams of language. If Ponge's authorial positions and writerly practices have worked actively to inhibit readings of the subjective, the critical recuperations of Ponge's poetry by Sartre for phenomenology, in the 1940s, and by Sollers for Tel Quel, in the 1960s, deepened that inhibition.[1]

Emerging from the bipartisan cleft of the mid-twentieth century, the critical study of Ponge's work opened to embrace the diversity of contemporary approaches, from semiotics and linguistics to visual theory and genetic analysis. Since the 1980s, the insights of Bernard Beugnot, Jacques Derrida, Michael Riffaterre, Jean-Pierre Richard, Michel Collot, Ian Higgins, Jean-Marie Gleize, and Philippe Met have done most to enrich our readings of Ponge, sustaining a critical tradition that is as intellectually probing as it is passionately textual.[2] However, with the recent exception of Michel Collot, critics have resisted reading subjectivity in Ponge.[3] The reasons for that resistance appear self-evident: the Ponge of celebrated memory is the author of *Le Parti pris des choses*, the verbal energizer of material objects; he is a self-proclaimed twentieth-century Lucretius who guides our attention towards surface and substance, delighting in the palpable thickness of things and the deep texture of language. The 'poetry of objects' diffuses the euphoria experienced in the everyday things that make up our world and that Ponge gathers into his writing, there to unfold in the generous, generative play of language. In poetry that moves between those settled states of joy, happiness, admiration, certainty, and a sense of complicity with the world, questions of problematical subjectivity seem blissfully remote. The troubled and troubling qualities of equivocation and self-scepticism that define the most tantalizing texts of modernist expression leave Ponge's writing seemingly untouched. In a textual world brimming with 'things,' the dreaming, fantasizing, yearning, unresolved self of modern sensibility appears singularly – and disappointingly – absent.

Yet, precisely because Ponge's euphoria in things appears so confidently to rule out expressions of disenchanted or pressured subjectivity, the very freight of writerly happiness and certainty in his poetry seems destined to provoke unease, suspicion even, in the reader raised on (post)modern scepsis and the belief that identity is pliant and problematical. Certainly, for those intent on bringing about a radical decentring of the subject in writing, Ponge would, at one level, appear to encourage the unquestioning perpetuation of a traditional model of selfhood founded in the fallacy of natural and necessary authority. Arguing for an anti-representationalist, anti-subjectivist poetics in 1963, Alain Robbe-Grillet denounced what he saw in Ponge as the pressing of human certainties onto material things, the untroubled 'complicity' between self and world that marked out an unreconstructed humanist: 'L'anthropomorphisme le plus ouvertement psychologique et moral que [Ponge] ne cesse de pratiquer ne peut avoir [...] pour but que l'établissement d'un ordre humain, général et absolu.'[4] Forty years on, Robbe-Grillet's reading of Ponge seems rather less controversial than quaintly outdated, a product of formalist assumptions and of more ideologically constrained times. What Ponge articulates is not facile anthropomorphism but a sense of the deep relationality between self and world, between subjectivity and materiality:

> [N]ous avons à nous épanouir, développer, à engendrer le monde qui nous environne—plongés donc, baignés dans le monde muet,—qui est notre milieu naturel, notre seule, notre véritable patrie; qui nous environne, nous traverse, nous alimente; dont nous faisons partie; dont nous ne sommes qu'un noeud [...] dont nous avons besoin comme il a besoin de nous; où nous respirons comme il respire par nous. (*Pour un Malherbe*, 71)

The displacements and the equivocations that inflect and alter this relationality are the visible traces of subjectivity in process, problematized. The purportedly affirmative world view imparted in Ponge masks an anxiety about the relation of self to culture, to hard things, and to language that persists across his oeuvre. As the clamour of twentieth-century heterodoxies is stilled and the desire to move beyond theory gathers pace, these questions are acquiring a new critical legitimacy. It is in this context that subjectivity makes an urgent return.

My argument is that the problematics of subjectivity is implicit in Ponge, but is more conspicuously dispersed, transposed, or displaced. Several examples, drawn from markedly different phases of Ponge's writing, will illustrate this displacement. *Douze petits écrits* (1926), Ponge's first published collection of poetry, reveals subjectivity through the social codes, cultural practices, and discursive strategies by which citizens struggle to make sense of an alienating, topographically unfixed urban space. The resolute outwardness of *Le Parti pris des choses* (1942), invested in the third-person primacy of the object and its description, would appear to exclude a priori the forms of inwardness (memory, desire, fantasy) that define selfhood, yet it is here in these passionately 'objective' texts, in the movement of consciousness through material things and the fabric of language, that subjectivity affirms itself as process. In 1951, Ponge sets about 'writing Malherbe.' Published in 1965, *Pour un Malherbe* probes the anxiety and the pleasure of writerly influence in a part-celebration, part-critique of literary-paternal authority that gives rise to a fragmentary, fractured poetics and an elliptical self-appraisal. *Pour un Malherbe* is a deeply unresolved text, for if it deflects the temptations of solipsistic expression and works to displace the autobiographical urge via a biographical and literary homage to the *grand siècle* reformer of French poetry, it reveals self-writing desire as deeply embedded and unstoppably eruptive.[5] Questions of voice and identity, authority and self-scrutiny intrude tellingly into the *hommage*, where Ponge announces his unease with the psychological tradition and characterizes the relation between his own writing and his inner self as one of salutary alienation:[6]

[J]e conçois tout naturellement et dès l'abord (dès que je les entreprends) mes écrits comme détachés de moi, vraiment comme des objets. J'ai l'impression qu'il s'agit de fragments de la littérature française vue objectivement ou historiquement. Je me parais donc trop mince pour ce rôle, si bien que, parlant au nom de la littérature entière, je dois employer le *nous*.

C'est encore peut-être parce que je ne m'intéresse plus, c'est un fait, aux auteurs qui emploient le *je*. Ils me paraissent minces et ridicules; naïfs, vains, exagérément prétentieux, fantomatiques, et sans intérêt comme tels. Je ne voudrais pas perdre *notre* temps avec l'un d'eux. (*Pour un Malherbe*, 208)

For Ponge the ideal balance – canonical, literary, moral, historical – is weighted towards 'objective,' autonomous writing that would deny a place to the fragile, insubstantial self. In *Pour un Malherbe*, Ponge exchanges the vulnerability of 'je' for the collective authority of 'nous' that emerges from the consolidation of author (Ponge), object (Malherbe), text (*Pour un Malherbe*), and reader. By sidestepping the marginalizing trap of selfhood, Ponge seeks to resolve the anxiety of ontological slightness with a denser, more capacious configuration of identity inextricable from the practices of writing and reading: 'puisque tu me lis, cher lecteur, donc je suis; puisque tu nous lis (mon livre et moi), cher lecteur, donc nous sommes (Toi, lui et moi)' (*Pour un Malherbe*, 203). Self-identity is thus intentionally displaced on to other and object and text, a process which recognizes that displaced, de-individualized subjectivity is constituted in language, the product of poetic discourse and of its readerly reception. *Pour un Malherbe* brings forth a more permeable self formed in the intertextual mesh of historical, literary, and readerly practices. Ponge's 1977 text *Comment une figue de paroles et pourquoi* is, arguably, of all his works, the most consciously *self*-formative in subjective, material, and writerly terms. Here the act of textual constitution repeatedly invokes the process of ego-formation and the generative pleasure of infant orality ('Nous l'aimons [la figue], nous la réclamons comme notre tétine').[7] Chosen to be the mesmerizing object of Ponge's 'consolation matérialiste,' the fig materializes the desire mentally to 'mordre dans les choses et de s'en nourrir,' a principle celebrated in reiterated intertextual tribute to the sixth-century philosopher Boethius's *Consolation of Philosophy*. But much more strikingly here than in *Pour un Malherbe*, the (auto)biographies of author, model (Boethius), and matter (the fig) are subsumed in the autobiography of the text, the patient constitution of *tous ses états*. Ponge demonstrates *how* and *why* knowing the material and the subjective is a process inextricable from the genesis of the text:

Le *comment* est l'éloge du travail et de la production à l'intérieur du monde dans lequel nous sommes enfermés; c'est-à-dire le monde de la parole. [...] [En ce qui concerne le *pourquoi*,] il s'agit de la matérialité de la langue et de la matérialité du monde extérieur; je suis quelqu'un pour qui le monde extérieur existe, comme disait Théophile Gautier; mais il provoque des émotions! Par exemple j'aime les figues, mais j'ai perdu toute illusion de parler vraiment de la figue du modèle intérieur. C'est le paradis perdu.[8]

This chapter offers a reading of the earlier part of Ponge's poetry set in the wider context of his art criticism, his literary essays, and certain key texts of the later period. This will provide a focused study of the period up to and including *Le Parti pris des choses*, and allow us to make some critical connections across the broad span of Ponge's rich, multi-genre output. My study begins where the displacement of subjectivity first registers in Ponge: in the deep cultural dysphoria of his earliest texts, *Douze petits écrits*, the series of satirical monologues and portraits where any sense of coherent, self-generating individuality is neutralized by the impersonal structures of social and economic life, where subjective consistency is replaced by dislocation and the fractured, fractious voices of a Hamletian narrator and his disaffected interlocutors. In an anonymous, featureless urban space, these disenchanted citizens struggle to make sense of the social, economic, affective, and discursive relations that define their existence. Their everyday alienation is refracted through the reified structures of employment and production, dysfunctional family relations, emotional isolation, and commodity fetishism. Their exasperated voices speak of the impoverishment of human relations and of the severely depleted opportunities for individual creativity or self-transformation. The culture critique emerging in these texts has more profound connections than is generally assumed with Ponge's subsequent writing, for it projects through the abstractions and macro-structures of economic and social life a problematics of subjectivity that resurfaces immediately in the material, the particular, and the small-scale things of *Le Parti pris des choses*, and seeks regeneration there in the rich folds of language. This argument is likely to unsettle those readers who feel that I am giving disproportionate emphasis to an inferior, stylistically immature set of poems whose political undertow is unrepresentative of the purer Ponge of *Le Parti pris des choses* and the later collections.[9] The same readers, for the same reasons, may react with scepticism to the suggestion that, in certain critical ways, these early satirical pieces anticipate the later writing. Their scepticism serves to underline the creative tension that drives Ponge's early writing from *Douze petits écrits* to *Le Parti pris des choses* and beyond: the passionate engagement with the world (material

things, social structures, ideology, perceptual experience) and the struggle to bring that engagement to language. That tension is the subject of
the chapter that follows. First, however, I want to reflect on the relative
poetic quality of the earlier texts, and consider some key connections
between this critically underexposed satirical series and Ponge's most
celebrated collection of poetry.

The satirical series has its unarguable source in the anti-bourgeois revolt of the young anarchist idealist, but Ponge's achievement in *Douze
petits écrits* is resolutely poetic, for these texts distil vituperation, they
offer sensitive, elliptical portraits of human disconsolation, and they
rarefy revolt through measured allegory. The oppressively vacant city
that looms in *Douze petits écrits* fills with the Rimbaldian echo of certain
of the *Illuminations*. The stylistic detachment and subtle poignancy of
these texts expose the profoundly human motivation of an inaugural
series whose critique is as much cultural and linguistic as it is social and
economic. Here, Ponge exposes the dystopia – moral, linguistic, human,
material – for which he will seek a corrective throughout his subsequent oeuvre.

Ponge himself appears equivocal about the significance of these texts
to his later work. In a parenthesis within the preface to *Le Grand Recueil*,
he indicates that he had almost forgotten that his poetic project origi-
nated, not with *Le Parti pris des choses*, but with *Douze petits écrits*. If the
poet's self-correction draws our attention to the neglect of *Douze petits
écrits*, by the same token it hints at the need to relate these early works
to the rest of the oeuvre. Ponge goes on to make a more unequivocal
connection in his published interviews with Philippe Sollers, where he
confirms that the socio-cultural critique of *Douze petits écrits* resurfaces
in *Le Parti pris des choses*, and where he reveals its autobiographical
source in the bitterly oppressive experience of paid employment. Here,
he recalls the brutalizing daily routine that he endured at the Messageries
Hachette between 1931 and 1936: 'Ce bagne, je l'ai décrit dans un texte
qui s'appelle "R.C. Seine" et qui est publié dans *Le Parti pris des choses*.
[...] [O]n y travaillait, on y vivait dans des salles surveillées par des
gardes-chiourme qui circulaient dans les couloirs, des policiers de la
maison. [...] C'était quelque chose d'extraordinaire. Les dactylos étaient
punies d'amendes si elles ne faisaient pas tant de frappes dans la
journée' (*Entretiens avec Philippe Sollers*, 76). The text to which Ponge
refers, 'R.C. Seine n°,' forms a socio-critical diptych with 'Le Restaurant
Lemeunier' (the latter described by Gabriel Audisio in an unpublished
letter as 'accablant de vérité').[10] As critical exposés of social contain-

ment, cultural reductionism, and the everyday desolation of the urban serf, these texts take forward the style and substance of the *Douze petits écrits* in a more developed narrative form. By embedding in *Le Parti pris des choses* a very conspicuous *condensé* of the socio-cultural critique exposed throughout *Douze petits écrits*, Ponge invites us to read across the boundaries between collections – and between poetic styles – usually considered autonomous and distinct. At the same time, the connection between the two collections is deeper, more subtle, and more generalized than is suggested by the localized reprise of socio-cultural critique in two contiguous texts of *Le Parti pris des choses*. Indeed, the early texts propose a culture critique that anticipates the project of *Le Parti pris des choses* in less overtly signalled and more profound ways. Ponge himself infers these deeper connections between the political and the aesthetic when he affirms his desire to give voice to what is overlooked, be it the worker or the pebble:

> [A]u fond ce que j'aime, ce qui me touche, c'est la beauté non reconnue, c'est la faiblesse d'arguments, c'est la modestie.
>
> Ceux qui n'ont pas la parole, c'est à ceux-là que je veux la donner.
>
> Voilà où ma position politique et ma position esthétique se rejoignent.
>
> Rabaisser les puissants m'intéresse moins que glorifier les humbles (m'intéresse pourtant: *Compliment à l'industriel* et *Tire tire tue tire sur les autos*)
>
> Les humbles: le galet, l'ouvrier, la crevette, le tronc d'arbre, et tout le monde inanimé, tout ce qui ne parle pas.
> ('Je suis un suscitateur' [1942], Cahier de l'Herne, 17)

Unrecognized beauty, modesty, silent things, and the need to speak these things – this is the familiar Ponge – but what comes strikingly into focus in this text is the relationality between the socio-cultural and the material, and the expressed urgency of bringing that relationality to language.

Reading Ponge through the displacements of the subjective onto the larger structures and systems represented in *Douze petits écrits*, or through the material and perceptual fabric explored in *Le Parti pris des choses* encourages us to revise some of the critical *partis pris* that have shaped and, sometimes, constrained readings of Ponge. To read Ponge's critique of urban culture in *Douze petits écrits* and related texts is to challenge the assumption that the tradition of city poetry leaves the poet's work untouched; it is to uncover Ponge's bitter exposé of the situation of the 'individu social.'[11] I argue that the analogical project of *Le Parti pris des choses* takes forward the cultural structures – material and linguistic – that define objects for us and shape subjectivity in the process: thus, 'cageot' presents itself to the narrator-as-reader first as a dictionary item (a product of the reading process) and subsequently as the signifier of an object that the narrator-as-writer resituates materially in an economy of urban-based consumption and wastage. Certain 'ravissements de citadin devant l'étrangeté vivace de la nature,' Ponge recalled in 'Seconde méditation nocturne,' had prompted his first poetic descriptions.[12] The configuration of the cultural, the material, and the subjective persists beyond *Le Parti pris des choses*. References to the wartime scarcity of soap and the imposition of an inferior substitute in *Le Savon* infer the specific historical and cultural determination of the object. Likewise, an intensely subjective experience of the pinewood ('Le Carnet du bois de pins') or the meadow (*La Fabrique du pré*) solicits analogies with cultural structures and materiality of a conspicuously non-contiguous kind (cosmetics, factory production, church, auditorium, operating table, billiard table, board-room meetings).[13] Ponge's writing implies that to achieve a more exact description of nature demands immersion in the breadth and diversity of human experience.

Culture and Subjectivity

The satirical series *Douze petits écrits* (1926), Ponge's first published collection, is my primary focus here, but I will also be considering related socio-critical texts of the 1920s and 1930s dispersed across his oeuvre in *Le Parti pris des choses* (1942), *Proêmes* (1948), and *Lyres* (1961). *Douze petits écrits* offers a bleak reflection on the human situation as a succession of disenchanted citizens drift through a topographically indeterminate modern metropolis, their vulnerability and their impotent vituperation surfacing in monologues, portraits, and fragmentary first-person narratives. Identity is revealed as functional and operative: individuals are reduced to generic types, indistinguishable from their economic status or occupation. Subjectivity is constituted in the intractable structures of social and symbolic organization: employment, sociability, the laws of economic exchange, the codes of language, and erotic relations.

Ponge is not content simply to describe the corrosive effects of capitalist conditioning; his writing actively probes the (albeit limited) potential for destabilizing the prevailing ideologies and asserting individual freedom. *Douze petits écrits* stages the movement of consciousness against habit, functionalism, and the standardizing structures of everyday experience. The anonymous spaces of modernity fill with the clamour of ironic or disenchanted voices: those of an embittered office worker, an acerbic anti-capitalist, a frustrated vacationing couple, and a sceptical narrator. These twelve little textual incendiaries expose and explode the everyday forms of cultural, economic, and linguistic containment.[14] Ponge returns to the dehumanizing effects of commerce and capitalism in *Le Parti pris des choses*, where 'R.C. Seine n°' and 'Le Restaurant Lemeunier rue de la Chaussée-d'Antin' present searing evocations of material dystopia and spiritual emptiness, symptoms of modernity endured rather than chosen. Together, these texts chronicle and critique the homogenization of human experience, exposing the severely diminished possibilities for individual expressivity.

Already in *Douze petits écrits*, everyday existence is synonymous with order and routine, with uniformity and reductionism. Here, the office worker begins his monologue:

> Sans aucun souci du lendemain, dans un bureau clair et moderne, je passe mes jours. [...] Je gagne la vie de mon enfant, et je gagne ma vie, paisiblement. Je peux aller, vers le milieu de la journée ensoleillée, manger; et manger encore le soir quand l'activité de la ville, après une période d'intensité considérable, décroît et meurt avec la lumière.   ('Monologue de l'employé,' *Quatre satires*)

The flat prose style of the 'Monologue,' aggravated by the unrelieved monotony inscribed in the present tenses, registers the levelling of human experience and the constraint of quotidian routine. The voice of the office worker echoes that of the desultory citizen of Rimbaud's topographically standardized city-space as he confronts the neutralization of surprise, paradox, individuality, and difference:

> Je suis un éphémère et point trop mécontent citoyen d'une métropole crue moderne parce que tout goût connu a été éludé dans les ameublements et l'extérieur des maisons aussi bien que dans le plan de la ville. Ici vous ne signaleriez les traces d'aucun monument de superstition. La morale et la langue sont réduites à leur plus simple expression, enfin!   ('Ville,' *Illuminations*)[15]

Ponge exposes the world of everyday entrapment, where lives are compartmentalized by social class and family relations, and where existence is regulated by the unrelenting rhythm of employment. If, in the first half of the monologue, the speaker appears to rationalize, endorse even, the smooth linearities connecting the worlds of paid work and of private life, the reiterated expressions of self-contentment seem strained. Some modestly meliorative adverbs ('paisiblement,' 'soigneusement') call attention to what is as yet unexpressed – the welling disenchantment of a self under conditions of severe pressure. Soon, however, controlled dysphoria flares into a resentful critique of social reifications in the second half of the monologue, where the office worker's revolt erupts in the competing discourses of self-analysis, socio-political insight, religiosity, and pomposity:

> Cependant le soir, libre de mon temps, je prends conscience d'être un homme pensant [...] Dans ce moment, une amertume coutumière m'envahit et je me prends à songer que vraiment je suis un être humain supérieur à sa fonction sociale. Mais je dis alors une sorte de prière où je remercie la Providence de m'avoir fait petit et irresponsable dans un si mauvais ordre de choses.

Ponge's office worker veers between exasperated petulance and consuming complacency, appeasing his uncertainties through the repetition of shibboleths:

> Et je tourne encore mon esprit vers mon enfant qui me lie à l'ordre social, et dont l'existence aggrave ma condition de serf. Je pense aussi à cette femme... Alors ma respiration devient tout à fait régulière car la tranquillité m'apparaît comme le seul bien souhaitable, dans un monde trop méchant encore pour être capable de se libérer, d'après ce que disent les journaux.[16]

This Pongean Prufrock, alternately biddable and critical, is conscious of the lexical, ideological, and personal choices open to him, but fails to use language creatively; he resorts, instead, to miming the available discursive options. By staging the refuge sought in cliché and second-hand language, 'Le Monologue de l'employé' reveals discourse, as much as physical routine, to constrain individuality and usurp personal potential. Any sense of a coherent subjectivity breaks down here, leaving only the fractured discourse of an urban individual alienated from his inner self and from the collective structures to which he submits. The office worker responds to the reifications of his world with language whose centre does not hold; he loses himself in a discursive drift that thickens into the slag of ideologies, formulae, and clichés confronted in 'Sur un sujet d'ennui' (*Trois apologues*): 'Il s'est formé des tas de corps lourds à traîner, des tas d'expressions, de choses à dire.'

The office worker belongs to those urban hordes for whom dislocation and disempowerment are the ransom of petit-bourgeois reason, denounced by the narrator in 'Trois poésies: I': 'Pour la ruée écrasante / De mille bêtes hagardes / Le soleil n'éclaire plus / Qu'un monument de raisons.' Written in the 1920s – a period of intense political awakening for Ponge that anticipates his active involvement in trade unionism and his brief membership of the Parti communiste – these texts portray not the politically self-organizing classes, but instead the bureaucratically regulated masses whose uniformity and resignation are relieved only by modest aspirations, malice, and sporadic in-fighting. The 'peloton de petits employés à la fois mesquins et sauvages' denounced in 'R.C. Seine n°' (1939) embodies Ponge's deep scepticism towards concepts of class consciousness and collective action, and sharpens the masses/ classes dialectic, prefiguring the poet's disillusionment with idealistic proletarianism.[17]

The wavering consciousness of the office worker probes the parameters of everyday containment, only to turn back upon itself, gripped by inertia. In contrast, a resolute, ideologically focused anti-capitalist speaker serves up the acidic 'Compliment à l'industriel' (*Quatre satires*): 'Sire, votre cerveau peut paraître pauvre, meublé de tables plates, de lumières coniques tirant sur des fils verticaux, de musiques à cribler l'esprit commercial.' The ironic conflation of material and mental structures lays bare the fetish-images crowding a mind-turned-metacommodity, and exposes, in the process, the alienation of the capitalist from his inner self. The industrialist's car bears the trashy signs of consumerist excess ('un fleuve de platine, où pend la tour Eiffel avec d'autres breloques célèbres').[18] This automotive parade of cliché and gimmickry traces the journey of the fetish-object back to its point of origin in 'vos usines, déposées au creux des campagnes comme autant de merdes puantes.' The references to scatology and pollution subsequently migrate from the site of production to the owner of the means of production when the industrialist enters a soiree and instantly attracts a swarm of silken seductresses ('des mouches vertes'). The swirl of economic, scatological, and erotic values around the figure of the capitalist entrepreneur identifies him with the irreversible force of entropy that saps material energy and moral will. These are the signs of an ethical Ponge, whose concern with ecology, anti-capitalism, and the critique of patriarchy denounces the mesmerizing prevalence of commodity fetishism, its irresistible infiltration of consciousness, and its regulatory impact on material and erotic exchanges.[19]

In *Le Parti pris des choses*, 'R.C. Seine n°' revisits the industrial dystopia from the exasperated perspective of an impotent insider-subject. This raw, intensely personal voice evokes a disturbing, Célinean world of dehumanization and physical obliteration ('nous approchons à une allure de grains de café de l'engrenage broyeur'). Work is portrayed as an all-consuming, pulverizing machine that turns human subjects into ranks of automata. The metaphors of scatology are deployed now in ways that are not simply associative and reassuringly disconnected from the individual: instead, human subjects are described as part of a vast excrementary process, their bodies passing through a sphincter-like channel into a rigidly compartmentalized office ('Chacun en est ainsi aussitôt expulsé, honteusement sain et sauf, fort déprimé pourtant, par des boyaux lubrifiés à la cire, au fly-tox, à la lumière électrique'). Images of disease, desiccation, and decay conjure visions that paralyse the animate and bring the ordinarily inert frighteningly to life:

[L]'on se trouve alors, dans une atmosphère entêtante d'hôpital à durée de cure indéfinie pour l'entretien des bourses plates, filant à toute vitesse à travers une sorte de monastère-patinoire dont les nombreux canaux se coupent à angles droits, — où l'uniforme est le veston râpé.

Bientôt après, dans chaque service, avec un bruit terrible, les armoires à rideaux de fer s'ouvrent, — d'où les dossiers, comme d'affreux oiseaux-fossiles familiers, dénichés de leurs strates, descendent lourdement se poser sur les tables où ils s'ébrouent.

The cultures represented in Ponge's *Douze petits écrits* and the related satirical poems are – like the texts themselves – fractured, atomized, and deeply enmeshed in the socio-economic structures that form them and which they critique. The compounding of social fragmentation and discursive breakdown, registered in the conscious stylistic disjointedness of these texts, anticipates Henri Lefebvre's vision of 'subcultures' that fail to cohere into a single, unitary culture.[20] What binds together Ponge's disconnected worlds is the ordinary experience of disenchantment. But where Lefebvre defines everyday life in performative terms as a series of actions intended to transform the everyday, in Ponge the refuge sought in acquiescence or revolt – essentially static responses – places limits on the individual's potential to transform his or her disenchantment.

'Le Restaurant Lemeunier rue de la Chaussée-d'Antin' (*Le Parti pris des choses*) is revealing in this respect, for it dramatizes the failed struggle of the office workers of 'R.C. Seine n°' to transform their disenchantment beyond the controlled regime of work in what is supposedly the freer, more negotiable space of off-duty sociability. Temporarily released from their grinding routine, the workers enter the fantasy realm of the restaurant, lured by its multifarious visual, culinary, and interpersonal attractions. The narrator reconstructs the scene in tones that range through neutrality, empathy, and irony:

> Rien de plus émouvant que le spectacle que donne, dans cet immense Restaurant Lemeunier [...], la foule des employés et des vendeuses qui y déjeunent à midi.
> La lumière et la musique y sont dispensées avec une prodigalité qui fait rêver. Des glaces biseautées, des dorures partout. L'on y entre à travers des plantes vertes [...] dans une salle aux proportions énormes [...] où vous accueillent à la fois des bouffées d'odeurs tièdes, le tapage des fourchettes et des assiettes choquées, les appels des serveuses et le bruit des conversations.
> C'est une grande composition digne du Véronèse pour l'ambition et le volume, mais qu'il faudrait peindre tout entière dans l'esprit du fameux *Bar* de Manet.

The narrator actively invites the reader to imagine his 'composition' suffused with the *spirit* of Manet's 1882 depiction of the bar at the Folies-Bergère, thereby summoning the ideology that informs the painter's portrayal of petit-bourgeois sociability and leisure in a capitalist society.[21] The proposed refraction of the pictorial through the verbal activates the criteria that subtend Manet's representation of the Folies-Bergère bar. If Ponge's text is a verbal analogue to Manet's visual description, there is more to the relationship than mere thematic complementarity, founded on parallel representations of a physical space regulated by the rhythms of erotico-social exchange and material consumption. Manet's placing of the viewer in a deeply unresolved relation to the represented scene, mediated through the blank stare of the barmaid, at once reflects the outsider status of the implied viewer and presents no block to his/her participation or critique. Ponge's first-person narrator-observer in 'Le Restaurant Lemeunier' occupies a similar liminal position, at once inside and outside the frame of commercialized sociability: he/she is both critic and participant, caught up in the swirl of social relations and dizzying reflections, and curiously cut off ('Comme dans une grotte merveilleuse, je les vois tous parler et rire mais ne les entends pas').

Ponge asks us to hold in our minds, simultaneously, Manet's depiction of petit-bourgeois leisure and his own study of white-collar appetites temporarily unleashed and enduringly constrained. The hullabaloo of the Restaurant Lemeunier, like that of the Folies-Bergère bar, is underwritten by a set of entirely ritualized jollifications where snobbery and affectation vie with cynicism and indifference. Spontaneity and improvisation are eschewed in favour of vignette performances that pastiche upper-class manners and modes of consumption: here an anxious lover seeks to seduce, with the spectacle of lavish desserts, 'une dactylo magnifiquement ondulée'; there a blasé diner makes a conspicuous show of his simpler tastes before capitulating to his greedy appreciation of sweetmeats; elsewhere, customers feign indifference to luxury as a sign of their presumed distinction. This animated and profoundly inauthentic world of jostling desires is committed as much to the signalling and the provisional reassignment of social identities as to the material satisfaction of its acquisitive urges. In this respect, Ponge's depiction of the lunching workers proceeds in ways not dissimilar to Zola's narrative critique of the codified behaviour that passes for spontaneous sociability at every level of Second Empire society, whether in the satirical set pieces of *nouveau riche* interaction in *La Curée* or in the humorous portrayal of lower-class mores in *L'Assommoir*.[22] In Ponge, as in Zola and Manet, glimpses of authenticity are dispiritingly rare. One exception prompts the narrator's direct appeal to a young salesman to nurture the potential for intimacy and genuine affective reciprocity ('Jeune vendeur, c'est ici, au milieu de la foule de tes semblables, que tu dois parler à ta camarade et découvrir ton propre coeur. Ô confidence, c'est ici que tu seras échangée!').

While sociability is a space wrested free from the pressures of production and regulated labour, the same power protocols (male/female, richer/poorer, stronger/weaker) invade off-duty space and regulate interpersonal exchanges. The workers may struggle to assert their individuality and to re-create themselves in their own eyes and in those of colleagues and lovers, but Ponge's narrative exposes their stultifying dependence on code and cliché.

Everyday culture in Ponge is synonymous with the perpetuation of ritualized practices, ossified language, and atrophying routine. It is perceived less as something to transform (to change from the *inside*) than as a condition to be endured. Thus, the will to pleasure, to creativity, and to self-reconnection – such as it is – promotes limited forms of escapism the terms of which are, inevitably, socially and culturally dictated.

The limited possibilities for transforming disenchantment emerge most urgently in the portrait poem 'Le Patient Ouvrier' (*Quatre satires*), the text that engages most visibly with the everyday (in terms of a conspicuously 'flat' lexis, a shabby setting, and a lowly protagonist). The workman, Fabre, inhabits a featureless wasteland, unremittingly silent apart from a creaking cart, a world of proto-Beckettian disconsolation. In this study of material dystopia, the daily existence of the patient workman is picked out in the signs of physical neglect ('Mal assis, Fabre, à l'estaminet, bouge sous la table des souliers crottés la veille'; he wipes a potato-encrusted knife on his bread, gulps sour wine, and pushes his creaking road-cart through incessant rain, his repetitive activity summed up by 'd'autres charges'). Fabre dreams of withdrawing from the everyday, of seeking a cessation of his activity (all activity perhaps) in retirement (with all that the semantically resonant 'retraite' seems to promise in terms of escape). Retirement is a modest utopia, the passport to which ('le papier de la caisse des retraites') is tucked, fetish-like, in his pocket, betokening happiness of an entirely rationed, bureaucratically managed variety.

The workman's pension statement finds its analogue in the pages of romantic fiction devoured by the vacationing Julie in 'Le Martyre du jour ou "Contre l'évidence prochaine."' Julie's utopia – that nowhere-space of true-love narrative – is quickly reclaimed by the everyday when her husband's consumerist concerns cut short her readerly rapture:

> Dans une anthologie romantique, Julie, la peau dorée, les cuisses aérées sous une robe légère, lisait. [Oscar] la bouscule devant un bazar. On y voit des tapis étalés comme des campagnes, et des bronzes dessus comme des rochers. Des coffrets ouvrés ressemblent à des villes. De l'or des genêts, du violet des bruyères une carpette est brochée. 'C'est trop, dit Oscar, et pas cher dans le Catalogue moderne.'

Love relations, aggravated by the excesses of consumer fetishism, take an acutely vicious turn in 'Dimanche, ou l'artiste' (*Lyres*), where commercial assault is imaged as a violation of the body of the city:

> Brutalement, à midi, la clameur des affiches, la réclame des avertisseurs, plante sa hache barbare dans la masse de Paris.
> Elle tranche d'un coup cent grands murs verts et rouges, elle fend des rues où grincent à vif les rails nerveux, elle écartèle les carrefours roués et démembrés. Cornez, trompettes discordantes! Croulez, gares!

The processes of dislocation and fracturing migrate from the commercial sphere to the space of intimate relations, inducing the mental breakdown of the male protagonist, Lucien. This provokes a scene of domestic assault triggered by linguistic discord and a surge of antipathy:

> Mille cubes dans [la] pensée [de Lucien], heurtés, escaladés, composés, s'écroulaient d'un coup. Mais de lui vers Alice simplement un mince et ridicule filet de paroles coulait vite, comme une gamme de fifre, comme un jockey qui galope au déboulé de Saint-Cloud.
> Il se tut et Alice leva les yeux. [...] Le regard, les cheveux mal traversés par la lumière, l'abattement d'épaules faibles, les mains pointues, tout en elle exprimait le mensonge.
> Comme une grande rafale fut ressentie par Lucien. L'enthousiasme le saisissait. Dans un élan qui emportait tout son poids, il gifla trois fois fortement la femme. Révoltée, précipitée, hurlante, pleurante; puis soulevée sur un coude, face à la vitre, elle montre des yeux lavés. Elle sourit.

What reads at one level as a disturbing sign of female acceptance of violence, emerges as more problematical and less intelligible in the retrospective light of 'tout en elle exprimait le mensonge.' The closure of the poem in the aporia of the victim's indeterminable smile reproduces in the narrative structure the unresolvability of intersubjective relations and the insurmountable isolation of the individual.

Ponge's cultural critique exposes the profound disaffection and cynicism pervading all areas of human activity – private and public, official and informal, economic and affective, industrial and social. In this series of monologues, narratives, fragmentary satires, and pen portraits, drawn from across his oeuvre, Ponge reveals a crisis of subjectivity as he sounds the deep alienation of the individual from the defining structures of capitalist society and its institutions, and from his or her inner self. In their unequal struggle against everyday disenchantment, Ponge's people shuttle between two positions – break up or break out – but these positions only sharpen their sense of containment and offer little transformative potential. The burden of disenchantment, assumed by the drift of disconsolate characters and the poet-narrator, comes through in the stylistic and syntactic disturbances manifest in the texts. But if the mixing of styles and the dislocation of syntax reproduce the deep cracks in the smooth outer surface of structures and systems, the narrator's work on language tends to repeat the positions – retreat or revolt – adopted by his characters. Like them, he veers between discursive escapism ('Forcé souvent de fuir par la parole') and verbal destructiveness ('le défigurer un peu ce beau langage').

The explicit identification of a crisis in language as the source of the fractured subjectivities and competing discourses of *Douze petits écrits* has clear implications for Ponge's project in *Le Parti pris des choses*. Yet where *Douze petits écrits* traces alienation back to the fixed mantle of words that cloaks us and that we fetishize, other texts anticipate the dismantling of the monumental drapery of cliché and readerly assumption. 'L'Avenir des paroles' (*Proêmes*) affirms the forward momentum of Ponge's project for language: 'Quand aux tentures du jour, aux noms communs drapés pour notre demeure en lecture on ne reconnaîtra plus grand-chose sinon de hors par ci nos initiales briller comme épingles ferrées sur un monument de toile.'

The culture critique emerging most visibly in Ponge's earliest texts articulates the profound dislocation of the individual – from society, from language, and from a richer experience of inwardness. The urgency of transforming that experience of dislocation solicits the reconnection of self and world through language and the generative play of analogy in *Le Parti pris des choses*. A textual key to the transition between *Douze petits écrits* and Ponge's subsequent work is provided by 'Les Écuries d'Augias,' written in 1929–30 and published in *Proêmes*. 'Les Écuries d'Augias' begins with a scathing reprise of the culture critique of the early satirical texts. The exasperated inaugural cry '[l]'ordre de choses honteux à Paris crève les yeux, défonce les oreilles' unleashes visions of tumult, hyperactivity, aggression, and individual subjugation to the pressures of industrial production and the market economy. The insistent rhythm imparted by the repeated demonstratives mimes the hypertrophic swell ('monstruosité') of commerce with its cynical transactions and desolating practices:

> Ces ruées de camions et d'autos, ces quartiers qui ne logent plus personne mais seulement des marchandises ou les dossiers des compagnies qui les transportent, ces rues où le miel de la production coule à flots [...] cette autre sorte d'hommes qui ne sont connus que par leurs collections, ceux qui se tuent pour avoir été 'ruinés,' ces gouvernements d'affairistes et de marchands.

What makes 'Les Écuries d'Augias' a summative text is the aggrieved recognition of the incontrovertible relationality between the cultural order and subjective condition, the coincidence of material dystopia and forms of inward affliction: 'Hélas, pour comble d'horreur, *à l'intérieur de nous-mêmes, le même ordre sordide parle.*' This reciprocal mirroring of world and self, exteriority and subjectivity, underlined by the poet's italics, is crucial to an understanding of the relationship between the earlier socio-critical texts and the project of reconnection unfolding in *Le Parti pris des choses.* The citizens of Ponge's anonymous metropolis suffer profound alienation – from themselves, from the social structures imposed from without, and from the palpable things so conspicuously absent from the systematized world represented in the satirical and socio-critical texts. The city-dwellers are embittered or embattled, but whether their response to alienation takes the form of revolt or capitulation, it coincides invariably with the realization that the resources of language have become severely depleted or devalued: '[N]ous n'avons pas à notre disposition d'autres mots ni d'autres grands mots (ou phrases, c'est-à-dire d'autres idées) que ceux qu'un usage journalier dans ce monde grossier depuis l'éternité prostitue.' 'Les Écuries d'Augias' begins by revisiting our dislocation from our milieu and from our inner selves; it moves on to embrace the possibility of regeneration through language. Because we have no other words or ideas than those that everyday familiarity has polluted over the centuries, regeneration demands a creative recycling of language. Ponge's revision of the Herculean cleaning of the Augean stables urges the repainting of those stables by means of their own slurry. Only by plunging his brush into the familiar pot can the painter of words inscribe bold new traces on a blank surface.

Le Parti pris des choses proposes a profound reconnection between self and world in the experience of freedom, solace, creativity, and the desirable reciprocity of things and of language. I argue, in what follows, that the poetry of *Le Parti pris des choses* offers a corrective to the abstractions exposed in *Douze petits écrits* by summoning the expressivity of subjective and perceptual plenitude to counter a world where human lives atrophy and language is depleted.

Discussing *Douze petits écrits* and *Le Parti pris des choses* invites critical metaphors that are contrastive and complementary: where the satirical series calls up terms such as 'abstraction,' 'depletion,' 'standardization,' 'levelling,' and 'repetition' (itself a process of 'wearing thin'), *Le Parti pris des choses* solicits 'richness,' 'thickness,' 'generosity,' and 'expansiveness.' In order to examine more closely the relationship of contrast and complementarity between these two contiguous phases of Ponge's writing, I first take a detour via *L'Atelier contemporain*, where the poet's elliptical reflections on Giacometti's whittled figures raise crucial questions of subject–body–world relationality.[23]

In *Douze petits écrits*, individuals are overwhelmed by abstractions (alienation, exploitation, routine) that they barely tolerate and to which they offer no effective counterweight or real resistance. Their diminished lives find an unexpected material analogue in the acutely pared bodies of Giacometti's sculptures, about which Ponge writes movingly and sparingly in 'Joca seria: Notes sur les sculptures d'Alberto Giacometti.' Ponge focuses on the paradoxical embodiment of figures whose grotesquely overweighted feet and atrophied torsos evoke at once the immobilizing burden of existence and the unbearable erosion of subjective complexity. He evokes Giacometti's brilliant and disconsolating materialization of the ponderous and the imponderable, of existential heaviness and the sublime fragility of being. At once excessively slight and intolerably heavy, existence is bodied forth as instability and disequilibrium.[24] The complex appeal of Giacometti for Ponge lies in the translation of that existential unease into bodily form, for consciousness – for Ponge as for Giacometti – is inescapably embodied. The poet's sensitive, searching study of flesh and form in Giacometti alerts us to how stunningly undervisited the body is in critical readings of Ponge's work: I want to address this corporeal blind spot in what follows. More than this, however, Ponge's empathy with the sculptor's deeply affecting representation of precarious human identity, existential vertigo, and the slightness of being can illumine the keen study of dystopia (*Douze petits écrits*) and its poetic corrective (*Le Parti pris des choses*): the physical 'thinness' of Giacometti's figures translates the diminished subjectivity exposed in *Douze petits écrits*; at the same time, those harrowed figures, in their lack, seem to strain after the replenishment proffered in *Le Parti pris des choses*.

As we saw in *Douze petits écrits*, individual or collective subordina-
tion to abstract structures has its corollary in the existential starkness
that is figured by the absence of particular, palpable objects (and the
corresponding preponderance of fetishized emblems). Alienated subjectivity defines itself in terms of the failure to embrace things and a
corresponding inability to move beyond the repetition of flattened discourses and embrace the regenerative potential of language. These
ideas are amplified in 'My Creative Method' (*Méthodes*), where Ponge
expressly presents his preoccupation with things as the corollary of his
aversion to systems and abstractions. Ponge evokes the pleasure afforded by the material and palpable, the individual and particular
(landscapes, events, objects, people), precisely as a remedy for alienated subjectivity. Things make the poet what he is, and in the process
they give rise to other new things in the form of writing and text.
Connecting with material things is the means of reconnecting with
language, the way of making new:

> Les idées me demandent mon agrément, l'exigent et il m'est trop facile de
> le leur donner: ce don, cet accord ne me procure aucun plaisir, plutôt un
> certain écoeurement, une nausée. Les objets, les paysages, les événements,
> les personnes du monde extérieur me donnent beaucoup d'agrément au
> contraire. [...] Leur présence, leur évidence concrètes, leur épaisseur, leurs
> trois dimensions, leur côté palpable, indubitable, leur existence dont je
> suis beaucoup plus certain que de la mienne propre, leur côté: 'cela ne
> s'invente pas (mais se découvre)' [...] [T]out cela est ma seule raison d'être,
> à proprement parler mon *prétexte*; et *la variété des choses est en réalité ce qui
> me construit.* [...] [S]'il faut donc que j'existe, à partir d'[une chose], ce ne
> sera, ce ne pourra être que par une certaine création de ma part à son
> propos.
> Quelle création? *Le texte.*   ('My Creative Method,' *Méthodes*, 12–13)

Being on the side of things is a way of countering vertigo and assuaging
anxiety, and a means of (re)generating self through writing. Faced with
the abyss of self-doubt, Ponge turns his gaze on familiar objects, on
irreducible, obstinately non-standard things: 'la forme des choses les
plus particulières, les plus asymétriques et de réputation contingentes
[...] [J]'y trouve tout mon bonheur' ('La Forme du monde,' *Proêmes*).
Just as the displacement of subjectivity onto material things signals a
retreat from social systems, so it averts the temptations of inwardness
via a more expansive, more outwardly generous project of self–world

relationality. In his essay 'Braque le réconciliateur,' Ponge affirms that man can only nourish himself by forgetting his *self*, by thinking of himself as a simple element in the functioning of the world:

> Il nous est arrivé de constater que pour nous satisfaire, ce n'était pas tant notre idée de nous-mêmes ou de l'homme que nous devions tâcher d'exprimer, mais en venir au monde extérieur, au parti pris des choses. Et qu'enfin l'homme—son chant le plus particulier il ait des chances de le produire au moment où il s'occupe beaucoup moins de lui-même que d'autre chose, où il s'occupe plus du monde que de lui-même. [...] Disons qu'il arrive à l'homme de s'oublier, pour considérer le monde, et croire y découvrir quelque chose. Et jamais plus qu'alors il ne se montre homme, jamais il ne répond mieux à sa définition, ou destination. Jamais il ne rend mieux compte de lui-même.   ('Braque le réconciliateur' [1946], *L'Atelier contemporain*, 62–3)

The displacement of subjectivity has its source in the yearning after things external to ourselves, in transitive desire: 'Notre âme est transitive. Il lui faut un objet, qui l'affecte, comme son complément direct, aussitôt. Il s'agit du rapport le plus grave (non du tout de *l'avoir*, mais de *l'être*),' ('L'Objet, c'est la poétique,' *L'Atelier contemporain*, 221). The activation of transitive desire demands a special kind of object, not the kind that we routinely colonize and domesticate, but the kind of object that places itself beyond fetishistic or economic recuperation, that resists reifying assimilation: thus Ponge retrieves the wooden crate ('Le Cageot,' *Le Parti pris des choses*) at the precise point where it passes out of economic circulation, its utility exhausted and its symbolic value irrecoverable. The flow goes in the opposite direction too, for transitive desire implies a yearning for objects that will confront and judge us in turn. As if to emphasize this two-way flow, Ponge reverses the usual direction of the transitive proposition and provides a humorous lesson in modesty when he asks how objects might see us. His conjecture? As great red monkeys obeying our defining whim, which is to speak. His conclusion? That we are no greater or more interesting in our verbal expression than objects and creatures in their silence ('Tentative orale,' *Méthodes*, 247–8).

Transitive desire surges in moments of optimal perceptual contact between subject and world, the body forming the material seam between inner self and exterior surface. In Ponge, the intense pleasure of perception (not unmixed, sometimes, with disgust) implies a profoundly embodied rush of consciousness ('un milliard de petites pompes aspirantes que l'on peut fouler, non refouler,' *La Fabrique du pré*, 201).[25] Such moments are at once disruptive – for they tear us free of self-assuring complacency – and enriching – for they provide illuminating lessons in visual and verbal appraisal, and prompt new creation in the form of poetry. The fraught and energizing coincidence of the conscious body with things is the source of the richer subjective and linguistic experience to which Ponge's poetry aspires.

Subjectivity and the Material

The body is inextricable from desire, as Ponge reminds us in passionately corporeal – and resolutely masculinist – language: 'Tendre au maximum sa vie et sa lyre. Son désir et son expression. Somme toute, il faut désirer, aimer, bander et jouir (tout cela aussi ardemment et rigoureusement que possible).'[26] My purpose is not to debate the broader gender ethics raised by the provocative discourse of a literary program, but to consider the body and desire in the more fluid, indeterminate, and inclusive filtering of a poetic vision; on that basis I shall assume that Ponge's call to erotic energy may be extended, metaphorically, to all writers and readers in their experience of texts.[27]

Ponge reminds us that the body is the sublime surface across which desire rushes; it is the site of voluptuous contact with things located beyond itself. The body connects us with other and with object; it enables what is on the outside to enter via sensation and perception, and it makes visible what is interior (thought, emotion, consideration) in the form of a physical gesture, a facial expression, or the words inscribed on the page. Ponge evokes the deep relationality of the body, desire, and writing:

> Ce qui est intéressant dans le phénomène de l'homme qui parle pour dire quelque chose, c'est le fait que tout se passe en somme corporellement [...] Tout passe à l'intérieur du corps et s'exprime également de cette façon-là. J'ai dit parfois que mon porte-plume m'apparaissait comme une espèce d'organe supplémentaire, vraiment attaché à mon corps, la trace à bout de bras de ce qui vient du fond, c'est-à-dire de *l'éros qui fait parler*.   (Interview with Marcel Spada, *Magazine littéraire*, December 1988, 26; my emphasis)[28]

'L'Orange,' one of Ponge's most beautiful and subtly erotic texts, reveals the irrepressible surge of the body towards things. Here, the desire for possession embraces the yearning to absorb and internalize things ('un liquide d'ambre s'est répandu, accompagné de rafraî-chissement, de parfums suaves, certes') and the urge to alter the world beyond self, to change it materially and poetically. '[L]'épreuve de l'expression' is the exasperating struggle for physical and verbal pos-session that bodies forth in the passionate excesses perpetrated on the flesh of the fruit ('ses cellules ont éclaté,' 'ses tissus se sont déchirés'). Comparable acts of erotic violence – or fantasies of fragilization and penetration – are repeated on the passive fibres of the potato –

> Entre le gras du pouce et la pointe du couteau tenu par les autres doigts de la même main, l'on saisit – après l'avoir incisé – par l'une de ses lèvres ce rêche et fin papier que l'on tire à soi pour le détacher de la chair appétis-sante du tubercule.   ('La Pomme de terre,' *Pièces*)

– and on the irresistibly resisting *figue-tétine*:

> [La figue] n'est qu'une pauvre gourde, d'un caoutchouc desséché juste à point qu'on puisse en accentuant un peu incisivement la pression des dents franchir la résistance (ou plutôt d'abord la non-résistance) de son enveloppe pour les lèvres déjà sucrées (en quelque façon récompensées) par le sucre d'érosion superficielle qui la saupoudre, jouir de l'autel scin-tillant en son intérieur qui la remplit toute d'une pulpe de pourpre grati-fiée de pépins.   (*Comment une figue de paroles et pourquoi*, 109)

The resistance of things to opening is captured in the intractability of the oyster or the impenetrable intactness of the orange's pip as it asserts '[s]a dureté relative et [s]a verdeur' against the masochistic passivity of the pulp. Resistance aggravates desire and intensifies imaginary vio-lence as the blade of the knife prises apart the oyster shell, and fingers dig into the skin and flesh of the orange. The fantasy of sadistic pleasure played out in 'L'Orange' coincides with the desire of the would-be torturer, in turn, to be entered and possessed by the object; to become the object of his object. Reciprocity brings appeasement: the blissful diffusion of sensation and the physical articulation of that sensation (as the larynx opens to let the word and the juice pass through) produce pleasure that is simultaneously physical and linguistic as world and word coincide in the body.

The indivisibility of body, subjectivity, and writerly necessity comes through in 'Témoignage' (*Proêmes*), an elliptical meditation on autobiography, materiality, and the struggle for poetic language. This text is worth quoting in full for it captures the relation between body and consciousness in Ponge, and stresses subjectivity as a process inextricable from the process of writing the material:

> Un corps a été mis au monde et maintenu pendant trente-cinq années dont j'ignore à peu près tout, présent sans cesse à *désirer* une pensée que mon devoir serait de conduire au jour.
> Ainsi, à l'épaisseur des choses ne s'oppose qu'une *exigence* d'esprit, qui chaque jour rend les paroles plus coûteuses et plus urgent leur besoin.
> N'importe. L'activité qui en résulte est la seule où soient mises en jeu toutes les qualités de cette construction prodigieuse, la personne, à partir de quoi tout a été remis en question et qui semble avoir tant de mal à accepter franchement son existence.

Consciousness in Ponge is active in the deep of things ('l'épaisseur des choses'): it coils itself into the shell of the snail, explores the glassy chamber that is the shrimp, pierces the gleaming wood of the greengrocer's crate, circulates in the 'immense laboratoire' of vegetation illuminated by heavy rainfall. The movement of consciousness through things probes infinite variety and variability, and bodies forth in forms of visual, acoustic, or tactile activity that reach beyond erotic pleasure to a fuller perceptual voluptuousness – that of the voice which caresses and passes over things; that of the eye which struggles to see or gain a fuller perspective from the dark underside of ferns ('Rhum des fougères'); that of the lips which kiss the table and consecrate the poet's 'Tentative orale' (*Méthodes*, 262). Ponge evokes the profound pleasure afforded by intense moments of bodily contact with the material world, like the subject-to-surface sensuality of the encounter with the yielding weight of a door ('Les Plaisirs de la porte,' *Le Parti pris des choses*). But such ephemeral pleasure ('ce corps à corps rapide') incites more longing as new desire is left unappeased by the fracture and separation of body and material that occurs when the subject moves through and beyond the door. Those corporeal instances of self–world exchange and alteration are abundant and momentary in Ponge's writing: the body rubs up against the world, the skin makes contact with the object, and, reciprocally, the material thing makes its bodily incursion in the form of an image on the retina or a tactile sensation to which poetic language gives voice. Poetry stages a deep fascination with the very moment when the embodied consciousness meets and is altered by matter, and in turn leaves its imprint on the world and in words, like the beating wings of a bird that instantly set the air rippling or the sudden blink of a human eye.[29] Desire is constituted in the urgency of making contact with the world, of inscribing the surface of things with traces whose origin is perceptual and whose perpetuation brings forth analogy and allegory.

In his meditation on memory and lithography, Ponge finds an analogue for the imprint of words on the lithographer's stone in the visible traces of a thought on the face of someone speaking, in the capacity of the flesh to inscribe meaning: 'Voilà donc une page qui vous manifeste immédiatement ce que vous lui confiez.'[30] The bodily propensity to exteriorize feeling or memory or thought stirs a textual obsession with the body's outer surface and its boundary, with the skin – the exquisitely receptive and articulate site of sentient experience. The skin's quality as a communicative, meaning-producing surface gives rise to successive investments in the outward material texture of things, in the 'face' they present to the world:[31] the post-partum mother ('Quelques jours après les couches la beauté de la femme se transforme. Le visage souvent penché sur la poitrine s'allonge un peu. [...] Les bras et les mains s'incurvent et se renforcent. [...] Le ventre ballonné, livide, encore très sensible; le bas-ventre s'accommode du repos, de la nuit des draps,' 'La Jeune Mère'); the crust of bread ('[une masse amorphe] s'est façonnée en vallées, crêtes, ondulations, crevasses...,' 'Le Pain'); the steaming fibre of freshly cut meat ('Chaque morceau de viande est une sorte d'usine, moulins et pressoirs à sang. Tubulures, hauts fourneaux, cuves y voisinent avec les marteaux-pilons, les coussins de graisse. La vapeur y jaillit, bouillante,' 'Le Morceau de viande').

The notion of a miraculous seam of contact between inner and outer, between self and world, world and text, is deployed through a dazzling extended metaphor in the opening essay of *L'Atelier contemporain*, 'L'Atelier.' Here the artist's studio is figured as a fragile, taut, translucent film of skin erupting into light-diffusing bubbles of incomparable sensitivity ('l'aspect bullescent, ou bullulé').[32] 'Ampoule' brings into coruscating fusion notions of vitreous transparency, luminosity, and the bodily blister ('entre verrière et verrue'). This vitreous bubbling or blistering of surface is the sign of the repeated, reciprocal rubbing (and healing) of self and world that produces the therapeutic eruption of creativity – 'une dialectique subtile de l'usure et de la réparation (voire de la fabrication)'. The translucent, crystalline studio offers a metaphor for the activity of the poet as he shapes and perfects his project in the workshop of words, and strives towards optimal reciprocity and verbal transparency (what Ponge calls *adéquation*) between object and language.[33]

The relationality between subjectivity (in its consciously embodied forms) and things presupposes a specific object of desire capable of provoking sensation and generating language. What drives the poetic project in *Le Parti pris des choses* and beyond is the urge to explore how things engage the subject and how, in turn, the subject, impelled by writerly desire, seeks verbal *jouissance* in the description of things: 'Il faut du désir, donc un objet, un objet sensible, un objet de sensations, pour qu'il y ait départ et persistance de la parole.'[34] Ponge selects material things as the site of an ideal coincidence of subject and world whose physical boundaries shape the parameters of conscious selfhood ('le contour de la "chose," de l'objet constitu[e] alors *l'horizon* de l'être').[35] The mediating encounter of self with a particular object or phenomenon is key to the poetic mapping of a fresh reciprocity of self and world.

The implied surge of the desiring, sentient body towards things raises questions about the compelling nature of the objects explored and about the particular ways in which those objects may be known and be brought to language. In order to consider the particularity of language in Ponge, we need first to probe the poet's preoccupation with the specificity and singularity of things.

Ponge urges us to look afresh at objects to which we have become anaesthetized – intellectually, aesthetically, and perceptually. His 'parti pris des choses' is a commitment to engage subject and object in invigorating new ways, and thus challenge normative modes of viewing and naming; his writing chronicles the struggle to bring to language the dazzling or disturbing quality of an object ordinarily perceived as unexceptional. And, as if to reaffirm the bidirectional flow of transitive desire, Ponge again reverses the habitual 'subject-to-object' direction of affectivity when he exhorts the object to stir itself and rouse a dormant consciousness: 'Bois de pins, sortez de la mort, de la non-remarque, de la non-conscience.' ('Le Carnet du bois de pins,' *La Rage de l'expression*). This imagined empowering of the material and non-sentient imparts the urgency of resisting the disappearance of objects (and human subjects) into the colonizing structures of the levelling consciousness exposed in *Douze petits écrits*. The will to dismantle the socio-cultural structures critiqued in the early satirical series finds more ample and affirmative expression now in the desire at once to enliven things – the subjective perception of things – and to 'undeaden' language. Ranging across socio-cultural and linguistic concerns in the programmatic text 'Introduction au "Galet"' (*Proêmes*), Ponge deplores (somewhat hubristically) '[le] peu d'épaisseur des choses dans l'esprit des hommes jusqu'à moi,' and goes on to provide four instances of what he considers platitudinous literary evocations of pebbles and stones (drawn from Diderot, Saint-Just, and Rimbaud).[36] Resistance to linguistic and cultural levelling is thus figured *materially*, as a search for depth and density, a yearning for 'thickness-in-things' that finds its poetic correlative in the deeper texturing of words:

> Je propose à chacun l'ouverture de trappes intérieures, un voyage dans l'épaisseur des choses, une invasion de qualités, une révolution ou une subversion comparable à celle qu'opère la charrue ou la pelle, lorsque, tout à coup et pour la première fois, sont mises au jour des millions de parcelles, de paillettes, de racines, de vers et de petites bêtes jusqu'alors enfouies. O ressources infinies de l'épaisseur des choses, *rendues* par les ressources infinies de l'épaisseur sémantique des mots! ('Introduction au "Galet,"' *Proêmes*)

Ponge seeks, in the manifest surfaces and the hidden recesses of objects ordinarily neglected and 'naturalized,' a remedy for linguistic depreciation and diminished subjective experience. As the beneficiary of a radically reappraising gaze, the object that was dulling our perception – and which our dulled perception was dulling the more so – becomes a *captivating* object, one that solicits and rewards perceptual investment; one that stirs language as it stirs consciousness.

What specific things imprint themselves on the Pongean consciousness and leave their traces in language? To revisit the poet's corpora of everyday things is to be struck by the selectivity that favours the domestic, the natural, the modest, the minimally processed: the candle, the bar of soap, the bilberry, the cigarette, the 'almost nothing' that is the glass of water. Holding up, one after the other, a series of outwardly simple things, Ponge confronts and strives to resolve, or at least relieve, the crisis in subject–object relations.

For Ponge, the most familiar things are those most lost to sight and to experience, obscured by the self-regarding gaze of a materially abstracted sovereign subject ('Rien n'a été dit des moindres choses, puisque tout ne l'a jamais été que du point de vue de l'homme seulement').[37] Ponge explicitly challenges the humanistic model of pre-given subjecthood and urges us to turn our gaze upon what is outside of ourselves as a means of retrieving things from neglect and, in the process, replenishing subjective experience. Ponge's project is driven by the indeflectible desire to turn outwards, to nourish subjectivity in exteriority: by displacing attention from abstract systems to superficially simple yet profoundly complex things, the concept of sovereign subjecthood vested in 'l'homme' is displaced by the process of subjectivity. Ponge explicitly relates the rescue of the small-scale and singular to the crisis of subjecthood in advanced modernity. He outlines a situation where subject authority is pressured, fragilized, overwhelmed, and he proposes a remedy, not in theoretical abstraction, but in an invigorated contact with the material and unbounded receptivity to new, fragmentary forms of knowledge:

> J'ai dit, dans un texte intitulé "Introduction au galet", qu'il était impossible, pour un homme de notre époque, de saisir l'ensemble des connaissances et, par conséquent, de faire quelque chose qui soit comparable aux cosmogonies des Grecs présocratiques, parce que les sciences se sont développées de telle façon et divisées de telle façon qu'il y faudrait plusieurs vies d'homme, et alors, à ce moment-là, j'ai dit: le plus simple est de reprendre tout du début, s'allonger sur l'herbe, et recommencer, comme si on ne savait rien.   (*Entretiens avec Philippe Sollers*, 105)

Knowledge, Ponge proposes, is located in the encyclopedia of everyday things, in the raw of simple existence. He implies that the pressures of an increasingly fractured, impossibly morsellized world can only be alleviated if we transfer our gaze to rare, relatively unprocessed fragments of material life. The poet's corpora admits only the simplest things for they are already so materially full and linguistically *prégnant* as to be utterly sufficient: '[L]a richesse de propositions contenues dans le moindre objet est si grande, que je ne conçois pas encore la possibilité de rendre compte d'aucune autre chose que des plus simples: une pierre, une herbe, le feu, un morceau de bois, un morceau de viande' ('Introduction au "Galet,"' *Proêmes*).

Ponge intimates a wondrous folding of the world into the poem in the stunning singularity of things. 'La Fin de l'automne' (*Le Parti pris des choses*) opens with an allegory of the contraction of abstract subject matter (autumn) to a single material signified unfolded by the generative play of metaphor: 'Tout l'automne à la fin n'est plus qu'une tisane froide. Les feuilles mortes de toutes essences macèrent dans la pluie.'

'La Fin de l'automne' presents a fragmentary illustration of an idea limned in 'Bords de mer' (*Le Parti pris des choses*), that of a salutary contraction or 'whittling' of the abstract that would bring about a breathless expansion of the material and small-scale. In 'Bords de mer,' the vast flatness of the sea fractures into a thousand individual waves, and deposits its dross of pebbles and shells in an allegory that celebrates the expressivity of the particular as a counter to the terror of limitlessness:

> La mer jusqu'à l'approche de ses limites est une chose simple qui se répète flot par flot. Mais les choses les plus simples dans la nature ne s'abordent pas sans y mettre beaucoup de formes, faire beaucoup de façons, les choses les plus épaisses sans subir quelque amenuisement. C'est pourquoi l'homme, et par rancune aussi contre leur immensité qui l'assomme, se précipite aux bords ou à l'intersection des grandes choses pour les définir.
> [...]
> [...] [L]e flot venu de loin sans heurts et sans reproche enfin pour la première fois trouve à qui parler. Mais une seule et brève parole est confiée aux cailloux et aux coquillages, qui s'en montrent assez remués, et il expire en la proférant; et tous ceux qui le suivent expireront aussi en proférant la pareille, parfois par temps à peine un peu plus fort clamée. Chacun par-dessus l'autre parvenu à l'orchestre se hausse un peu le col, se découvre, et se nomme à qui il fut adressé. Mille homonymes seigneurs ainsi sont admis le même jour à la présentation par la mer prolixe et prolifique en offres labiales à chacun de ses bords.

Simple things, in their retrievable richness and affecting singularity, satisfy the competing urges of diminished subjectivity: they respond to the longing for equilibrium, however fragile, and they counter mental inertia with the invigorating play of paradox.[38] Simple things present a compelling mix of the reassuringly familiar and the intriguingly singular, of the culturally contained and the poetically untapped: '[le sens de mon oeuvre] est d'ôter à la matière son caractère inerte; de lui reconnaître sa qualité de vie particulière, son activité, son côté affirmatif, sa volonté d'être, son étrangeté foncière (qui en fait la providence de l'esprit), sa sauvagerie, ses dangers et ses risques' ('Le Verre d'eau,' *Méthodes*, 158). Ordinary objects call forth extraordinary acts of retrieval and discovery: they urge us to retrospective action – to recover what has been depleted – and they move us prospectively to open up fresh perceptual and lexical seams. This backwards and forward momentum traverses the object as writerly desire surges to retrieve what is overlooked or exhausted, and make it new in language.[39]

The 1967 essay *Le Savon* offers an enraptured lesson in the recovery of an object that has become lost to sight, a symptom of a more generalized crisis in a consumer economy where material desires are routinely met, and the movement of supply and demand is precisely calibrated.[40] Selecting for scrutiny the domestic soap-bar, Ponge contrasts the perceptions of this simple substance prevailing in the materialistic mid-1960s with attitudes to soap during the years of war rationing. He contrasts the unthinking, indifferent 'naturalization' of soap in an economy of plenty with the investment of the same commodity with qualities of uniqueness and distinction in a period of material scarcity. Ponge observes that the rareness and the rarefaction of soap effectively transform the experience of material deprivation into one of perceptual enrichment, an experience that empowers the beholder to view the object afresh, actively, to see it for itself and not simply to (ab)use it. More than this, the recovery or reinvestment of the object assists us to see ourselves differently, for when the world engages us in arresting ways (baffling us, beguiling us), our value changes in our own eyes. The transitive relationship between humans and things is immeasurably optimized here. The euphoria of the encounter between a perceptually invigorated human subject and the beneficiary object materializes in the exuberance of soap. The solid object escapes our physical grasp but its wake of cloudy blueness tantalizes the gaze and stimulates writerly desire; the soap bar exhausts itself in the very act of self-generation, yet leaves its visible traces on the world and in the flurry of signifiers that capture it for poetry: 'Ce galet inerte est presque aussi difficile à tenir qu'un poisson. Le voilà qui m'échappe et comme une grenouille replonge au bassin... émettant aussitôt à ses dépens un bleu nuage d'évanescence, de confusion ...' (*Le Savon*, 24). Celebrated as a source of knowledge ('ce que nous savons faire'), soap dispenses, not only a lesson in how to live – energetically, independently, and unarrestably – but a model for how to write.[41] Soap and its startling capacity to foam and froth, to expand and self-generate – its material 'volubilité' – finds its analogue in a humorous, consciously effervescent verbal style ('En raison des qualités de cet objet, il me faut [...] le faire mousser à vos yeux').[42] Ponge's writing captures the performative quality of this 'pierre bavarde' whose expressivity momentarily dissolves the differences between language and materiality, poetry and metapoetry, subject and substance:[43]

Pierre magique!

...Plus il forme avec l'air et l'eau des grappes explosives de raisins parfumés.

L'air, l'eau et le savon alors se chevauchent, jouent à saute-mouton, forment des combinaisons emphatiques et légères qu'un souffle, un sourire, un rien en trop de vanité intérieure, la moindre exagération font exploser...

Ou une catastrophe des eaux.

On sent que j'ai exagéré les développements, les variations; qu'il y a là comme un style savonneux, moussant, écumeux, – comme la bave aux naseaux du cheval qui galope –.

Je l'ai naturellement fait exprès.

Sachant qu'il me suffirait d'un paragraphe de raison (ou d'ironie?) pure pour nettoyer, dissoudre et rincer tout cela.   (26–7)

Soap – or rather the process of soaping – is like poetic language as it self-transforms, proliferates, disperses, dissolves, and falls silent. In this brilliant, tender portrait, soap emerges as an intensely affecting substance. It proffers a compelling materialization of paradox, for it generates its own effervescence and in the process consumes itself. The acrobatic activity of the soap-bar, in both physical and rhetorical terms, describes the subtlety and the precariousness of the writing project that begins with mundane things (ordinary objects and familiar words), and achieves poetry of luminous, sublimely fragile intensity.

As Ponge's essay on soap performs the pleasure and the plenitude experienced in the particular of things, it engages with the need to make things *present* and not simply to represent (repeat and duplicate) them: 'il ne s'agit pas de "rendre", de "représenter" le monde physique [...] mais de *présenter* dans le monde verbal quelque chose d'homologue' (*Entretiens*, p. 48). *Présenter* is the desire to capture in words the rush of consciousness at the point of contact with the world. The temptations of euphoric or orgasmic 'débordement' are moderated by the recognition of the sheer material necessity of things, and the urgency – and sometimes, briefly, the joy – of finding structures (verbal, subjective) to articulate that necessity:

> [C]e qui me paraît vraiment merveilleux [...] c'est le fait même que n'importe quelle structure [celle des mots, des personnes, des machines, du monde entier] puisse se concevoir comme telle, s'accepter et s'avouer, se déclarer hautement pour ce qu'elle est, c'est-à-dire (avec à la fois orgueil et humilité) comme conventionnelle par elle-même; eh bien! si elle peut trouver le signe de cela, à ce moment-là il y aura une espèce de transmutation, alors vraiment heureuse, jubilante: c'est ce que j'appelle l'*objoie*.
>
> Il y a là une sorte de morale qui consiste à déclarer qu'il faut qu'un orgasme se produise et que cet orgasme ne se produit que par l'espèce d'aveu et de proclamation que je suis ce que je suis, qu'il y a une sorte de tautologie.
> [...]
> La beauté est la beauté, ce n'est que la beauté, et il ne s'agit que de développer cela, et de structurer cela, cette tautologie, qui est, au fond, contenue seulement dans le *nom*; il s'agit de développer cela dans la joie, dans la jubilation.   (*Entretiens*, 190–1)

Ponge suggests that by neglecting deceptively simple things and the lessons that inhere in those things, we neglect ourselves and we neglect language. Only by recovering the forgotten and the overlooked can we begin the process of restoring plenitude to language and bringing new depth to subjective experience. Coming towards the end of Ponge's oeuvre, *Le Savon* offers an extended reprise of the object as a model for our self-change, an idea that I would argue, originates in *Le Parti pris des choses*, for it is here that the desire for knowledge (and self-knowledge) seeks out the instructive, inspiriting qualities of material things and of sentient life forms. This is a question to which I will return, but I want at this point to consider a seam of anxiety running through Ponge's receptivity to things.

The poetic treatment of material things reveals a degree of uncertainty as to whether the individual object signifies metonymically as a representative fragment of the real or is embraced in its particularity, acknowledged for its unique lesson in beauty, symmetry, tenacity, and transparency. Ponge's poetry brings both readings into play such that the ordinary object is perceived by the reader to oscillate between its unassailable specificity and its representative, generic value in the order of everyday things.[44] The (generally) euphoric engagement with the singularity of things is tracked by the fear of lapsing into generalities *around* the object: this becomes a site of unresolvable tension. The task of describing the apricot in *Pièces* poses specifically this problem for Ponge. In his essay 'La Pratique de la littérature,' he presents his struggle to express the colour specificity of the apricot as a stand against generality, failing which the descriptive imperative would capitulate to the generic pathos and vulnerability of all soft fruits: 'il ne fallait pas me contenter de dire ce qui m'émeut profondément dans l'abricot, et qui est valable pour tous les fruits. [...] [J]e voulais faire un abricot seulement. Alors je suis obligé de chercher la couleur et de chercher encore bien autres choses, sans dire quasi un mot du pathétique du fruit.'[45]

The complex allure of the most simple things, their material and representational volatility, and their resistance to description are a source of both writerly pleasure and difficulty (a difficulty that is not inherently unpleasurable for Ponge). The poet's memories of the Algerian landscape provide an ample illustration of his pursuit of the obstinate singularity of things and his struggle to equal that singularity in language by means of a painterly concern for gradations of colour and for the precise capturing of perception. Again in 'La Pratique de la littérature,' which is part travel journal, part aesthetic meditation, Ponge chronicles his successive efforts to name the specific shade of pink ('un certain rose') bathing the foothills of the Atlas Mountains.[46] He charts his patient progress to 'rose sacripant' ('peccant pink'), after a deviation via the exposed heels of the heavily veiled women, an erotic charge that produces a further chromatic complication where natural beauty became indistinguishable from its artificial enhancement:

> Et alors il y avait ce rose. Il y avait aussi un côté fard. J'ai cherché cette couleur rose, un rose ardent, intense, un peu violet et j'avais fini par trouver des mots de couleur. Ça ne marchait pas. Rose cyclamen, non, non, rose polisson, coquin, à cause du fard, à cause du côté sensuel de la chose: ça n'allait pas. [...] Finalement j'ai trouvé un mot, il existe, je ne l'ai pas inventé, parce que c'est mon honneur de vouloir travailler justement avec cette mauvaise peinture, alors: sacripant, un rose sacripant. C'est un mot qui n'est pas très rare en français, qui veut dire un peu polisson. [...] Sacripant. Le mot me plaît. Rose sacripant. Ça y est.[47]

A felicitous dictionary search provides intertextual validation, by way of Ariosto's *Orlando furioso*, for 'sacripant.' This literary-lexical search allows Ponge to loop back to those pink-red foothills, and achieve the relative satisfaction of a sense of writerly arrival ('Sacripante, personnage de l'Arioste, tout comme Rodomonte. Rodomonte, qui signifie, "rouge montagne" et qui était Roi d'Alger. Voilà la preuve. Quand on a ça, on est sûr. [...] [L]e sentiment d'avoir le mot était justifié').[48]

But, these meditations leave unanswered the tantalizing question as to what draws Ponge to one material or substance, and makes him bypass another. What motivates a poetics of selective recovery? Ponge's art criticism, in its reciprocal embedding of poetic and painterly meditations, may help us towards an answer.

In 'L'Objet, c'est la poétique,' Ponge affirms his preference for objects that elude our gaze, for things that are not biddable ('des objets véritables, objectant indéfiniment à nos désirs,' L'Atelier contemporain, 224). These are precisely the kinds of objects to which we should turn our attention, for they resist assimilation into habitual, culturally defined perceptions. Objects that *object* are the obstinate antithesis of those compliant accessory objects that we bend to our desires and that reflect us back to ourselves, and in which, ultimately, we lose ourselves: 'L'homme, le plus souvent, n'étreint que ses émanations, ses fantômes. Tels sont les objets subjectifs. Il ne fait que valser avec eux, chantant tous la même chanson; puis s'envole avec eux ou s'abîme' (224). The subjective inclination to colonize the material world in a bid for a reassuring but illusory self-identity with objects has to be resisted. This may explain Ponge's sporadic aversion to things that fail to resist, his dislike of alterable liquids, viscosity, and states of softness and saturation, and his preference for solid objects, for a salutary 'hardness-in-things.' Rigid and semi-rigid things promise durability, detachment, and a certain internal necessity; above all, they can bear weight and so they offer the necessary corrective to both the excessive fragility of existence and a sense of ontological overburden ('Lourds ou légers [...] je ne sais, nous avons besoin d'un contrepoids,' ibid., 223).

The particularity of Ponge's preferred objects lies in their resilient autonomy, yet their allure inheres in their unpredictability and unevenness. Objects are uneven in their beauty, unpredictable in the responses they bring forth: admiration, awe, curiosity, humour, love, remembrance, pleasure, disgust. Poetry is the struggle to bring their 'qualité différentielle' to language.[49] To recognize the uneven beauty of things and to seek to express that particularity in poetry is to oppose flattening and standardization.[50] In the proem 'La Forme du monde,' the narrator contrasts the systematizing models favoured by philosophers, cosmogonists, and mathematicians with his fascination for what obtrudes materially, for what refuses to be regulated and homogenized, and translates into the asymmetrical and uncontainable. These qualities surface in material things as they coincide and collide with the body in a series of alterations and cancellations. Thus, 'la conscience amère d'une expulsion prématurée de pépins' interrupts and redefines the delicious liquid eruption of 'L'Orange.' The same process of perceptual and linguistic revision is at work in descriptions of more indirectly apprehended phenomena. The variability of rain, for example, is enacted in the series of analogical adjustments and substitutions unfolding in 'Pluie' (Le Parti pris des choses):

> Au centre [de la cour] c'est un fin rideau (ou réseau) discontinu, une chute implacable mais relativement lente de gouttes probablement assez légères, une précipitation sempiternelle sans vigueur, une fraction intense du météore pur. A peu de distance des murs de droite et de gauche tombent avec plus de bruit des gouttes plus lourdes, individuées. Ici elles semblent de la grosseur d'un grain de blé, là d'un pois, ailleurs presque d'une bille.

The richly allegorical, fragmentary study 'Le Verre d'eau' (1948) celebrates the unpredictable symmetry of disparate things – vitreous ('dur et fragile'), verbal ('ces pierres précieuses, ces merveilleux sédiments'), and aqueous ('point de matière').[51] Their shared qualities of sublime beauty and rarefaction form a relationship of unbreakable reciprocity and transparency ('La meilleure façon de présenter l'eau est de la montrer dans un verre. [...] [L]a meilleure façon de présenter un verre (dans l'exercice de ses fonctions) est de le présenter plein d'eau').[52] Throughout his study, Ponge reaffirms the urgency of rendering the particular beauty of the glass and the water it contains, differentiating this project from his earlier discrete descriptions of water in 'De l'eau' (Le Parti pris des choses) and La Seine:

> L'eau du verre est une eau particulière, proche de certaines autres, bien sûr, surtout de l'eau de la carafe, de celle du bol, de l'éprouvette, différente d'elles pourtant, et très éloignée, cela va sans dire, de celle des fleuves, des cuvettes, des cruches et des brocs de terre; plus éloignée encore de celle des bénitiers.
> Et, bien entendu, c'est sa différence en tous cas qui m'intéresse.

> La nature de l'eau est qu'on ne puisse guère la considérer en dehors de son récipient. Certes, cela est vrai d'à peu près tous les fluides, mais l'eau,

de par sa transparence, de par aussi sa viscosité et sa densité propres, enfin surtout de par son manque de qualités même, se trouve plus qu'aucun autre affectée par son récipient: elle attend à vrai dire d'être affectée par lui, elle attend de lui beaucoup de ses qualités.

C'est aux dents propres, fraîches et polies du verre que se marient le mieux les lèvres de l'eau, puis la langue et soudain l'âme profonde de l'eau, quand à ce verre j'appuie ma propre bouche.   (*Méthodes*, 128–9)

In thrall to the mesmerizing translucence of the solid-liquid alliance, Ponge illumines the power of each substance to optimize the beauty and purity of the other. In the process, poetry enacts the blissful coincidence of body and substance in 'Le Verre d'eau' as the reciprocal qualities – 'fraîcheur,' 'liquidité,' 'limpidité,' and 'transparence' – fill the body with freshness, and a sense of subjective integrity is miraculously restored ('votre identité, votre moi').[53] Cool radiance and deep pleasure are the gift proffered by the almost-nothing of the water-in-its-glass, and its invigorating textual equivalent. Each new encounter with the object gives rise to a fresh confrontation with language, thus 'Le Verre d'eau' moves consciously between a reflection on (and of) the material relationality of things and a meditation on the challenge of bringing that relationality to language. As it unfolds the phases of its self-refracting struggle with its cherished object and with language, Ponge's text becomes a model for the search for transparency (*adéquation*) in the description of things (*Méthodes*, 127).[54] The study of the glass of water unfolds its allegory of the difficulty and the delight of moving between object and poetic form, between the container (recipient, glass, text, signifier) and its content (substance, water, idea, signified):

Le mot VERRE D'EAU serait en quelque façon adéquat à l'objet qu'il désigne... Commençant par un v, finissant par un u, les deux seules lettres en forme de vase ou de verre. Par ailleurs, j'aime assez que dans VERRE, après la forme (donnée par le v), soit donnée la matière par les deux syllabes ER RE, parfaitement symétriques comme si, placées de part et d'autre de la paroi du verre, l'une à l'intérieur, l'autre à l'extérieur, elles se reflétaient l'une en l'autre.
[...]
Dans VERRE D'EAU, après VERRE (et ce que je viens d'en dire) il y a EAU. Eh bien, EAU à cette place est très bien aussi: à cause d'abord des voyelles qui le forment. Dont la première, le E, venant après celui répété qui est dans

VERRE, rend bien compte de la parenté de matière entre le contenant et le contenu, – et la seconde, le A [...] rend compte de l'œil que la présence de l'eau donne au verre qu'elle emplit (œil, ici, au sens de lustre mouvant, de poli mouvant).   (*Méthodes*, 127–8)

Relationality and Reciprocity

'Le Verre d'eau' and *Le Savon* affirm the eruptive and formative momentum of Ponge's poetics as the object comes dazzlingly to sight and to language as if for the first time; the deep reciprocity between appraising subject and the material thing appraised is thus revealed. The physical object becomes the beneficiary of an act of perceptual and verbal generosity, and the viewing subject is rewarded in that what he or she was bypassing *in error, in blindness*, is opened up in fresh, undreamed ways.

In return for the gift of descriptive and readerly attention, inert objects and everyday living forms offer lessons in living and in writing. The most memorable *art de vivre* and *art d'écrire* is that offered by snails. In the traces they leave on the world and the earthy imprint the world presses upon them, the discrete shell-bearing creatures illustrate that optimal relationality between subjectivity and material things so fundamental in Ponge. Their determined, gentle movement across the earth offers an allegory of the poet's struggle to possess and transform the world through patient trace-leaving activity on language:

> [L]es escargots aiment la terre humide. *Go on*, ils avancent collés à elle de tout leurs corps. Ils en emportent, ils en mangent, ils en excrémentent. Elle les traverse. Ils la traversent. C'est une interpénétration du meilleur goût parce que pour ainsi dire ton sur ton – avec un élément passif, un élément actif, le passif baignant à la fois et nourrissant l'actif – qui se déplace en même temps qu'il mange.   ('Escargots')

As the poem takes forward the example of snails – slowly, deliberately, in celebratory mimesis – the lesson in how to live thus becomes inseparable from a model of creativity that Ponge would evoke in his essay on the virtues of Malherbe:

> [C]ette bave d'orgueil ils en imposent la marque à tout ce qu'ils touchent. Un sillage argenté les suit.
> [...]

[L'escargot] colle si bien à la nature, il en jouit si parfaitement de si près, il est l'ami du sol qu'il baise de tout son corps, et des feuilles, et du ciel vers quoi il lève si fièrement la tête, avec ses globes d'yeux si sensibles: noblesse, lenteur, sagesse, orgueil, vanité, fierté.

[...]

Rien n'est beau comme cette façon d'avancer si lente et si sûre et si discrète, au prix de quels efforts ce glissement parfait dont [les escargots] honorent la terre!

The capacity of ordinary, familiar things to enhance life, whether of themselves, in their paradoxical beauty, or as models of education or creativity, should move us to invest them with language, and by speaking them give them voice.[55] The relationality between subject and the material object is affirmed, then, in the bestowing of reciprocal benefit. The fuller perceptual attention turned on the habitually overlooked object finds its reward in beauty, surprise, joy, learning, recognition – forms of subjective regeneration that unfold in the deep texture of analogy. This transforms a situation of diminished value into one of mutual restoration as poetry works to right a wrong, to repair a flaw, to remedy a lack. Recovery and repair, so crucial to Ponge's own poetry, is the ethical touchstone of his appreciation of Braque's bid, not to transform the world, but more modestly to restore the world *in its fragments* ('Braque – Dessins,' *L'Atelier contemporain*).[56] In the recurrent references throughout his art criticism to craft, modesty and a material aesthetics, Ponge is speaking passionately for his own creative purpose and for a writerly project invested with affect:

[J]amais le monde dans l'esprit de l'homme n'a si peu, si mal *fonctionné*.

Il ne fonctionne plus que pour quelques artistes. S'il fonctionne encore, ce n'est que par eux.

Voilà donc ce que certains hommes seuls sentent, et dès lors leur vie est tracée. Ils n'ont plus qu'une chose à faire, plus qu'une fonction à remplir. Ils doivent ouvrir un atelier; et y prendre en réparation le monde, le monde par fragments, comme il leur vient.

Tout autre dessein désormais s'efface: pas plus que d'expliquer le monde, il ne s'agit de le transformer; mais plutôt de le remettre en route, par fragments, dans leur atelier.'

('Braque – Dessins,' *L'Atelier contemporain*, 106)

This ethical aesthetics emerges modestly and memorably in 'Le Cageot' as Ponge salvages the discarded object (wooden crate) and recovers its referent ('cageot') from the dictionary where it languishes in the vicinity of more conspicuous sites of containment ('cage' and 'cachot'). The process of material and verbal recovery is driven by the need to make the object 'different' again, to recover its surprise quality, the strangeness that time and familiarity have factored out. If there is an echo of Apollinaire's *surnaturalisme* and the surrealists' *merveilleux*, Ponge's 'found objects' remain more grounded in the specificity of the material: his poetry explores the inside and the exterior of things, and probes their existence both within and beyond the structures of everyday practice. So, objects are appraised in their cultural context (in relation to commercial practices in the instance of the crate) and returned to that context, but between those liminal points (which coincide with the beginning and the end of the text of 'Le Cageot') they are approached in ways that tip them over, change their status, destabilize their normative integrity, and present them afresh. Thus, the crate is revealed as less enduring and more unaffectedly precious than the prized perishables that pass in and out of it; the relation of durability (container) to vulnerability (contents) is as if suddenly reversed. The qualities of tenderness, beauty, and luminosity inherent in the fruit make a miraculous migration to the wooden crate:

A tous les coins de rues qui aboutissent aux halles, il luit alors de l'éclat sans vanité du bois blanc. Tout neuf encore, et légèrement ahuri d'être dans une pose maladroite à la voirie jeté sans retour, cet objet est en somme des plus sympathiques — sur le sort duquel il convient toutefois de ne s'appesantir longuement.

By restoring something of the fullness of lost or depleted objects, poetic description refreshes material perceptions and in the process stimulates more writerly desire whose satisfaction is deferred by the censoring authority of the clausula. The meliorative implications of the subject-object encounter invite closer attention.

The act of material and verbal recovery is also crucially an act of self-recovery. In 'Préface aux *Sapates*' (*Proêmes*) Ponge outlines his aim to 'saisir presque chaque soir un nouvel objet, [...] en tirer à la fois une jouissance et une leçon.' Objects provide pleasure and instruction; the benefits – perceptual, sensual, ethical, linguistic – that inhere in objects are deeply formative. Making contact with material things thus becomes a means of re-investing self.[57] Ponge's aim is to return to the world of things in order to re-nurture human subjectivity: 'Notre raison d'être est, certes, en premier lieu, de nous retourner décidément vers le monde (parti pris des choses) pour y re-nourrir l'homme' (*Pour un Malherbe*, 26). This is one-half of the project, of which the other, indissociable half is the desire to bring the silent world to language. The question of subjective fulfilment and self-recovery through things has crucial implications for language.

For all the formulaic certainty of Ponge's aphorisms ('le monde muet est notre seule patrie'), the process of self-recovery is not straightforward or untroubled.[58] Subjective experience fluctuates between contentment and yearning, stability and unease, and the source of that fluctuation is as much in language as it is in things. If the experience of pleasure figures prominently in Ponge, it is pleasure mingled with disquiet, where the strangeness of things erupts in what is routinely perceived as stable and inalterable. Ponge imparts the inert quality of matter falling away to reveal the pliancy and the uncanniness of things, their power to move, disturb, and enthral us. His texts track the altering structure of perceptions; they reveal the experience of beauty as fragile and provisional at the point where euphoria tips over into unease and anxiety. Reading 'Le Pain,' we descend from the luminous, craggy heights of the crust of bread (via analogies with the Alps, the Taurus Mountains, and the Andean Cordillera) to the 'mollesse ignoble' of the bread's inner crumb. The arrival at 'ce lâche et froid sous-sol' hastens the moment of material and writerly rupture, when the summons to break bread precipitates the breaking-off of the descriptive project. Pleasure in the deep perception of things is not unmixed with the anxiety, perceptual and writerly, that things induce – both of themselves and by their resistance to representation.

The subjective experience fluctuates between anxiety and self-assuredness in things and in language, between desire and nourishment, between arousal and appeasement. This instability is itself beneficial. In 'Le Murmure (condition et destin de l'artiste)' (1950), it is the sheer volatility and paradox of perceptual experience that provides the antidote to abstractions and the means by which the human individual can work towards self-regeneration:

[S]cience–éducation–culture: tout risquerait de finir par une soif inextinguible de repos, de sommeil, de nuit, voire de sauvagerie et de mort, si n'intervenait [...] quelque antidote de même niveau, qui ravisse et comble d'un coup l'homme entier, le trouble et le rassoie dans son milieu naturel, l'en affame et l'y nourrisse, et à proprement parler le récrée. (*Méthodes*, 184–5)

Subjectivity is glimpsed in its expanded potential, in the capacity of the individual to embrace, deep within self, the extremes of experience. Before turning to look further at the specific relation between subjectivity and the material, I want to stay for a moment with these extremes of experience, particularly with Ponge's embrace of destabilization and unease. Such forms of alteration are habitually viewed as negative and synonymous with a loss of centredness and self-consistency. But Ponge subjects these aversive connotations to affirmative revision; he conceives of a therapeutic necessity in violence and the violation of normative assumptions. In the poet's succinct formulation: '[I]l ne s'agit pas d'arranger les choses (le manège) [...] Il faut que les choses vous dérangent' ('Tentative orale').[59] As a generator of displacement and disturbance, the encountered object provokes a therapeutic shift in the patterning of perceptions. This appeal to an active, *activating* strangeness-in-things places Ponge indisputably in the tradition that gathers momentum with Baudelaire and extends through Lautréamont and the surrealists. My concern, though, is not with specific intertextual echoes and influences, but with a feature of modernity and postmodernity that leaves its visible imprint on Pongean poetics: the dismantling of the traditional concept of subjecthood by a process of subjectivity founded in receptivity and the pliant activity of consciousness-in-things. Ponge's elliptical meditations in 'L'Objet, c'est la poétique' track subjectivity as a fluid process of self-generation and negotiation through material things: '[Q]u'est-ce *l'être*? – Il n'est que des façons d'être, successives. Il en est autant que d'objets. Autant que de battements de paupières.'[60] The texts enact the displacement of subjectivity towards things that is crucial to Ponge's purpose, for if the human individual is to achieve a reconciliation with the material world, the world must overwhelm the individual to the point where he or she can break free of reifying structures, and begin to invent a new language:

Il suffit d'abaisser notre prétention à dominer la nature et d'élever notre prétention à en faire physiquement partie, pour que la réconciliation ait lieu. Quand l'homme sera fier d'être non seulement le lieu où s'élaborent les idées et les sentiments, mais aussi bien le noeud où ils se détruisent et se confondent, il sera prêt alors d'être sauvé. L'espoir est donc dans une poésie par laquelle le monde envahisse à ce point l'esprit de l'homme qu'il en perde à peu près la parole, puis réinvente un jargon.   ('Le Monde muet est notre seule patrie')[61]

If the material world offers uneven surfaces for the eye to explore, disparate objects to (be)hold and to question, the traffic goes in the opposite direction too, for things 'talk back': 'Et plus on ouvre de grands yeux, plus ça ouvre de grands yeux. Plus ça vous questionne' ('Courte méditation réflexe aux fragments de miroir').[62] The movement of the subject–object relation against inertia and towards pliancy optimizes equality between subject and object. Their reciprocal probing may be disturbing or inspiriting, but it is always profoundly enabling in bringing us – and things – afresh to language. Ponge reflects on that crucial movement of object and subject, together, into language in his encounter with the Chiffa pebble, an instance that begins with equivocation as to the generic or specific value of the object beheld, and quickly moves to a more crucial discovery. The subject-object encounter urgently calls into question the humanistic concept of stabilized subjecthood and holds up, in its place, a model of subjectivity that is at once perceptual and writerly, affective and textual:

[N]'importe quel caillou, par exemple *celui-ci*, que j'ai ramassé l'autre jour dans le lit de l'oued Chiffa, me semble pouvoir donner lieu à des déclarations inédites du plus haut intérêt. [...] [C]e galet, puisque je le conçois comme objet unique, me fait éprouver [...] un complexe de sentiments particuliers. Il s'agit d'abord de m'en rendre compte. Ici, l'on hausse les épaules et l'on dénie tout intérêt à ces exercises, car, me dit-on, il n'y a là rien de l'homme. Et qu'y aurait-il donc? Mais c'est de l'homme inconnu jusqu'à présent de l'homme. Une qualité, une série de qualités, un compos de qualités inédit, informulé. Voilà pourquoi c'est du plus haut intérêt. [...]
Me voici donc avec mon galet, qui m'intrigue, fait jouer en moi des ressorts inconnus. Avec mon galet que je respecte. Avec mon galet que je veux remplacer par une formule logique (verbale) adéquate.   ('My Creative Method')[63]

The desire for *adéquation* gives rise to the urge to write the intensity of visual, tactile, or kinaesthetic experience in the unpredictability of that experience. This calls forth the pliancy of analogy as habitual perceptions are transformed, and the diversity and openness ordinarily denied the object illuminatingly restored. As the pendulum so long 'arrested' on the side of pre-given subjecthood swings towards objects invigorated by a receptive consciousness-in-language, an imbalance is righted and the concept of a sovereign self suffers an overdue, irreversible loss of prestige.

From Subjectivity as Process to Things-in-Process

Recognizing the displacement of the static freight of subjecthood by a process of subjectivity constituted in visual, tactile, or kinaesthetic sensation enables us to locate the origin of Ponge's writerly project in the coincidence of self and other ('other' defined as everything that exists beyond the boundaries of self). Ponge's own assertion of self–other relationality contests, indirectly, the tendency of critics to factor out subjectivity and perpetuate the distorting 'poetry of objects' frame:

> J'éprouve une émotion très violente à la rencontre aussi bien d'une personne, d'un être ou d'une chose [...] Tout mon travail consiste à [...] rendre compte de la force de cette première émotion, de la puissance et de la nécessité [...]
> [...] Quand je parle d'une rhétorique par objet, c'est vraiment la trace humaine à bout de bras.   (*Magazine littéraire*, December 1988, 31)

The affective tenor of Ponge's language ('force,' 'puissance,' 'nécessité, 'émotion très violente') reaffirms the shock of the subjective–material encounter, and the need to make that shock reverberate across the traditional separation of subject and object. His texts describe an itinerary of desire that moves across the external surface of the object and delves deep into its interior texture. The opening poem of *Le Parti pris des choses*, 'Pluie,' illustrates this. If, initially, 'Pluie' identifies the source of the visual project in the first-person narrating voice ('je'), any sense of a stable subject is quickly eclipsed by a continuous and more diffuse process of subjectivity invested in perceptual experience ('Je la regarde tomber'): thus, the myth of a world-mastering subject is displaced by subjectivity defined as receptivity to the world and the urge to approximate that receptivity in language. Subjectivity surges in the selectivity of analogy and metaphor, and in smaller units of language. Adverbs act to refine meaning, to supplement value ('parfaitement vertical') or subtract it ('relativement lente'); they function as markers of subjective evaluation. Verbs like 'sembler' are attempts at approximation, forms of mediation that register the inescapable truth that language may be in excess of its object or may be deficient, but it is always intractably *inadéquat*. Poetry works to compensate the vain ideal of *adéquation* by means of an analogical project, a chain of substitutions that enact the repeated deferral of the imaginary moment at which full possession of the object might be achieved.

The process of subjectivity finds a complement in the pliancy of objects. The wonder of things – material objects and the poems that stand in their place – lies in our experience of them as process – the cigarette-as-it-burns, the poem-as-it-is-read, or the pinewood as it self-generates ('En série, industriellement, mais avec une lenteur majestueuse ici se fabrique le bois,' *La Rage de l'expression*).[64] Ponge's desire to bring material things to language has its source in a deep fascination with the self-altering object or thing. He studies living forms that expand and contract, like the gymnast whose elasticity registers both in the coiling-uncoiling letters that make up 'Le Gymnaste,' and in the described whorls of the gymnast's moustache and the swirl of his forelock (*Le Parti pris des choses*). Ponge tracks matter-in-process, such as the candle whose guttering flame alters the relation of light to shadow – 'La nuit parfois ravive une plante singulière dont la lueur décompose les chambres meublées en massifs d'ombre' ('La Bougie') – before consuming itself, and the writing and the reading experiences, in the act of self-liquefying: '[L]a bougie, par le vacillement des clartés sur le livre au brusque dégagement des fumées originales encourage le lecteur, – puis s'incline sur son assiette et se noie dans son aliment.'

Ponge's commitment to capturing material alterability in the analogical fluctuations of the text, his urge to convey the inner, self-generating process at work in the world and in language, is brilliantly evoked in the painterly reconstruction of the tessellation and texturing of the Algerian sky in 'Pochades en prose':

> Dès le matin,
>   le ciel se dalle, se marquette, se pave, se banquise, se glaçonne, se marbre, se cotonne, se coussine, se cimente, se géographise, se cartographise...
>   (La forme pronominale convient bien ici, car ces formes *se* créent, en vérité: de l'intérieur.)   ('Pochades en prose,' *Méthodes*, 73)

Ponge concludes by celebrating the material process of self-alteration and the capacity of language to iterate the idea of process in reflexive forms. The material thing invites us to know it – and to write it – as a process. Clouds are tracked in their multifarious transformations; the disturbing dance of black motes before ageing eyes is an analogue to the 'confusion marine' that defines the sinuous darting of indeterminable shrimps; moss is monitored in its military-style occupation of bare rock and its growing susceptibility to elimination:

Les patrouilles de la végétation s'arrêtèrent jadis sur la stupéfaction des rocs. Mille bâtonnets du velours de soie s'assirent alors en tailleur.

Dès lors, depuis l'apparente crispation de la mousse à même le roc avec ses licteurs, tout au monde pris dans un embarras inextricable et bouclé là-dessous, s'affole, trépigne, étouffe.

Bien plus, les poils ont poussé; avec le temps tout s'est encore assombri.

[...]

Or, scalper tout simplement du vieux roc austère et solide ces terrains de tissu-éponge, ces paillassons humides, à saturation devient possible.

('La Mousse')

The text captures the moment of turning towards the object; it narrates the movement of consciousness as it becomes arrested by the object and it (re)enacts the surge of subjectivity towards the thing beheld or remembered. Writing unfolds its bid to take imaginary possession of the object through analogy; and finally it marks the point of turning away from the object, the rupture between subjective and material that takes the form of a cancelling wave of indifference or anxiety, weariness or aversion. The process of the object – its surge and its lapse, its eruption and its fading – coincides with, precipitates even, the exhaustion of the writing and reading processes.

The poem takes forward the process of the object, its making and its unmaking, its happening and its ceasing in the world as in text. The descriptive project hastens towards the culminating point at which mesmerizing or invigorating contact with the object is suddenly broken off by a surge of humour, irony, or a sudden distancing of the narrator from the object under scrutiny (never more prosaically than in the abrupt 'Il a plu' that ends 'Pluie'). The clausula is the rhetorical marker of deflection or discouragement; it responds to the exasperated recognition of the limitations of description, and reasserts the object's poetic limitlessness. Particularly salient in this respect is 'Le Cageot,' where the end of the life cycle of the object coincides with textual closure as if to affirm that material and poetic usefulness is exhausted, and to warn both writer and reader against overloading the significance of this particular descriptive venture ('sur le sort [du cageot] il convient toutefois de ne s'appesantir longuement'). The clausula brings closure: it offers the refuge of indifference, brings relief in the form of humour, or proposes (the appearance of) a conclusive moral lesson (in 'La Fin de l'automne'). The clausula fractures the contact between subject and object; it situates the narrator beyond the phenomenon, on the other side. While the ironic, humorous, pseudo-moral, or playfully self-reflexive clausula brings disengagement, it sows the suspicion that this rhetorical release-mechanism may be triggered by an inability to continue or a refusal to confront desire. Thus, the corrective issued at the end of 'Le Pain' seems all too brusquely to reassert the rights of the body over the imperatives of description as the material urge suddenly quells writerly desire ('[le pain] doit être dans notre bouche moins objet de respect que de consommation'). Paradoxically, the brusque interruption of the perceptual and writerly processes serves to remind us more acutely of the encounter between embodied consciousness and its object, and of its capacity to make us see differently. As the clausula delivers the shock of separation, it affirms that there is no predetermined point at which our contact with the object would break off naturally, and reminds us that the moment of looking can stretch forward indefinitely, for looking always encourages more looking, and writing incites more writing.

Consciousness-in-Things and the Writing Process

When Elaine Scarry affirms that 'beautiful things have a forward momentum [... inciting] the desire to bring new things into the world,' she identifies a principle of aesthetic (and moral) generation that is paralleled in Ponge's poetry in the progress of consciousness as it moves from its source object towards other, remembered things made textually present through analogy.[65] This is the expression of the generative, capacious desire that seeks at once to know the particular and to approach the world through its fragments. Consonant with Braque's creative purpose, Ponge's writing proceeds at once fragmentally and expansively, embracing the struggle outwards, the move against containment, and affirming the deep pleasure of the particular and palpable.

The forward momentum from the original object to other absent objects takes the form of a writerly *décontraction*, the unfolding of consciousness through metaphor and analogy.[66] The desire to 'flesh' description with analogies is a textual extension of the profound bodiliness of perceptual experience. Analogies are the verbal equivalent of the body's repeated efforts to hold the object in the fullness of perception. In 'L'Orange,' the sudden realization of verbal lack is assuaged by successive attempts to express the colour-dense, light-bearing, supple perfection of the fruit:

> Et l'on demeure au reste sans paroles pour avouer l'admiration que mérite l'enveloppe du tendre, fragile et rose ballon ovale dans cet épais tampon-buvard humide dont l'épiderme extrêmement mince mais très pigmenté, acerbement sapide, est juste assez rugueux pour accrocher dignement la lumière sur la parfaite forme du fruit.   ('L'Orange')

As the poem affirms the impossibility of ever definitively possessing its object, materially or linguistically, it begins to construct its fantasy of overcoming that impossibility through the generative activity of description. Analogies retrace the movement of consciousness in a rush of brilliant leaps or in the patient yet passionate work of *adéquation*. Analogies are always mediations, verbal bids to move closer to things via other, often staggeringly disparate things ('comme si l'on avait à sa disposition sous la main les Alpes, le Taurus ou la Cordillère des Andes').[67] But the variable gap – here wider, there narrower – between tenor and vehicle underscores the enduring resistance of objects to description, imparts their tenaciously unbiddable quality. The succession of analogies inscribes the constant displacement of desire from source object to other absent objects along the chain of signifiers: by this act of deferral, writing simultaneously nourishes desire and provokes anxiety, aggravates the difficulty and heightens the pleasure of describing things. The text is, then, the event of describing the object and the struggle for expanded knowledge of that object: it is a struggle whose limitations and pressures coincide with those of language.

Analogical activity is figuratively expansive for, as it takes forward the desire to extend the boundaries of perception, it draws in the protean qualities of absent, often extraneous things. A key instance of the figurative expansiveness of analogy is provided by the raft of references to cultural practices, artefacts, human behaviour, and social exchanges. Thus, in 'Le Papillon' the crystallization of nectar in flowers is compared to the formation of a sugary residue in unwashed cups; in 'La Mousse' the fabric of moss on a rock is compared punningly – stunningly – to velvety fibres arrayed 'en tailleur.' Analogy takes forth the desire to resituate the natural in the cultural world; it articulates the affective contiguity of materiality and subjectivity, and imparts a sense of the possible empathy of the individual (as a social and cultural being) with his physical environment. Thus, perceptions of rain incite comparisons with multifarious human activities: play ('billes'), domesticity ('Sur des tringles, sur les accoudoirs de la fenêtre, la pluie court'), confectionery ('berlingots convexes'), and mechanics ('Le tout vit [...] comme une horlogerie dont le ressort est la pesanteur d'une masse donnée de vapeur en précipitation'). Objects are things-in-themselves; they are also, Ponge insists, things-in-the-world: the candle is the strange plant that turns furnished rooms into mountain ranges as the memory of the external world is brought indoors, and a new relationality between the natural environment and the built space is brought to language.

Analogy memorializes the object beheld or remembered, superposing on it the traces of a subjective encounter with other things and, in the process, intimating the extensivity of human experience: thus, fascination with the wasp conjures up (principally) the sound experience (dry, crackling) induced by a passing electric tram:

> Quelque chose de muet au repos et de chanteur en action. Quelque chose aussi d'un train court, avec premières et secondes, ou plutôt motrice et baladeuse. Et trolley grésilleur. Grésillante comme une friture, une chimie (effervescente).
> Et si ça touche, ça pique. Autre chose qu'un choc mécanique: un contact électrique, une vibration venimeuse.   ('La Guêpe,' *La Rage de l'expression*)

We touch here on a further source of anxiety, for analogical activity is subtended by two competing desires – on the one hand, to bring things closer to each other and, on the other, to preserve the differences between things so that the defining singularity of the object prevails. Analogies are inherently aporetic, for their purpose is to exist in order to be eclipsed; their value lies not in their capacity to deliver sameness, but in their capacity to fall away and allow the place they vacate to fill with the object's *qualité différentielle*: 'Les analogies, c'est intéressant, mais moins que les différences. Il faut, à travers les analogies, saisir la qualité différentielle' ('My Creative Method').[68] The unfolding of analogies reveals not the ressemblance of the wasp to the tram, but the insect's enduring particularity. Thus, analogies (like candles) cancel themselves in the process of revealing – or at least, not obstructing – the illumination of difference: 'Mais son corps est plus mou – c'est-à-dire en somme plus finement articulé – son vol plus capricieux, imprévu, dangereux que la marche rectiligne des tramways déterminée par les rails' ('La Guêpe'). The expansive movement that leads analogically from the wasp to the tram forces consciousness to fold back upon itself as it precipitates a return to the source object. So, the *décontraction* of analogy produces *contraction* when the forward momentum that produces the description triggers a reverse movement that invites us to look again, longer and lovingly, at the original object. While analogies take us outwards in a breathlessly expansive flight, the surge of the *qualité différentielle* produces a tightening of the text around the object as consciousness returns more resolute, more illuminated, more nourished to its object. We touch here on the paradox of analogy: by its outward action, analogy hastens the reverse effect of binding consciousness to the original object, thickening the bonds between mind and material. There is, then, a subjective optimization of the object, suddenly made dense, plentiful, enthralling.

Ponge's poetry records the transaction between self and world, self and word. It takes forward the human desire to alter the world by leaving traces on material surfaces and by leaving imprints in the form of texts. The analogous trace-making activity of snails and of poets is a deeply affective and materially fragile manifestation of this desire:

> L'expression de [la] colère [des escargots], comme de leur orgueil, devient brillante en séchant. Mais aussi elle constitue leur trace et les désigne au ravisseur (au prédateur). De plus elle est éphémère et ne dure jusqu'à la prochaine pluie.
> Ainsi en est-il de tous ceux qui s'expriment d'une façon entièrement subjective sans repentir, et par traces seulement, sans souci de construire et de former leur expression comme une demeure solide, à plusieurs dimensions. ('Escargots')

Perceptual awakening to the sheer materiality of things and the urge to bring that bodily experience to language drive the project of *Le Parti pris des choses*. Set in the wider context of Ponge's literary essays, his fragmentary aesthetics, his (auto)biography, and his art criticism, *Le Parti pris des choses* emerges as a corrective to the diminished subjectivity and the alternately totalizing and reductive culture exposed in *Douze petits écrits*. Where the satirical series focuses the unalleviated symptoms of modern subjecthood – ideological pressure, affective vacancy, cultural depreciation – *Le Parti pris des choses* signifies a surge of creativity against the forces of cultural and linguistic entropy through a passionate contact with things and a desire to materialize the rich possibilities of language. The humanistic concept of subjecthood – whose beleaguered representatives populate the cityscape of *Douze petits écrits* – is displaced in *Le Parti pris des choses* by a process of subjectivity inextricable from the ceaseless effort to articulate the coincidence of self and world, of materiality and consciousness. Ponge's texts articulate the desirability of reciprocal recognition, for, at the same time as objects are being spoken, being given voice, they are in some sense speaking us, revealing our passage through the world. And so, as objects come into language, subjectivity becomes constituted in the play of signifiers and the mobility of analogy. The process of subjectivity (desire, sensation, affect) is generative of the process of the text.

The material demands to be thought, and consciousness seeks its materialization through analogy, allegory, and metaphor, whose texturing makes almost palpable the deep, uneven pleasure of perception. The integrated reading of *Le Parti pris des choses* I have offered here suggests, in this respect, a closer relation between the 1942 collection and the later texts than is generally acknowledged by critics, or indeed by Ponge when he contrasts the 'closed' forms of *Le Parti pris des choses* with the 'open' texts of *La Rage de l'expression* (1952) and, by implication, the writing that follows. Thus, in an interview with Sollers, Ponge affirms '[dans] mes textes de *La Rage de l'expression* [...] je mets sur la table la pratique scripturale, l'acte textuel'; in a subsequent exchange with Sollers he identifies 'L'Oeillet' as a pre-eminent example of the 'forme ouverte.'[69] I would argue that the textual 'tabling' of the process of writing comes through already, albeit in less explicit ways, in *Le Parti pris des choses*, in the constant shifting between the temptations of real-world referentiality and the aspiration to analogical equivalence, in the ceaseless bid to bring forth the *qualité différentielle*. *Le Parti pris des choses* may lack the scriptural self-absorption of later texts (*Comment une figue de paroles et pourquoi*), but it reveals a consciously writerly project centred on the verbal extendibility of things and, by implication, the material extendibility of texts.

Thus, the fascinated contemplation of the mollusc produces a text ('Le Mollusque') in thrall both to the reciprocal adherence of the creature and its shell, and to the generative capacity of the mollusc-text to illuminate, via certain cultural comparisons ('gond,' 'blount,' 'porte'), the indissociability of language and the human body:

> [Le mollusque] n'est à vrai dire qu'un muscle, un gond, un blount et sa porte.
> Le blount ayant sécrété la porte. Deux portes légèrement concaves constituent sa demeure entière.
> Première et dernière demeure. Il y loge jusqu'après sa mort.
> Rien à faire pour l'en tirer vivant.
> La moindre cellule du corps de l'homme tient ainsi, et avec cette force, à la parole, – et réciproquement.

Texts generated by the encounter with things self-extend to become texts about the making of text: this is the lesson illumined by those dazzling reconstructions of the painstaking, pleasure-generating attempts to describe the pine forest, the bar of soap, the fig, or the meadow. Where *Le Parti pris des choses* anticipates the later poetry – the poetic journals – in terms of textual self-generation and the pull from the material to the writerly, the same texts reveal something of a reverse movement whereby the material becomes reaffirmed in the very conscious constitution of the text as body (through fracturing, growing, grafting, and regrafting). The later poetry is not so much in retreat from materiality as actively self-materializing. Even as the later works revel in their multi-layered textuality, they reveal a materializing consciousness that puts the subjective and performative principle to work in the act of writerly self-constitution: 'Je me regarde écrire. Des textes comme la *Creative Method* ou *Le Verre d'eau* sont significatifs à cet égard.'[70] As the poet watches himself write, he holds up his writing practice to the world as a model of self-constitution founded on the material pleasure of words: 'L'amour des mots est le chemin à la création littéraire, poétique, c.a.d. aussi bien le chemin à la self-création' (*La Fabrique du pré*, 17).

4 Sweeping the (Sub)urban Savannah: Everyday Culture and the Rédean Sublime

The critique of rationalized post-industrial urban space and the celebration of cultural alternatives through inventive praxis ('arts de faire') developed by Michel de Certeau and the post-*Annales* school turn fascinated attention to the active agency of the city, its capacity for resistance and for self-transfiguration, and the altering power it exercises over those I shall be referring to as 'artisans of the everyday.' The following extract from the essay 'Les Revenants de la ville,' co-authored by Certeau and Luce Giard, proposes a metaphorical mapping of the city that is consonant – metaphorically and conceptually – with the urban and suburban topographies traced by Jacques Réda in his poetry and his prose-writing:

> [C]et urbanisme [a] plus détruit que la guerre. Pourtant, même pris dans ses filets, d'anciens immeubles survivaient. Ces vieilleries qui semblaient dormir, maisons défigurées, usines désaffectées, débris d'histoires naufragées, elles dressent encore aujourd'hui les ruines d'une ville inconnue, étrangère. Elles font irruption dans la ville moderniste, massive, homogène, comme les lapsus d'un langage insu, peut-être inconscient. [...] [C]es îlots créent des effets d'exotisme à l'intérieur. Tour à tour ils inquiètent un ordre productiviste et ils séduisent la nostalgie qui s'attache à un monde en voie de disparition. Citations hétéroclites, cicatrices anciennes, ils créent des aspérités sur les utopies lisses du nouveau Paris. Les choses anciennes se rendent remarquables. Un fantastique est tapi là, dans le quotidien de la ville. C'est un revenant, qui hante désormais l'urbanisme.[1]

Certeau and Giard's appraisal of the city's eruptive creativity and its potential to surge against the ideologies of flattening provides a salient frame for focusing Réda's poetry and prose-writing from *Les Ruines de Paris* (1977) to *Accidents de la circulation* (2001).[2] A critical, passionate city-explorer, Réda probes the resistance to the sleek colonizations of modernity that erupts in a culture of unevenness and recalcitrance; as a poet and chronicler, he proposes writerly and affective resistance in the form of myth, metaphor, humour, fantasy, colour practice, and the search for an urban sublime. Certeau and Giard's essay illuminates many of the ideas that I will be exploring in this chapter.[3] Their remarkable metaphorical range embraces the geographic and the cutaneous, the eruptive and the systemic, order and organicity, the fantastic and the economic, the exotic and the writerly, roughness and smoothness, the utopian and the geological, the familiar and the unknowable. The figurative pliancy in Certeau and Giard's writing is paralleled in Réda's material and metaphoric work on the city, in his probing of debris and decrepitude, his affinity with stubborn marginality, his passion for places and practices that resist the reductive reifications of capitalist consumerism, and his celebration of the extraordinariness of the ordinary. Like Certeau and Giard, Réda is in thrall to the active, intractable charm of the city's 'ruines,' their capacity to disrupt normative ways of looking, and their boundless vision-altering potential. Réda's ruins metaphorize the city's irresistible infiltration of gaze and consciousness, its figurative and myth-generating qualities, its everyday mediation of fantasy.

For the poet of *Les Ruines de Paris*, as for the cultural historians, the figure of 'ruines' extends beyond physical sites and the material tesserae of human lives to the potential of transformative desire and the yearning for a city sublime. Réda's 'ruines' figure the resistance of superseded objects or anachronistic practices to the homogenizing encroachments of the new; as metonymy and as metaphor, 'ruines' offer a constant incitement to imaginary construction and forms of hybrid creativity that challenge the levelling doxa of advanced modernity.

Ruins, rubble, debris, and stubborn proliferations of vegetable life all provide zones of resistance against colonization, pockets of oxygen against the stifling of individuality and marginality. Opposing a culture of transparency, standardization, streamlining, commercial monopoly, and urban redevelopment, the material of dereliction offers refuge and inscrutability. '[O]n voit la végétation vigoureuse des ruines qui recroît' (*RP*, 45) captures the oxymoron of generative mess that vitalizes Réda's city poetics through visions of resistant decrepitude and productive obsolescence.

Réda's exploration of fertile ruins maps the city in terms of human actions both in physical space and in the symbolic arena: artisanal recycling, marginality, empathy, cussedness, the privatization of space, illicit practices, identity-formation, and poetry-writing. Submerged and (sometimes) subversive practices are the sign of consciousness at work on material things: altering, quoting, ripping, wounding, resisting, loving, gleaning, reclaiming, appraising, colouring, sifting, and fantasizing.

A passionately material poet, Réda revels in incidents, physical objects, wildernesses, streets, debris, walking patterns, architectural changes, social exchanges, habits, light conditions, ambiance, bodies and faces, economic transactions, individual negotiations, and cultural practices. It is above all the particular that captivates the poet as he turns ear and eye to the affective infiltration of the material density of the city, where human contour ceaselessly redefines anonymous volume: 'Je remonte et m'en retourne vers la Butte: Place Paul-Verlaine, rue des Cinq-Diamants. A travers l'épaisseur, on entend appeler déjà les gosses pour qu'ils rentrent, qu'ils se lavent, qu'ils mangent; ce sera long' (RP, 81).

Réda calls attention to the rips and tears in the flat weave of repetitious ordinariness; he captures the eruptive complexity of human meaning that is bodied forth in the gesture of the driver in the instant before he collides with a statue in the Rue Serpollet: 'le chauffeur [...] étend les bras dans un geste où l'effroi, l'enthousiasme et l'abandon extatique au désastre se combinent' (AC, 80).

Just as human subjects invest places with physical actions and symbolic exchanges, so the affective qualities that inhere in a locality irresistibly alter those who pass through. Thus, in 'Dans le huitième' (AC, 37–42) the poet celebrates a kind of therapeutic unevenness as the folds of the physical terrain and the fluctuations of the ambient atmosphere disrupt expectations and elicit new subjective responses: '[L'arbitraire des lieux] crée des espèces d'enclaves engendrant de l'émotion. Alors qu'on circule dans un milieu urbain à peu près homogène, on éprouve tout à coup un changement de climat et de densité' (AC, 37).

As subjectivity alters and is altered through contact with the material, the body emerges in Réda's writing as an exquisite seam of contact between self and world. The sheer corporeality of the self–world encounter provides the starting-point of this chapter. The focus in Réda's poetry on the adventures of the body (the story of its possibilities and its constraints) has been neglected in critical terms, despite – or perhaps because of – the obsessive attention paid to walking per se. The two-way contact between self and world gives rise to writing that folds those corporeal adventures into its deep metonymic and metaphoric textures. The concept of pliancy is critical in Réda's texts: the pliancy of embodied subjectivity and its duplication in stylistic pliancy. Réda's textual imaging of the body captures its fluctuations, its recalcitrance, its flexibility, and its subjective articulacy.

Corporeal pliancy implies mental *disponibilité*. The resolute out-wardness of Réda's poetry brings forth a protean first-person subject-narrator whose boundless physical 'circulations' around the city are mappable to the multifarious identities of ethnographer, urban cowboy, marginal, misfit, memorialist, polemicist, gleaner, autobiographer, walker, stalker, culture critic, and social historian. Selfhood is configured, then, not as autonomous and exclusive, but as interactive and inevitably fractured, as a mosaic of subjectivities backlit by the practices and performances of other artisans of the everyday. Réda's project constantly moves beyond the self-defining experience of the first-person narrator to connect with the analogous practices of the gleaners and recyclers of the material city. He records their actions on the world and he traces – and invites us to trace – analogies with his own work as he translates their activities into poetry; this aspect of intersubjective action will be the focus of the second part of this chapter.

Corporeal and subjective pliancy is a prerequisite for the peripatetic poet, but an excess can tip the balance, altering self-perceptions and precipitating ontological anxiety. In a humorous example of Réda's fresh analogical style, the self-sceptical narrator reflects on this excessive pliancy, prompted by a destabilizing encounter with a folding stepladder-stool combination: 'Je me voyais comme un être un peu trop facilement transformable, à l'instar de l'escabeau-tabouret [...] Je me déplie et puis je me replie, et une fois replié, je ne songe qu'à déplier de nouveau ma petite volée de marches. Tantôt vers le passage où invite la rue du Retrait, tantôt au gré de mes relations avec autrui qui, sous leurs apparences de civilité, tissent un réseau secret dont chaque agent est à la fois le tabouret et l'escabeau de machinations obscures' ('Roman de l'escabeau,' AC, 24–5). This vivid analogy, prompted by the pliancy – linguistic and physical – of the two-way alterable 'escabeau-tabouret' (or 'tabouret-escabeau') raises key questions about subjective pliancy, its possibilities and its limitations, and about intersubjective relations. Crucially, the pun on 'steps' ('ma petite volée de marches') reminds us that the subjective engagement with the real is inescapably embodied. And it is bidirectional, for our bodies take us out into the world ('Voici dix ans que chaque jour je me frotte à ces rues,' 'Une lettre de Vaugirard,' *CCA*), and the world makes its imprint on the body in the form of an altered perception, impression, gesture, and language ('un vent qui me pousse ou me freine / [...] me fait redécouvrir mon volume et mon poids,' 'Bonjour, adieu,' *SM*).

Self–body relations, in their pliancy and their capacity for reciprocal altering, have a mythic extension in Réda's vision of the city as a vast organic consciousness, or, more often, a self-ramifying unconscious. His pursuit of 'une certaine poétique de l'espace, qui n'obéit pas aux critères des administrations' tracks the fertile migrations between the embodied consciousness of the urban explorer and the latent myth-generating potential of certain places. Subjectivity emerges here as receptive and generative, mobile and intersubjective, for this expansive consciousness appears to dissolve the boundaries between the mind of the poet-explorer and the indefinable, self-transfiguring city beyond. As the poet moves through the city, the city simultaneously stalks him, propels him, rushes him, such that subjective agency appears to migrate to the other side, to the side of the material and physical. Michael Sheringham, in his reading of *Châteaux des courants d'air*, identifies this state of extreme subjective *disponibilité* (which is no less than giving oneself up or making oneself over to the creative potential of physical space) as the crux of Réda's poetry:

> The secret designs of the *promeneur* reveal themselves to involve anonymity and self-dissolution, a desire to become no more than an instrument serving to reveal the city's own reality. The moves and gambits of the *promeneur* serve to vary the angles at which the city is refracted through the prism of his mind, moods and words.
> [...]
> The city needs to find expression by being filtered through the homologous zone of the *promeneur*'s mind, and the *promeneur* feels compelled to externalize what the city is doing to (and in) his head. In doing so he also realizes a clearly marked desire for self-dissolution.[4]

The preoccupation with the city as an organic consciousness, mesmeric and destabilizing, continually altering the explorer's self-perceptions, is reaffirmed in Réda's recent writing in the language of subjective *disponibilité* and corporeal displacement:

Il y faut certainement une participation subjective assez intense de l'observateur, mais la réalité qui la provoque n'a rien d'imaginaire. Ces enclaves sont comme les casiers d'un jeu de l'oie spécifique de Paris. On croit progresser normalement dans une direction assurée, à travers une région dont l'unité provient du retour de certaines variables, et voilà qu'on tombe brusquement dans un casier imprévu, qu'on est réexpédié dans un autre espace, et, peut-être, dans un temps différent.   ('Dans le huitième,' *AC*, 38)

Réda probes the unfathomable, compelling, and propitious quality of the city, its seductive mingling of the mundane and the metaphysical, the resistant and the redundant, the obtrusive and the furtive. The active magic of the city inheres in its tantalizing indeterminacy, its lack of a centre, its destabilizing and self-transfiguring potential. In this, Réda relays the tradition of a modernist city poetics that originates with Baudelaire's ironic, allegorical vision of Paris, extends through Rimbaud's luminous phantasmagorias, erupts in Apollinaire's *surnaturalisme*, and opens out into the reality-shattering visions of surrealism. In *Accidents de la circulation* the fickle magic of the city is at once revealed and withheld in a kind of *fort-da* game that exposes the intersubjectivity of self and other, of explorer and city, as at once anxiety-inducing and deeply pleasurable:

[I]l m'était enseigné une fois de plus que les lieux où la ville autorise à déceler un de ses centres métaphysiques, par là même communiquent métaphysiquement entre eux pour édifier les monuments et ouvrir les carrefours d'une autre ville insaisissable. Peut-être figurent-ils aussi l'obstacle que la masse hétéroclite de la ville concrète oppose à nos tentatives d'embrassement. Ces sont des lieux contradictoires où, du même mouvement, elle a l'air de nous tendre une clé magique et la dérobe.   ('Dans le huitième,' *AC*, 41)

Implicit in the migration between human subject and the sublimity of the quotidian world is an active consciousness moving ceaselessly across the thresholds of the perceptual and the metaphysical, delving deep into the minutiae of the everyday, and stretching towards the rarefied as material solidity dissolves in the generous play of colour and light, form and fracture.

The desire to merge with the material metropolis implies a willing abdication of individual subjectivity, or at least a temporary ceding of that subjectivity to the acutely receptive consciousness of the city. Self becomes seamlessly incorporated as the object (or outcome) of the fantasizing work of the city. Finally, in 'Au beau milieu' (CCA, 14), subjectivity is absorbed into a prism of light and colour sensations:

> Ma tête qu'elle contient devient l'étendue que la ville arpente, où les quartiers glissent les uns sur les autres comme les fragments de verre lumineux dans un kaléidoscope, y recomposant à l'infini de nouvelles figures dont on ne sait au juste qui décide, mais qui laissent à l'observateur l'illusion d'en être le seul milieu. Mais qu'il se déplace encore ou s'en tienne à cette immobile rêverie, ce sont les figures qui l'absorbent parmi leurs lignes et leurs couleurs.

In the final section of this chapter, I shall take the crucial question of 'self-dissolution' (Sheringham) or 'désubjectivisation' (Pinson) in the underexplored direction of Réda's colour-work, and link it to the yearning for the sublime.

My purpose here is to bring forward a sense of the connective tissue between the poet's immersion in the material and the metaphysical desire that materializes in coruscating visual instances. The resolute outwardness of Réda's writerly project, in both its embrace of the material and its straining after the sublime, implies a deflection from self-driven subjectivity that is consonant with a poetics of 'self-dissolution,' with poetry where questions of selfhood are displaced by the eruptive culture of the everyday or absorbed into the city envisioned as a roaming consciousness. Yet, the poetic processing of the material and the real – its selection, sifting, memorializing, fantasizing, ironizing, and the sheer wondering at things – reveals a continuous, pervasive subjective coloration, an alternately enthralled and critical, ironic and empathetic engagement with physical things, material practices, and human actions on the world.

Le Corps incontournable

In Réda, the movement of consciousness and of language is vested most insistently in the body, the exquisite interface between self and the world, between consciousness and its objects, material and symbolic. The body is the transformer of sensory signals into an intricate mesh of impressions, memories, fantasies, and yearnings. In the title narrative of his collection Le Lit de la reine (2001), Réda amplifies his thoughts on the corporeal imprinting of memory, marvelling at how the tips of his fingers have stored a sequence of musical notes which they can play back without the poet referring to the musical score.[5] The transformation of the everyday idiom into 'apprendre par corps' captures the inscription of memories ('souvenirs') in flesh as each zone of the body becomes a storehouse of images to be reactualized at will. Réda's reflection on the location of memory in the physicality of bodily sensation and specifically at the point of contact with palpable things – fingers touching the keyboard, feet pressing on the pedals of his Solex – has important implications for the relation between the sensory and the phantasmatic, subjectivity and the material.

Subjectivity, in Réda, is profoundly embodied. The body is active in a series of peripatetic processes and kinetic modes that are linked to the need both to make visible what has become lost to sight and to visualize (through fantasy and dream-work) as a means of healing the Cartesian rift between body and mind. Walking, for example, is always a matter of walking the gaze; excursive desire generates visual prospecting untrammelled by solipsistic agendas. At the beginning of Le Citadin, in the sequence 'Automne,' walking is presented as a process of self-dissolution and it is this productive 'loss of self' that enables authentic viewing to take place: 'Il arrive qu'à force de marcher [...] juste en déambulant, on perde peu à peu le sentiment de son identité propre. En même temps on promène son regard à droite, à gauche, devant soi, derrière (on se retourne), et puis surtout en l'air, car c'est souvent dans la hauteur qu'une merveille se déclare' (CiT, 11). To walk is, ideally, to become the gaze: '[J]'oublie peu à peu ma propre identité. [...] [J]e deviens un simple regard qui se pose impartialement partout' (CiT, 20).

Excursive desire demands bodily responsiveness in an assortment of kinetic modes that take forward the poet's visual project: summed up as circuler, these encompass leaping, roaming, jumping, walking, dancing, lurching, stopping, starting, deviating, crossing, digressing, skipping, hesitating, hovering, stumbling, samba-dancing, slipping, and rolling ('marcher,' 'déambuler' [LR, 106], 'rôder' [RP, 106], 'sauter' [RP, 115], 'sursauter' [AC, 38], 'arpenter' [SM, 90; LR, 48], 'baguenauder,' 'errer' [BS, 22; LR, 158], 's'aventurer,' 'franchir' [LC, 47], 'sortir à quatre pattes' [CCA, 16] 'savater' [RP, 39]). These bodily modes have mechanical extensions in Solex-riding and train-travelling (though conspicuously not in metro-hopping, which offers only a narrow-line gaze and a very literal form of tunnel vision).[6] Kinetic modes are triggered by the desire to externalize a gaze dulled by obsessive introspection. In 'Un

Citadin' (La Course), the poet struggles to dispel the cumulus of self-absorption and nostalgia through revitalized visual activity: 'Je m'applique assez bien à ce délicat exercise / Pour que très vite mon regard cesse d'appartenir / À l'amas nuageux d'espérance et de souvenir / Auquel j'aurai donné mon nom' (LC, 11). Excursive desire is desire rerouted from the solipsistic dead end of personality towards extrospective viewing activity. A passionate engagement with material objects and physical places nurtures an expansive curiosity that is alive to the strangeness and unevenness of the most mundane things: the poet feels an affinity with the postman who is stunned ('sidéré') by the sheer exuberance of the world (RP, 34). The relation between the peripatetic self and the world is dazzlingly revealed in moments of intense visual contact with things, moments that generate empathy, irony, wonder, surprise, and humour.

Excursive desire demands unfettered corporeal co-operation, but embodied subjectivity makes its own insistent claims. The intractability of subjective–corporeal relations prompts a caveat and a disclaimer from one who aspires to the bliss of impersonality, but fails to dislodge the burden of subjectivity that makes itself felt in acutely corporeal terms: 'Quand Je ne peut plus se souffrir, hop il tente ce détour avec astuce ou rage vers un zénith obscur où clame Personne. Mais qui s'arrache? Ma peau à moi reste collée et brûle' ('Langue maternelle,' CV).[7] Underlying this humorous vision of a corporeal cauldron of bubbling, spluttering selfhood is a serious point about the inextricability of subject–body relations, for at the very moment when the subjective charge overloads, triggering the safety cut-out of impersonality, the body makes its truculent presence felt and reminds us that subjectivity is inextricably embodied.

The body, through the grammar of its gestures, its kinetic and perceptual modes, assumes an autobiographical function: it tells the story of how we've got to where we've got, and reassures us or not (most likely not in Réda's case) as to who we are. In 'Bords du treizième' (AC, 68–75), the body that comes to a halt at the corner of the Boulevard Saint-Marcel and the Boulevard de l'Hôpital provides a literal answer to 'où suis-je?,' but the more troubling question 'que suis-je?' prompts an extended reflection on origins and identity. Scrutinizing the bas-relief depiction of evolution encircling the exterior walls of the Institut de Paléologie Humaine, the poet confronts the acute feelings of alienation that set him apart from the human species, like some alien interloper ('délégué à des fins d'espionnage, de sabotage, de désinformation'). His anxiety is compounded when he senses a split between his inner self and his 'vraie peau,' which has become indistinguishable from the mask that he wears out of habit and the desire for social assimilation. This 'agent double incapable, grillé des deux côtés' feels intensely that he belongs neither to the human race nor to the alien world. Yet, if the nowhere space he occupies seems a desolating void, it is transformed briefly into a performative arena where the potential for self-fictionalizing is actualized in the seasonal hell of mid-summer Paris: '[J]e me crée un personnage d'un satanisme fumeux' (AC, 73). Suspended between the competing pressures of the real and the fantastic, prehistory and modernity, body and self, humour and self-irony, the poet's experience of his own subjectivity is inherently anxious and unstable: '[J]e flotte. Entre deux eaux, entre deux mondes, je suis le demi-noyé de la profondeur immobile et limpide des rues' (AC, 73).

Self–body relations may be productive or problematic, alternately powering or impeding excursive momentum. The source of this un-evenness can be traced to the body's eruptive expressivity and to the subject's precipitate desires, both material and metaphysical.

The body's simple physical needs and everyday longings generate the forward momentum, peripatetic and poetic, that takes the writer into myriad city neighbourhoods, explorations that in turn stimulate new desire and new writing. Cravings for wine or cigarettes, the search for a particular cheese or some elusive sheet music, sensuous yearnings, or simply the need to refuel a spluttering Solex, propel one who is, by nature, 'pantouflard et pusillanime' into the labyrinth of the city and into a series of commercial transactions and poetic interactions. Physical and mental *disponibilité* is duplicated in stylistic pliancy as the sublime rivals with bathos, and self-irony jostles with fantasy. In 'On ne sait quoi d'introuvable' (RP, 65–73) the lure of possession – material and scopophilic – sets in train a series of dizzying oscillations between pleasure and reality principles. Libidinal interest is stirred at the tobac-conists' ('à cause du regard que je ne peux pas ne pas plonger dans le corsage toujours béant de [...] Joëlle') and sublimated in visionary poetry ('Joëlle aux yeux gris comme la pluie sur la candide dépravation de la mer'), while fetishistic desire is countered by the 'fée ou sorcière castatrice' at the model-collectors' shop who derides his fondness for lead soldiers (RP, 69).

In 'On ne sait quoi d'introuvable,' the body's material needs give rise to a series of topographical and commodity-based twinnings ('Rue du Bac, deux cahiers écoliers à réglures simples'), as successive *étapes* inject shopping anecdote and social observation with irony, confession, real-ism, humour, self-parody, myth, prosiness, cultural commentary, and even anti-car polemic.[8] It is body-work and the strenuous exercise of pedalling a now fuel-less Solex that brings the poet (and the reader) to the final destination where the bathos of the sweating cyclist is trans-figured in the mythic vision of a disconsolate savage crouching amid the phosphorescent pools and gravel mountains of a deserted building site, a critical witness to the entropic frenzy of the 'civilized' *polis*. In the metaphorical sublimity of this material wilderness, the poet surveys the city and his preoccupation with bodily desires spirals off into a reflection on corrosive modernity and metaphysical emptiness:

> Sommes-nous [...] tous à ce point semblables en solitude; tant de grossière frénésie, si peu d'amour, rien que ce renfrognement qui présage la misère du dimanche au fond de nos coeurs? — Peu à peu le silence, la charitable obscurité. Tel un barbare déçu, je demeure accroupi sur mon tertre, adossé aux ruines de Paris. (*RP*, 72–3)

Réda's texts take forward competing reflections on the body, its pow-erful articulacy, its capacity for generating and for obstructing excur-sive desire. Where the examples from 'On ne sait quoi d'introuvable' reveal self–body relationality that is positive, fulfilling physical needs and producing instances of metaphorical and metaphysical intensity, self–body relations are often more problematic. This registers in the fluctuations of excursive desire as the world continually grazes the surface of the body producing sensation and impression, causing rip-ples. 'Que le Nord transcendantal du poète' (*RP*, 120) tracks the surges and lapses of excursive desire on a search for the absolute in the city's northern suburbs. The epidermis, that acute receiver of what is on the outside of ourselves, is the catalyst for the poet's metaphysical search: 'Un frisson m'avertit que je dois sans le moindre délai [...] suivre [les rails], et non pas un vague tressaillement de l'âme ou de l'intellect: l'authentique chair de poule, sur ma peau le souffle même du Nord présent en vérité' (*RP*, 120). But here, as in numerous self-debunking instances, the recalcitrant body ultimately blocks the excursive project and diminishes perceptions of subjective agency. Unerringly percipient in anticipating (or inducing?) the poet's discouragement, bodily signals trigger the realization that metaphysical aspirations are unrealistic. The warm wave that surges through the poet confirms that the game is indeed up, but exacerbates, in the process, inner conflict: 'J'ai chaud de honte et de soulagement comme un prédestiné qui flanche' (*RP*, 121). If the poet's body is complicit here with his deep longing to be done with his quest, elsewhere the power balance shifts. When the ecstatic wanderer, in thrall to feelings of immortality, capitulates to a yearning for transcendence, it is his legs that assume the corrective task of resituating the self in the here-and-now, carrying it back to the embankment and setting it down gently to deflate:

> Il règne ici la paix qui succède aux profonds cataclysmes, quand leur souvenir même est perdu, et que le ciel de nouveau préhistorique pâture avec une lenteur innocente l'ampleur en fin de compte extatique du dégât. L'être antérieur au temps contemple avec les yeux de ma tête, mes jambes le soulèvent et le transportent machinalement sur un remblai. J'y cherche en vain le soleil dans cette pulvérisation de la lumière, un peu plus dense au bout des rails aplatis vers le nord.   (*RP*, 121–2)

The body sets material limits to metaphysical desire by derailing, redefining, or simply slowing the progress of the excursion. In more prosaic instances, the body's need for physical protection applies a brake to the circulatory project. The corporeal risks may be no greater than the sum of quotidian hazards encountered by all who venture out, but the very sight or sound of untethered dogs induces a near-pathological fear. Predictably marked in Réda's most recent work, particularly *Accidents de la circulation*, are deep anxieties over physical frailty and mortality. The body's perceived susceptibility to lapses and collapses prompts an ironic and deflationary self-view that consolidates and lends a new poignancy to the 'comic heroic' identity that is a playful constant of Réda's writing. In peripatetic and textual terms, a sense of physical vulnerability leads to shortcutting and backtracking, to hesitation and to reorientation, but now, increasingly, the body's own story (the chronicle of its events and, particularly, its mishaps) supplies an alternative narrative to the intended *récit*. This is seen close up in 'Dans le dixième' (*AC*), when the poet realizes that his Dali-esque refiguring of the renovated Porte Saint-Martin as 'une géante motte de beurre' is motivated by a lurking anxiety about his own corporeal consistency (or the lack of it) brought on by sensations of giddiness attributable to a marked fall in his blood pressure. This sudden alertness to physical fragility launches a narrative of the body's vertigo when a sudden swell of distorted perceptions destabilizes self-identity, causing him not only to lose his literal and ontological 'footing,' but to question the stability of the external world:

> [L]es images, que mes yeux enregistrent, rencontrent dans les profon-
> deurs aveugles de mon corps une sorte de houle qui les ballotte, les
> déforme et me donne le mal de mer. Je me sens pris entre deux espaces:
> un intérieur agité de mouvements imprévisibles comme un radeau, un
> dehors que je m'efforce encore de juger ferme et stable.
> [...]
> [Mes semelles] se désolidarisent du trottoir, et reprennent contact avec un
> sol trompeusement élastique où je vais m'enfoncer comme dans une
> épaisseur de coton.   (*AC*, 48–9)

Physical malaise precipitates an ontological crisis and prompts a textual turning point. Whether to go on or to turn back at this point is
decided by the propitiatory action of attempting to light a cigarette. The
abdication of intentionality and the embrace of contingency (or predes-
tination as the poet-quester prefers to construe it) reroutes surrealist-
derived *disponibilité* along Réda's favoured comic-heroic mode. And so
he recalls his adolescent observation of a man in the street whose efforts
to light a cigarette appeared (to a bemused thirteen-year-old muddling
the medical and military implications of 'une attaque') to be the catalyst
of the man's fatal stroke. Reading his own success in lighting a cigarette
as prophesying his short-term survival, the poet quells memories of
pharmacists proffering faulty blood-pressure gauges and alarming di-
agnoses. He extends his excursion (and his text) into the heart of the
10th arrondissement, transforming his more anxious maritime metaphors ('la houle') to conjure up a scene of pleasurable coasting ('caboter,'
'à bâbord, à tribord') as he skirts the territories of erotic yearning ('Rue
du désir') and arcadian delight ('la cour de la Ferme-Saint-Lazare').
However, the contemplation of an intriguing illusionist mural representation of Saint Vincent de Paul then destabilizes his sense of self, captured in the oscillation between the assertion and the cancellation of
perceptions ('la figure existe, n'existe pas'). Only the poet's dawning
impression of an uncanny facial resemblance between the represented
saint and his own trusty cardiologist returns the body and its owner to
the certainty of properly calibrated blood-pressure readings, and as-
sures the reader of a continuing supply of text.

Whether sustaining or blocking excursive desire, the body is startlingly articulate, expressing desires and fears, longings and frustra-
tions, constantly externalizing its subjective charge. Just as the body

makes itself *felt* (in episodes of giddiness, shivers, hunger, taste, spasms, sweats), so it makes itself *heard* in ways that affirm unevenness and the subjective contouring of the material. The experience of hearing the echoes of his own cough bouncing across the nave of the Église Saint-Sulpice prompts the poet to reflect on this ordinary corporeal reflex and its extraordinary capacity to alter the relations between self and world. By setting the air in sound waves that fill the nave, 'the visitor' (Réda's third-person impersonality blurs the distinctions between self and other in a characteristic intersubjective move) seeks to give voice to his sense of self through the cadences of his coughing: 'La toux réflexe du visiteur n'a d'abord d'autre motif que de l'assurer de soi dans un volume dont l'ampleur obscure l'excède; où, aussi dur qu'il soit, le noyau de l'être tend à se vaporiser comme un brouillard' (*CCA*, 81–2).[9] But the attempt to affirm self by making the body sound is derailed by the fractured trajectory of the sound waves – now splitting apart, now colliding – which disconnect the series of coughs from their corporeal source. The sense of self, unable to reconnect with its material trace, ends up destabilized, fragilized:

> Mais ce bruit aussitôt lui échappe, s'enfuit circulairement, s'enfle, un instant paraît mourir, puis, répercuté par les voûtes, revient multiplié de telle manière que le tousseur ne sait plus si c'est lui qui a toussé. Il croyait affirmer ou du moins localiser et délimiter sa personne; or le retour de son propre son le déroute et l'abolit. Simplement garde-t-il la conscience d'une espèce de vide, que la toux a désobstrué, autour duquel il flotte comme un vase de densité faible, neigeuse, d'une extrême fragilité.   (*CCA*, 82)

The urgent, uneven articulation of self through the body's rhythms connects coughing with other rhythm-shaping activities that extend through walking, jazz swing, and poetry-reading. Rhythm connects self to what is exterior – object and other – via a series of actions that reveal consciousness as deeply embodied but ceaselessly working across the boundaries between self and world. A signal example of this is provided by Réda's *vers mâché*, which, as he explains in the notes to *La Course*, is the importing into poetry of the tendency of French speakers north of the Loire to elide mute 'e's. Thus, the bodily and the ethnographical, the particular and the geographical inform the very rhythm and texture of poetry. The action of coughing, the reading aloud of poetry, and, for the jazz-loving poet, the playing of a tenor saxophone produce a subjective trajectory traced in sound whose kinetic analogue is walking, with its cadences and syncopation. Réda's concern for the surge of subjectivity captured in rhythm reverberates across his poetry and his reflections on literature. Thus, in *Celle qui vient à pas légers*, a collection of essays on language and poetry-writing, Réda distances himself from the poetics of impersonality and embraces the subjective urgency of rhythms surfacing in writing: 'l'anonyme, l'impersonnel, quelle contradiction avec tout ce que j'aime: le ton unique d'un être résumé dans ses cadences, ma joie à Cingria ou à Montaigne, la rencontre d'un coeur intact sous l'épaisseur et les transparences du style.'[10] Cadences – whether those of coughing, poetry-making, jazz syncopation, or walking – are instances of creative unevenness that challenge the smooth order of things.

The body alters and is altered by the world, to the point where the two seem to coincide inextricably, such that an ideal intersubjectivity is occasionally glimpsed and the Cartesian separation between the mind and its objects, self and other, is provisionally overcome: 'Je suis sûr que le monde avance avec mes jambes / Pense avec mon cerveau, regarde avec mes yeux' (*Retour au calme*, 122). Yet self–world relations, in their mediation through the body, are rarely so blissfully symmetrical; in the event, they tend to be more productively uneven. The body's kinetic activity bears the imprint of that unevenness in its modes of circulation. Physical variability, as we shall see, maps to the stylistic pliancy of Réda's writing.[11] I begin, though, by focusing on the body's circulations.

Circuler implies the bodily freedom to go around, and annexes the urge to explore the unfamiliar and the unfathomable: 'il faudrait circuler librement dans ce dédale' (*CCA*, 54). Peripatetic freedom is founded on a transgressive opposition to regulation: 'je circule en sens interdit' (*RP*, 72). The defiant first principle of Réda's excursive credo insists on the pleasure of unbounded exploration, the delight of going against the flow, of embracing disorientation. While there are surrealist affinities in his celebration of modes of transgressive walking, Réda is often closer to the anxious, self-ironizing postmodern quester who persists with his efforts to get lost: 'je [rate le bus] aimant mieux essayer encore un moment de me perdre' (*RP*, 109); 'Ma méthode qui consiste à prendre à gauche, à droite, / pour éviter le trafic assassin des boulevards, / fait qu'assez vite je me perds' ('La Course,' *LC*, 54). Réda's aspiration to multidirectionality and simultaneity, his desire to embrace multifarious experiences, proposes a kinetic variant on Apollinaire's simultanist practice: 'Et mentalement ou non, j'agite les bras et les jambes, comme pour partir dans tous les sens' (*LR*, 47). Taking forth the urge to radiate in a mix of modernist and postmodernist perspectives, Réda's call to *circuler* proposes a counter to the somnambulism of city dwellers who walk unconsciously, unstoppingly, their reactions 'pétrifiées ou stérilisées par l'habitude' (*AC*, 38). Flat, undifferentiated walking translates a mental state of non-pliancy, unreflectiveness, even inertia. Such modes of 'smooth walking' are challenged by the poet's 'sursauter,' his gleeful leaps and jumps, and his propensity to explore space in a series of jolts and collisions. Réda's culture critique mobilizes repeatedly the opposition between linear and circular modes of negotiating space, linking bodily disposition to particular ways of being in and thinking about the city. First, we need to consider further the modes for which *circuler* offers a corrective.

Utilitarian modes are characterized by repetition and minimal disruptiveness, streamlining and the 'tracking' of movement, and forms of false (unconscious, unreflecting) mobility. Thus, 'applied' walkers – as opposed to those marginal, misfit walkers like the poet – embody the despairingly pedestrian in their flowing, virtually imperceptible movement.[12] Routine-bound, they are more moved along than actively moving; their unhampered *parcours* inscribes their lack of obstinacy or volition and their unreflective adherence to productivist assumptions. Réda's self-preoccupied passers-by inherit the cynical indifference of Rimbaud's modern citizen and the complacency of Ponge's urban serfs. In their self-absorption, they neglect sources of magic and condemn real streets to totalizing neighbourhood blandness: 'Une vraie rue-rue [Rue Titon] que le passant annule par l'acte distrait de son passage, et qui se fond dans l'anonymat typique du onzième arrondissement' (*AC*, 58). Their mechanistic locomotion diminishes them physically and subjectively; they are, in every sense, 'de très petits passants' (*RP*, 38). The zero-degree walking of the ordinary pedestrian has its accelerated variant in the quantifiable (and consequently false) mobility of the athlete. Thus, the sight of a running track under construction elicits a parenthetic blast from the poet against those who would curtail the freedom to walk without a socially sanctioned purpose: '(courez en rond tant que vous voudrez mais ne rôdez pas)' (*RP*, 115). The sleep-walking pedestrian, the officially regulated athlete, and other urban automata are complicit in repetitive, unspontaneous locomotion. Their kinetic perpetuation of externally imposed rules and social mores is the antithesis of Rédean pliancy. Their movement, barely distinguishable from stasis, has its equivalent in visual inertia: 'la curiosité retombe à cause d'un besoin général d'indifférence et de lenteur' (*RP*, 20). In tropes that recall the flattened metropolis of Ponge or Rimbaud, gestural automatism and physical sclerosis relay mental unreflectiveness ('tête tuméfiée du dimanche,' *RP*, 20) and communicative aridity ('les gens [dans la salle à boiseries] remuent à peine, ne parlent pas,' *RP*, 63). Bodies veer between excessive heaviness (wooden people in wooden rooms) and impalpability figured by the insubstantial, phantomatic presences of anonymous citizens more acted upon than acting. The virtual imperceptibility of their bodies (a perception repeatedly troped) betokens their nonpercipience. They pass abstractedly across the surface of the city (and of the page), embodiments of the diminished subjectivity that Réda's poetic project sets out to challenge.

Only by walking freely, fully conscious, unconstrained by social and solipsistic agendas, can people dispel their anomie: 'Le désespoir n'existe pas pour un homme qui marche, à condition vraiment qu'il marche, et ne se retourne pas sans arrêt pour discutailler avec l'autre, s'apitoyer, se faire valoir' (*RP*, 14). Pure, unhampered walking is Réda's antidote to the corrosive effects of cultural repetition and social compliance mimed in metaphors of smoothness and stillness. To walk or engage in related circulatory activities is to embrace unpredictability and unevenness, peripatetic qualities that spill over into the multifarious materiality explored by Réda and relayed through the stylistic pliancy of his writing. Kinetic flexibility – turning and tumbling, lurching and veering – is duplicated in the generative unevenness of Réda's writing, its hybrid, improvised quality.

The pliancy of embodied consciousness has its analogue in the unpredictable oscillations of metonymy and metaphor, prosiness and phantasmagoria, anecdote and allegory, realism and the sublime, cultural critique and comic heroics, reportage and colour practice, colloquialism and the language of metaphysical desire. Everyday idiom and colloquialism relay the poet's contact with the real, imparting a sense of spontaneity and directness: '[J]e prends tout à coup les sentiers que signale une pancarte jaune marquée de lettres au pochoir en noir un peu de traviole: DANGER TERRAIN MILITAIRE ACCÈS INTERDIT, car je me fous pareillement et plus de ces pancartes' (*RP*, 156). 'Straight' observation of the real often receives a wry or sarcastic twist: hence elderly shopkeepers, 'pour atteindre ce qu'elles ont placé je ne suis comment à l'étalage, ces vieilles dames d'ailleurs pas abusivement aimables doivent d'abord se jucher sur un petit banc' (*RP*, 70); the account of killing time between trains at Laroche includes the vignette of a café proprietress: '[C]ette dame menue d'allure cependant dynamique (genre paquet de nerfs à l'âge où, sur le goût de séduire, l'emporte décidément le pur cynisme féminin) m'a-t-elle laissé finir sans hâte un sandwich aux rillettes, servi un second verre de beaujolais' ('Les Gris,' *AC*, 121). Humour often based on caricature is imparted via onomatopoeia that mimics the exploits of the narrator-turned-urban hero in his daily struggle against homicidal taxi drivers: 'L'autre jour j'ai combattu de l'Alma jusqu'à Raspail contre une de ces terreurs. Vraoum à tous les verts il croyait me clouer sur place, et moi qui ne dispose d'aucune marge d'accélération, pototof-pototof au rouge suivant le réobsédait mon même profil de marbre' ('Du jour au lendemain,' *RP*, 55). Fresh humour has its source in vivid analogy, as in *Le Citadin*, where medical and musical metaphors enliven the chronicle of his street exploration: 'Du *Rendez-vous des clowns* à la piscine, j'aurais dû facilement parcourir toute la rue Oberkampf avant la nuit. Mais à force de changer de trottoir pour ausculter des porches, et tenter des combinaisons sur leurs petits claviers, le temps passe' (*CiT*, 69). Metaphor nourishes fantasy-work, prompting a temporary transfiguration of the real, but always one that imparts an acute sense of texture, colour, or form, as in this example of Rédean anthropomorphism: '[L]es faces bleues de strangulation des choux observent par-dessus les clôtures' (*RP*, 109). Réda mixes stylistic modes by way of ironic or humorous interjection or incongruous analogy; this conveys improvisation, quickness, and flexibility. Stylistic fluctuations take forward a subjectively pliant experience of the real, thus social commentary segues into painterly evocation in 'Orage à Saint-Cloud' (*LC*, 42):

Les dîneurs sont assis avec des couvertures
Sous leurs tables, pour le confort des lévriers
Chagrins, de pékinois nourris de confitures
Mais prêts à mordre au cas où vous vous lèveriez
Brusquement sous l'éclair bleu qui photographie
Le pré jaune où deux petits enfants
Cu'butent. Vers Meudon le ciel se tuméfie.

The opening of 'Au printemps' (*CCA*, 62) reveals Réda's characteristically hybrid, careering style as banal topographical notation instantly gives rise to a witty anthropomorphic fantasy: 'Se trouver juste devant la plaque de la psychanalyste, ça ne trouble pas ce figuier. Au contraire sans doute. Je n'en avais encore jamais vu d'aussi jeune à Paris, ni d'aussi dépourvu de complexes.' Humour veers to erotic reverie –

On approche de la fin d'avril, et [le figuier] gonfle déjà très gaillardement ses figues qui (malgré la comparaison d'habitude féminine qu'appelle ce fruit) me font penser [...] à des couilles pleines de jus. C'est donc ma propre libido qu'il faudrait que je surveille.

– which is quickly dispelled by a sour personal recollection and the pleasurable, if paradoxical, resurgence of a literary memory:

Ces figues mûriront-elles? L'été dernier, j'en ai mangé de bien bleues (bleu outremer) dans une impasse privée de la rue de la Tombe-Issoire: la cité Annibal, je crois, si bien que l'idée de Carthage (*des figuiers entouraient les cuisines*, lit-on dans le Festin de *Salammbô*) rachetait un peu leur goût de vernis qui m'infestait la bouche.

The creatively uneven itineraries of the urban rummager, both peripatetic and mental, invite writerly rule-breaking and risk-taking, the crossing of stylistic boundaries, as the poet in 'Au printemps' reflects, suddenly jolted out of his literary-gustatory reminiscence: 'Cependant je mélange tout, puisque ces réflexions m'escortent présentement dans le XVe à deux pas des Objets Perdus, près de l'endroit où ce figuier prospère.' Here, poetic and excursive imperatives, always coextensive in their space-occupying, time-extending momentum, coincide in launching his *périple* through the city's southern arrondissements.

It is in terms of a certain salutary unevenness that the title of Réda's 2001 collection *Accidents de la circulation* has to be read; it intimates, not a catalogue of road-traffic horrors (even if one such catastrophe is only narrowly avoided in the opening text 'Ménilmoto'), but the mesmerically uneven terrain of events, incidents, exchanges, happenings, and obtrusions that constitute the subjective relief map of the city's topography. When the body steps out, it registers its coincidence or collision with the real by picking up and transmitting signals in irregular kinetic patterns: the blips, jolts, shudders, interruptions, eruptions, and surges that make up the material experience of the (sub)urban explorer and whose percipient physicality is their epicentre. The body inscribes (in its waves and surges) the moments when the real impinges on consciousness, disrupts smooth linearities, shatters continuity – thus, the poet's jack-in-the-box leap from the delivery wagon figures the propitious moment when self and the world collide, and embodied consciousness is set in a different rhythm (*RP*, 111).

Surges of consciousness are mappable to the coincidence of self and world in forms of unevenness: 'Dans ce couloir où mon / Envergure se cogne aux murs (j'avance oblique)' ('Un passage,' *LC*, 33); 'ma tête cogne contre un bec de gaz' (*RP*, 15). The experience of stumbling upon things (in both senses) calls attention to the positive coincidence of self and the material where the body registers the moment of apprehending the real as a therapeutic jolt.[13] When a path takes a steep dip and sends him rolling down an embankment, material adventure and poetic venture are launched: 'Sous le pont en béton comme prévu je perds tout d'un coup l'équilibre, et je me ramasse parmi des lambeaux de matelas et de pneus' (*RP*, 108).

Bumps, rolls, little shocks and knocks punctuate the collision of self and world. Jumpiness, jerkiness, careering, and lurching – the body's fractured rhythms disrupt the smooth linearities of routine and repetition. The city explorer who is gleefully thrown off course or who actively deviates from routine and repetition feels an instant affinity with the woman cycling in from the suburbs whose sudden wobble registers the moment of contact between self and the material; a quickening surge of consciousness seems to ripple through the 'indéfinissable verdure' protruding from her bag (*RP*, 27) and flickers onto the page in the tender portrait of organic resistance in face of the systemic city.

Corporeal pliancy and mental *disponibilité*, brought forth in a poetics of pliancy and hybridity, embrace the unpredictable and the variable ('*accidents* de la circulation'). It is unpredictability and improvisation, linked to an ethical cussedness, that set the practices of the poet and other urban gleaners and recyclers against those of town planners and architects, property developers, and corporate entrepreneurs, promulgators of a culture of blandness and over-processing, of the self-same and the endlessly reproduced. We will return to the homogenizing projects that factor out the city's magic in the name of progress in the next section, 'Tenacious Practices, Tender Objects'; let us stay for the moment with unevenness.

Réda sets out to ruck the sleek fabric of urban homogeneity. Stumbling, colliding, lurching, and forms of awkwardness connect here with activities – skipping, acrobatics, gymnastics – that are more familiarly construed as their agile antithesis. Awkwardness and pliancy are complementary here, not antithetical, for they map flexibility and individuality to a surge of creativity and to the desire to counter the doxa of levelling in performative ways.

Particularly marked in the incipits of Réda's texts is the explicit embrace of spontaneity and chance. The poet launches his text and relaunches his peregrination with this *in medias res* introduction: 'Mais quelquefois aussi je ne songe qu'à poursuivre l'espace et, en plein midi, un détour imprévu peut me plonger au coeur de la métropole' (*LR*, 50). Physical disruption and kinetic unevenness thus signal a consciousness-shifting incident that is propitious for poetry-making. '*Chutes répétées*' (*LR*, 97–102) is a narrative of productively disrupted circulation. The text is inspired by a succession of falls which, when the poet plots them on a map of the city, form a scalene triangle whose centrepoint (in the 3rd arrondissement) inspires the excursion that produces the poem before us, '*Chutes répétées.*' This new itinerary, whose source is traced textually to the topography of the original falls, itself 'falls down' when it is halted (briefly) in its tracks, due to the closure of the museum of the Conservatoire des Arts et Métiers. The aborted itinerary makes possible the rerouting of the narrative excursion through a fantasy reconfiguration of the sexual characteristics of the display mannequins in shop windows, and some humorous analogical play:

> [L]'on doit pouvoir remplacer facilement le bassin d'un homme au complet par le ventre d'une femme enceinte, effectuer d'autres permutations de savant pervers ou de chirurgien fou. À de rares exceptions évoquant le jus de tomate ou le sorbet à la pistache, les mannequins [...] ont cette teinte d'un rose pâle chimique et uniforme qu'on rencontre aussi dans le tarama de certains traiteurs, les rubans adhésifs en usage chez les électriciens et les infirmières.   (*LR*, 100–1)

The practice of productive disruption and the related forms of pliancy foregrounded in Réda find their echo in Pierre Mayol's description of the creative activities of a city neighbourhood assumed to be a space in which freedom may be wrested from the levelling effects of utilitarian recuperation through a series of improvisations: 'La pratique du quartier introduit de la gratuité au lieu de la nécessité; elle favorise une utilisation de l'espace urbain non finalisé par son usage seulement fonctionnel. À la limite, elle vise à accorder *le maximum de temps à un minimum d'espace* pour libérer des possibilités de déambulation.'[14]

Gratuitousness and playfulness characterize the time-spinning, space-filling activities unfolding across Réda's poetry: improvisation is bodied forth in a random sequence of steps ('avancer pizzicato,' *RP*, 114) or in the samba performed across railway sleepers. The poet's bouncing steps give material form to the tactic of creative irregularity as he leaps and hovers, pauses to critique or celebrate, to retrieve and to invent. To stop is to give creativity a chance; to move on is to resume quotidian routine and seek (reluctant) reintegration into normative patterns and practices. Freedom is paced as deviation, digression, looping back, and fertile interruption. Moving against the unthinking flow and countering smoothness demand disruptiveness: stopping and starting, lurching and hesitating. Cadences bear the imprint of subjectivity; they also inscribe alternative patterns (of walking, of writing) based on variability, deviation, and the fertile alternance of expansion and contraction.

Children's skipping games have a special appeal for Réda in this respect because they interiorize the anti-utilitarian paradox of simultaneously moving and not moving, and because they combine bodily movement and creative language-making (*RP*, 23). Like the poet, the children respond to the urgency of breaking up temporal and spatial linearities by generating their own subjective rhythms and bringing these to language:

> Avant le refrain qui disait:
>> *En avant, la femme du sergent,*
>> *En arrière, la femme du pompier,*
>> *Tout autour, la femme du tambour,*
>
> se déroulait un motif indéfiniment répété (croche, noire pointée, double croche, soupir, et encore la croche, etc.) à la fois monotone et fascinant comme le bourdonnement rythmique d'un rouet ou d'une machine à coudre.

Children skipping are 'activement poétique[s]': they embody kinetic and verbal pliancy because skipping prompts singing (just like walking triggers writing), and as they mix and recycle French and American cultural influences, the children generate new forms of hybridity, like the poet and other artisans of the everyday. To walk, to skip, to samba, or to invent a song is to imprint on life the rhythms of purposive play.[15] By generating forms of circular creativity (the ropes goes round and round; the incantation is repeated over and over), the actions of the children collapse the frames of history and culture, and hold past and present, the eternal and the contemporary in a compelling synthesis. Thus, the mythic quality of the everyday is reaffirmed: 'Et ce motif [à la fois monotone et fascinant] arrivant du fond des âges serait transmis, d'autres gamines de sept ans avec leur frénésie austère de bacchantes, leur autorité de prêtresses, maintiendraient la célébration du vieux Pan sur les trottoirs sourds de Paris' (*RP*, 23).

The poet's own combination of moving and remaining in the same place (literally, for a while on the same tiled square) takes the form of his 'gymnastique étroite,' across the chequered floor of the Galerie Véro-Daudat ('Un passage,' *CCA*). As with the girls' skipping game, kinetic activity is subjectively patterned and language-shaping, in this case by the moves the poet permits himself in an imaginary game of chess or hopscotch enacted across the floor of the arcade, whose monochrome tile-pattern prompts fantasy-work: 'Noir, blanc, blanc, noir. [...] Blanc, noir, noir, blanc: poursuivant cette bizarre marelle, j'entrais en communication avec d'autres épaisseurs de silence et d'obscurité' (*CCA*, 93–4). Here the body of the 'chess player' moves minimally, but imaginative pliancy allows him to infiltrate a variety of phantasmagorical sites ('palais mal connus'), the poet's equivalent of 'le monde souterrain des enfants' (*RP*, 22). His obscure spaces are cavernous like the Bibliothèque Nationale in the rue Richelieu, intriguingly decrepit like the theatres of the 2nd arrondissement, and unfathomable like the Hôtel des Postes with its unceasing commerce in life-altering intimations. All are places mesmerically abstracted from real life, pleasurably obscure; these fertile and troubling zones reverberate with repressed longing and ever-present anxiety; the atmosphere is redolent of Mallarmé ('meubles orphelins et l'inanité des bibelots'). Exploring these shadowlands turns the poet into a phantom, insubstantial and uncertain. Myth-generating and language-producing, his phantasmatic activity is short-circuited by a sense of futility and desolation: '[J]e pouvais avancer longtemps encore, en esprit, dans un monde dont toutes les choses s'évanouissent pour m'ouvrir une interminable impasse.' But he resists the enduring temptation to quench lack and desire through fantasy in order to return to the everyday and the real, and concludes his text by intimating a new horizon in the Gare de l'Est.

In Réda, as in Certeau, the relation between walking practices (including skipping and samba-dancing) and writing practices exceeds that of simple analogy; the two sets of practices are imbricated in the subjective construction of the city. The cross-fertilizing actions of circulating physically and of producing text emerge most vividly in 'Un Citadin' (*La Course*), where Réda folds embodied subjectivity, city, and language into a capacious mobile consciousness:

Il faut aussi qu'un sentiment de bonheur absolu
Se prononce comme en dehors de ma propre personne,

Au point que la rue elle-même à ce moment soupçonne
Qu'elle, toute la ville et son espace irrésolu
Ne font qu'un avec le réseau mobile mais fidèle
Des phrases que nos pas écrivent quand nous circulons.   (*LC*, 11)

Réda combines excursive and discursive strategies in ways analogous to Certeau's 'rhétoriques cheminatoires,' as he holds together the relations between walking and the language-structuring activities of writing, speaking, and dreaming.[16] For Certeau, the walking itinerary is refreshingly irregular, punctuated by pauses and deviations; Réda's poetic practice is similarly shaped by fluctuation and pliancy, and can be illuminated through Certeau's 'rhétoriques cheminatoires.'

Certeau deploys the terms 'synecdoche' and 'asyndeton' to expose the relation between those textual moments that undergo a pleasurable expansion (synecdoche) and those that are passed over fleetingly (asyndeton). The writerly itinerary involves hesitation – the pleasure of narrative movement arrested, intense instants when wonderment, awe, or a sense of the sublime suddenly floods the everyday, contingency is overruled, and a rarefied moment is captured in synecdoches of colour, form, and movement. When the marvellous subsides and synecdoche retreats, movement, which was briefly arrested, is resumed. Movement, here, implies *moving on*, a form of writerly nimbleness that entails shortcutting and bypassing, sliding and eliding, such that certain sights and surfaces are only minimally described or passed over. These instances of structural and syntactical ellipsis are summed up, for Certeau, by the rhetorical figure of asyndeton. While synecdoche indulges in delectable dilatoriness, asyndeton is its precipitate partner, rushing past, skipping over, and always hastening the next moment of pleasurable arrest. The two figures are correlative, rather than in any sense contrastive, because the capturing of the sublime or the rarefied (in synecdoche) demands the curtailment of pedestrian discursiveness (by means of asyndeton).

In Réda, pleasurable expansion follows a fortuitous disruption to plans or expectations. In 'Rue Serpollet' (*AC*, 76–81), the futile search for the eponymous street and its remarkable statue to Léon Serpollet is rapidly curtailed, peripatetically and textually, in this example of asyndeton: '[J]'ai vainement cherché la rue Serpollet pendant une demi-heure. Je ne m'en plains pas. Autrement je n'aurais pas parcouru certaines voies que d'habitude on néglige et dont le nom nous poursuit à tort ou à raison parfois comme un remords' (*AC*, 76). The physical, mental, and textual space thus opened up by the digression begins to fill with the poet's reflections on the anomalous relation between intriguing street names and the banal or dispiriting atmosphere of the streets themselves. This synecdochic instance is expanded further by Réda's humorous speculation on a toponymic curiosity: the multiple military identities amassed behind the name 'Rue des Colonels-Renard' and spilling forth in possible explanations of promotion, dynasty, statistics, and fraternal relations. Then, suddenly reminded of his original purpose, the poet quickly halts his peripatetic and textual digression, and as the synecdochic instance fades, the quest narrative is resumed: 'Perdu parmi les réflexions de cet ordre, j'en avais presque oublié la rue Serpollet. A proximité de l'église, j'abordai tour à tour deux personnes susceptibles de me renseigner' (AC, 77).

Rédean *disponibilité* is the readiness to alter the course of a walk or a poem on a whim, or to respond to the almost bodily grip of a cherished preoccupation: 'Parti pour voir du neuf mais *ressaisi* par mes habitudes, j'aboutis encore rue Leblanc' (RP, 93; my emphasis). This real-time curtailment (and textual elision) of the anticipated departure enables the poem to fill with the metaphysical desire experienced in the disused Citroën buildings, visited only two poems and three weeks earlier. Disruption to the planned itinerary both in 'plot' terms and in textual terms is repeatedly inscribed in tangents broken off, unexpectedly resumed, or redefined. This emerges (by default) in the striking textual compression or elision of the actual *event* of moving on or altering course: 'Ayant raté mon train, je circule autour de Saint-Lazare' (RP, 87). Digression and deviation, and rushing over things in order to embrace serendipitous pleasure produce a balance between the fleeting economy of asyndeton and the space-filling, time-slowing action of synecdoche. Developing the metaphorics of rhythm, we can map the two mutually balancing moments to the complementary movements of systole and diastole: contraction (asyndeton, speeding up, 'passer') and expansion (synecdoche, slowing down). I will return to the slow, beautiful, expansive deployment of synecdoche in Réda's colour-work and his search for the sublime.

Réda strives to capture the synergy between the city and the body unburdened by inwardness ('en dehors de ma personne'). This synergy surfaces in a series of mergings and meanderings, shifts and slippages between the real and the imaginary. What is remarkable in Réda's later writing, as Michael Sheringham has noted with reference to *Châteaux des courants d'air*, is the structural displacement whereby subjectivity is seen to inhere less in the human individual than in the city itself.[17] The fertile, fluctuating consciousness of the city comes dazzlingly into view here in the miraculous migration of imaginative potential from human agency to city entity, then follows its reverse flow in forms of (sublimely) altered subjectivity:

> [J]e sens mieux, la nuit, [...] quelle dimension mentale [certaines rues] ajoutent au corps de la ville: rues en perpétuel mouvement comme dans les rêves, où c'est la ville qui se rêve et navigue en tout sens à travers les strates de pierre, de vie et de mémoire qui forment son épaisseur, réinventant à mesure les lois de son instable gravitation. Car si Paris semble devenir par instants une ville imaginaire, [...] elle est avant tout une ville imaginative [...] sans cesse en quête d'elle-même sous le front rassurant que nous tendent les monuments de sa gloire. Sans doute redevable de ces dispositions aventureuses à la proximité de la mer (la lumière y est de sable et d'écume, l'air volumineusement libre et vert), peu à peu ses métamorphoses influent sur le promeneur. Il se pressent à son tour imaginé, promené comme l'antenne vagabonde et réflexive de la ville dans ses humeurs passagères.   (CCA, 13)

This is not the Paris of the individual *promeneur*'s fantasy, but urban space as the generator of desire and myth, an organic entity endowed with transformative potential and the power to infiltrate and shape the consciousness of its explorer. As the subject becomes a pliable object for the space it inhabits, selfhood as familiarly constituted is temporarily abdicated and consciousness yields to the formative desire of the city.[18] The displacement of the normative subject-as-subject by subject-turned-object for the generative consciousness of the city involves a pronominal shift as first-person agency cedes to an active third-person impersonality ('la ville,' 'elle,' 'l'espace'). Subjective freight is discharged through mythopoeic visions that endow the city with the power to make its own incursions into the mind of the explorer. It is in these terms that we need to understand Réda's anthropomorphism: not as a trivializing prop, but as a mode that strives to duplicate the sublime intensity of the relation between individual mind and the city's organic consciousness.

To walk the city is to be stalked, rushed, possessed, and ultimately displaced by the subjectivity of the city. This emerges in the evaporation of volition and the consequent self-dissolution, even self-abdication, that is a signal feature of Réda's writing. This extreme point is reached in *La Liberté des rues*, where the narrator announces that his self-perception has altered with his altering view of the city to such a degree that he has become absorbed into the vast libidinal network of urban space, where he is more acted upon than acting:

> À pied ou à vélo, j'ai d'ailleurs cessé de croire que je circule au gré de ma fantaisie. Je ne pense pas davantage obéir, en circulant, à quelque plan préétabli pour me guider ou me perdre. Il me semble plutôt que sans se préoccuper de mon cas, ce sont les rues elles-mêmes qui se déplacent, s'ébattent – et je me laisse remuer, prenant discrètement ma part du plaisir qu'elles échangent.   (*LR*, 59)

Walking (like other peripatetic activities) involves – necessitates, even – separation and alteration if the wanderer is to be optimally receptive and bring forth new mythopoeic responses. Exploring the city is figured as a kind of mutilation for the walker, whose physical actions and mental dispositions are disrupted by new spatial configurations: the walker is left 'amputé d'un morceau de sa mémoire' (*CCA*, 18); 'rue du Retrait [...] une de ces lacunes imprévues me déséquilibra presque physiquement. Les démolisseurs avaient aboli jusqu'à l'image, ne laissant dans ma mémoire qu'un trou' (*LR*, 32).

The peripatetic project, experienced as a series of risks, gains, and losses, solicits forms of pliancy that are ultimately less corporeal than imaginative. Thus, streets whose everyday significance has evaporated retain a mythic power that infiltrates the conscious and the unconscious mind: 'Ayant perdu leur territoire, [ces rues] en cherchent un autre dans l'espace de vos rêves les plus singuliers' (*AC*, 21). There is a tense reciprocity here, for as the city invades his mind and possesses his body, so the poet leaves his traces on the city. Embodied consciousness is altered by the city, and in turn alters the city, cutting things out and passing things over, excising and neglecting: '[L]e regard du promeneur s'éduque et détruit ce qui le contrarie, ou passe sereinement à travers' (*CCA*, 42). Subject and the city are mutually mutilating in the search for new configurations capable of altering our sense of the real and of language.

I began by looking at how subjectivity comes forth in corporeal circulations that imprint and alter perceptions of urban space via a series of kinetic and poetic moves. This reading uncovered Réda's capacious description of subjectivity unfixed from personhood and absorbed into the city itself, figured as a consciousness infiltrating and shaping the thoughts of the individual explorer. In Réda, subjectivity is always intersubjective, defined by the action of altering the world and being altered by it. Turning now to the circulation of material things around the city, I want to consider further the mutually formative relations between human subjects and physical objects, locations, and incidents. In taking forward this reading of Réda, I ask: how does subjectivity shape the representation of material things (taken to include mess, debris, human actions and practices, everything that may be said to constitute the real)? How, in turn, is subjectivity altered through contact with the material? These questions have implications for writing that explores the capacity of physical things to provoke action, material and metaphoric, pragmatic and poetic. Working on material things – preserving them, reclaiming them, transforming them – has its analogue in the action of the poet, exploiting the rich resources of metaphor, myth, allegory, and irony as he generates text.

Tenacious Practices, Tender Objects

In her documentary film *Les Glaneurs et la glaneuse* (2000), Agnès Varda seeks out those who make recuperative or transformative contact with superseded things, those who bend down in order to pick up what is discarded by advanced consumer society, those who sift and retrieve, and ultimately regenerate. Like Varda, Réda feels a broad affinity with all who practise forms of urban gleaning: a street-sweeper gathering debris; a retired sewer-man recycling junk; Tunisian grocers overseeing their eclectic, teetering stock; allotment-holders tending their plots. For Réda, as for Varda, gleaning is an activity profoundly marked by transformative desire, whether formed in poverty, political choice, or aesthetic purpose. The poet describes himself and his companion as '[a]vançant comme deux glaneurs dans ces ruines aplaties de la rue de Belleville, nous ne cherchons rien, puis nous ramassons n'importe quoi' (*RP*, 18). Yet, gleaners have to resist the temptation of total, non-discriminating possession: 'On voudrait tout sauver, mais ce ne serait que provisoire au fond de nos caves, et encore plus navrant' (*RP*, 19). There is a capacious desire to salvage everything, but proper gleaning implies sorting, selecting, and rejecting, as Varda's beautiful film lovingly, gleaningly, depicts. Like Agnès Varda, and her sifters and gatherers, lavishing attention on the beauty and the utility of advanced society's quotidian dross, Réda finds in the work of artisans of the everyday an analogue of his work on the world and on language, of his nurturing of poetic materials ('[J]e dois être essentiellement un glaneur, et dans tous les domaines. J'envie un peu ceux qui cultivent et moissonnent, mais j'ai grand plaisir à glaner').[19]

By aligning himself with street-sweepers and other urban gleaners, Réda distinguishes his low-level, 'hands on,' non-elitist approach from the cultivated approach of the aesthete-*flâneur* whose obsession presupposes a readiness to withdraw things from material circulation, to fetishize or museumize. Such abstractions are, of course, the very antithesis of Rédean joy in contingency. For the poet, as for the filmmaker, the material of contingency claims its place, and asserts its simple tenaciousness and its resistant beauty in life, in film, and in poetry. In ways comparable to Varda as she transforms her beloved, misshapen potatoes – the rejects of commercial calibration – into the tender objects of a digitally produced still-life, Réda celebrates and performs in poetry his own *art de la récupération*.

Gleaning is a series of actions that involve walking around, stopping at things, holding and beholding them, sifting and ultimately transforming them into image and pattern. As Varda's film and Réda's writing show powerfully, the bodily action of reaching out to marginal things extends into non-material space and connects with ways of tending symbolic wealth (collective values, social justice, democracy, mutual respect). Réda celebrates the quotidian gleaner, the black municipal street-sweeper who represents individual dignity and multiculturalism in action; he embodies the ideal of 'res publica,' tending the public domain, applying himself to the city's detritus (*RP*, 32–3). The street-sweeper interrupts the flow of contingency, and affirms order and necessity. His expansive gestures and his close work are analogous to the alternately generous and precise movements of the poet. Each pursues his patient search for the trivial and the displaced, reaches into corners, reclaims what others have passed over; at the same time, each is spurred by the desire to gather up and make new.

The sublime sweeper of the (sub)urban savannah, Réda gathers thematic materials, filters perceptions, gleans impressions, and registers the human and cultural moment made palpable in physical things and incidents.[20] He traverses city space with a broad sweep: his recuperative activity is visually discriminating and materially attentive as he transforms the facticity of quotidian existence into memory and fantasy, myth and metaphor. Réda's rummaging in 'ruines' turns up material things whose cultural pertinence has lapsed with advancing technologies and transformations in taste, but which reveal all the more clearly the passage of human desire and need: 'des saletés flottent dans le canal au-dessous du pont mobile, avec ses engrenages empâtés de graisse qui n'ont presque plus de dents. On identifie encore aisément une bouteille, mais des formes molles et mortes que le clapotis de l'eau rend vivantes figent le coeur' (RP, 34).

In their refusal at once to integrate – or remain within – the normative circuits of taste, consumption, and visibility, ordinary curiosities provide a model of defiant constancy and eruptive creativity; they offer a symbolic defence against the material and cultural erosion induced by commercial standardization. Hence Réda's affinity with the Tunisian grocers whose crammed, chaotic shops attend to simple, everyday needs and, in the process, create pockets of regenerated authenticity and sociability, like the îlots celebrated by Certeau and Giard.

In 'Et avec ça?' (CCA, 18) Réda explores how, in an ethnically diverse city, changes to the economic landscape bring forth new socio-cultural practices as resistance to the monopolizing 'grandes surfaces' sparks a new pliancy in neighbourhood retail practices and consumer mores. Eclecticism, disorder, and spontaneity release autochtone citizens from their Cartesian rationalist inheritance; in the chaotic profusion chez le Tunisien, they become less mannered and more open-hearted ('à travers tant de changements, perdure à Vaugirard une figure humaine de l'épicerie,' CCA, 21). Neighbourhood shopkeepers, like other artisans of the everyday, are a further source of the productive symmetry between the material and the subjective that emerges in the circulating oxymorons of everyday exoticism and the extraordinary ordinary: '[D]es négoces [...] concourent solidairement à la mise en circulation de richesses indispensables' (CCA, 22–3). Réda is alive to the cultural changes nurtured in the city's ethnic or spatial margins, noting them and celebrating them, at once ethnographer and full participant. His 'Oui, tout change ...' (CCA, 18) is an unmistakable echo of Baudelaire's 'Le Cygne,' but the ethnographic change that Réda notes is affirmative, for alternative retail practices thriving in clusters of small shops enrich intersubjective relations: 'au contact de l'Orient nos cités se civilisent' (CCA, 20).

Réda's conspicuous choice of the small-scale and the ordinary, like Varda's, is explained by the capacity of the quotidian to persist and to obtrude, precisely because of its superseded status or perceived superfluousness, and its consequent availability as a filter of desire, memory, and fantasy. Just as the poet chooses trivia, so trivia attaches itself to him like the window display of ties that seem to absorb the flow of thoughts, gestures, memories, and images generated by the poet and by other passers-by: '[L]'esprit se servait de n'importe quoi, et au besoin de cravates, pour entretenir une veilleuse dans certains recoins du souvenir' (LR, 52). If the capacity of the lowly object to act as a filter for the consciousness of the narrator solicits a Proustian memory excursion, Réda moves in a specifically intersubjective direction by speculating on the potential of the material to open up the network of desires, attitudes, anxieties, and expectations beyond the containments of self:

> [P]eut-être discernerait-on, dans le jeu de ces discrets phénomènes, un code donnant accès au réseau de tous les destins, au fond de chaque mémoire; comprendrait-on l'enchaînement fatal ou aléatoire des causes et des effets. Telle à présent cette main posée sur un comptoir de cuivre, et dont je devine les tâtonnements dans l'ombre d'une chambre vers une épaule qui luit.   (LR, 51)

The landscapes of affectivity are relayed through a single, simple object. Gleaning material or imaginary things brings pleasure and fulfils a psychic necessity. Urban dystopia and individual disenchantment are temporarily assuaged by the creative, phantasmatic work triggered by a passionate (usually visual) contact with things. Here, the movement of self towards other, and the migration of consciousness in the opposite direction, are directed through the mediating object:

> J'ignore si cette jeune femme s'intéresse vraiment aux cravates, ou si elle ne cède pas elle-même au même genre d'attraction. Si par l'intermédiaire de ces huissiers des âmes distraites, nos relais individuels ne communiquent pas plus profondément qu'on ne penserait. De telle sorte qu'au prix d'un effort mental nullement gênant pour elle, je pourrais m'aventurer dans son univers intérieur, tandis que le mien se découvre à elle peut-être – à elle, à l'un ou l'autre des passants plus pressés qui nous bousculent, dont chacun enregistre ici ou là (des bijoux ou des souliers plutôt que des cravates), un de ces relais singuliers dont les connexions se mélangent dans l'ensemble en perpétuel mouvement qui nous contient. Je me demande alors qui circule, qui songe, qui se souvient de quoi. Voilà ce qui suffoque, mais se transforme en un sentiment dilatant de liberté dans l'infini, vivant possible.   (LR, 52)

Material things abound in Réda's world, as in Varda's, but, conspicuously, it is not the brilliant, sophisticated objects of late-twentieth-century consumer society that captivate them, but the flotsam of every-day living. The referential framework in Réda is constituted in the un-remarkable commodities that satisfy bodily need or offer gratification: the ubiquitous *boules Quies*, *gauloises* cigarettes, clothes drying on a washing line. Réda retrieves and recycles, metaphorically, things that have become naturalized, banalized, and, in the process, lost to sight. These are things that seem neither to require nor invite any explanation; they are things about which there is no mystery and, on the face of it, no compelling attraction, commercially or aesthetically. He chooses them because they expose the inert gaze that is the product of repetitive modes of viewing. By temporarily arresting the flow of things in order to select particular objects for fresh appraisal, Réda offers lessons in looking anew.

Réda is attracted to mess, waste, debris, trivia; he is drawn to those objects that exist de-fetishized, untended, and unclaimed; their marginalized or anachronistic status (what he prefers to call 'objets *perdus*' rather than 'objets trouvés') is a material correlative of the solitary, marginal poet who eschews the networks of social circulation and community. Réda returns repeatedly to what contingency washes up, drawn not to second-hand books and 'collectables,' but to valueless plastic toy-figures and assorted tat: 'des chasseurs alpins en tenue de neige, avec des cors, des charrettes vert pomme garnies de bonbons poussiéreux' (*RP*, 20). Rummaging in skips on the rue de Belleville, he is alert to the formidable resistance put up by paltry things, the material remnants of individual desire and action:

> Plusieurs [cartes postales] sont adressées à Jeanne ou à Louise Forgeron. Elles datent du début de ce siècle. Signés de prénoms féminins et mon-trant *La Belle Georgette* enveloppée de voiles transparents, elles nous sem-blent équivoques bien que désuètes. [...] On trouve ailleurs des cahiers de géographie tenus à la perfection, des débris de jouets (un chien, un rail de chemin de fer mécanique), des trumeaux et des marqueteries d'un travail très ancien. (*RP*, 19)

The debris of education, manual work, play, and domestic architecture bears the traces of its own history, the succession of breaks and disloca-tions that mark the gradual dereliction of things. Their physical surface reveals the preserved inscriptions of human effort and application, imagination and creativity. The poet is fascinated by the persistence of objects (across time, through space), and by their power to articulate subjectivities and provoke new readings (historical, intimist, biographical, social, cultural, ethnographical, visual). Other postcards written at the turn of the century are poignant vestiges of separation and longing. They are autobiographical traces; they articulate the desire to heal spatial and affective dislocation: '[J]e m'attache moins aux images qu'aux textes, quand il y en a: *Maman*, supplient Marcel et Claude (à Chaumont-sur-Tharonne, Loir-et-Cher, en juillet 1935), *écris-nous des lettres parce que ont s'ennuis et pour cela nous vourions bien revenir'* (*RP*, 118). These human inscriptions illustrate Certeau and Giard's concept of 'citations hétéroclites.' They connect with the output of the graffiti artists who are the subject of 'Le Chantier' (*LC*, 34). The *tagueurs'* drawings are actualizations of narrative potential, markers of the obstinate desire of individuals to leave their traces on the world, to alter the perceptions of others. The graffiti artists have painted emaciated figures that the poet imagines coming to life at night – like the statues he imagines stepping down from their plinths in 'Un passage' (*CCA*). The *tagueurs'* finished work provides the raw material for the poet's imaginative project, proffering a model of aesthetic recycling and sustaining a chain of creativity that extends from social gestures and cultural critique, through personal anecdote and ethnography, to memory, longing, and (sub)urban youth culture: all deeply affective, creative responses to the city. The relations linking the artisans of the everyday (Dédé, Tunisian grocers, graffiti artists) to makers of text are more than simply analogical; they are connective and generative because they nourish fantasy (other people's, the poet's) and bring forth poetry.

Contingency simply washes around, but what washes up in Réda's texts is not insignificant driftwood bobbing on the urban tide, but the precious wreckage ('ce naufrage,' *RP*, 19) of human circumstance and individual history; or what Certeau and Giard refer to, in the opening quotation of this chapter, as 'débris d'histoires naufragées.' Strewn across the landscape of quotidian existence and memory, the dross of other people's lives exists beyond the reach of fetishistic reclaim.

Réda's ecology of the ordinary and the small-scale needs to be set in the wider context of the culture critique that surfaces in his writing. Trivial objects put up a tenacious resistance to the cultural flattening that diminishes subjective experience and replaces material diversity with the pre-packaged and streamlined. While Réda explicitly eschews any specific political purpose (*RP*, 33), his critique of the arbiters of cultural taste regularly detonates a polemical charge:

[L]'aplatissement résulte d'une autre volonté qui s'exerce, méthodique partout, principalement où s'opposent de l'amour et de la colère; un spectre humanisé à distance dans ses contours – ces vêtements et ces gestes, ces regards et ces voix sans un pli qui jugent et qui décrètent – pour faire croire que l'humain coïncide avec son trafic; vous laissant libre d'épiloguer alors qu'il vous nie en sourdine; vous prescrivant en cas de malaise la dose suffisante de poison sous forme d'argent, de tranquillisants, de honte et de vitamines.   (*RP*, 76)

Réda launches humorous or vituperative blasts against the new imperialisms, whether the aggressive assault of the retail trade or the colonizations perpetrated in the name of real estate ('cette architecture actuelle fait rayonner le néant imaginatif des automates qui l'ont conçue,' *AC*, 19). His scathing critique turns on the urban planners and commercial developers – makers of 'la ville moderniste, massive, homogène'[21] – and focuses on the material habitat – thin, anaemic constructions of social housing – and the diminished lives that attach to it. The sterile echo of the falsely salubrious 'grands blocs de blocs' (*CCA*, 65) amplifies notions of anonymity and dehumanized existence, and connects with a metaphorics of the city-as-pathology. The city as a body fragilized and flattened finds graphic representation in the figure of the motorway proposed for Montparnasse ('[qui] s'abattrait en travers comme une grande matraque de béton,' *RP*, 43; 'l'existence [...] laminée,' *CCA*, 59). Sickness, atrophy, violence, and death are reflected too in the opulent dystopia of bourgeois habitation (concretized in the 'progression inexorable des immeubles de luxe funéraire du Front de Seine,' *RP*, 94). Ersatz luxury claims its hygienized, aestheticized space in the seamless, serial repetitions (Certeau and Giard's 'utopies lisses') of high-rise blocks or the dehumanizing uniformity of streets where *immobilier* is synonymous with contagious immobility and mental vacancy (*CCA*, 44).[22] Bourgeois authority is constructed on the spectacular reifications of its speculative, totalizing, and, ultimately, entropic drives. The architectural refiguring – disfiguring – of the 15th arrondissement's riverside is emblematic of a cultural moment, and a mental crisis, for the radical renovation of the built environment brings sharp recognition of the wearying permanency of change. Symptoms of enforced modernity – anomie, despair, solitude, indifference, hypocrisy and pretension – surface in Réda's acute observations of mores and mannerisms, individual behaviour and social interaction: he captures the dully gazing woman who obsessively runs her hand through her hair in preparation for a social encounter redolent with Baudelairean spleen ('la veuve Éternité (qui radote) au salon,' *RP*, 74). In certain districts at certain times of day, the normative ideology of uprightness and sterility turns into almost palpable compliance, thus around St-Lazare, 'le néant très correct s'y déclare en fermes contours. En somme un néant coopérateur' (*RP*, 87). The smooth, pure-surface luxury of the 17th arrondissement is epitomized by 'cette personne entièrement chanélisée' (*AC*, 84). The discrepancy between states of exterior opulence and inner sterility nourishes a profound sense of lack.

Where alienation finds an outlet in modes of polite sociability and the hollow rectitude of certain bourgeois localities, a comparable sense of self-dislocation feeds destructive impulses in forsaken youth struggling to give meaning to their disconsolating experience of urban space in 'Les Visiteurs du samedi soir': 'mal assurés d'eux-mêmes, de la réalité de la ville' (*CCA*, 47). Vandalism and violence are a response to the need to produce an event, to claim a space of one's own, to assert a subjective position, but the futility of such gestures bodies forth in metaphors of sickness and desolation, brittleness and fracture:

> *Ils transbahutent leur malaise tels des déménageurs,*
> *L'air blasé, mais troublés par ce qui scintille et rutile:*
> *Vitrines et cinés, le hall flambant du* King Burger
>
> *Ils y restent longtemps avant d'oser manger des frites,*
> *Traînent ensuite leur ennui brutal sur les trottoirs,*
> *Surpris, fâchés que rien n'arrive, et de ne pas savoir*
> *Trouver ce qu'ils cherchaient dans la nuit qui déjà s'effrite*
> *Et qu'il leur faut aider maintenant à finir, en cassant*
> *N'importe quoi sur le chemin du retour où dimanche*
> *Commence à vomir sa lueur livide entre les branches*
> *Et lancer par endroits une éclaboussure de sang.*   (CCA, 47)

Responses to the experience of urban space veer from *refoulement* to *défoulement*: where the superfluous gestures of the bourgeois woman mime the need to bring the body under control, dispossessed youth resorts to self-unleashing in acts of violence. Class differences may be indelibly marked in gesture and disposition, but the thwarted subjectivities captured by Réda cut across the distinctions of culture and social territory. In ironic portraits and poignant vignettes of atrophied lives, Réda maps a landscape of affective desolation to an architecturally desolate environment. This bleak vision is proposed and continually challenged in poetry that brings to language the restorative richness of overlooked materiality. In this respect, Réda's poetry reveals a passionate and very Certelian concern with how artisans of the everyday create and preserve subjective territory. Réda brings forth pockets of resistance ('îlots de résistance,' CCA, 92) and the creative practices and fantasies that they nourish. To quote Certeau, '[C]es îlots créent des effets d'exotisme à l'intérieur.'[23]

Seeking solace and an authentic place of his own, Dédé, the retired sewer-man, is the model of an individual mapping his personal territory in opposition to the encroachment of the new 'Résidences' with their ethos of streamlining and standardization (RP, 108).[24] The maker of his own habitat ('palais hun'), Dédé is representative of the generalized resistance ('une réaction de calfeutrage hostile,' RP, 109) that takes the form of 'bedding down' and immersion in obscure, semi-licit, or organic practices whose diversity is captured in the jostling of material references and the intrusion of everyday speech-features: 'On n'attaque pas impunément l'indépendance d'orgueilleux maraîchers-ferrailleurs experts en forçage du bégonia, rafistolage des carrosseries, et conscients du droit de l'homme à ne rien foutre sinon fumer des jours durant' (RP, 109). The sewer-man's shack, distinguished unerringly by the poet as 'bas et [...] complexe,' materializes the stubborn inscrutability of the 'riverains ombrageux.' First among them is Dédé himself, the one-time explorer of man-made, subterranean channels, whose name seems to call up the underworld river Léthé. The obscure mesh of underground rivers once worked by Dédé connects metaphorically to all those abandoned passages, barely accessible recesses, tunnels, thickets, railway sidings, concealed spaces, and the hidden Bièvre River, sites crucial to Réda's concept of an organic city consciousness. As articulations of the meandering pleasures of creativity and fantasy, they link the practices of the sewer-man and his fellow *riverains* to the 'monde souterrain' of childhood inventiveness and freedom, and to the poet's own fantasy-work in the Véro-Daudat Arcade, the commercially superseded and fantasy-generating tunnel of iron and glass explored in *Châteaux des courants d'air.*

The defiance towards homogenization and authority that informs the actions of Dédé and his neighbours extends from the city to the suburbs and to activities that flourish beyond the reach of officialdom and regulation. Réda brings recalcitrant practices to writing and captures the *prégnance* of material marginality in its economic, subjective, topographical, and symbolic significance.

In 'Tôlerie peinture' (*Beauté suburbaine*), territory is staked out according to the alternative but no less rigorously enforced customs and practices of unofficial trading. Power and resentment are mobilized in the preservation of a space – that of a backstreet car-body repair shop – and sovereign authority is bestowed on the owner, 'un homme / Dont le poil et la corpulence annoncent les Balkans.' This master of the symbolic is defended by menacing red-eyed curs and by 'la fille en flanelle, à la lippe de reine, / Qui m'observe et qui semble ignorer ce ramdam / Car dans son fief aucun moteur ne ronfle.' There develops, around the medieval connotations of 'fief' and the regal tawdriness of the flannel-clad secretary, an allegory of modern myth-making founded on the trio of the Balkan master, his baroque queen, and the mongrel Cerberus patrolling their territory. Réda thus presents the new heroes of the everyday, formidable opponents of the mainstream and homogeneous; they transmute mundaneness into mythic power, and define marginality as a space of self-regeneration. To explore the everyday is to make destabilizing and fertile incursions into a cultural underworld and into the recesses of suppressed desire and anxiety. This potent metaphorical conflation of backstreet business premises and Balkan fiefdom, of banality and baroque beauty, of suburban curs and Cerberus clones, articulates fear and admiration, respect, and a sense of the narrator's outsider status as he watches the scene illicitly and becomes the disempowered object of scornful scrutiny: 'Je sais bien l'air que j'ai (naguère on disait: un quidam).'

Réda probes, in the alternative urban practices of marginalized citizens, modernity's epic dimension and subjects it (and himself) to the ironic undercut of postmodernity. A sound like a battle cry calls up the epic struggle between Achilles and Hector, the legendary memory abruptly relativized when the poet, '[r]etombant des hauteurs de l'épopée,' glimpses itinerant potato-sellers haranguing reluctant customers. But the eruption of the everyday (in the form of an acoustic event) is instantly recognized as the material of contemporary legend: 'Je descendrais [dans la rue] même si leur prix atteignit le double, ému comme si c'était Rimbaud fourguant de vieux Remingtons' (*RP*, 48–9). Postmodern irony and self-debunking are mixed with empathetic admiration for these 'révoltés' of the commercial world whose piercing 'tintouin' temporarily demarcates subjective space (in this street, beneath these windows); their raucous obstinacy is a selling strategy and so the potato-sellers' incongruous embodiment of the rural and the mechanical, the manual and the motorized, presents a pocket of resistance. In this hybrid configuration of myth and bathos, irony and empathy, Réda captures for poetry the eruptive quality of the everyday and the potential of alternative material practices to bring forth fresh subjective possibilities and inspire new urban legends.

Réda works constantly to move his poetic horizons beyond the built environment in order to articulate the city as a lived space, endlessly inflected by gestures, practices, habits, sounds, rituals, and forms of human resistance, sometimes of an economic or cultural kind, but often rather more obscure or symbolic. The coincidence of 'une matérialité de plus en plus convaincante' and 'une véritable substance humaine' ('*Paris spiral*,' *LR*, 67–8) is at the generative centre of Réda's poetics.

The labyrinthine streets of the Butte-aux-Cailles exude quiet, but tenacious, resistance: '[O]n se sent haut et retranché, familier d'un dédale, (rue Samson, rue Jonas) où les silhouettes qui se défilent supposent une épaisse touffe de peuple encore ici concevable, opiniâtre dans sa façon furtive de se cramponner' (*RP*, 78). The poet returns to 'la farouche autonomie de la Butte-aux-Cailles' (*CCA*, 12), evoking a space at once imprinted with the collective memory of the Commune and suffused with a spirit of obstinate self-determination. Such places are experienced as pleasurably dense, for their resistance is at once almost palpable and unfathomable. The antithesis of the monumental transparency and thinness of the Front de Seine, the Rue Daguerre in the 14th arrondissement is full of murmur and memory in contradistinction to the still, comatose silence of neighbouring streets:

une rue où le silence se met à vivre, à respirer, à chuchoter sous quantité de pieds qui pantouflent. [...] Comme quelques autres maintenant interdite à l'automobile, telle est la rue Daguerre avec ses riches commerces de victuailles qui débordent sur les trottoirs, et dont l'abondance révèle sans doute un changement de la population. Mais le climat reste populaire, d'un populaire ancien à dominante d'artisanat. (*CCA*, 60)

Such places are synonymous with muteness and depth, qualities that suggest forms of subjective intractability (toughness of attitude, resilience, obstinacy). The poet is repeatedly drawn back to places where the sheer accumulation of material things, often in the form of detritus and mess, betokens a wider culture of entrenchment that places the neighbourhood beyond normative reducibility or official recuperation. Thus, the resistance of the rue Camulogène to urban speculators is materialized in its rampant dereliction: 'Frigos, loques, sommiers / Cartons, chats morts' (LC, 20). The signifying chaos of domestic debris mixed with evocations of pullulating nature ('cormiers,' 'roses,' 'l'air embaumé d'échalotes') conjures up a vision of intense, unbounded organicity. Réda reads, in the pleasurable overflow of contingency, the memorial traces of ancient resistance, that of Camulogenes the Gaul against Caesar, and its contemporary analogue in the barricades of redundant household goods and debris with which the quartier's present-day residents meet the assault of the new colonizers. History and micro-history, legendary Gallic resistance and the quotidian recalcitrance of a backstreet in the 15th, are pressed together in Réda's empathetic evocation of this obscure pocket of resistance. Such places obtrude on the city's smooth utopian surface, challenging the pretensions of progress.

The aggressive extension of the boundaries of urban development implies an enforced contraction of the space available for subjective reclamation. This explains Réda's obsessive immersion of his poetry in *impasses*, the physical interstices and recessive practices that elude the censoring gaze or totalizing claims of urban planners and commercial developers. (For Réda, the walk is itself an interstice – 'il faudrait d'ailleurs distinguer entre le voyage d'obligation [...] et la promenade dont l'intérêt tient en entier dans l'intervalle,' 'Éloge modéré de la lenteur,' RaP, 85.) These interstitial refuges exist beyond the reach of utility or rationalist accommodations; they offer respite from the futile frenzy of the normative; they are synonymous with trespass and with transgression. Subjectivity is nurtured in what is inchoate, discarded, unreclaimed. Whether Dédé's shack or the Balkan's fiefdom or, for the poet, an anonymous building site or the old Vaugirard hospital building ('un palais du cauchemar,' CCA, 36–7), obsolescent or as yet unformed places are elective sanctuaries. These lapsed or improvised spaces may fail to impinge on the consciousness of the preoccupied citizen; they may not yet feature on city plans or may soon cease to figure, but they are the material on which the poet and other artisans of the everyday plot their subjective cartographies. The pleasure of exploring these improbable sanctuaries derives from the act of crossing boundaries: transgressive desire connects kinetic practices of 'going across' to the urge to infringe symbolic codes, whether collective ('accès interdit au public') or individual ('[n']importe la façon dont le plan cadastral le nomme: On comprend que ce territoire est autonome,' BS,

14). This links the peripatetic poet to recyclers of urban material, those whose passion and persistence are expressed in their predilection for crossings, hybrids, mixings, and migrations, both physical and symbolic.

The disused Citroën factory is one such sanctuary in a text that mixes medieval romance mystery and the wasteland topography of postmodernist irony. The factory is a 'nef' (*RP*, 94), a metaphorical conflation of the marine and the architectural that connects the metaphysical promise of a spiritual site to the fabulous ships of Arthurian imagination; it is the sublime space the poet enters like a quester in search of an unknowable Grail. The auratic experience of the urban wanderer-turned-mariner of the metaphysical surges against complacency and indifference, generating in their place understanding or trepidation. The poet senses a metaphysical quickening in his contact with place and atmosphere (this, as we will see, resurfaces in his evocation of the effects of colour and light), but here, as in the Église Saint-Sulpice, his resonating voice is an implacable reminder of his own embodied, time-bound subjectivity:

> J'entre dans cette nef et j'appelle: ho, ho. L'écho me gratifie aussitôt en stéréophonie de la seule réponse distincte mais décevante dont me juge digne l'Inconnu: ma propre voix, tournant dans ce fatras condamné de palans et de poutrelles. Et je songe à tant d'hommes qui n'ont même pas fini là-dessous de purger quelle peine, puisqu'il faut recommencer ailleurs. Et que peut-être on devrait sauvegarder certains de ces sanctuaires, pour faire comprendre ou pour faire peur, quand on va se croyant seul à l'abri de la menace, un dimanche, sous le libre ciel.   (*RP*, 94)

In search of a 'divinité sauvage des lieux' (*RP*, 103), Réda hante the spaces that are neglected by mass tourism when it sets people down to gawp at the designated sites of Green Guide cultural approval: in the church at Hérou '[les visiteurs] viennent s'émouvoir sur les tombes' ('Aux environs,' *RP*, 103). Their vacuousness and metaphysical desolation find compensation in fetishistic overflow ('ce chaos de garde-meuble de marbre, de chérubins de faïence, de béton'), the material translation of 'des tonnes d'ennui et d'incroyance fondamentale sur l'espoir d'une résurrection' (*RP*, 103).

As a counter to sites of metaphysical flattening (the 'sinistre écrasement monothéiste' of *hauts lieux* spirituality in 'Aux environs'), the poet proposes wastelands, disused hospitals, building sites, derelict premises, and the defunct Petite Ceinture railway line whose dips and recesses offer solace and a space for self-regeneration.[25] Despite their provisional, precarious status (the building site will be superseded by the new construction whose completion it exists to advance; the disused industrial premises will be obliterated to allow development), these places possess an unbiddable quality that challenges the forces of homogenization. They offer obscurity in the double sense of being occluded from view *and* resistant to rationalist appropriation as they stimulate desire for sublimity and nourish fantasy. It is the propitious *disponibilité* of such places – their affective and poetic potential – that links the poet's exploration of the disused Citroën factory to other stages of his *périple*, such as the excursion to Gentilly, where he tries to share his sense of the extraordinary with a sceptical elderly inhabitant: 'Je lui prédis qu'un jour ces faubourgs rejoindront ceux de Marseille [...] ajoutant que si j'aime malgré tout ce ravage et cet envahissement de désordre (sa cabane, son jardin, une usine, un ruisseau, deux immeubles, une folie, une futaie, trois cents pneus), c'est à cause de ma certitude qu'une révélation s'y prépare, ou sa promesse au moins' (*RP*, 115–16).

If obsolescent materiality and marginal symbolic practices are signs of subjectivities coming into being, occupying territory and configuring space according to rules invented rather than inherited, what analogical implications do these actions and objects have for poetry-making, and how do they impact on the identity-formation of the first-person narrator? Dédé, the Tunisian shopkeepers, and the suburban *rafistoleurs* transform their disenchanted or marginalized experience of the city through their work on the material world and, in the process, they confront and assuage feelings of dislocation and alienation. Their individual acts of creativity fill space or flash across it, expanding or contracting it. Activities of *bricolage* and *rafistolage*, like the haphazard hybridity of Tunisian shopkeeping, provide models for how to inhabit space (actively and generatively) that have implications for the poet's shaping of his habitat: language.

Where the artisans of the everyday tell their stories through the language of materials (the ramshackle 'palais hun,' the makeshift body-work premises), the poet articulates his subjectivity through the material of language. Like the language of materials, the material of language is susceptible to composition and cumulation, to alteration and transformation. Material *bricolage* and hybridity have their writerly equivalent in Réda's mixing of styles and modes from realism through fantasy, anecdote and irony, to culture critique.

The texture of Réda's writing is precarious and pliant, singular and eruptive, resistant and fragile, like the materials of the artisans. The embrace of contingency and improvisation that shapes these marginal subjectivities is captured in the fluctuations of an explorer who is alternately assertive and hesitant, critical and dreaming, humorous and curious, empathetic and ironic. The sense of self as an outsider and an intruder, as a transgressor and an adventurer, playfully disregarding code and convention, like the backstreet wheeler-dealers, emerges in Réda's free-wheeling style: in the jostling and switching of tones, the lurching and looping of voices. Practices of lurking and looking ensure that the world *beyond* self is continually foregrounded; this favours the swapping of multifarious guises and identities, a practice whose analogue is stylistic pliancy. Through its myriad competing modes, this protean voice takes forward a variety of performative possibilities in the personae of ethnographer, obstreperous citizen, intruder, observer, social geographer, chronicler of the everyday, culture critic, marginalized self, and postmodern quester. As the producer and the product of competing discourses (ideological, affective, painterly, ludic, nostalgic, socio-critical, polemical), the first-person narrator resists recuperation to any fixed identity-position. Rather, the eruptions of this de-individuated self destabilize the well-rounded, properly grounded subject of humanistic assumption.

In the guise of observer-intruder-infiltrator, the poet is intent on maximizing the visibility of things usually obscure or neglected, while minimizing his visibility to others. Signs of affirmative communication with others are consequently rare and then only glancing. His outsider status is reflected not only in a state of mind (a very real one for Réda that involves going against the flow, whether of traffic, of bourgeois utilitarianism, or of cultural complacency), but also in the desire to subvert stable identity-formations. First-person subjectivity is constituted as a series of displacements and creative appropriations, analogous to the uneven surfaces of the sewer-man's hut or the pell-mell display *chez les Tunisiens*.

In the same way that materials are provisional and contingent – found objects, everyday debris – so identities are tradeable and trashable. A playful, postmodern irony attends the performance and the putting aside of roles and personae. Hubristic self-inflation provokes a collapse into bathos triggered by similes that actively undercut relationality or ressemblance, proposed or supposed. The poet identifies with a stowaway when merely going out to buy cigarettes ('By Night,' *CCA*, 15), while the underground pass of Ouest-Ceinture makes him feel like a spy or an escapee ('Au seuil de l'inconnu,' *CCA*, 49). Here, a desire for transgressive adventure is stimulated by the prospect of 'crossing over' or hovering on forbidden thresholds, but the poet repeatedly hijacks his own attempts to suffuse the banal with mystery, to spin an aura around himself. He sets about dismantling the illusion (fiction, myth) by revealing the gap (usually via the echoing hollowness of 'comme') between self and the assumed or fantasized persona:

> Certains jours et à certaines heures, on croirait en effet être le seul à [...] connaître et à [...] emprunter [le couloir souterrain], et c'est comme un évadé ou comme un agent secret qu'on y pénètre, qu'on se hâte de le parcourir. Car il est sinistre et sordide, bien dans le ton du roman qu'on joue à se raconter.   (*CCA*, 49)

The poet's intruder-identity is destabilized when the resurgent reality principle (purveyed by upholders of the rational and the linear) cuts short the performative pleasure that inheres in living out fantasies, in articulating these, sometimes out loud and in public: at the *traiteur*'s he claims that the motivation for his visit is mystical rather than gastronomic, and is 'éconduit sans autre débat,' made to leave 'à quatre pattes,' a metaphor that solicits the real (and a dose of irony) when a stray dog promptly materializes at his heels (*CCA*, 15–16). Self-deflationary humour tips over into postmodernist self-parody whose source is the poet's vision of himself as an everyday buffoon and louche lurker, in contradistinction to the heroes of modernist peripatetics, whose transgressive practices are underpinned by an unwaveringly serious intent, as in the surrealist classic *Le Paysan de Paris*. Self-debunking strives to conceal – and in the process exposes – a deeper anxiety about the identity and the possibilities of self.

Réda's writing reveals a strong sense of self constituted in language (myth, legend, history), the product of an intertextual fiction that is as much of other people's making as it is of his own. Thus, in 'Une lettre de Vaugirard' (*CCA*, 28), the poet excuses himself to a friend for not wishing to visit; if he had remained 'fidèle à [s]a légende,' he would have leapt on his Solex and crossed the city. Here he confronts and dismantles his persona as a contemporary quester, situating himself in contrast to the heroes of the *polis*, ancient or modern. Playful, parodic, and self-inventing, he continually assumes, conflates, swaps, and revises successive literary and cultural models of identity. Comic-heroic buffoonery erupts in his battle with the taxi-driver as the Solex rider proclaims 'je ne suis que le cow-boy de Saint-Ouen' (*RP*, 54–5). The clash of culture-derived heroics with the facticity of the everyday, with its limitations and its pressures, triggers conscious self-irony. At the same time, the ceaseless displacement of identities points up the lack of any stabilized position and imparts an enduring sense of ontological vacancy.

The affirmative value of an ungrounded, free-floating self depreciates when the status of marginality, so often productive, suddenly becomes inhibiting. While the activity of looking is (ideally) liberating, the experience of being looked at is invariably constraining, debilitating even, when it relays fear or contempt. Here, the poet lingers in a square where he intuits a strong initiatory power, and distractedly picks up an abandoned toy: '[J]e sens qu'on m'observe avec trop d'insistance. Il est temps de partir, non sans avoir remis en place le petit camion jaune, que je manipulais distraitement, et dont le propriétaire [...] se demandait comment faire pour le reprendre à ce grand maboul' (*RP*, 92). Fear that others will misinterpret his presence and his purpose ('rôder') curtails the quest and forces a deferral of excursive desire. In 'L'Été' (*CCA*, 66–72) anxiety over the perceptions formed by others temporarily stalls the intended itinerary of the poet's thoughts and his text, and presses him into a ludicrous role play:

> [J]e débouche devant le parc à sable où une jeune femme solitaire surveille ses deux enfants. Comme la surprise me fige moi-même dans une posture de Sioux, il est bien normal qu'elle s'alarme, lâche plusieurs mailles de son tricot. Je me retiens de filer aussitôt en sens inverse, pour ne pas aggraver son inquiétude ni justifier sa suspicion. [...] Elle ne s'apaise vraiment qu'en me voyant tirer de ma sacoche un livre qui, de loin, peut ressembler à un missel. [...] [C]'est une contenance que je me donne parce qu'on m'observe toujours. (*CCA*, 66–7)

His scope for trespassing and infringement is powerfully constrained by the gaze of others. This reins in excursive desire and writerly impulse, such that a text about exploring the city neighbourhood becomes rerouted via an account of the social pressures that block circulatory desire. In *Châteaux des courants d'air*, a nagging fear that his own open-air activity will be misconstrued as that of a potential child-abductor or an *exhibitionniste* connects with a recurring meditation on statues of male personnages that appear to be 'flashing' at passers-by; Bartók is mentioned in 'XVᵉ magique' (*CCA*, 38) and in 'L'Été' (*CCA*, 70), where the composer is joined in involuntary self-exposure by the figure of Pierre Mendès France. The censoring or mistrustful gaze of others induces debilitating self-doubt, confirming subjective experience as inescapably intersubjective and invariably anxious.

Subjectivity, then, is lived as a series of displacements, exposing an underlying ontological void that the adoption of a variety of discardable personae, far from addressing, appears to aggravate. Veering between two extremes, subjectivity is alternately overloaded with the sheer facticity of embodied existence or too light, evanescent, like a ghostly apparition caught on photographic film: 'doté [...] de juste assez de consistance pour troubler vaguement l'émulsion d'une pellicule photographique' ('Souvenirs de Cambridge,' Actes de Pau, 10). This anxiety over ontological inconsistency is integral, perhaps even necessary, to Réda's mythopoeic construction of the city.

Réda attributes a sense of self-dispossession and vacancy to his perception of the city as a void. In 'Bords du treizième,' having pondered the question of self-identity, the poet reaches a provisional conclusion: '[O]ù suis-je? que suis-je? [...] [C]es questions sans réponse naissent de la vacuité de la ville en cette saison' (AC, 70). The seamless consciousness that binds self and the city, generating creative, fantasy-making momentum, carries its own freight of anxiety and shared desolation: '[La ville] s'interroge confusément sur sa raison d'être [...] D'où son angoisse, et le retentissement qu'elle provoque chez l'être isolé dans son désert' (AC, 70).

The reciprocity of self and city responds to the desire to resist overly solipsistic recuperations while affirming subjectivity as a fluid, intersubjective process. This relates to the identity problematics explored by Michael Sheringham in Parisian Fields. Sheringham attends scrupulously to the subjective experience of the city as a mesmerizing flow of impressions and sensations, as an activating, self-reflexive process, yet his definition of self-dissolution as 'a desire to become no more than an instrument serving to reveal the city's own reality' would appear to factor out the fate of subjectivity.[26] Sheringham acknowledges Réda's bid to de-reify the self, but where he constructs this as an 'escape from self,' I see self-dissolution less as a negation or abdication than as a series of migrations and cross-fertilizations, connections and collisions between the pliant consciousness of the city explorer and the self-transforming entity that is the city.[27]

The problematics of subjectivity is complicated by Réda's intriguing discussion of impersonality. In the essay 'L'Intermittent' (reprinted in *Celle qui vient à pas légers*), Réda proposes 'l'impersonnel' as the antithesis of subjective rhythm and affective cadence. As the essay unfolds, however, he amplifies and nuances his perspective on impersonality, bringing forward a subjectively contoured, deeply embodied variant:

[L]'impersonnel n'est pas le neutre, l'insignifiant. Encore moins le résultat d'une abstraction, ce détour obligé vers sa lumière et qui ne s'effectue qu'en nous, à travers la nuit matérielle de nos organes, par l'espace mouvant des rêves et de la mémoire, par les degrés de notre histoire et des passions (les plus humbles d'abord: voir, entendre, toucher, retrouver constamment l'étonnement d'être sous la couleur du ciel toujours pour la première fois!). Tel est le paradoxe: qu'à la crête d'impersonnel qui danse et nous échappe, on n'atteindra qu'en épousant la singularité de sa propre cadence. On ne se perd qu'en s'accomplissant.[28]

Impersonality, Réda suggests, is not a negation or abdication of self, but a more pliant, more creative *process* of self-constitution: self-dissolution is predicated on poetic plenitude. Here, the values of subjectivity and *l'impersonnel*, usually proposed antithetically, coincide in the language of desire and memory, sensation and creativity, materiality and movement, colour and light. Réda explains: '[U]ne dépersonnalisation du "sujet" est nécessaire pour que sa personnalité même puisse se transformer en langage, entrer aussi loin que possible dans ce domaine qui ne lui est pas personnel, mais où il ne saurait se fonder sans être le plus possible à lui-même. Il y a en somme simultanéité entre l'accès au personnel et le passage à l'impersonnel qui, en ce sens, n'est donc pas l'anonyme.'[29] Figuring impersonality as a ridge or a high place in 'L'Intermittent,' Réda holds together, in a precious and precarious balance, notions of subjectivity and the sublime. Through the verb 'épouser' he solicits their active reciprocity, their capacity for mutual altering in the luminous, expansive quickening of perception. Réda appears, then, not to abdicate subjectivity, but to propose its inextricable oneness with the material and the bodily, in poetry. Strikingly evoked in the passage above is a plea for attentiveness to the affective rhythms of colour and light. Réda celebrates perceptual acuity and the quickened contact between self and world that surges in language.

In Réda's colour-work, subjectively contoured impersonality and materiality are transposed in the coruscating play of prismatic light.

'Me voici du côté de la véritable lumière': Colour and the Material Sublime[30]

Réda lists, among his favourite painters, the great colourists Gauguin, Matisse, Bonnard, Poussin, and the medieval miniaturists.[31] To read Réda is to immerse oneself in the rich, undulating texture of colour description; it is to participate in the intense and pleasurable work of bringing colour to language. Working across the imprecise divide between the perceptual and conceptual implications of colour, Réda reveals a line of connection that reaches directly back to Baudelaire as he sounds the rich, synaesthetic depths of colour experience, and reflects on the unceasing struggle of poetic language to represent that experience. Réda extends the synaesthetic dimension through his rapt attention to colour as material sensation, endlessly modulating and altering. In his evocation of the variable texturing of colour, Réda's writing presents analogies with the work of modern colour theorists in their search for verbal equivalents of visual and haptic experience.[32] I stress 'analogies' (nothing more) because Réda is unequivocal when he states, '[J]e n'ai aucune "philosophie" de la couleur.'[33] In the translation of chromatic instances through the metaphorics of materiality, Réda's colour-work reveals its subjective contour.

The intense, painterly quality of Réda's writing has, to date, received minimal critical attention. The neglect of the intense chromatic quality of the poet's work is paradoxical, for, as Michael Sheringham points out, 'les allusions aux couleurs sont très abondantes dans tous les états de son écriture.'[34] Réda's work reveals a passionate, painstaking struggle to find verbal equivalents of mesmerizing visual sensations. What I shall be calling Réda's colour practice – his exquisite evocations of colour and light, and his active problematization of colour-in-poetry – forms a seam in his writing that is perhaps most vivid and intense in *Les Ruines de Paris* and *La Course*, but is continuous across his poetry and prose-writing. In his colour practice, he eschews pure, Fauve-style abstraction in favour of the deep, almost palpable texturing of colour and light sensation: 'Je ne veux que [...] cette bonne lumière crayeuse où s'incruste le moindre détail' (*RP*, 93); 'la lumière s'est épaissie comme la chair d'une reine-claude' (*CCA*, 58). Descriptions of immaterial light 'thicken' with suggestions of violence and beauty, asperity and sensuousness, quickness and stasis. Colour reverberates with the rhythms of human and industrial activity, and meteorological fluctuation. This brings forth a complex, even paradoxical beauty:

D'une vivacité de forge luttant contre un vent d'asphyxie, rouge est cette lueur qui dure au-dessus du Luxembourg. Mais rouge signifie mal, il faudrait dire *rapide*, bien qu'elle semble en même temps pour toujours immobile – et justement: rien ne peut mieux convenir qu'une notion de suspens vertigineux inclus par la vitesse, engendrant le cramoisi foncé et qui fonce de cette lueur. (*RP*, 30)

Réda engages actively, speculatively with colour as lived experience, exploring its effect on himself and on others. His urgent concern with subjective perspective in colour composition, and its deep relatedness to questions of language and communication, is everywhere patent and sometimes explicitly formulated. What appears like an everyday poetic struggle ('chercher les mots pour le dire') becomes, in this context, a stimulating and predictably frustrated search for visual-verbal correspondence when the poet recognizes that the word for the tonal subtlety of a particular green escapes him and that the everyday lexical palette lacks the necessary discrimination: 'vert appelé vert faute de mot pour la nuance' (*RP*, 104). Passing or pleasurably prolonged reflections on the difficulties that language poses for the verbal colourist point up the conscious painterliness of Réda's writing. In 'Bleuâtre? Jaunâtre?' (*CiT*, 161–6), the process of *representing* colour perception, as much as the material sensation itself, is subject to equivocation. That writerly process begins analogically, proceeds by contrastive contiguity, and concludes with simultanist abstraction:

Bleuâtre? Jaunâtre? Difficile de décider. C'est une velléité de couleur qui n'est pas sûre d'elle-même, et va rester dans cette hésitation. Un peu malade. On rencontre des gens de cette teinte impossible dans les couloirs des hôpitaux. Elle a décomposé le noir d'une encre garantie indélébile, et précisément à l'endroit où j'avais figuré d'un rond la tête d'une jeune fille assise par terre [...] Une goutte [de pluie] a éclaté en plein au milieu du cercle, et à ce moment, la jeune fille avait relevé la tête, toute rose entre un bonnet de laine vert et le jaune vif de son anorak. [...] Je ne garderai d'elle qu'une grosse tache à la fois bleu et ocre, et le souvenir d'un coup d'oeil glacial. (*CiT*, 161–2)

In *Retour au calme*, a momentary hesitation produces a descriptive tremble as words compete in the rush to expressivity, triggering a Ponge-like revision: 'Un sentier couleur d'os ou d'orange' (59). The generative paradox at the centre of Réda's poetics – the extraordinariness of the ordinary – is reaffirmed in his colour practice, where the very impossibility of achieving verbal correspondence ceaselessly renews the longing to bring impalpable colour experience to language. The embrace of that paradox and its generation of repeated verbal *steps* to colour expressivity launches 'Le Pied furtif de l'hérétique,' the startlingly beautiful opening poem of *Les Ruines de Paris*. This text inaugurates a poetics of creative unevenness, as the poet stumbles towards chromatic revelation and achieves a description of sublime, colour-saturated affectivity:

> Vers six heures, l'hiver, volontiers je descends l'avenue à gauche, par les jardins, et je me cogne à des chaises, à des petits buissons, parce qu'un ciel incompréhensible comme l'amour qui s'approche aspire tous mes yeux. Sa couleur à peu près éteinte n'est pas définissable: un turquoise très sombre, peut-être, l'intense condensation d'une lumière qui échappe au visible et devient le brûlant-glacé de l'âme qu'elle envahit.   (*RP*, 9)

The urgency of bringing visual desire to language through colour expressivity forms a constant in Réda's work, generating speculation on the relativity of viewing. The poet reflects on how others see things, and wonders how the same blue sky would appear to the 'yeux analphabètes' of the poor (*RP*, 101). A preoccupation with the interrelation of colour expression and the cultural experience of the viewer extends Réda's dual engagement with the sublime and the everyday, the beautiful and the banal, sensation and subjectivity. In 'Rose framboise ardent' (*RP*), the desire to bring to language the complex, world-altering experience of colour perception emerges in a series of corrections, refinements, nuances, modulations, and analogies. In Sheringham's words, 'le langage tente une saisie, toute performative, d'une expérience':[35]

> Rose framboise ardent mais d'un rose de sorbet — de sorbet tombé de son cornet et qui roule dans la poussière — le soleil est en proie à une dilatation qui ferait peur, s'il n'y avait en plus cette couleur de fond de jour de fête, et bientôt de soie ancienne qui s'effrite au lieu de craquer. L'indifférence des passants est totale, je ne comprends pas.   (*RP*, 24)

Réda expresses incomprehension towards those who neglect colour and light and the stunning materialization of the sublime in the everyday. Colour expresses sublimity shaped by human affect, never abstract, always relative; it corresponds to a surge of desire, to the visualization of yearning. The eruption of mesmeric colour captures a moment of enhanced being, where the quickening of consciousness is matched by the slowing of kinetic action: this maps to synecdoche as poetic space becomes saturated with luminous description. Such instants figure the fracturing of the time continuum, when human activity is stilled, and visual and affective freedom is ripped from quotidian constraint. The evocation of the provincial landscape reveals the sublime as an event of visual making, a chromatic allegory of the desirability of libidinal and poetic possession:

> Bien avant Bar-le-Duc, il fait nuit deviendra le seul terme approprié à cette glace d'un bleu épais qui prend pour se fendre en étoiles sur les coteaux. [...] Entre-temps des buées d'or rose ont monté des chaumes et des maïs, restituant le nectar de la couleur comme on sent le chaud de l'été s'évaporer des pierres. Un petit groupe de toits de tuiles et les murs aussitôt ensuite d'une usine de briques accomplissaient l'amour. Non la fornication aveugle qui pompe vers un orgasme, mais le suspens incandescent où lévitent pour une seconde et sans terme ensemble deux corps. L'amour n'a pas de nom, pas de borne; il s'infuse.   (*RP*, 144)

The rarefying of experience is borne forth in an epiphanic moment of visual and atmospheric intensity: libidinal energy, dissolving through the play of translucent and saturated colour textures, is finally decanted into sensuous sublimity. In 'La Course' (*LC*, 54–5) the poet's gaze is suddenly arrested by the coincidence of colour and form:

> Et, tout à coup,
> du haut de la rue Pasteur m'apparaît une colline
> de ce bleu de Prusse très foncé des bois par temps pluvieux,
> mais elle porte au sommet l'émeraude, qui s'illumine,
> d'une prairie suspendue à même le gris des cieux.

The perception of colour contiguities (blue, emerald, grey) prompts self-questioning. Is the poet's haphazard wandering, disorientation even, the serendipitous means to a discovery wholly external to himself, or is his 'égarement' (the purest instance of physical and mental *disponibilité*) the precise source of his illumination? The question is tantalizingly unresolvable:

Etait-ce pour la trouver qu'il fallait que je m'égare,
ou bien a-t-elle surgi du fond de mon égarement?
Elle plane.

Réda's colour-work and its affective saturation have implications for his pursuit of impersonality. As Réda affirms in *Celle qui vient à pas légers*, in his affective contouring of *l'impersonnel* the dissolution of subjectivity (in the rhythms of colour and light) assuages anxiety and betokens the longed-for absorption of the weight of existence into luminous imponderability. Emerging from the metro onto a deserted esplanade, the poet envisions a release from the deadening burden of pessimism and self-doubt: 'Seul le drame lumineux du soir s'y déroule à travers des nuées, comme la métamorphose en mouvement d'une rumeur délivrée des sons, la sublimation en or vivant du plomb de l'âme et de la matière' (*LR*, 34). It is as if the freight of selfhood has been miraculously discharged and existential inertia transmuted in desire-quickening pools of vivid gold. Colour practice responds luminously to the urge to contour a space of bliss. Self-dissolution through colour and light affectivity, then, is not equivalent to self-abolition in Réda's poetry; rather it is synonymous with the subjective permeation of indefinable moments when the weight of the material and the quotidian suddenly falls away; it is here, in the intense interplay of saturated colour and liquid light, that pleasure takes form.

Visual lushness and exquisite longing come together in the earth tones of 'Éloge de la brique' (*La Course*): 'Quant à moi, je m'y gorgerais du vin de la couleur / Et dénombrerais cette masse énorme, brique à brique / Pour endormir la dent creuse de ma douleur' (*LC*, 37). Here dissolved subjectivity re-forms in the evocation of material density and volume. Réda's colour-work intimates a rich sensuousness, where light is figured as shimmering vibrancy and saturated materiality as in 'Vers l'automne': 'le poids lumineux d'un soir de septembre ardent comme l'érable et croulant du raisin' (*CCA*, 53).

Colour and light sensations correspond to moments of visual freedom, expressions of desire momentarily captured, fleetingly eroticized. In 'Un jardin' (*CCA*, 80) Réda tends colour with painterly preciseness, patiently constructing his palette of colour adjectives: 'bouquets d'épaules roses, brunes, ocre, ébène.' Flesh and flowers mingle in Réda's landscape of desire, the coincidence of the material and the subjective producing a tantalizing tremor in his writing. Again, impersonality bears a deep subjective charge through colour that flows over the boundary between the human and the horticultural.

The poet alternates the dense sensuousness and ecstatic lushness of his colourist treatment with more fractured forms. Descriptions of brittleness and fragmentation impart a material edge to the Rédean sublime: an alley is described as 'escarpé comme un couteau noir qui s'ébrèche' (RP, 99); elsewhere, 'un nuage / S'était déchiré dans le ciel' (LC, 53). Fractured colour, lacerated light, and jagged surfaces capture the arresting, consciousness-shifting potential of the subjective encounter with the material world. Réda's syncopated chromatism is the visual correlative of his beloved jazz cadences. Vivid and eruptive, such instances bear the bodily imprint of rhythm: in 'Le Pied furtif de l'hérétique,' the image of 'claudication de cristal' transposes the perception of uneven beauty into the translucent tremor unsettling the night sky (RP, 12). The colour and configuration of the night sky intimate a silently expressive human drama where alertness to hue and gradation bears the imprint of the body's fragilization:

> Ce que je veux, c'est ne pas résister à la volonté de la lune, et rester le plus longtemps possible en arrêt plus loin comme une bête au milieu du pont. Car une déchirure vers le nord s'est produite dans la lie, élargissant un golfe glacial où deux étoiles émettent en télégraphe optique leurs brefs signaux. Je regarde ces rivages qui s'en vont en charpie et fument horizontalement devant l'astre. Bleue et bistre il y a deux meurtrissures en forme d'anneaux tout autour. Elles phosphorent sur les nuages. Un chien préoccupé qui passe m'évite comme si j'étais un loup. Et je pourrais hurler à mon aise, étant là seul au monde.   (RP, 13)

Beauty is contused – 'les tons du ciel virent à l'eccymose' (RP, 38) – in a characteristically modernist treatment that imprints the sublime with the traces of fractured subjectivity. It is here in colour expressivity that the two extremes of Réda's poetic project – rummaging in the real, envisioning the sublime – coincide.

From its immersion in the everyday, Réda's poetry seems to pull away, drawn to rarefied instances captured in mesmeric colour. Yet, Réda's sublime expresses, not a yearning for the absolute, for empty transcendence, but rather the transposition of the everyday with its freight of weariness and longing. The Rédean sublime is not a denial of the real and the affective; it is, in the words of Jean Pierrot, the luminous trace of Réda's 'capacité à *soulever* la vie quotidienne vers autre chose' (my emphasis).[36] This intense colour expressivity breaks through in 'Un drame au Luxembourg' (*LC*, 14), where a young woman looks up at the sky, and form and colour coincide in the liquid light of unutterable longing:

> [La mère] regarde le ciel,
> Qui détient encore en liquide un riche potentiel,
> Ouvrir dans sa grisaille une petite crique
> De bleu phosphorescent.

While there is a kind of structuring reversibility in Réda's poetry (now delving deep, now lifting high), a deeper continuousness forms in the urge to exteriorize affect in colour-work. It is this desire always to turn outwards, whether in quick, vivid contact with the material and the everyday or in the yearning for a horizon beyond the world's palpable surfaces, that defines Réda's writing. This outwardness draws together the diverse strands of Réda's poetry: excursive pliancy and the corporeal adventures of the urban rummager; the everyday practices that are sites of human desire and resistance; the affective freight of colour and light that presents an analogue to those more palpable forms – material space and physical objects – that the poet invests with resistance and desire, creativity and cussedness.

Summations, Speculations

In this study I have put to work on the writing of four modern French poets reading practices more often reserved for studies of narrative fiction. My approach was spurred by a perceived reciprocity. Critical practices formed in such distinct, but increasingly overlapping disciplines as visual theory, gender studies, art history, and cultural history have much to offer modern poetry generally, and in particular such permeable, pliant writers as Rimbaud, Apollinaire, Ponge, and Réda. In return, modern poetry, in its reflexivity, its fracturing momentum, and its conscious experimentalism, reaches out to theory, exploring in playful and self-ironising ways theory's preoccupations, even striving at times to theorize itself.

Through my readings of their texts, I have tried to reflect the receptivity and the capaciousness of Rimbaud, Apollinaire, Ponge, and Réda. As this book has developed, I have moved further towards reading poetry as if it were a cultural history or an ethnographical text, viewing it as a material event, appraising it as if it were physical object, scrutinizing it as one might a painting or a sculpture. Such acts of generic disobedience seemed legitimate, desirable even, to bring about productive engagements with writing that works ceaselessly between poetry and politics, art, work, history, social life, cultural practices, and visuality. Boundary-moving poets invite risk-embracing readers.

The writing of a book, particularly one that covers several time-separated authors, involves substantial ground-shifting and many smaller actions of sifting and synthesizing. It seemed a bold yet necessary step to align Réda with such canonical figures as Rimbaud, Apollinaire, and Ponge. Réda's writing articulates the synergy and the symmetry between the uneven complexity of (sub)urban culture and the fluctuating fate of the modern or postmodern self at once detached and deeply affective, impersonal and intractably embodied. The breadth of Réda's vision, his textual enfolding of the material and the sublime, his coruscating treatment of colour and light, his fresh, invigorated language, his tonal suppleness, his lyric generosity, and the piercing precision of his writing determine that reading – and rereading – Réda is as pleasurably intense as it is urgent. His indisputable importance in the development of modern and contemporary French poetry makes Réda's inclusion in the canon – and consequently in this study – timely.

My objective, at the outset, was to give the representation of the body, at the centre of so much recent critical thinking (in gender studies, psychoanalysis, cultural theory, art-historical criticism), its proper place in modern French poetry studies. To a greater degree than I anticipated, the body – and by extension, embodied consciousness – has provided the connective tissue between my readings of the four poets. The body is inextricable from our sense of self and of other, and our corporeal awareness is crucial to our understanding of what it is to inhabit modernity, to live with(in) it and to live against it, sentiently self-present and cutaneously alert to our own interpenetrating positions, as subjects creating from within and as objects apprehended and appraised from without. The narrative of the body is integral to the autobiographical project that surfaces in all the poets explored here, whether in the exasperated physicality of Rimbaud's traveller through hell, in the sensuous dream-work of the soldier-poet, in the voluptuous visual and haptic fabric unfolded analogically by Ponge, or in the kinetic and poetic pliancy of Réda. There emerges in the work of each writer a keen sense of the body forming the interface between self and the world, turning a series of subtle or overwhelming engagements with the material and the real into intricate narratives of pleasure and of pressure. The body trope, obsessively scrutinized in studies of the novel, proves a no less privileged site of representation and resistance in modern poetry. An acute sense of the body *in* language and *as* language produces a remarkable parallel between poetic expressivity and the powerful corporeal articulacy of contemporary culture, both in conceptual or performance art and in its anthropological or popular forms. A shared sense of the boundless representational potential of the flesh and of the urgency of making it speak connects the subversive image-work of Robert Mapplethorpe and Cindy Sherman to the epidermal experimentation of quotidian artists of the tattooed and pierced body.

Subjectivity is a process *subject to* and straining against social pressures and cultural constraints. Expressed in sustained or discontinuous ways in the writing of all four poets is the need to reflect critically and to act performatively on the structures (social, economic, affective, aesthetic) that contain us and that materialize in our discursive drift. Each writer engages (explosively in the case of Rimbaud and Ponge) with modernity's constraining abstractions and its reifications; each exposes and subverts the ideologies in which we live and which live in us. Through radical approaches to syntax and metaphor, structure and lexicon they work to dismantle the stale habitat of quotidian discourse, and by making innovative new constructions in language, urge us to rethink our modern condition, to view it not as natural, but as alterable and transformable, like language itself. Rimbaud's prescient vision of the obscure, obscurantist world of modern bureaucracies betokens a twentieth-century literature of alienation whose most ample and devastating expression has been, unarguably, the novel. Ponge's nightmarish critique of mass production in the 1920s segues into the industrial dystopia of Céline's *Voyage au bout de la nuit*, while his atrophied workers prefigure Queneau's automata. The hallucinatory visions of Rimbaud and Ponge span a long twentieth century, reaching down as far as the terrifying accretions of body and industrial machine visualized by the contemporary American photographer Lee Friedlander. The poetry of Rimbaud, Apollinaire, and Ponge is the product of particular historical pressure points. The shockwaves of the Franco-Prussian war shudder through Rimbaud's writing as the young poet dissects the pullulating cadaver of France's Second Empire. The brimming, brilliant compositions of Apollinaire's *Ondes* series constructs a multi-layered representation of the Belle Époque city, captivating in its everyday magic, inspiriting in its epic potential. Apollinaire's vision, alternately expansive and intimist, communicates the thrill of the pre-1914 metropolis and probes its human poignancy as the aura of material modernity disperses in zones of disenchantment. In the poet's experimental series, cubism's impersonal structures, newly freighted with affect, chart the oscillations of a modern consciousness alternately quickened by a sense of boundless possibility and shattered by equivocation and a deep yearning for the irrecoverable past. Writing directly from the Western Front, the poet-turned-soldier tells his story, history made personal, through the fractured and fantasized structures of an autobiographical text. The war poetry of *Calligrammes* bears private witness to world-shaping events through the tonal modulations of a soldier-self who is at once warrior, comrade, lover, memorialist, patriot, dreamer, and poet.

With a metaphorical range that probes terror and rapture, the joy of belonging and the rawness of longing, the soldier-poet explores his desire to write, to love, to feel, to remember, to make and re-create, and to reaffirm human passion and plenitude amid the waste of war. It is, paradoxically, under the most pressured conditions that poetry finds an extraordinary suppleness of voice and vision, as if to work with the moving, beautiful shards of language was a first step to repairing the fractured world.

Ponge the resister is the poet who silences the war in order to voice the urgency of healing the broken self through scrupulous attention to things and the rich verbal articulations they inspire. Acts of perceptual generosity are poetically and existentially generative in reinvigorating things-in-language and assisting us to view the world afresh. Réda explores the often superseded spaces of contemporary subjectivity. He is a witness to a less convulsive, more diffuse time and the critical observer of a culture seemingly in thrall to the effects of its own stream-lining and homogenization. In an age strangely empty of history (post-industrial, postmodern), Réda is alert to the proliferating micro-histories of the *quartier*, the suburban neighbourhood, the street, the industrial wilderness, the railway embankment, the alleyway. He tends, in language that is vivid and precise, the detail of ordinary lives, cultural practices, commodities, the self-altering city, social ritual, the natural world, the built environment, the circulatory adventure of the body. Réda roams the post-industrial *terre gaste* and lingers in suburban spaces, capturing creativity in the margins inhabited by allotment holders and unlicensed traders, *bricoleurs* and tag-artists. The hands-on work of those who salvage and recycle finds its analogue in Réda, who carefully reworks tropes of materiality to reveal the eloquent poignancy of the familiar and the forgotten. The rapt gaze turned by the city explorer upon the unspectacular and unmemorable, mess and the mundane, reveals the material as integral to the desires, memories, and practices that surge against the new economic, spatial, and cultural contingencies. Réda feels an affinity with those who oppose the doxa of material modernity, and who sign their resistance to flat-lining and main-streaming. In his attention to their alternative practices, Réda takes forward Apollinaire's concern to register the creativity of everyday life and the search for magic exemplified by his fortune tellers and street performers. Where ethnographical, sociological, and new historical approaches have nourished studies of the nineteenth-century novel, fertile cross-readings of cultural history and the poetry of the everyday can also be reciprocally enriching, as my partial comparative approach to Réda and Certeau suggests. At the same time, Réda is much more than a material poet. As his writing draws us down into the real and the particular, so that movement is suddenly reversed and our attention is lifted towards those immaterial spaces that seem to absorb descriptions of the metaphysical and the sublime. Yet Réda's sublime is never remote or fathomless, but always informed by unnameable desire that intense evocations of colour and texture render almost palpable.

Striking across the writing explored here is the poets' preoccupation with how we make things, and more crucially how they make us, and the ways in which that relation may brought to language. The traces we make as we move through the world and the power of poetry to capture those traces is a phenomenon to which Jacques Réda, rummaging in the debris of the building site, and Guillaume Apollinaire, deep in his domesticated dugout, are extraordinarily alert. In its concern to gather into language things that are discarded and de-fetishized, modern poetry seems to share contemporary art's desire to reclaim and relish ordinary objects, and to extend their life through texts or visual images. Modern poetry shares contemporary art's concern for the inchoate and the unperfected, and suddenly connections seem viable between, for example, Réda (the other poets could make equal claim) and the debris art exemplified, at its extreme, by the scandalously dishevelled bed of Tracy Emin or the visceral materiality of Louise Bourgeois's installations. Imbricated in narratives of resistance and regeneration, the representation of the everyday generates tropes of mess and dross, revelling textually in matter that refuses to be ordered or absorbed.

In modernism, the metaphorics of debris marks the productive coincidence of trope and structure: modernism is synonymous with a culture of hybridity, anti-linearity, synchronicity, overflow, fragmentation, and indeterminacy. Modernism's structural spillage produces a single, powerful line of descent connecting Rimbaud, through the compositional fractures of Apollinaire, via cubism and abstract expressionism, to the junk-based combines of Robert Rauschenberg. We see repeatedly in modern poetry, as in other media, the tendency for the language of materiality to roll into the materiality of language. Thus, Rimbaud's writing reveals an acute sense of language constantly emptying and refilling, producing its debris of words. *Une Saison en enfer* theorizes its own production as much as it betokens a Beckettian world of desolation and aridity where the constructions of language disintegrate into stones and dust. Rimbaud draws our attention to language reduced to the preverbal energy that anticipates the jagged rhythms of Stravinsky ('Faim, soif, cris, danse, danse danse, danse!'). If Rimbaud touches the extreme point at which the harsher momentum of modern poetry runs out, he also begins in crucial ways to map the challenging territory beyond, the space that will be claimed by Joyce, by postmodern narrative, by conceptual art, or by the experimentalism of the contemporary French playwright Valère Novarina. In poetry, the energy generated by Rimbaud's language in the raw flows into Apollinaire's noisist performance ('La Victoire'), and galvanizes the disrupted syntax of Ponge as he works to register the eruptive quality of things in disarticulations of grammar, verbally contouring the series of adjustments demanded as hand or eye struggles to hold an object in its multifarious complexity.

Visuality has remained too long the predictable preserve of the art historian. If narrative studies are beginning to benefit from visual readings (we think of Mieke Bal's remarkable study of Proust and Jean Duffy's important work on art in the novels of Claude Simon), poetry studies have much to gain from scrupulous attention to the visual modes of text.[1] Forty years before the shock of 'Les Demoiselles d'Avignon,' Rimbaud's shattering and rebuilding of perspective in the *Illuminations* boldly predicted cubism's multiple viewpoint, while the disturbing beauty of the poet's figurative work opened the way to the unfathomable visual mysteries of surrealism. Colour practice (particularly in Rimbaud and Réda) spans the beginning and the end of this study. Réda's elliptical meditation on the difficulty of turning colour sensation into words takes forward a project that originates with Rimbaud's exploratory 'Voyelles': the ravishing colour practice of poets separated by over a century asks urgently, 'How does colour mean?' and 'How can visual sensation be articulated?' In an age visually saturated (sated?) with multimedia images, Rimbaud's visionary project continues to baffle and beguile. Colour is no more pure or empty in Réda, where it reverberates with desire or disconsolation, where the mineral, fractured quality of colour is charged with sometimes violent, sometimes voluptuous intensity. Eschewing colour theory, Réda speaks simply and eloquently of his appreciation of 'les mille nuances du bleu,'[2] but a deep concern for prismatic distinctness and discernment informs fleeting reflections on the difficult pleasure of bringing colour to language. For all its fragmentation and ellipsis, the colour-work of Réda is mesmeric and reveals unexpected affinities with the auratic meditations of Rothko or the deep immersions of Yves Klein, the sublime practitioner of blue. Discipline-defining essayists of the modern in art, Apollinaire and Ponge may be primarily concerned with questions of structure and texture in a world of cubist and abstract configuration, but both seek to capture the rugged luminosity of the object, its arresting immediacy. Apollinaire strives to synthesize the polychromatic abstraction of Delaunay's painting, while Ponge charts his writerly struggle to hold in language the opalescent oyster ('brillament blanchâtre'). It is Ponge's superb gifts of slow looking and rich verbal texturing that take forward, for poetry, the work of the still-life painter or the sculptor as he struggles to capture the compelling, complex unevenness of things. The singular power of the poet is to make us relive, in language, perceptual experiences of brilliance and hardness, depth and liquidity, in their uncompromising particularity. And when the analogical momentum prompts a sudden tilting of the object's description towards a sublime and unexpected vastness, this produces an effect comparable to the painter's abstraction. There emerges an unbroken if uneven line reaching all the way from Rimbaud, via Apollinaire, to Ponge and Réda: its source is their rapt attention to the chaos of lines, the intractability of surfaces, the movement of colour, the astonishing density of things. The power of poetry is to articulate the thickened, deeply seamed world that suddenly opens up to the alert gaze, the acute act of listening, or the slowed touch. The subtle texturing of the poetic wor(l)d renders the unceasing shifts of a consciousness alive to the infinite variability of the material world.

To this infinite variability of things and the pliant consciousness it forms in us, modern poetry responds with its own variable pacing. Poetry rushes along in the stream of its own broken structures (Rimbaud) or takes infinite pleasure in the amplitude of *adéquation* (Ponge). Poetry's two tempos coincide in its capacity to shift our consciousness into another gear, now quickening in a bid to capture the rapidity of visionary activity, now slowing, exquisitely, unbearably almost, to guide us in the ways of richer appraisal. Ponge's model for writing is also a model for reading up close, for attending to and taking pleasure in verbal detail, imperatives that we must balance with our desire to embrace poetry's greater ambition. This is the lesson proffered by Ponge and retraced by Jean-Daniel Pollet in *Dieu sait quoi* (1993), his film homage to Ponge.[3]

The narrative of the body, culture critique, the appraisal of the material object, and visuality have provided the substance of an integrated reading of four complementary, but utterly distinctive, voices in modern French poetry. In an age informed by critical theory, but no longer constrained by it, the demands of sophistication and accessibility need to be balanced. In exploring materiality and subjectivity, I have sought to impart a sense of the experiential and 'lived' quality of modern French poetry. With the desire to communicate something of the startling beauty and the raw urgency of writing, too often judged exasperatingly abstract and remote from our quotidian concerns, comes the hope that new readers may sense the quickened pulse that runs through modern poetry, and be encouraged to nourish their own readings, tending texts with patience and with passion. With that thought uppermost, I leave the last word to Jacques Réda:

> [L]'histoire commence par une jeune femme avec un arrosoir. Et tandis qu'elle humecte ses fleurs, on distingue derrière elle un pan de cuisine laqué, ou l'angle adouci d'une chambre, l'amorce d'une vie et puis de mille vies à partir de là qui s'enchevêtrent en réseaux infinis de bifurcations, d'interconnexions, de circuits d'émotions et de pensées, irradiant toute la ville vibrante sous son poids d'eau. ('Je rapporte...,' *Les Ruines de Paris*)

Notes

Introduction

1 A substantial number of single-author studies have been devoted to Rimbaud, Apollinaire, and Ponge. However, in respect of Rimbaud and Apollinaire, much of the critical commentary remains of a traditional nature: a rare exception is Timothy Mathews's deconstructionist *Reading Apollinaire* (Manchester: Manchester University Press, 1987). A re-evaluation of these poets through contemporary theoretical approaches is now overdue.

2 To date, two collective volumes (both in French) have appeared: *Approches de Jacques Réda: Actes du Colloque de l'Université de Pau*, ed. Christine Van Rogger Andreucci (Pau: Publications de l'Université de Pau, 1994); and *Lire Réda*, ed. Hervé Micolet (Lyon: Presses Universitaires de Lyon, 1994).

3 Nathaniel Wing, *The Limits of Narrative: Essays on Baudelaire, Flaubert, Rimbaud and Mallarmé* (Cambridge: Cambridge University Press, 1986) and Hans-Jost Frey, *Studies in Poetic Discourse* (Stanford: Stanford University Press, 1996), for example, retain an exclusively nineteenth-century focus on modernity, with chapters on Baudelaire, Rimbaud, and Mallarmé.

Chapter 1

1 Rimbaud's obsessively interpreted formulation derives from his letters of 13 and 15 May 1871 to Georges Izambard and Paul Demeny, respectively. See *Oeuvres complètes* (henceforth *OC*), ed. Antoine Adam (Paris: Gallimard, 'Pléiade,' 1972), 249, 250. Graham Robb, *Rimbaud* (New York and London: Norton, 2001), 83–4, summarizes some of the multifarious readings, while glossing Rimbaud's formula as an attempt to define a space for the id in

retreat from a superego synonymous with parental (maternal) authority. Kristin Ross, *The Emergence of Social Space: Rimbaud and the Paris Commune* (Minneapolis: University of Minnesota Press, 1988), 110, 113, interprets Rimbaud's device in terms of a heightened consciousness of the body as radically other, and the dispersion of individual subjectivity in collective formations.

2 In critical engagements with subjectivity in Rimbaud, two broad tendencies prevail: the post-structuralist and socio-cultural (Bersani, Murphy, Ross, Wing), and the humanistic and thematic (Bonnefoy and Ahearn). Nathaniel Wing, *The Limits of Narrative*, focuses on *Une Saison en enfer* as a modernist autobiographical narrative that foregrounds the constitution of subjectivity in language. Leo Bersani's 'Rimbaud's Simplicity,' in *A Future for Astyanax: Character and Desire in Literature* (New York: Columbia University Press, 1984), 230–58, is a brilliant deconstructive reading of the *Illuminations*. Steve Murphy, *Le Premier Rimbaud: Ou l'apprentissage de la subversion* (Lyon, Paris: Presses Universitaires de Lyon / CNRS, 1991), offers a closely argued study of the dismantling of normative cultural, social, and linguistic structures in selected early poems. Kristin Ross, *The Emergence of Social Space*, takes a broader approach to the nexus of poetry and politics across Rimbaud's writing. In *Rimbaud: Visions and Habitations* (Berkeley and Los Angeles: University of California Press, 1983), Edward J. Ahearn retrieves 'theme' from the post-structuralist trash can in the name of a profoundly human project in Rimbaud. Via a comparative reading that includes Wordsworth (primarily), Blake, and Nietzsche, Ahearn detects in – or constructs for – Rimbaud a Romantic and post-Romantic identity. Bridging the thematic and post-structuralist approaches, James Lawler's *Rimbaud's Theatre of the Self* (Cambridge, Mass., and London: Harvard University Press, 1992) stresses the performative and self-constitutive process of identity-formation in the visionary poetry. Through a series of persuasive close readings, Lawler probes intertextual connections with Baudelaire and Mallarmé. He sets out to correlate *Une Saison en enfer* and the *Illuminations* in terms of the action of self-constitution viewed as a 'project of self-dramatization' (p. 5). Eschewing the alienation thesis (and its tropes of fracturing and self-dispersal), Lawler argues for an 'existential project in Rimbaud' (81). André Guyaux, *Poétique du fragment: Essai sur les* Illuminations *de Rimbaud* (Neuchâtel: La Baconnière, 1985), proposes a comprehensive archaeology of the prose poems that explores chronology, manuscript variants, and textual analysis. Guyaux, *Duplicités de Rimbaud* (Paris and Geneva: Champion-Slatkine, 1991), offers a series of readings of the prose poetry, ranging across questions of reception, sources, formal features, and genealogy. John Porter

Houston, *The Design of Rimbaud's Poetry* (New Haven and London: Yale University Press, 1963), remains a valuable contribution to scholarship, combining literary history and close textual analysis, while Houston's ambitious study *Patterns of Thought in Rimbaud and Mallarmé* (Lexington: French Forum, 1986) maps the philosophical and aesthetic concerns of the two major poets of modernism, paying due attention to their nineteenth-century intellectual inheritance.

3 Karin J. Dillman, *The Subject in Rimbaud: From Self to 'Je'* (New York, Bern, Frankfurt am Main: Peter Lang, 1984), offers a linguistic study of the evolving first-person subject, and uses the celebrated formulae 'On me pense' and 'Je est un autre' as the theoretical basis for understanding the decentred subject of 'Le Coeur supplicié' and the '"je" in process' of the prose poem 'Aube.'

4 *OEC* (Adam), 250.

5 Ibid., 248.

6 The critical fire that once raged around the presumed chronology of *Une Saison en enfer* and of the *Illuminations* now merely smoulders. Rejecting the oversimplified diachronic model, the critical consensus focuses on two probabilities: that the writing of (some of) the *Illuminations* overlaps with the composition of *Une Saison en enfer* (dated by Rimbaud April–August 1873), and that *Une Saison en enfer* was not Rimbaud's farewell to poetry or was only one of a series of farewells (hence many of the *Illuminations* would postdate *Une Saison*). André Guyaux sums up the polemic pithily: '[L]es *Illuminations* [...] dateraient d'avant ou d'après *Une Saison en enfer* (la question est: avant ou après?; la réponse avant et après),' 'Généalogies du poème en prose de Rimbaud,' in *Duplicités de Rimbaud*, 47. See Robb, 239–40, for a summary of the chronological conundrum.

7 Lawler, 15.

8 Yves Bonnefoy, *Rimbaud* (Paris: Seuil, 1961), 58.

9 The quotations are taken, respectively, from 'Le Mal,' 'Accroupissements,' 'Le Buffet,' and 'Les Chercheuses de poux.'

10 Bersani, 243.

11 See Steve Murphy's closely argued reading of 'Le Forgeron' in *Rimbaud et la ménagerie impériale* (Paris, Lyon: CNRS / Presses Universitaires de Lyon, 1991), chap. 15, 'Fictions révolutionnaires: "Le Forgeron,"' 209–30.

12 See Kristin Ross on Rimbaud's 'swarm poesis' ('The Swarm,' 113, in *The Emergence of Social Space*, 100–22), and her study of the generative forces of intoxication, infestation, and hypersensitivity, all signs of working-class insurgency against bourgeois social and political structures.

13 Robb, 59–61.

14 Robb, 426.
15 There is a similar migration from alimentary pleasure to erotic awakening in 'La Maline,' where the fruit-laden scents, aroma of Belgian cooking, and fragrant patinas solicit the 'velours de pêche rose et blanc' of the serving-girl.
16 Bonnefoy (37) sees this poem, and related texts inspired by Rimbaud's travels in Belgium, as narratives of a healed or healing self.
17 See Ross on the individual and collective implications of epidermal stimulation in the *Poésies*; *The Emergence of Social Space*, 105–13.
18 Robb, 35.
19 The origins of this poem lie in a schoolboy Latin translation exercise, 'Invocation à Vénus.' See *Rimbaud: Oeuvres complètes*, ed. Pierre Brunel (Paris: Livre de Poche, 1999), 124–5.
20 *OC* (Adam), 252.
21 Courbet's painting is reproduced and discussed by Peter Brooks in *Body Work: Objects of Desire and Modern Narrative* (Cambridge, Mass., London: Harvard University Press, 1993), 142–3.
22 Robb (192) argues for a specifically auto-erotic reading of the baker's action.
23 Brunel (*OC*, 196) notes that the order of colours evoked in 'Les Éffarés' corresponds to the prismatic sequence described in 'Voyelles.' That order is however disrupted by other colour and tonal indications ('blond,' 'grise'), and extended by 'jaune' and 'roses.'
24 *OC* (Adam), 245.
25 Ibid., 249.
26 While acknowledging the voyeuristic fracturing of the girls' bodies, Kristin Ross (82–3) proposes a contrastive and bipartite reading of 'À la musique' that distinguishes the space of anti-bourgeois contestation (stanzas 1–6) and an 'alternative space [...] of affect and of possible (latent) event' (stanzas 7–9) (82).
27 Robb, 433.
28 Michel Collot, 'Quelques versions de la scène primitive,' *Circeto* 2 (1984), 15–26, prises psychoanalytic angles on the locked cupboard, and concludes that the text functions as a screen memory providing glimpses of a primal scene. Pierre Brunel (*OC*, 126) identifies the numerous Hugolian echoes in 'Les Étrennes des orphelins.' Steve Murphy, *Le Premier Rimbaud*, 25–50, sees the poet as reproducing the bourgeois world in order to twist and quietly savage it, under the influence of Coppée's subversive depiction of emotional poverty and family breakdown. Murphy focuses on the material displacement of affect onto the text's multifarious metonymies:

the cupboard as a sign of lost joy rather than of anxiety; the gifts as fetish-substitutes for the absent mother; the toys, in their conflation (in the childrens' minds) with funerary objects, as signs of the bourgeois preference for hollow representations over real actions.

29 Murphy, *Le Premier Rimbaud*, 87–124, views 'Les Premières communions' as inseparable from Rimbaud's communard poetry in its denunciation of abusive ideology (including misogyny) and its repudiation of establishment control. Murphy underscores the dislocation between the first section of the poem, set in the rural world, and the second, located in the city. The first section explores the resistance of the peasantry, through sexuality and pagan pleasure in nature, to the Church's stultifying grip; the second describes the hysteria of the young communicant who somatizes her psychosexual crisis and sublimates erotic desire through the social channelling of metaphysical aspiration.

30 Murphy, *Le Premier Rimbaud*, 94, interprets this as an allusion to child cruelty or sexual abuse rather than as a description of the rite of confirmation.

31 Bonnefoy, 38.

32 Bonnefoy links 'Vénus Anadyomène' to 'Le Forgeron' as part of the poet's multi-pronged attack on the culture of the Second Empire and its Third Republic succession.

33 Wendy Steiner, *The Trouble with Beauty* (London: Heinemann, 2001), relates the avant-garde perception of feminine beauty as an exhausted icon to the development of a self-absorbed aesthetics of alienation and negativity.

34 The critique of the bourgeois mindset is present in less overtly developed instances, for example, in 'Les Reparties de Nina,' where the sensual idyll, lingeringly unfolded, is suddenly aborted by the intrusive reminder of Nina's 'bureau.'

35 David Trotter, *Cooking with Mud: The Idea of Mess in Nineteenth-century Art and Fiction* (Oxford: Oxford University Press, 2000), tracks the productive outflow of the mess-narratives of nineteenth-century fiction and painting into the non-representational (or anti-representationalist) 'mess art' ('abstraction,' *papiers collés*) of the twentieth century.

36 Murphy, *Le Premier Rimbaud*, 69–85, relates the celebration of dirt, filth, and auto-eroticism to Rimbaud's rejection of the discourses of hygiene (corporeal and moral) and his critique of hypocritical concealment (as revealed by obsessive euphemism).

37 As a fantasy of self-autopsy, an anatomical variation on the *carpe diem* theme, 'Honte' (*Vers nouveaux*) reprises the tropes of visualization and subcutaneous examination foregrounded in 'Vénus Anadyomène,'

Rimbaud's autopsy on art: 'Tant que la lame n'aura / Pas coupé cette cervelle, / Ce paquet blanc vert et gras / À vapeur jamais nouvelle, / [...] / [l'enfant gêneur] / Ne doit cesser un instant / De ruser et d'être traître.'

38 'Le Bateau ivre' gives visionary momentum to the desire to rupture the smooth surface of things and leave traces: the image of the drunken boat *puncturing* the reddening sky materializes into the vision of a wall bedecked with solar lichens and azure snot.

39 Murphy, *Le Premier Rimbaud*, 77–8, relates the young poet's masturbation ('il tirait la langue, les deux poings / À l'aine, et dans ses yeux fermés voyait des points') to his creative urge ('Et pour des visions écrasa[it] son oeil darne') through the literal manipulation of visual activity.

40 Inserted in the May 1871 ('voyant') letter to Izambard, 'Le Coeur supplicié' is an exercise in therapeutic (and obscurantist) obscenity that is intended, not only to provoke its direct recipient, but also to launch an aggressive assault on Parnassian thematic and syntactic integrity. See Murphy, *Le Premier Rimbaud*, 269–316.

41 Robb identifies 'crapule' as signalling a 'perverse eulogy [...] to the proletariat of the French Revolution' (79).

42 *OC* (Adam), 251. Michel Collot, 'Rimbaud lecteur de *L'Homme qui rit*,' *Parade Sauvage* 2 (1985), 94–6, argues for a more nuanced examination of Hugo's influence on Rimbaud's espousal of tropes of mutilation and his understanding of monstrosity as the modern face of beauty. Collot detects a possible source for 'Je est un autre' in Gwyneplaine's reaction to regaining his name and social status: 'c'était bien à lui-même qu'on parlait; mais *lui-même était autre.*'

43 Kristin Ross (83–93) argues that 'Ce qu'on dit au poète à propos de fleurs' is a sustained satire on Parnassian hypertrophic exoticism, at both signifier and signified levels.

44 Wing, 80.

45 Critics tend to pass over the choice of 'détacher' as opposed to the more apposite 'arracher' with its suggestions of exasperation. Margaret Davies, *Une Saison en enfer d'Arthur Rimbaud*, Archives Arthur Rimbaud no. 1 (Paris: Archives des Lettres Modernes, 1975), 14, draws attention to the irony of the attitude of *détachement* in an address to Satan that is both sarcastic and self-debunking.

46 Guyaux, 'Alchimie du verbe,' in *Poétique du fragment*, 31–41, considers the uneven integration of the verse poems, with some texts meshed with the prose argument (as evidence or illustration) and others more tenuously related to the framing discourse. He argues that Rimbaud's purpose in 'Alchimie du verbe' is to review, not only the visionary project, but his

entire verse output (even if the intercalated poems date from 1872). In a brief study of the variants, Margaret Davies (77–84) indicates in 'Larme' the introduction of religious references and expressions of nostalgia, and signals in 'Bonne pensée du matin' the stress on artifice. 'Chanson de la plus haute tour' is, according to Davies, offered as an illustration of 'la vieillerie poétique.' Davies's suggestion that the embedded 'Faim' reads as a repudiation of the aversive does not correspond unequivocally to the framing narration, where recourse to direct speech blurs the distinctions between recollection and prospective longing ('"Général, [...] bombarde-nous avec des blocs de terre sèche [...] Fais manger sa poussière à la ville"').

47 Bonnefoy (111) stresses the episodic construction of *Une Saison en enfer*. 'Mauvais sang' (written in May 1873) introduces the narrative of three failures: 'Nuit de l'enfer' recounts the failure to be true; the failure of morality or charity produces 'Vierge folle' of 'Délires I'; the aborting of the visionary project is treated in 'Délires II: Alchimie du verbe.' This rather overdetermined reading factors out the tendency, evident throughout *Une Saison*, to treat multifarious questions concurrently; thus the failure of language (which Bonnefoy does not discuss) is a constantly erupting preoccupation of the narrator.

48 Mario Richter, 'Échos baudelairiens dans le "prologue" d'*Une Saison en enfer* de Rimbaud,' *Parade Sauvage* 5 (November 1998), 86–90, departs from the standard identification of rejected Beauty as Parnassian. Richter argues instead that the narrator is here recalling his *false* repudiation of sublime beauty (false because it failed to conform to the cultural expectations he had internalized). Read from this perspective, the act of casting out Beauty is therefore not progressive and revolutionary, but reactive; the narrator's recollection of his earlier dismissal of radical beauty is bitter and self-critical. Margaret Davies (8) raises the possibility of a Parnassian referent but, in the absence of textual confirmation, aligns her interpretation with a more abstract, synthetic concept of beauty.

49 Bersani, 231.

50 I am drawing here on the model of cursive/recursive alternance mapped by Jewel Spears Brooker and Joseph Bentley in *Reading 'The Wasteland': Modernism and the Limits of Interpretation* (Amherst: Massachusetts University Press, 1990).

51 Robb (112–13, 127–8, 151, 168) offers a graphic catalogue of Verlaine's actual and attempted assaults on Mathilde, including incidents of hair-burning, punching, throwing to the floor, and strangulation.

52 Wing, 80.

53 *OC* (Adam), 249.

54 Robb (208–9, 245–6) speculates on Rimbaud's experience as a teacher of the French language (among other subjects) in London in June 1873. This period coincides with the writing of *Une Saison en enfer*.

55 Bonnefoy, 131.

56 See Wing (95) on the significance of the impersonal mode and the future tense linked to the extendibility of autobiographical narrative.

57 Jean-Pierre Guisto, *Rimbaud créateur*, Littératures 13 (Paris: Presses Universitaires de France / Publications de la Sorbonne, 1980), taking a thematico-psychocritical approach, suggests persuasive parallels between *Une Saison en enfer* and certain of the *Illuminations*. He subscribes to the view, however, that *Une Saison en enfer* is Rimbaud's testament and the final text in the chronological series, a view now widely refuted or nuanced (by Brunel, Guyaux, et al.).

58 Wing, 78–9.

59 Bersani, 247.

60 Lawler (43–53) opposes the view shared by the traditionalist (Étiemble) and the post-structuralist (Kittang) that 'Voyelles' is empty of meaning. Lawler argues that 'Voyelles' aims to make language 'an instrument of body, mind and soul' (46), and endorses Valéry's description of Rimbaud's 'verbal materialism' in 'Calepin d'un poète.' Lawler sees 'Voyelles' as the production of a textual object composed of interrelated networks of image and suggestion. Similarly, Ahearn (121–2) stresses the conjunction between the poem's exploration of the body and its probing of language.

61 'Voyelles' tantalizes because it simultaneously opens up and forecloses the possibilities for meaning, so I will resist adding to the overweighted raft of interpretations of this poem. Peter Collier, 'Lire "Voyelles,"' *Parade Sauvage* 5 (1989), 56–102, provides a detailed *condensé* of exegeses of this much-disputed sonnet.

62 Robb (102–5) reminds us of the chronological proximity of the May 1871 'seer' letters and 'Le Bateau ivre' (September 1871). He underscores the 'controlled associative process' and the meaning that is 'allowed to leap across synapses formed by coincident sounds and memories of other texts so that the poem appears to write itself as it goes along' (103). Bonnefoy reads 'Le Bateau ivre' (60–1) as exposing the myth of the visionary project, its unrealizable projections, and its inevitable failure when Promethean desire is quelled and the longing for the familiar resurfaces. For Bonnefoy, modernist equivocation ('cette extase plus anxieuse') is, however, a sign of textual weakness.

63 Sergio Sacchi, 'Portrait de l'artiste en grand magasin,' *Parade Sauvage*

(Actes du Colloque 'Rimbaud ou "La liberté libre,"' 11–13 September 1986), 119–35, explores 'Métropolitain' through the tropes of consumer culture, cinematic processes, and realism, exposing Rimbaud's equivocal attitude to the modern metropolis.

64 The textual mimesis of cultural flattening is a critical preoccupation in the writing of Apollinaire, Ponge, and Réda, as I shall argue in subsequent chapters.

65 Focusing on 'Ouvriers' and 'Ville,' Ahearn reads the gradual 'deconstruction of the poetic self' as symptomatic of acute alienation (315).

66 Reinhard H. Thum, *The City: Baudelaire, Rimbaud, Verhaeren* (New York, Bern, Frankfurt am Main: Peter Lang, 1994), views 'Les Ponts' as 'a mental construct obeying its own laws' (177), but neglects to consider the text's visual analogue in abstractive painting.

67 Bersani (242) defines the 'floating a-sociability' of the *Illuminations* as the exclusion of '*all* systems of definition, whether they be systems which define things through their relations to other things, or whether they assume that each thing has a separate, unique essence which its relations may obscure.' Bersani argues that the conditions for meaning have been abolished but, as the examples I give here reveal, affective meaning continues to surface, however elliptically or fragmentally.

68 André Breton, *Nadja* (Paris: Gallimard, 1928).

69 Steve Murphy, ed., *Oeuvres complètes*, vol. 1, *Poésies* (Paris: Champion, 1999), 566–7, acknowledges the probable chronological proximity of 'Vénus Anadyomène' and 'L'Étoile a pleuré rose...'

70 Michel Leiris, *Brisées* (Paris: Mercure de France, 1966; repr. Gallimard, Folio 'Essais,' 1992), 52–3, reflects on the etymology of 'débâcle' and reclaims the concept's liberating implications and its power to reverse the effects of petrification and alienation.

71 Rimbaud's sublime is never divorced from affect, an equivocation that conflicts with Wendy Steiner's reading of the avant-garde sublime as synonymous with dispassion (12, 31).

72 Bersani (256), sees the abolition of a structuring personality as leaving space for a more collective and more fragmentary representation of desire in which 'depersonalized fantasies' merge and disperse.

73 Bersani, 237.

74 Ahearn, 196.

75 For Bersani, the process of theatricalizing enables Rimbaud to cast off the burden of 'reflective subjectivity' and properly achieve the 'subversion of the subjective self' (255).

Chapter 2

1 I use 'modernity' to refer to the range of material, social, cultural, and ideological criteria that define early-twentieth-century metropolitan experience. These include accelerating technological processes, widening geographical and cultural horizons, loss of centredness, declining religiosity, and a more complex and subsequently more fractured subjectivity. I reserve the terms 'modernism' and 'modernist' for individual aesthetic responses to the perception of altered conditions. Such responses are characterized by paradox, equivocation, a tendency to problematize perspectives, and formal experimentalism. I view Apollinaire's position as generally closer to the tradition of independent modernism than to the unequivocal, doctrinaire, and primarily collectivist values summed up by the category label 'avant-garde.' I discuss this matter in 'Naming the Modernist: The Ambiguities of Apollinaire,' in C. Berg, F. Durieux, and G. Lernout, eds, *The Turn of the Century: Modernism and Modernity in Literature and the Arts* (Berlin, New York: De Gruyter, 1995), 450–9.

2 See Marjorie Perloff, *The Futurist Moment: Avant-Garde, Avant-Guerre and the Language of Rupture* (Chicago and London: University of Chicago Press, 1986); Timothy Mathews, *Reading Apollinaire: Theories of Poetic Language* (Manchester: Manchester University Press, 1987); and Claude Debon, *Apollinaire après Alcools: Calligrammes, le poète et la guerre* (Paris: Minard / Lettres Modernes, 1981) and *Guillaume Apollinaire, Alcools et Calligrammes,* ed. C. Debon (Paris: Imprimerie Nationale, 1991).

3 See Anne Hyde Greet and S.I. Lockerbie (Berkeley, Los Angeles: University of California Press, 1980). Gilbert E. Jones, *Apollinaire: La Poésie de guerre* (Geneva, Paris: Slatkine, 1990), discusses *en passant* many of the pre-1914 poems ('Liens,' 'Les Fenêtres,' 'Lundi rue Christine,' and 'Le Musicien de Saint-Merry').

4 Apollinaire's enthusiasm for visual-verbal cross-fertilization is implicit in his appreciation of Delaunay's Orphism: 'Delaunay est un des artistes les mieux doués et les plus audacieux de sa génération. Sa dramatisation des volumes colorés, ses ruptures brusques de perspective, ses irradiations de plan ont eu beaucoup d'influence [...] Il recherche la pureté des moyens, l'expression de la beauté la plus pure' (*Oeuvres complètes* [Paris: Balland and Lecat, 1964–6], 4 vols, IV, 309, from 'Chronique d'art,' published in *Montjoie!* 18 March 1913). Hereafter, references to this edition are abbreviated to *OC*, followed by the relevant volume and page numbers.

5 Apollinaire criticism, still under the sway of historico-biographical approaches, has much to gain from new theoretical approaches to a poetics

of the material constituted in the pliancy of subjectivity. The probing of a
'poetics of objectivity' has been productive in readings of Reverdy (*Les Ardoises du toit*) and Ponge (*Le Parti pris des choses*), but its pertinence remains
largely untapped in Apollinaire studies. The materiality of the image-texts
(*idéogrammes lyriques*) has generated illuminating approaches in comprehensive readings by Jean Burgos, *Pour une poétique de l'imaginaire* (Paris:
Seuil, 1982), and Pénélope Sacks-Galey, *Calligramme ou écriture figurée:
Apollinaire inventeur de formes* (Paris: Minard / Lettres Modernes, 1988). See
also Willard Bohn, *Apollinaire, Visual Poetry and Art Criticism* (Lewisburg,
London, Toronto: Bucknell University Press and Associated University
Presses, 1993), which, although not directly concerned with the concrete
poetry of *Calligrammes*, offers a perceptive discussion of the *idéogrammes*
that Apollinaire contributed to the Survage-Lagut catalogue.

6 'Les Collines' is a post-1916 poem, placed at the centre of *Ondes* to provide
a symbolic link between the experimental series and Apollinaire's final
poems.

7 See Ezra Pound, *ABC of Reading* (New York: New Directions, 1960).

8 The simultanist dynamic driving 'Zone' has its origins in cubism's collapse of spatial and temporal frames, and the simultaneous availability of
competing perspectives. 'Zone' opens out to a global sensibility, a desire to
relay the immediacy of an expanded and increasingly fragmented world
through the jostling surfaces and fractured structures of a non-linear text.
'Simultanéïsme' is appropriated and variously deployed by Robert and
Sonia Delaunay, Apollinaire, and Cendrars, as well as by the Italian and
Russian Futurists, to describe, *inter alia*, the effects of rhythmic colour
harmony, splicing techniques, and the capturing of a trans-world consciousness in randomly distributed textual instances. See Perloff, chap. 1,
'Profond aujourd'hui,' for the salience of simultanism in the Delaunay-Cendrars collaboration on *La Prose du Transsibérien et de la petite Jeanne de
France*.

9 *OC*, IV, 907.

10 *OC*, IV, 902.

11 'Les Collines' anticipates the visionary claims of surrealism and is placed
out of chronological order in *Ondes* with the aim of situating the radical
experimentalism of 1912–14 relative to a more enduring program of
aesthetic renewal. 'Les Collines' forms a trilogy with the late poems 'La
Victoire' and 'La Jolie Rousse,' in which Apollinaire works towards a
definitive synthesis of the diverse strands of his modernism.

12 Barthes, 'Sémantique de l'objet,' in *Oeuvres complètes* (Paris: Seuil, 1966–73;
repr. 1994), 65–73.

13 Barthes, *Oeuvres Complètes*, 66.
14 Ibid.
15 The quotations are taken from 'La Cravate et la montre' and 'Lundi rue Christine,' respectively.
16 'Nous avions loué deux coupés dans le transsibérien / Tour à tour nous dormions le voyageur en bijouterie et moi' ('Arbre'); 'Et je partis moi aussi pour accompagner le voyageur en bijouterie qui se rendait à Kharbine / Nous avions deux coupés dans l'express et 34 coffres de joaillerie de Pforzheim / De la camelote allemande "Made in Germany"' (*La Prose du Transsibérien*, in *Blaise Cendrars, Oeuvres complètes*, 16 vols, ed. R. Dumay and N. Frank (Paris: Le Club français du livre, 1968–71), I, 16–32.
17 Barthes, *Oeuvres complètes*, 66. Barthes's vision of material saturation/ obtrusion stresses aversiveness and is mapped to 'une sorte d'absurde' illumined by Ionesco, Sartre and, implicitly, Robbe-Grillet. In its dysphoric moments, Apollinaire's poetry reflects the same resistance to material excess, but it diverges from the Barthesian model in countering this with euphoric responses.
18 The term is proposed by Apollinaire, who presents a typology of the different tendencies of cubist painting in *Les Peintres cubistes* (1913) (Paris: Hermann, 'Savoir,' 1965; repr. 1980).
19 For Apollinaire, as for Delaunay, the aeroplane is a sublime example of the materialization of the myth of Icarus, hence the importance given to the theme of aviation in *L'Esprit nouveau et les poètes*.
20 'La Petite Auto' is discussed below, 87–9.
21 I am consciously widening the 'material' category to include, in addition to physical objects, events and situations, and the language constitutive of human experience.
22 The quotation from Cendrars is the opening line of 'Contrastes,' from the 1919 collection *Dix-neuf poèmes élastiques* (*OC*, I, 56–7).
23 Michael Sheringham, 'Attending to the Everyday: Blanchot, Lefebvre, Certeau, Perec,' *French Studies* 54, no. 2 (2000), 187–99, examines rival and overlapping constructions of the everyday as a model of creativity explored in philosophy and in literary narrative.
24 Michel de Certeau, *L'invention du quotidien*, vol. 1, 'Arts de faire' (Paris: Gallimard, 1980; repr. 1990), 143.
25 Certeau celebrates walking as a supreme mode of everyday creativity. Apollinaire identifies repeatedly with the figure of the walker as 'flâneur des deux rives,' urban drifter in 'Zone,' 'mal-aimé' haunting the streets of south London, and Wandering Jew. Explaining to Henri Martineau his preferred mode of producing poetry, Apollinaire evokes the coincidence of

peripatetic and prosodic rhythms: 'Je compose généralement en marchant et en chantant sur deux ou trois airs qui me sont venus naturellement' (*OC*, IV, 768, letter of 19 July 1913).

26 In May 1912, Picasso abandoned analytical cubism for synthetic cubism. This represented a return to 'l'humanité de l'art' and to more figurative representation, values that Apollinaire, behind his defence of the first cubist experiments, had implied were lacking in the analytical phase: 'Un Picasso étudie un objet comme un chirurgien dissèque un cadavre,' in 'Les Trois Vertus plastiques' (1908) (*Les Peintres cubistes*, 60).

27 Cf. *Les Ardoises du toit* (1918), in *Plupart du temps*, vol. I (Paris: Gallimard, 1944).

28 Quoted by Michel Décaudin in his study 'Apollinaire critique d'art,' in *Apollinaire critique d'art* (Paris: Paris-Musées/Gallimard, 1993), 196.

29 It is virtually impossible to account for modernist form and style without using descriptors that, in other contexts, would have negative connotations. My use of terms like 'unevenness,' 'dislocation,' and 'discontinuity' to describe poetic structures, is intended neutrally.

30 André Breton, *Entretiens avec André Parinaud: 1913–1952* (Paris: Gallimard, 1952), quoted by Claude Debon in *Guillaume Apollinaire après Alcools*, 126.

31 The surrealists were the first, but not the last, to berate Apollinaire for his failure to articulate an unequivocal ethical position through his war poetry. Among first-generation Apollinaire scholars, Marie-Jeanne Durry condemned the poet for his apparent indifference to the horror of war (discussed by Debon, *Guillaume Apollinaire après Alcools*, 126).

32 André Breton, *Nadja* (Paris: Gallimard, 1928; repr. 1964), 18–19.

33 The suggestion that Apollinaire is morally indifferent to war is misleading both in biographical and literary terms. Debon's *Guillaume Apollinaire après Alcools* offers a major rehabilitation of Apollinaire post-1914. The dedication of *Calligrammes* to his fallen comrade René Dalize and the content of certain letters to Madeleine in *Tendre comme le souvenir* reveal how deeply affected Apollinaire was by his close experience of suffering and loss.

34 The ahistoricity of modernism manifests itself in the prevalence of mythic structures where cyclical and achronological patterning prevails over diachronic and linear development.

35 In his founding study *Le Pacte autobiographique* (Paris: Seuil, 1975), Philippe Lejeune proposes the taxonomic bases of the genre (see, in particular, pp. 14 and 245). His hesitations over the status of poetry are revealing. In the chapter entitled 'Michel Leiris, autobiographie et poésie,' Lejeune appears initially to nuance his stance, but concludes by reaffirming the incompatibility of poetry and autobiographical writing: '[il y a] peut-être

quelque arbitraire à repousser, comme je l'ai fait, hors des limites du genre autobiographique des oeuvres comme *Les Contemplations* [...] tout dépend en fait des habitudes de lecture d'une époque. Le degré de "poésie" que le lecteur juge compatible avec le pacte autobiographique peut varier, et, s'il est élevé, engendrer des clauses annexes au contrat, le lecteur [...] acceptant volontiers comme licence poétique à l'intérieur du contrat les stylisations et les manières de parler propres au genre. Cela, s'il lit le texte comme autobiographie: mais dans la plupart des cas le "je" des poèmes est un "je" sans référence, dans lequel chacun peut se glisser; c'est le "prêt-à-porter" de l'émotion. La subjectivité universelle du lyrisme est assez différente du discours autobiographique, qui, lui, suppose une attitude de communication entre deux personnes distinctes et séparées [auteur et lecteur].' In his study of Leiris, Lejeune goes on to explore the poeticity of autobiography. In discussing Apollinaire's war poetry, my aim is, in part, to reverse the terms and look at how poetry can be autobiographical. While the relationship of autobiographical writing and poetry is, clearly, not unproblematic, there is sufficient convergence between aspects of Apollinaire's war poetry and the taxonomic criteria describing autobiographical writing to validate this approach.

36 Letter to Henri Martineau of 19 July 1913, *OC*, IV, 768.
37 See Paul John Eakin, *Fictions in Autobiography: Studies in the Art of Self-Invention* (New Jersey: Princeton University Press, 1985), 151.
38 This is less of a change of stylistic direction than the continuation of the modernist aesthetic that informs the earliest poems and, signally, 'La Chanson du mal-aimé.' Its features are the fracturing of identity, polyphony, and stylistic plurality.
39 The poetry of *Calligrammes*, responding to both autobiographical and experimental urges, combines document, dream-text, art, allegory, the epic, fantasy, irony, pathos, and humour. See Michael Sheringham, *French Autobiography: Devices and Desires* (Oxford: Oxford University Press, 1993), 12–14, on hybridity as a generic, structural, and stylistic feature of autobiographical writing.
40 The pet name of Apollinaire's mistress Louise de Coligny-Châtillon is inscribed in 'Saillant' and in 'C'est Lou qu'on la nommait'; references to 'Madeleine' (in 'Veille') and to 'Rouveyre' (in 'La Petite Auto') further highlight the referential basis of autobiographical poetry.
41 Michael Levenson, *Modernism and the Fate of Individuality* (Cambridge: Cambridge University Press, 1991).
42 Paul John Eakin, *Touching the World: Reference in Autobiography* (Princeton: Princeton University Press, 1992), explores the fraught interrelation of

public and private in autobiography in terms of 'the tension between the intractable, broken reality of twentieth-century history and the irrepressible drive of the poet's imagination' (175).

43 The referential pact has been probed by Lejeune in *Le Pacte autobiographique* (36–7). The *histoire* (in both senses) of the self-writing subject is imbricated in externally verifiable and historically specific circumstances. Here, the relationship of the soldier-self to the material 'real' of war is mediated through represented objects, sensations, events, memories, and discourse; these construct the referential pact in terms of subjective criteria of selection, relativity, and partial reconstitution.

44 Commentators of the war poetry of *Calligrammes* have identified occasional instances of error and misrepresentation in the technical vocabulary deployed by Apollinaire. See, for example, Claude Debon, 110, and her article (published under the name Tournadre) 'Notes sur le vocabulaire de la guerre dans *Calligrammes*,' in *Guillaume Apollinaire*, 13 (Paris: Minard / Lettres Modernes, 1976), 65–75.

45 Philippe Hamon, in his essay 'Un discours contraint,' in R. Barthes et al., eds, *Littérature et réalité* (Paris: Seuil, 1982), 119–81, discusses the constraints on realist discourse in terms of the accessibility of the technical lexicons it exploits. Soldier slang poses the same problems of transparency for the reader, and raises an interesting paradox: the deployment of the comradely lexicon is key to the referential pact, yet that pact is not undermined where the reader fails to understand a given term, provided that the language of the soldierly group is recognizable as forming the prevailing code.

46 The metaphor of thickening is appropriate to the material embedding of 'real' signs (postal franking marks, signatures, and graffiti) in Apollinaire's ideogrammatic poems. This is a material variation on the traditional construction of the textual/extratextual relationship in terms of permeability and transparency, for which see Hamon, 150.

47 The *idéogrammes lyriques* are reproduced from Greet and Lockerbie's edition of *Calligrammes*.

48 Designations of status and job specification reveal a rigidly stratified world: soldiers are defined hierarchically by rank ('officier,' 'capitaine,' 'chef de section,' 'maréchal des logis'), and differentially by category ('fantassins,' 'dragon,' 'territorial') and specialism ('pointeurs,' 'servants,' 'conducteurs,' 'canonnier,' 'tirailleur,' 'bombardiers,' 'signaleurs,' 'brancardier,' 'vaguemestre').

49 Physical and mental geography is redrawn for military purposes as space is designated, apportioned, and coded. Thus, the title of the *idéogramme*

'SP,' the abbreviation of 'secteur postal,' signifies a defined administrative zone and a closed cultural space accessible only to those initiated into the mysteries of trench-war communication. Topographical imprecision is consistent with the need to safeguard military intelligence ('Secteur 59 je ne peux pas dire où' in 'Les Soupirs du servant de Dakar') and defend fighting positions ('aux créneaux' in 'La Nuit d'avril 1915,' 'rameau central de combat' in 'Guerre,' 'la zone des armées' in 'Désir').

50 The soldier-self cannot change the world, but he can indent and shape its surface by fashioning small objects from the detritus of war. On imprinting the world, see Elaine Scarry, *Resisting Representation* (Oxford: Oxford University Press, 1994), esp. chapter 2, 'Participial Acts: Working – Work and the Body in Hardy and Other Nineteenth-century Novelists.'

51 The representation of the soldier's world relies frequently on techniques of morsellization. Glimpses of ordinary existence and allusions to domestic trivia have a naturalizing effect. This may invite the charge that 'bite-size' realism obscures the horrors of war. Seen from that angle, the metonymic focus on the 'ordinary things' of war would deflect readerly attention from the absence of moral articulation. However, if we reverse the perspective, we can read in the preference for the small-scale an attempt to chip away at the unknowable whole of war, and a rejection of the temptations of a totalizing vision.

52 Micro-history is defined by Antoine Compagnon in 'Biography, Prosopography, Microhistory' (*New Comparison* 25 [Spring 1998], 71–82) as the post-*Annales* 'history of minutiae [...] symptomatic of the state of a discipline after theory, that is after years of taboo against subjectivity' (76).

53 See Jack Murray, *Landscapes of Alienation* (Stanford: Stanford University Press, 1991) 110 ff. on the absorption of the external world into the inner realm, and its refashioning as a space of counter-cultural subjectivity in the novels of Kafka. Apollinaire's description focuses on the particular attributes, atmosphere, organization, and decoration of the trench shelter or dugout, and their translation into dream and metaphor.

54 Lockerbie and Greet (434) clarify the reference to 'bobosses' ('fantassins à bosses') in their commentary on the poem.

55 The foregrounding of the informal sociolect of comrades places constraints on readerliness owing to the frequent confusion of literal and metaphorical meanings. This has influenced the course of much of the critical commentary on Apollinaire's war poetry. Tournadre elucidates the hermeticism of soldier discourse in 'Notes sur le vocabulaire de la guerre dans *Calligrammes*,' 65–75.

56 The incorporation of metaphorical aspects of soldierly discourse makes

reading and interpretation more problematical, with objects mediated through a code accessible only to the initiated. As textual hermeticism increases, so the sense of front-line war experience as self-contained and self-referential is made more acute. Metaphorical work on the transparent, metonymic vocabulary of war renders something of the creative response of the soldier as he grapples to make sense of a complex, technology-driven situation. While linguistic authenticity promotes the illusion of transparency, of unfiltered 'soldier-speak,' it also exposes that illusion, drawing attention to the processes of selection and organization that guarantee linguistic coherence and intelligibility for the soldierly group. The selection of the informal register places a visible (audible?) textual frame around the cultural interpretation of war by participants, the development of a comradely ethic derived from the dominant military ideology, and the psychological responses of ordinary men in exceptional circumstances.

57 Klaus Theweleit's classic study of the making of military masculinity, *Male Fantasies: Women, Floods, Bodies, History* (Minneapolis: University of Minnesota Press, 1987, trans. Stephen Conway), explores the historical and cultural negotiations, mediations, and appropriations implicit in the process. Eve Kosofsky Sedgwick's celebrated work *Between Men: English Literature and Male Homosocial Desire* (New York: Columbia University Press, 1985; repr. 1992) exposes the drive in homosociality to deny homo-erotic desire and, by over-focusing representations of the feminine, to strengthen male bonds defined as explicitly heterosexual and (at the very least) implicitly homophobic. In its affirmation of male camaraderie invested in relations of heterosexual exchange, remembered or fantasized, Apollinaire's war poems may be seen to collude in the suppression of homosexual desire. Yet, just as codes of masculinity are performed, so they are also resisted in *Calligrammes*. Apollinaire does not endorse the conservatism of the positions deconstructed by Sedgwick. Rather, his poetry tests the homosocial and its alternatives, refuses to stabilize positions, and explores the phantasmatic creativity of the protean self.

58 Sheringham, *French Autobiography* (96), notes the tendency in autobiographical writing for the subject to historicize experience via an alternative narrative that promises a transformed self in a context removed from the banality and constraints of the here-and-now.

59 Anthony Cascardi, *The Subject of Modernity* (Cambridge: Cambridge University Press, 1992), 72.

60 Here Apollinaire subscribes to the modernist practice of incorporating traditional material (legend, myth, biblical sources, canonic literature) for

the purposes of ironizing or relativizing the situation or the perspective of the protagonists. This practice finds its fullest expression in the work of Eliot and Joyce.

61 Representations of the castrating trench connect with disturbing images of ambivalent gardens whose beauty articulates cruelty and whose 'civilized' nature brings forth barbarity: 'la grenade est touchante / Dans nos effroyables jardins' ('Les Grenadines repentantes'). The garden is envisioned as a place of sacrificial sadism, a site of bodily exasperation ('totos' irritate the soldier's neck) and aggravated fear ('Les avions bourdonnent ainsi que des abeilles,' in 'À l'Italie'). The mesmerizing coincidence of death and the erotic, rapture and terror, in the garden is exquisitely expressed in 'Fête': 'Il songe aux roses de Saadi / Et soudain sa tête se penche / Car une rose lui redit / La molle courbe d'une hanche / L'air est plein d'un terrible alcool / Filtré des étoiles mi-closes / Les obus caressent le mol / Parfum nocturne où tu reposes / Mortification des roses.'

62 Apollinaire's treatment of themes of suffering and death differs markedly in this respect from that of the English war poets, with their realist representation of the body's trials.

63 See Marina Warner, *Monuments and Maidens: The Allegory of the Female Form* (London: Weidenfeld and Nicholson, 1985), for a historico-cultural critique of the iconicity of feminine embodiment.

64 Woman is appropriated in the project of masculine self-idealizing; she is wrapped in ideological value as the abstract embodiment of desire's sublimation. The discourse of mastery figures Woman as an absolute and as allegory, an idealization endlessly repeated in the structures of collective masculinity in order to perfect a soldierly self-image that, at the extreme, vaporizes and achieves sublime de-materialization ('Signe plus pur que l'Arc-en Ciel / [...] / Ô nous les très belles couleurs,' in 'De la batterie de tir').

65 Forms of desire are legitimated and contained within the male homosocial framework of military life. The textual 'framing' of the pun 'LES CÉNOBITES TRANQUILLES,' in 'Du Coton dans les oreilles,' inscribes the tension between the demands of homosocial context (figured by the collectivist asceticism of the Cenobite monastic order) and unsatisfied erotic desire.

66 Real female bodies are figured as chaotic, linked to tropes of debility, and thus placed beyond desire. The bodies may be infected and infecting, like that of the 'putain de Nancy,' or debilitated, like that of the wife of the territorial. Whether sexually threatening like the tyrannical Lou, or physically diminished like the wife-back-home, women are the object of deep male alienation.

67 Fetishistic investment in part-objects as a strategy for compensating for the unavailable 'body whole' was theorized by Melanie Klein. Juliet Mitchell offers a useful account of Klein's thought in *The Selected Melanie Klein* (Harmondsworth: Penguin, 1986).

68 The fracturing of the feminine body contrasts with the synecdochic representation of male participants, in terms of both motivation and effect. Where the female body undergoes a *depreciation* via the obsessive attachment to eroticized body parts, the synecdochic treatment of the male body in 'À Nîmes' and other texts (discussed pp. 99–101) is consistently *appreciative*, and integral to a project of idealization; hence the conflation of male physical and metaphysical values.

69 Wendy Steiner, *The Trouble with Beauty* (London: Heinemann, 2001), is a brilliant exposé of the twentieth-century avant-garde's deeply mistrustful relation to feminine beauty, and an assessment of contemporary culture's gradual work of freeing representations of beauty from the gender entanglements of that century.

70 Writing an imaginary body is a mediation towards the impossible situation where the self would have real power over an actual body. Here, anxieties over the real-time fragilizing of the male body are compensated by the feminine body that dream-work brings into being. The fantasized female body alleviates the heaviness of existence, in contrast with the intractable materiality of the sick wife of the territorial or the syphilitic prostitute from Nancy.

71 Eakin, *Touching the World*, 103.

72 'Notes sur les Otages, peintures de Fautrier,' in *L'Atelier contemporain* (Paris: Gallimard, 1977), 11–12.

Chapter 3

1 Sartre and Sollers converge in their resistance to reading subjectivity in Ponge. In 'L'Homme et les choses' (*Situations*, I [Paris: Gallimard, 1947]), Sartre detects in *Le Parti pris des choses* a desire to see the human disappear. Ponge refutes this view in 'L'Homme à grands traits' (1945–51) – an extension of 'Notes premières de l'homme' (*Proêmes*) – affirming that the human self is, together with 'words' and 'things,' one of the three defining terms of his writing. Celebrating objects is, for Ponge, precisely a way of reaffirming the human.

2 Among the numerous monographs devoted to Ponge, the following are essential reading. Bernard Beugnot, *Poétique de Francis Ponge: Le palais diaphane* (Paris: PUF, 1990), explores the regeneration of allegory in Ponge,

paying particular attention to rhetoric and textual genetics. Written to
honour Ponge at the 1975 Cerisy-la-Salle conference, Jacques Derrida,
Signéponge (Paris: Seuil, 1988; bilingual ed. New York: Columbia University Press, 1984), is a boundlessly inventive speculation on the generative
processes of signature, self-signing, and textual inscription in Ponge. Jean-
Marie Gleize, *Francis Ponge* (Paris: Seuil, 1988), is an important bio-critical
exploration of the motivation and philosophy of Ponge that ranges across
the poet's political inclinations and activity, the philosophical undertow
of his work, and the influence of culture, education, nature, and literary
figures from Paulhan to Breton. Michel Collot, *Francis Ponge: Entre mots et
choses* (Seyssel: Champ Vallon, 1991), is discussed in note 3. Ian Higgins,
Francis Ponge (London: Athlone Press, 1979), remains an indispensable
introduction to the corpus. While it is impractical to list here more than a
tiny selection of articles on Ponge, mention should be made of essays by
Jean-Pierre Richard (*Onze études sur la poésie moderne* [Paris: Seuil (1962),
1981], 198–224; 'Fabrique de la figure,' in *Pages paysages – Microlectures II*
[Paris: Seuil, 1984]), and by Michael Riffaterre ('La surdétermination dans
le poème en prose: Francis Ponge,' in *La Production du texte* [Paris: Seuil,
1984]). Among contemporary readers of Ponge, Philippe Met combines
rigorous textual analysis and sensitivity to intratextual complexity (see
esp. 'Francis Ponge ou la fabrique du (lieu) commun,' *Poétique* 26 [1995],
303–18, and 'Poésie de résistance et résistance de/à la poésie: Le cas
Ponge,' *Dalhousie French Studies* 51 [2000], 109–20).

3 Michel Collot is the first critic to engage systematically with subjectivity.
In *Francis Ponge: Entre mots et choses*, Collot offers a critical 'third way,' a
means of bypassing the ossified opposition between 'Ponge – poet of
objects' and 'Ponge – worker on language.' Where Collot seeks to sidestep
the conflict between phenomenology and linguistics, I propose a reading
of subjectivity that works *across* the divide between objects and language –
probing objects through language and language through the referentiality
of objects. My purpose here is to consider how the disconnection consecrated by the Sartre/Sollers opposition is actively challenged by the
project of reconnection and regeneration that is at the centre of Ponge's
writing. In addition to the work of Collot, see Henri Maldiney, *Le Vouloir
dire de Francis Ponge* (La Versanne: encre marine, 1993), who acknowledges
the subjective dimension of Ponge's writing: 'Francis Ponge affirme,
proclame son horreur du pathétique, du "magma poétique" et de "l'idéo-
logie pâtheuse." [...] Mais [son] parti pris d'objectivité n'arrive pas à
dissimuler la dimension *pathique* qui fait le ton de son oeuvre. La mise à
distance de soi qu'elle suppose n'est pas un détachement. Il écrit dans

l'urgence. Et dans cette écriture un homme est en question sous l'auteur. Les titres auxquels il a songé un instant pour *La Rage de l'expression*, comme "La Respiration artificielle," sont ironiques sans doute, mais non pas dérisoires. Il s'agit de réanimation, c'est-à-dire de rappeler un homme à la vie — à commencer par soi-même' (143). Also of interest are Josiane Rieu, 'La Subjectivité dans *Le Parti pris des choses*,' in *Francis Ponge, Cahier de l'Herne* (Paris: L'Herne, 1986), 86–111, and Michael Riffaterre's study of subject–object relations and humour in 'The Primacy of Words: Francis Ponge's Reification,' in C. Minahen, ed., *Figuring Things: Char, Ponge and Poetry in the Twentieth Century* (Lexington: French Forum, 1994), 27–38.

4 Alain Robbe-Grillet, *Pour un nouveau roman* (Paris: Editions de Minuit, 1963), 60–4.

5 Monic Robillard's felicitous description 'autobiographie nouée' for *Pour un Malherbe* captures Ponge's meshing of self and other, biography and self-writing, critical celebration and self-evaluation ('*Pour un Malherbe* ou l'autobiographie nouée,' *Études Françaises* 17, nos. 1–2 [April 1981], 129–42).

6 The risks of bilingual conflation should be signalled here. The meaning(s) of 'subjectivity' deployed throughout my study are quite distinct from Ponge's occasional use of the term 'subjectivité' to excoriate the poetry of self-indulgent introspection. One important exception emerges in the preface to *La Fabrique du pré*, where Ponge declines 'subjectivité' etymologically, and raises precisely those questions of externalization, bodiliness, and desire with which this study is concerned. However, in general terms, Ponge uses 'subjectivité' as a synonym for 'sentimentalité,' a mode wholly at variance with his lyric practice and his patient, passionate struggle for a 'nouvelle rhétorique,' following Rimbaud and Lautréamont: '[I]l y a là une conception de la poésie *active* qui est absolument contraire à celle qui est généralement admise, à la poésie considérée comme une effusion simplement subjective, à la poésie considérée comme, par exemple, "je pleure dans mon mouchoir, ou je m'y mouche," et puis je montre, j'expose, je publie ce mouchoir, et voilà une page de poésie' (*Entretiens avec Philippe Sollers*, 27).

7 *Comment une figue de paroles et pourquoi*, p. 226.

8 Interview with Jean Ristat, *Comment une figue de paroles et pourquoi*, 276–7.

9 See Ian Higgins, 'Language, Politics and Things,' *Neophilologus* 63 (1979), 347–62. Other critics have been more appreciative: Groethuysen recognized the link between *Douze petits écrits* and *Le Parti pris des choses*, and the stirring of consciousness and language against the discursive hubbub: 'J'aime les douze petits poèmes de Francis Ponge, que le silence unit: le

mot balbutie et la pensée s'agite' (quoted by Robert Sabatier in *Magazine littéraire* 260 [December 1988], 34).

10 Audisio's letter is quoted in *Oeuvres complètes* (*OC*), I, 890–1.

11 Ponge distinguishes between personal and collective subjectivities when he celebrates the affinities of poets and painters in their capacity to bring forth '[un] art de vivre comme individu et [un] art de vivre comme individu social' (*Entretiens avec Philippe Sollers*, 91). The individual as a social being, as a product of economic, linguistic, and cultural structures, and the capacity of art – poetry, in this instance – to offer a critique of those structures, in anticipation of the 'art de vivre' of *Le Parti pris des choses*, constitute the fractured ground of the satirical *Douze petits écrits*.

12 *Nouveau nouveau recueil*, II (Paris: Gallimard, 1992), 31.

13 'Le Carnet du bois de pins' is published in *La Rage de l'expression* (1952), which is included in the first volume of the *Oeuvres complètes* and is also available in a Gallimard *NRF* paperback edition. *La Fabrique du pré* was the object of a beautiful illustrated edition in 'Les Sentiers de la création' series of Albert Skira.

14 Gleize evokes the explosiveness of *Douze petits écrits*: '[L]'écriture est ici déclarée, comme on dit "la guerre est déclarée," sous éclairage éthique. L'écriture, la poésie, la langue [...] ont à voir avec l'ordre des choses, ont affaire à l'ordre social. [...] Une arme et un outil. Masse cloutée, fouet de l'air, coup de style. Les *Douze petits écrits* visent très haut, très loin' (*Francis Ponge*, 42–3). For his part, Ponge reserved 'incendiary' metaphors to describe *Le Parti pris des choses*. He felt in retrospect that the early satirical poems were too overt weapons (like sabres or arrows) against a bourgeois target. His aim in writing *Le Parti pris des choses* was to produce something more subtle and more effective: 'Je voulais préparer [...] quelque chose de beaucoup plus clos, de beaucoup plus fermé, mais de beaucoup plus efficace [...] Du point de vue [...] de la *forme* même de mes textes, c'était la forme de la bombe, et [...] la longue préparation de la bombe qui m'intéressait' (*Entretiens avec Philippe Sollers*, 68).

15 Rimbaud, *Oeuvres complètes* (Paris: Gallimard, 'Pléiade,' 1972), 134.

16 The routine of office workers and clerks is evoked more equivocally in Apollinaire's 'Zone': here, euphoria mixes with whimsical irony to produce the indeterminate perspective of the outsider-narrator ('J'ai vu ce matin une jolie rue dont j'ai oublié le nom / Neuve et propre du soleil elle était le clairon / Les directeurs les ouvriers et les belles sténo-dactylographes / Du lundi matin au samedi soir quatre fois par jour y passent'). Ponge's abdication of the viewing/speaking position to the office worker

allows unmediated expression to the desolating experience of externally regulated routine.

17 Unless otherwise indicated, the chronology of the poems is that given in *OC*, I.

18 In the glitz and 'clinquant' of fetishized objects, there are echoes of Rimbaud's satire on the bourgeoisie of Charleville: 'Le notaire pend à ses breloques à chiffres' ('À la musique,' *Poésies*).

19 Complementing the satirical charge on the figure of the industrialist is 'Le Ministre' (*Lyres*, 1934), a sharp critique of the gestural and sartorial pretensions of the politician. Via the graphic and acoustic mutation of 'sinistre' into 'ministre,' the text proceeds through the discourses of entomologist and zoologist to dissect its specimen of study, a grotesque hybrid of human and subhuman features whose potent realization aligns the early Ponge with the long tradition of visual and verbal caricature.

20 *Everyday Life in the Modern World*, trans. S. Rabinovitch (London: Allen Lane, 1971).

21 See T.J. Clark's key analysis of the instabilities of class identity in Manet's 'Le Bar aux Folies-Bergère,' in *The Painting of Modern Life: Paris in the Art of Manet and His Followers* (London: Thames and Hudson, 1984).

22 In *La Curée* (1872) and in *L'Assommoir* (1877), Zola focuses on the concomitant modes of oral consumption and sociability: they reveal the space of leisure and pleasurable self-indulgence to be subject to the same processes of social dissolution and the same empty articulations as the 'on-duty' worlds of *nouveau riche* property speculators or lower-class laundresses.

23 Shirley Ann Jordan, *The Art Criticism of Francis Ponge* (London: Modern Humanities Research Association, 1994) is the first comprehensive study of *L'Atelier contemporain*, and an insightful exploration of Ponge's essays on Fautrier, Giacometti, and Braque.

24 In Ponge the constant yearning for equilibrium is expressed in recurrent figures of clockwork mechanisms. In 'L'Objet, c'est la poétique' (*L'Atelier contemporain*), Ponge asserts that if we were only bodies, we would balance with Nature. However, our soul is on our body's side with its freight of emotion, imagination, and memory, and this tips the balance. For Ponge, the activity of writing offers the possibility of equilibrium, for with every word we utter we lighten ourselves: language is a necessary counterweight to subjective overburden.

25 Ponge affirms the insistence with which the body impinges on consciousness in 'L'Homme à grands traits,' in the specific context of ageing. His

remarks are equally valid for the invigorating moment when self and world coincide, and a new sensory experience erupts: 'Hors quelques fulgurations dans la conscience, quelques poignants remords, on n[e] pense jamais [à son corps]. On ne s'en rend pas compte, on ne le prend en considération qu'aux moments de crise. En période d'évolution rapide. Quand le processus se précipite' (*Méthodes*, 179).

26 *Pour un Malherbe*, 174.

27 Ponge is not gender-blind or gender-indifferent; his use of gendered language tends towards the metaphorical and allegorical not the literalist. Throughout his essay on Malherbe, he deploys the discourse of male sexual power and pleasure to express writerly desire and the urgency of giving voice to the feminine-ascribed silence of things. Yet, his passion and aspiration envision the human and the creative: 'Nous donnons la parole à la *féminité* du monde. Nous délivrons le monde. Nous désirons que les choses se délivrent, en dehors (pour ainsi dire) de nous. [...] Nous suivons leurs contours, nous les invitons à se parcourir, à jouir, à jubiler d'elles-mêmes. Nous les engrossons alors. Voilà notre art poétique, et notre spécialité érotique' (*Pour un Malherbe*, 73).

28 The deep imbrication of the affective and the material, desire and the body, is evoked in more personal terms when Ponge describes his every-day writing practice to Philippe Sollers: 'Je travaillais en général les pieds sur la table, pour ne pas travailler comme on travaille à l'école, pour me mettre dans une espèce d'état second, dans lequel la nécessité *complète*, passant par mon corps et aboutissant à ma plume par l'intermédiaire de mon bras, ce que j'inscris est une sorte de *trace* de ce qu'il y a de plus profond en moi, à propos de telle ou telle notion. [...] J'avais une sorte de froideur vis-à-vis de ce que je faisais, que j'ai toujours gardée; froideur en même temps que l'ardeur qui vient du fond..., du désir, de l'Éros qui fait écrire' (*Entretiens avec Philippe Sollers*, 72–3).

29 'Nous battons du regard comme l'oiseau de l'aile, pour nous maintenir' ('L'Objet, c'est la poétique,' *L'Atelier contemporain*, 223).

30 'Matière et mémoire,' *OC*, 118.

31 The following three examples are taken from *Le Parti pris des choses*.

32 The twinning of the tropes of tautness and creative necessity recalls the tension on the lyre string that Ponge offers as a metaphor for the precision and economy of Malherbe's poetry and, by extension, his own. The quotations from 'L'Atelier' are taken from *L'Atelier contemporain*, 2.

33 The aspiration to *adéquation* is aporetic, for the process of seeking verbal equivalence is self-abortive and endlessly generative. If the thing – experienced as a composite entity, a combination of physical and immaterial,

substance and notion – exceeds the potential of language to describe it (as it always does), then language is 'inadéquat.' This failure to find equivalence prompts new bids at subjective penetration and writerly inscription in the potentially limitless extension of the textual process.

34 *Pour un Malherbe*, 182.

35 Ibid., 251.

36 Originally intended by Ponge as an introduction to *Le Parti pris des choses*, 'Introduction au "Galet"' exposes (and explains) the *grandes lignes* of his poetics. It reveals his aspiration to be a Lucretius for the twentieth century, his privileging of the unexceptional, the significance of transitive desire, and the mingling of materiality and subjectivity ('Tout le secret du bonheur du contemplateur est dans son refus de considérer *comme un mal* l'envahissement de sa personnalité par les choses,' *Proêmes*).

37 *Pour un Malherbe*, 173.

38 Ponge distinguishes between those artists and writers who (presumably in the tradition of Baudelaire quoted here) privilege the vertiginous and the plunge into the absolute, and those (like Ponge) who seek equilibrium in things as a way of countering existential angst: 'Je ne parle pas ici [...] de ces gens qui cherchent des sensations, plongent dans l'inconnu pour trouver du nouveau, demandent à être projetés, secoués, aiguillonnés, chatouillés, exaltés: ceux-là ne m'intéressent guère. Mais de ceux au contraire qui ressentent violemment le chaos et le dangereux balancement du monde, la légèreté de la personne, sa vertiginosité, sa tendance à sa propre perte, – et qui désirent violemment des moeurs d'équilibre' ('Braque le réconciliateur,' *L'Atelier contemporain*, 61).

39 Pendular momentum is a leitmotif and a structuring principle of *Pour un Malherbe*, representing Ponge's broad desire to reach backwards into the past for the benefit of the present and the future, and his more specific objective to make Malherbe modern and, in the process, align himself with the great tradition of French lyric renewal.

40 *Le Savon*, 122.

41 Ibid., 25.

42 Ibid., 28.

43 Ibid., 35.

44 The identification of an object-referent, announced (for the most part) by a definite article ('Le Gymnaste,' 'La Mousse,' 'Le Morceau de viande,' 'La Cheminée d'usine'), hovers between the designation of individual specificity (the pebble presently beheld) and the intimation of a generic or categorial value (the pebble as opposed to the rock or the stone).

45 'La Pratique de la littérature,' *Méthodes*, 283–4.

46 *Méthodes*, 281–3.

47 Ponge's stated commitment to working with 'cette mauvaise peinture' (*Méthodes*, 282) – a metaphor for everyday lexical materials and dictionary words – recalls his definition of his task in terms, not of cleaning the Augean stables, but of painting them 'au moyen de leur propre purin.' Ponge defines his poetics as a therapeutic recycling of the commonplace, the overlooked, and the obscured. Thus, he rejects tabula rasa purification.

48 In his Pléiade notes to 'Pochades en prose,' Bernard Beugnot underlines the Proustian echoes in Ponge's painterly evocations of the Sahel, and his narrative reconstruction of the struggle to bring colour and atmosphere to language (*OC*, 1093). Ponge passes over the connection between his 'rose sacripant' and Miss Sacripant, the subject of Elstir's portrait in *À l'ombre des jeunes filles en fleurs*.

49 *Pour un Malherbe*, 134.

50 Elaine Scarry, *On Beauty and Being Just* (Princeton, NJ: Princeton University Press, 1999) is a passionate, probing exploration of the uneven beauty of art and nature, 'unevenness' being defined as the capacity of things to prompt alterations of perception, revisions of judgment, and thus generate new acts of creativity.

51 *Méthodes*, 119, 120, 122.

52 Ibid., 123.

53 Ibid., 129.

54 Philippe Met, 'Les Censures du "Verre d'eau,"' *Genesis* 12 (1997) 49–66, examines the complex dialectic in the manuscript between the exposure and the erasure of the text's earlier versions.

55 'Oh! l'héroïsme de la moindre chose. Sa vertu. Sa patience. Sa volonté d'être comme elle est, comme elle attend qu'on vienne l'admirer; et l'aimer!' (*Comment une figue de paroles et pourquoi*, 67).

56 The greater part of Ponge's art criticism is devoted to Braque, with whom Ponge feels deep aesthetic (and human) empathy. The following extract from the essay 'Braque – Dessins' reveals a striking convergence between Ponge's appreciation of Braque and many of the key preoccupations of Ponge's poetic project (modesty in things, repair, the oscillation between fragmentary and expansive, the corrective potential of creativity): 'Pas plus que d'expliquer le monde, il ne s'agit de le transformer; mais plutôt de le remettre en route, par fragments, dans [son] atelier'; 'Chez Braque, c'est tout notre monde qui se répare, qui se remet à fonctionner. Il frémit et quasi spontanément se remet en marche. Il résonne. [...] [N]ous marchons dans les pas du temps, guéris' (*L'Atelier contemporain*, 106, 108).

57 'Préface aux *Sapates*' (*Proêmes*), originally intended as an introduction to *Le*

Parti pris des choses, was withdrawn and rewritten by Ponge after Paulhan objected to it.

58 The quotation is from *Pour un Malherbe*, 41.

59 *Méthodes*, 257.

60 *L'Atelier contemporain*, 222.

61 *Méthodes*, 197–8.

62 *L'Atelier contemporain*, 56. In his essay 'Nature, humanisme, tragédie' (*Pour un nouveau roman*, 45–67), Robbe-Grillet deplores in Ponge's poetry what he sees as an anthropomorphizing treatment of non-sentient objects. He attacks as a mannered, stylistically facile indulgence Ponge's bid to make us more attentive to the object in its physical particularity (for example, the fragility of the wooden crate) by freighting it with human affect (in this case, vulnerability). Ponge seems particularly drawn to objects that can be damaged, whose vulnerability impresses itself upon us. His material alertness and empathy span the differences between living things (the snail, the fronds of the fern) and inanimate objects, between sentient and non-sentient things. Whether enduring (like the pebble) or ephemeral (like the wooden crate), all trigger deep affect and are accorded respect, admiration, wonder, or curiosity.

63 *Méthodes*, 25–6.

64 *OC*, 385.

65 Scarry, *On Beauty and Being Just*, 46.

66 The centrality of pliancy or *décontraction* in Pongean poetics is summed up in *Comment une figue de paroles et pourquoi* as 'de l'élasticité à l'esprit des paroles – et de la poésie comme je l'entends' (84).

67 The quotation is from 'Le Pain' (*Le Parti pris des choses*).

68 *Méthodes*, 41–2.

69 The quotations are taken from *Entretiens avec Philippe Sollers*, 97, 120. Ponge refers to *Rage* as more of a poetic journal than poetry per se (see *Entretiens*, 106). Sollers sees the text as a description of its own production and thus as offering the fullest possible penetration of the external world. The repetitions of the signifying function impart the sense that the external world is being explored in the minutest detail.

70 *Pour un Malherbe*, 70.

Chapter 4

1 Michel de Certeau and Luce Giard, 'Les Revenants de la ville,' in Michel de Certeau, Luce Giard, and Pierre Mayol, *L'Invention du quotidien*, vol. 2, 'Habiter, cuisiner' (Paris: Folio, rev. ed. 1994), 189–90.

2 My reading focuses on the main collections of Réda's urban and suburban poetry, beginning with the 1977 collection *Les Ruines de Paris*, which established his reputation as a major contemporary poet. This chapter takes in Réda's city-based chronicles and narratives, such as *Accidents de la circulation* (2001), and draws on his writings on poetry and poetics. Reference to works by Jacques Réda are given in parentheses in the text, using the following abbreviations:

RP   *Les Ruines de Paris* (Paris: Gallimard, 1977; Coll. Poésie, 1993)
CV   *Celle qui vient à pas légers* (Montpellier: Fata Morgana, 1985; 1999)
BS   *Beauté suburbaine* (Périgueux: Fanlac, 1985)
CCA *Châteaux des courants d'air* (Paris: Gallimard, 1986)
RaP   *Recommandations aux promeneurs* (Paris: Gallimard, 1988)
SM   *Le Sens de la marche* (Paris: Gallimard, 1990)
LR   *La Liberté des rues* (Paris: Gallimard, 1997)
CiT   *Le Citadin* (Paris: Gallimard, 1998)
LC   *La Course* (Paris: Gallimard, 1999)
AC   *Accidents de la circulation* (Paris: Gallimard, 2001)

3 In a letter of 22 October 2002, Réda stresses that his interest in the quotidian and the material has its roots in literature, not in philosophy or the social sciences: 'Michel de Certeau n'a jamais été pour moi qu'un nom rencontré au hasard de quelques lectures. C'est une lacune que je me promets de combler. Si mon attachement aux aspects du "matériel" et du "quotidien" dépend d'une influence, elle est [...] plutôt d'ordre littéraire. Je citerais alors celle de Jean Follain, [de] Supervielle [...], [et des] romanciers américains (Saroyan, Steinbeck, Caldwell) chez qui les details de la vie quotidienne tiennent une place souvent déterminante. (J'ai été sidéré, à dix-huit ans, par la première scène de *Pylône*, de Faulkner.)'

4 Michael Sheringham, 'City Space, Mental Space, Poetic Space: Paris in Breton, Benjamin and Réda,' in M. Sheringham, ed., *Parisian Fields* (London: Reaktion, 1996), 104–5.

5 This text was originally published under the title 'Souvenirs de Cambridge' in Christine Van Rogger Andreucci, ed., *Approches de Jacques Réda: Actes du Colloque de l'Université de Pau* (henceforth abbreviated to *Actes de Pau*) (Pau: Publications de l'Université de Pau, 1994), 9–12.

6 One intriguing exception is to be found in the series of 'Grandes Expéditions' (*La Liberté des rues*), where the poet describes an abortive exploration of the tiny spermatozoa-shaped circuit of metro line 7B (144–7).

7 This essay first appeared in *Nouvelle Revue française* 214 (October 1970),

and was reprinted in *Celle qui vient à pas légers* as the chapter entitled 'Langue maternelle' (35–46); the quotation appears on p. 38.

8 In *Recommandations aux promeneurs*, in the chapter entitled 'Lecture portative,' Réda denounces the motor car as '[la] principale responsable d'un abêtissement des peuples dits civilisés' (77).

9 Behind the fanciful humour of Réda's claim to polyglottal fluency – based on the numerous international brands of cigarette he has smoked (*RP*, 66) – lies a serious point about the body's powers of articulacy.

10 From an essay originally published in *Cahiers du chemin* in 1969 and reprinted in *CV* (p. 11).

11 Among the critics who have examined the tropes of 'circulation' in Réda's work, Jean-Claude Pinson contrasts functional circulation (systematizing, reductive, synonymous with the reality principle) with poetic circulation (pleasurable, unpredictable, actively creative), which he relates to a Heideggerian 'désubjectivisation' or self-dissolution in the material and the quotidian. See 'Jacques Réda, poète de la circulation lyrique,' in *Lire Réda*, 125–33. In an important essay that draws on Baudelaire, Benjamin and the Surrealist legacy, Catherine Coquio situates Réda as a continuer of the *flâneur* tradition, a sublime melder of the peripatetic and the metaphysical ('Le Retour du flâneur' in *Actes de Pau*, 45–64).

12 I am grateful to Michael Sheringham for alerting me to Rebecca Solnit's *Wanderlust: A History of Walking* (New York: Vintage, 2000), a sprightly cultural survey of walking in its pure and applied modes, that spans ancient Greece and Kinder Scout, modes of religious pilgrimage and situationist drifting, Muir Woods, and the traditional repression of women's freedom to walk. Regrettably, Réda is missing from Solnit's reflections on Paris as a privileged terrain of 'the chief theorists of walking' (212). In *Recommandations aux promeneurs*, in a chronicle entitled 'Où, comment, quand, pourquoi?', Réda suggests that the walker should be prepared always to alter his/her itinerary: 'Mon avis est qu'il faut avoir un but, mais qu'on ne doit pas lui sacrifier sa liberté. Mobile, aléatoire, son rôle est un peu celui que l'hypothèse joue dans la recherche scientifique, où elle conduit parfois à de l'imprévu' (36). In *Recommandations*, Réda scampers through, or hovers around, topics as diverse as reading material, staying with friends who have renovated a country property, fishing, rain, slowness – all aspects of travelling experienced by him, particularly in the provinces on longer excursions.

13 The jolt is a Rédean and postmodernist variation on the necessary physical and imaginative 'saccade' announced by Breton at the end of *Nadja* (1928).

14 From the essay entitled 'Le Quartier' in the chapter 'Habiter,' in Michel de Certeau et al., *L'Invention du quotidien*, vol. 2, 23.
15 The children's production of kinetic and verbal rhythms illustrates the Rédean principle whereby quotidian inventiveness generates poetry. The democratic vision of poetry-making is affirmed in *Celle qui vient à pas légers*, in the essay entitled 'L'Intermittent' (first published in *Cahiers du chemin*, 6 [April 1969]), in terms of a depersonalization and new subjective unfreighting: '[la poésie est] l'inflexion fondamentale, commune aux voix les plus diverses [...] Cette plénitude intermittente, celui qui la connaît un peu sait bien qu'elle est dépossession. Dépossession heureuse, mais dépossession. De sorte que la poésie a toujours été faite par tous, ou par personne si l'on préfère' (9–10).
16 Michel de Certeau, *L'Invention du quotidien*, vol. 1, 'Arts de faire' (Paris: Folio, rev. ed. 1990), 151–4.
17 Sheringham, *Parisian Fields*, 102–9, esp. 105–7.
18 The human subject becomes object and material for the creative agency of the city. This migration of subjective authority from explorer to the territory explored also attends Réda's poetic construction of rural space. In remarkably similar terms, in the prelude to his Lake District texts, Réda evokes the depersonalization necessary if one is to be permeated by the atmosphere of a place: '[S]'il est vrai qu'on apprend mieux à se connaître quand on voyage, on y fait aussi l'expérience d'une certaine dépersonnalisation, comme si l'on se transformait en un libre espace dont celui qu'on explore devient à son tour le promeneur' (*SM*, 69).
19 Letter of 22 October 2002.
20 I am playing here on Réda's evocation of 'une sorte de savane suburbaine' (*RP*, 114).
21 Certeau and Giard, 'Les Revenants de la ville,' in Certeau et al., *L'Invention du quotidien*, vol. 2, 189.
22 The Front de Seine development provokes a similar reaction from Roger Caillois in his *Petit guide du XVe arrondissement à l'usage des fantômes* (Paris: Fata Morgana, 1977): 'Le quartier [de Grenelle] cependant se transforme avec une hâte fébrile. Les anciennes maisons sont abattues par dizaines et remplacées par de grands ensembles massifs et uniformes. Constitués le plus souvent d'éléments préfabriqués, ils présentent presque nécessairement une disposition stricte et mécanique. Elle entraîne une répartition orthogonale, donc intégrale, de l'étendue disponible, exigence économique à laquelle ce type de construction est précisément destiné à répondre' (31).
23 Certeau and Giard, 'Les Revenants de la ville,' 190.

24 Dédé is one of the rare artisans of the everyday to be named, for Réda is more concerned with subjectivities than with subjects, with human traces than with individual persons; hence the prevalence of generic affective instances over biographical particulars.

25 In 'Problématique de l'espace dans *Les Ruines de Paris*' (*Lire Réda*, 31–41), Jean Pierrot evokes the poet's fascination for wastelands and (after-hours) building sites, the underground Bièvre river, and places closed off from the incursions of the everyday real.

26 Sheringham, *Parisian Fields*, 104. Sheringham is, in this respect, close to Jean-Claude Pinson's 'désubjectivisation' in *Lire Réda*, 125–33 (see note 11).

27 Sheringham, *Parisian Fields*, 105.

28 'L'Intermittent' (*CV*, 12).

29 Letter of 27 January 2003.

30 The quotation is taken from 'La Lumière à Châtillon' in *Beauté suburbaine*.

31 Letter of 22 October 2002.

32 John Gage, *Colour and Meaning: Art, Science and Symbolism* (London: Thames and Hudson, 1999), 56, discusses the efforts of theorists to extend art-historical colour description.

33 Letter of 22 October 2002.

34 'Le Poète attentif: Les couleurs chez Bonnefoy, Jaccottet et Réda,' in J.-M. Maulpoix, ed., *Figures du poète moderne, Cahiers de RITM* 21 (2000), 208. Denise Gellini, 'La Porte, le seuil' (*Actes de Pau*, 35–44), makes passing reference to the conscious painterliness of 'Saint-Germain au musée' in *Beauté suburbaine*.

35 Sheringham, 'Le Poète attentif,' 209.

36 *Lire Réda*, 40.

Summations, Speculations

1 Mieke Bal, *The Mottled Screen: Reading Proust Visually*, trans. Anna-Louise Milne (Stanford: Stanford University Press, 1997); Jean M. Duffy, *Reading between the Lines: Claude Simon and the Visual Arts* (Liverpool: Liverpool University Press, 1998).

2 Letter of 22 October 2002.

3 See Shirley Jordan, 'Moving Still Life: Jean-Daniel Pollet's Francis Ponge,' *French Studies* 54, no. 4 (2000), 479–92.

Bibliography

Ahearn, Edward J. *Rimbaud: Visions and Habitations*. Berkeley and Los Angeles: University of California Press, 1983.

Apollinaire, Guillaume. *Alcools et Calligrammes*. Ed. C. Debon. Paris: Imprimerie Nationale, 1991.

– *Oeuvres complètes*. Ed. Michel Décaudin. 4 vols. Paris: Balland and Lecat, 1964–6.

– *Les Peintres cubistes*. Paris: Hermann, 'Savoir,' 1965; repr. 1980.

Bal, Mieke. *The Mottled Screen: Reading Proust Visually*. Trans. Anna-Louise Milne. Stanford: Stanford University Press, 1997.

Barthes, Roland. 'Sémantique de l'objet.' In *Oeuvres complètes*, 65–73. Paris: Seuil, 1966–73; repr. 1994.

Bersani, Leo. *A Future for Astyanax: Character and Desire in Literature*. New York: Columbia University Press, 1984.

Beugnot, Bernard. *Poétique de Francis Ponge: Le palais diaphane*. Paris: Presses Universitaires de France, 1990.

Bohn, Willard. *Apollinaire, Visual Poetry and Art Criticism*. Lewisburg, London, Toronto: Bucknell University Press / Associated University Presses, 1993.

Bonnefoy, Yves. *Rimbaud*. Paris: Seuil, 1961; new ed. 1994.

Breton, André. *Nadja*. Paris: Gallimard, 1928; repr. 1964.

– *Entretiens avec André Parinaud: 1913–1952*. Paris: Gallimard, 1952.

Brooker, Jewel Spears, and Joseph Bentley. *Reading 'The Wasteland': Modernism and the Limits of Interpretation*. Amherst: Massachusetts University Press, 1990.

Brooks, Peter. *Body Work: Objects of Desire and Modern Narrative*. Cambridge, Mass., and London: Harvard University Press, 1993.

Burgos, Jean. *Pour une poétique de l'imaginaire*. Paris: Seuil, 1982.

Caillois, Roger. *Petit Guide du XVe arrondissement à l'usage des fantômes*. Paris: Fata Morgana, 1977.

Cascardi, Anthony. *The Subject of Modernity*. Cambridge: Cambridge University Press, 1992.

Cendrars, Blaise. *Oeuvres complètes*. Ed. R. Dumay and N. Frank. 16 vols. Paris: Le Club Français du Livre, 1968–71.

Certeau, Michel de. *L'Invention du quotidien*, vol. 1, 'Arts de faire.' Paris: Folio, 1980; rev. ed. 1990.

Certeau, Michel de, Luce Giard, and Pierre Mayol. *L'Invention du quotidien*, vol. 2, 'Habiter, cuisiner.' Paris: Folio, rev. ed. 1994.

Clark, T.J. *The Painting of Modern Life: Paris in the Art of Manet and His Followers*. London: Thames and Hudson, 1984.

Collier, Peter. 'Lire "Voyelles."' *Parade Sauvage* 5 (1989), 56–102.

Collot, Michel. 'Quelques versions de la scène primitive.' *Circeto* 2 (1984), 15–26.

– 'Rimbaud lecteur de *L'Homme qui rit*.' *Parade Sauvage* 2 (April 1985), 94–6.

– *Francis Ponge: Entre mots et choses*. Seyssel: Champ Vallon, 1991.

Compagnon, Antoine. 'Biography, Prosopography, Microhistory.' *New Comparison* 25 (Spring 1998), 71–82.

Coquio, Catherine. 'Le Retour du flâneur.' In Christine Van Rogger Andreucci, ed., *Approches de Jacques Réda: Actes du Colloque de l'Université de Pau*, 45–64. Pau: Publications de l'Université de Pau, 1994.

Davies, Margaret. *Une Saison en enfer d'Arthur Rimbaud*. Paris: Minard / Archives des Lettres Modernes, 1975.

Debon, Claude. *Guillaume Apollinaire après Alcools: Calligrammes, le poète et la guerre*. Paris: Minard / Lettres Modernes, 1981.

Décaudin, Michel. *Apollinaire critique d'art*. Paris: Paris-Musées/Gallimard, 1993.

Derrida, Jacques. *Signéponge*. Paris: Seuil, 1988; bilingual ed., New York: Columbia University Press, 1984.

Dillman, Karin J. *The Subject in Rimbaud: From Self to 'Je.'* American University Studies, series II, Romance Languages and Literature, 23. New York, Bern, Frankfurt am Main: Peter Lang, 1984.

Duffy, Jean M., *Reading between the Lines: Claude Simon and the Visual Arts*. Liverpool: Liverpool University Press, 1998.

Eakin, Paul John. *Fictions in Autobiography: Studies in the Art of Self-Invention* Princeton, NJ: Princeton University Press, 1985.

– *Touching the World: Reference in Autobiography*. Princeton, NJ: Princeton University Press, 1992.

Frey, Hans-Jost. *Studies in Poetic Discourse*. Stanford: Stanford University Press, 1996.

Gage, John. *Colour and Meaning: Art, Science and Symbolism*. London: Thames and Hudson, 1999.

Gellini, Denise. 'La Porte, le seuil.' In Christine Van Rogger Andreucci, ed.,

Approches de Jacques Réda: Actes du Colloque de l'Université de Pau, 35–44. Pau: Publications de l'Université de Pau, 1994.

Gleize, Jean.-Marie. *Francis Ponge*. Les contemporains. Paris: Seuil, 1988.

Greet, Anne Hyde, and S.I. Lockerbie. *Guillaume Apollinaire: Calligrammes*. Berkeley and Los Angeles: University of California Press, 1980.

Guisto, Jean-Pierre. *Rimbaud créateur*. Littératures, 13. Paris: Presses Universitaires de France / Publications de la Sorbonne, 1980.

Guyaux, André. *Poétique du fragment: Essai sur les Illuminations de Rimbaud*. Neuchâtel: La Baconnière, 1985.

– *Duplicités de Rimbaud*. Paris and Geneva: Champion-Slatkine, 1991.

Hamon, Philippe. 'Un discours contraint.' In R. Barthes et al., eds, *Littérature et réalité*, 119–81. Paris: Seuil, 1982.

Harrow, Susan. 'Naming the Modernist: The Ambiguities of Apollinaire.' In C. Berg, F. Durieux, and G. Lernout, eds, *The Turn of the Century: Modernism and Modernity in Literature and the Arts*. Berlin and New York: De Gruyter, 1995.

Higgins, Ian. *Francis Ponge*. London: Athlone Press, 1979.

– 'Language, Politics and Things.' *Neophilologus* 63 (1979), 347–62.

Houston, John Porter. *The Design of Rimbaud's Poetry*. New Haven and London: Yale University Press, 1963.

– *Patterns of Thought in Rimbaud and Mallarmé*. Lexington, Ky.: French Forum, 1986.

Jones, Gilbert E. *Apollinaire: La poésie de guerre*. Geneva, Paris: Slatkine, 1990.

Jordan, Shirley Ann. *The Art Criticism of Francis Ponge*. London: Maney / Modern Humanities Research Association, 1994.

– 'Moving Still Life: Jean-Daniel Pollet's Francis Ponge.' *French Studies* 54, no. 4 (2000), 479–92.

Lawler, James. *Rimbaud's Theatre of the Self*. Cambridge, Mass., and London: Harvard University Press, 1992.

Lefebvre, Henri. *Everyday Life in the Modern World*. Trans. Sacha Rabinovitch. London: Allen Lane, 1971.

Leiris, Michel. *Brisées*. Paris: Mercure de France, 1966; repr. Gallimard, Folio 'Essais,' 1992.

Lejeune, Philippe. *Le Pacte autobiographique*. Paris: Seuil, 1975.

Levenson, Michael. *Modernism and the Fate of Individuality*. Cambridge: Cambridge University Press, 1991.

Maldiney, Henri. *Le Vouloir dire de Francis Ponge*. La Versanne: encre marine, 1993.

Mathews, Timothy. *Reading Apollinaire: Theories of Poetic Language*. Manchester: Manchester University Press, 1987.

Mayol, Pierre. 'Le Quartier.' In Michel de Certeau et al., *L'Invention du quotidien*, vol. 2, 'Habiter' cuisiner,' 13–185.

Met, Philippe. 'Francis Ponge ou la fabrique du (lieu) commun.' *Poétique* 26 (1995), 303–18.

– 'Les censures du "Verre d'eau."' *Genesis* 12 (1997), 49–66.

– 'Poésie de résistance et résistance de/à la poésie: Le cas Ponge.' *Dalhousie French Studies* 51 (2000), 109–20.

Mitchell, Juliet. *The Selected Melanie Klein.* Harmondsworth: Penguin, 1986.

Murphy, Steve. *Le Premier Rimbaud: Ou l'apprentissage de la subversion.* Paris, Lyon: CNRS / Presses Universitaires de Lyon, 1991.

– *Rimbaud et la ménagerie impériale.* Paris, Lyon: CNRS / Presses Universitaires de Lyon, 1991)

Murray, Jack. *Landscapes of Alienation: Ideological Subversion in Kafka, Céline and Onetti.* Stanford: Stanford University Press, 1991.

Perloff, Marjorie. *The Futurist Moment: Avant-Garde, Avant-Guerre and the Language of Rupture.* Chicago and London: University of Chicago Press, 1986.

Pinson, Jean-Claude. 'Jacques Réda, poète de la circulation lyrique.' In Hervé Micolet ed., *Lire Réda*, 125–33. Lyon: Presses Universitaires de Lyon, 1994.

Ponge, Francis. *Le Grand Recueil: Méthodes.* Paris: Gallimard, 1961.

– *Pour un Malherbe.* Paris: Gallimard, 1965.

– *Le Savon.* Paris: Gallimard, 1967.

– *Entretiens de Francis Ponge avec Philippe Sollers.* Paris: Gallimard/Seuil, 1970.

– *La Fabrique du pré.* 'Les Sentiers de la création.' Geneva: Albert Skira, 1971.

– *L'Atelier contemporain.* Paris: Gallimard, 1977.

– *Comment une figue de paroles et pourquoi.* Paris: Flammarion, 1977; repr. 1997.

– *Nouveau nouveau recueil.* Vol. II. Paris: Gallimard, 1992.

– *Oeuvres complètes.* Vol. I. Ed. Bernard Beugnot. Paris: Gallimard, 1999.

Pound, Ezra. *ABC of Reading.* New York: New Directions, 1960.

Réda, Jacques. *Les Ruines de Paris.* Paris: Gallimard, 1977; repr. Collection 'Poésie,' 1993.

– *Beauté suburbaine.* Périgueux: Fanlac, 1985.

– *Celle qui vient à pas légers.* Montpellier: Fata Morgana, 1985; repr. 1999.

– *Châteaux des courants d'air.* Paris: Gallimard, 1986.

– *Recommandations aux promeneurs.* Paris: Gallimard, 1988.

– *Le Sens de la marche.* Paris: Gallimard, 1990.

– 'Souvenirs de Cambridge.' In Christine Van Rogger Andreucci, ed., *Approches de Jacques Réda: Actes du Colloque de l'Université de Pau*, 9–12. Pau: Publications de l'Université de Pau, 1994.

– *La Liberté des rues.* Paris: Gallimard, 1997.

– *Le Citadin*. Paris: Gallimard, 1998.
– *La Course*. Paris: Gallimard, 1999.
– *Accidents de la circulation*. Paris: Gallimard, 2001.
Reverdy, Pierre. *Les Ardoises du toit* (1918). In *Plupart du temps*, I. Paris:
    Gallimard, 1944.
Richard, Jean-Pierre. *Onze études sur la poésie moderne*. Paris: Seuil, 1962; repr.
    1981.
– 'Fabrique de la figure.' In *Pages paysages – Microlectures*, II. Paris: Seuil, 1984.
Richter, Mario. 'Échos baudelairiens dans le "prologue" d'*Une Saison en enfer*
    de Rimbaud.' *Parade Sauvage* 5 (November 1998), 86–90.
Rieu, Josiane, 'La Subjectivité dans *Le Parti pris des choses*.' In *Francis Ponge,
    Cahier de l'Herne*, 86–111. Paris: L'Herne, 1986.
Riffaterre, Michael. *La Production du texte*. Paris: Seuil, 1984.
– 'The Primacy of Words: Francis Ponge's Reification.' In C. Minahen, ed.,
    Figuring Things: Char, Ponge and Poetry in the Twentieth Century, 27–38.
    Lexington, Ky.: French Forum, 1994.
Rimbaud, Arthur. *Oeuvres complètes*. Ed. Antoine Adam. Paris: Gallimard,
    'Pléiade,' 1972.
– *Oeuvres complètes*. Ed. Pierre Brunel. Paris: Livre de Poche, 1999.
– *Oeuvres complètes*, vol. 1, *Poésies*. Ed. Steve Murphy. Paris: Champion, 1999.
Robb, Graham. *Rimbaud*. New York and London: Norton, 2001.
Robbe-Grillet, Alain. *Pour un nouveau roman*. Paris: Éditions de Minuit, 1963.
Robillard, Monic. '*Pour un Malherbe* ou l'autobiographie nouée.' *Études
    Françaises* 17, nos. 1–2 (April 1981), 129–42.
Ross, Kristin. *The Emergence of Social Space: Rimbaud and the Paris Commune*.
    Minneapolis: University of Minnesota Press, 1988.
Sabatier, Robert. 'Son parti des choses.' *Magazine littéraire* 260 (December
    1988), 34–7.
Sacchi, Sergio. 'Portrait de l'artiste en grand magasin.' *Parade Sauvage*, Actes
    du Colloque 'Rimbaud ou "La liberté libre,"' 11–13 September 1986, 119–35.
Sacks-Galey, Pénélope. *Calligramme ou écriture figurée: Apollinaire inventeur de
    formes*. Paris: Minard/Lettres Modernes, 1988.
Sartre, Jean-Paul. 'L'Homme et les choses.' *Situations* (Paris: Gallimard,
    1947), I.
Scarry, Elaine. *Resisting Representation*. Oxford: Oxford University Press, 1994.
– *On Beauty and Being Just*. Princeton, NJ: Princeton University Press, 1999.
Sedgwick, Eve Kosofsky. *Between Men: English Literature and Male Homosocial
    Desire*. New York: Columbia University Press, 1985; repr. 1992.
Sheringham, Michael. *French Autobiography: Devices and Desires*. Oxford:
    Oxford University Press, 1993.

- 'City Space, Mental Space, Poetic Space: Paris in Breton, Benjamin and Réda.' In M. Sheringham, ed., *Parisian Fields*, 85–114. London: Reaktion, 1996.
- 'Attending to the Everyday: Blanchot, Lefebvre, Certeau, Perec.' *French Studies* 54, no. 2 (2000), 187–99.
- 'Le poète attentif: Les couleurs chez Bonnefoy, Jaccottet et Réda.' In Jean-Michel Maulpoix, ed., *Figures du poète moderne, Cahiers de RITM* 21 (2000), 193–211.

Solnit, Rebecca. *Wanderlust: A History of Walking*. New York: Vintage, 2000.

Steiner, Wendy. *The Trouble with Beauty*. London: Heinemann, 2001.

Theweleit, Klaus. *Male Fantasies: Women, Floods, Bodies, History*. Trans. Stephen Conway. Minneapolis: University of Minnesota Press, 1987.

Thum, Reinhard H. *The City: Baudelaire, Rimbaud, Verhaeren*. New York, Bern, Frankfurt am Main: Peter Lang, 1994.

Tournadre, Claude [Claude Debon]. 'Notes sur le vocabulaire de la guerre dans *Calligrammes*.' *Guillaume Apollinaire* 13, 65–75. Paris: Minard / Lettres Modernes, 1976.

Trotter, David. *Cooking with Mud: The Idea of Mess in Nineteenth-century Art and Fiction*. Oxford: Oxford University Press, 2000.

Warner, Marina. *Monuments and Maidens: The Allegory of the Female Form*. London: Weidenfeld and Nicholson, 1985.

Wing, Nathaniel. *The Limits of Narrative: Essays on Baudelaire, Flaubert, Rimbaud and Mallarmé*. Cambridge: Cambridge University Press, 1986.

Index

Adam, Antoine, 225–6n1
Ahearn, Edward J., 56, 226–7n2, 232n60, 233n65
Apollinaire, Guillaume, 4–8, 10, 62–112, 217–21, 223, 225n1; *surnaturalisme*, 77–8, 151, 169
– *Alcools*, 5, 7, 62–7, 70, 85; 'La Chanson du mal-aimé,' 63, 65–6, 84, 238n38; '1909,' 51, 70; 'Rhénanes,' 62; 'Le Voyageur,' 51, 62, 66, 70, 84; 'Zone,' 62, 65–7, 78, 84, 235n8, 236–7n25, 246–7n16
– *Calligrammes*, 5, 7, 62–112, 219; 'À l'Italie,' 98, 242n61; 'À Nîmes,' 87, 93, 100–1, 106, 108, 243n68; 'Arbre,' 63, 68–73, 80–1, 236n16; 'À travers l'Europe,' 69; 'Carte postale,' 90, 99; 'C'est Lou qu'on la nommait,' 101, 105, 238n40; 'Chant de l'honneur,' 103; 'Chant de l'horizon en Champagne,' 96, 103; 'Les Collines,' 67, 235nn6, 11; 'Dans l'abri-caverne,' 95, 101–2, 108; 'De la batterie de tir,' 105, 242n64; 'Désir,' 96, 106, 239–40n49; '2ème canonnier conducteur,' 96, 99, 105; 'Du Coton dans les

oreilles,' 91, 96, 105, 242n65; 'Échelon,' 92, 96, 97, 103; 'Un fantôme de nuées,' 70, 74, 76–8; 'Les Fenêtres,' 68–70, 72–3, 79–80, 234n3; 'Fête,' 93, 242n61; 'Les Feux du bivouac,' 110; 'Fumées,' 109; 'Fusée,' 96, 106; 'Les Grenadines repentantes,' 242n61; 'Guerre,' 96, 104, 239–40n49; 'L'Inscription anglaise,' 110; 'La Jolie Rousse,' 63, 84, 89, 111–12, 235n11; 'Lettre-Océan,' 68, 70; 'Liens,' 70–1, 234n3; 'Loin du pigeonnier,' 96; 'Lundi rue Christine,' 68–70, 73–5, 79–80, 234n3; 'Merveille de la guerre,' 87, 102; 'Le Musicien de Saint-Merry,' 77–8, 234n3; 'Mutation,' 93, 103; 'La Nuit d'avril 1915,' 96, 239–40n49; 'Océan de terre,' 102; 'Ombre,' 95; 'Oracles,' 92; 'Le Palais du tonnerre,' 94; 'Paysage,' 68; 'La Petite Auto,' 71, 84, 87–9, 238n40; '14 juin 1915,' 96; 'Saillant,' 95, 96, 238n40; 'Les Saisons,' 96–7; 'Les Soupirs du servant de Dakar,' 97, 239–40n49; 'Souvenirs,' 92; 'SP,' 96; 'Sur les

prophéties,' 75–6; 'Veille,' 238n40;
'Venu de Dieuze,' 96; 'La Victoire,'
74–5, 222, 235n11
– *L'Esprit nouveau et les poètes*, 66,
236n19
– *Les Peintres cubistes*, 80–1
Aragon, Louis, 82; *Le Paysan de Paris*,
206
Ariosto, Ludovico: *Orlando furioso*,
145–6
Audisio, Gabriel, 118
autobiography, and modernism, 85–
6, 98–107, 238n39; aspects of, in
Apollinaire, 219; —, in modern
poetry, 4–5, 7–8, 11–12, 14, 29–44,
59, 61, 81–112, 237–8n35

Bal, Mieke, 222
Barthes, Roland, 8, 67–9, 236n17
Baudelaire, Charles, 3, 24, 169, 198,
210, 225n3, 226–7n2, 249n38,
253n11; 'Le Cygne,' 193
Baudrillard, Jean, 83
Beckett, Samuel, 127, 221
Benjamin, Walter, 253n11
Bentley, Joseph, 231n50
Bersani, Leo, 15, 34, 45, 51, 55, 226–
7n2, 233nn67, 72, 75
Beugnot, Bernard, 113, 243–4n2, 250n48
body, representation of, in poetry, 4,
102–11, 218; in Ponge, 134–49; in
Réda, 9, 166–90; in Rimbaud, 7,
11–14, 18–19, 21–8, 30, 32–5, 37,
39–40, 43, 52
Boethius: *Consolation of Philosophy*,
116
Bohn, Willard, 234–5n5
Bonnard, Pierre, 210
Bonnefoy, Yves, 13, 19, 24, 43, 226–

7n2, 228n16, 229n32, 231n47,
232n62
Bouguereau, Adolphe William, 25
Bourgeois, Louise, 221
Braque, Georges, 79, 133, 150, 158,
250n56
Breton, André, 82; *Nadja*, 52, 82–3,
107, 253–4n13
Brooker, Jewel Spears, 231n50
Brooks, Peter, 228n21
Brunel, Pierre, 228n23, 228–9n28
Burgos, Jean, 234–5n5

Céline, Louis-Ferdinand, 25, 50, 124,
219
Cabanel, Alexandre, 25
Caillois, Roger, 254n22
Cascardi, Anthony, 99
Cendrars, Blaise, 69, 73, 235n8,
236nn16, 22
Certeau, Michel de, 9, 75, 164–5,
186–7, 193, 196–7, 199, 221, 236–
7n25, 252n3; *rhétoriques cheminatoires*, 187
Charroi de Nîmes, Le, 100
Chirico, Giorgio de, 50
city, representations of, in modern
poetry, 49–52, 65–6, 70, 76, 120,
164–216, 219
Clark, T.J., 247n21
Collier, Peter, 232n61
Collot, Michel, 113, 228–9n28,
230n42, 243–4n2, 244–5n3
colour, representation of, in
Apollinaire, 64, 69–70, 79–80; in
modern poetry, 4, 218; in Ponge,
145–6; in Réda, 10, 170, 188, 209–
16, 221, 222; in Rimbaud, 11,
13–17, 23–5, 46–7, 60–1, 222

Compagnon, Antoine, 240n52
Coppée, François, 228–9n28
Coquio, Catherine, 253n11
Courbet, Gustave: 'L'Origine du monde,' 19, 228n21
cubism: anticipated by Rimbaud, 13–15, 31–2, 44, 51; aspects of, in Apollinaire, 62, 79–81, 85, 98, 221, 223; —, in modern literature, 229n35
culture critique, aspects of: in Ponge, 117–31, 219; in Réda, 179–81; in Rimbaud, 20–9, 219

Davies, Margaret, 230n45, 230–1n46, 231n48
Debon, Claude, 64, 234n2, 237n33, 239n44
Delaunay, Robert, 64, 70, 223, 234n4, 235n8, 236n19
Delaunay, Sonia, 235n8
Demeny, Paul, 11, 19, 29, 225–6n1
Derrida, Jacques, 113, 243–4n2
Dillman, Karin J., 227n3
Duffy, Jean, 222
Durry, Marie-Jeanne, 237n31

Eakin, Paul John, 8, 238–9n42
Eliot, T.S., 8, 72, 241–2n60; 'The Love Song of J. Alfred Prufrock,' 122; The Wasteland, 36, 73, 231n50
Emin, Tracy, 221
Ernst, Max, 25, 52

Faulkner, William, 252n3
Fautrier, Gabriel: 'Otages' series, 111
Flaubert, Gustave, 59
Follain, Jean, 252n3
Frey, Hans-Jost, 225n3

Friedlander, Lee, 219
futurism, 63, 235n8

Gage, John, 255n32
Gauguin, Paul, 210
Gellini, Denise, 255n34
Giacometti, Alberto, 131
Giard, Luce, 164–5, 193, 196–7
Gleize, Jean-Marie, 113, 243–4n2, 246n14
Greet, Anne Hyde, 64, 234n3
Groethuysen, Bernard, 245–6n9
Guisto, Jean-Pierre, 232n57
Guyaux, André, 31, 226–7n2, 227n6, 230–1n46

Hamon, Philippe, 90, 239n45
Harrow, Susan, 234n1
Higgins, Ian, 113
Houston, John Porter, 226–7n2
Hugo, Victor: influence on Rimbaud, 230n42

Ionesco, Eugène, 236n17
Izambard, Georges, 12, 20, 40, 225–6n1, 230n40

Jones, Gilbert E., 234n3
Jordan, Shirley Ann, 247n23
Joyce, James, 36, 222, 241–2n60

Kafka, Franz, 240n53
Kant, Immanuel, 54
Klein, Melanie, 243n67
Klein, Yves, 222

Lautréamont, Comte de (Isidore Ducasse), 245n6
Lawler, James, 13, 226–7n2, 232n60

Lefebvre, Henri, 8, 124–5
Leiris, Michel, 54, 233n70
Lejeune, Philippe, 8, 237–8n35, 239n43
Levenson, Michael, 89
Lockerbie, S.I., 64, 234n3

Maldiney, Henri, 244–5n3
Malherbe, François de, 113, 149, 248n32
Mallarmé, Stéphane, 5, 225n3, 226–7n2
Manet, Édouard: 'Le Bar aux Folies-Bergère,' 125–6, 247n21
Mapplethorpe, Robert, 218
Marinetti, Filippo, 8, 72
Martineau, Henri, 236–7n25
Mathews, Timothy, 64, 225n1, 234n2
Matisse, Henri, 210
Mayol, Pierre, 184
Met, Philippe, 113, 243–4n2, 250n54
Micolet, Hervé, 225n2
Mitchell, Juliet, 243n67
modernism, 4; and autobiography, 85–6, 98–107; and poetry, 3, 6–8, 11, 65, 71–2, 83–5, 234n1, 237nn29, 34, 241–2n60
Murphy, Steve, 5, 226–7n2, 227n11, 228–9n28, 229nn29, 30, 36, 230nn39, 40, 233n69
Murray, Jack, 240n53

Novarina, Valère, 222

Parnassianism, 19, 60, 230n40, 231n48
Paulhan, Jean, 243–4n2, 250–1n57
Perloff, Marjorie, 64, 234n2, 235n8
Picasso, Pablo, 237n26; 'Les Demoiselles d'Avignon,' 107, 222; 'L'Homme à la pipe,' 44

Pierrot, Jean, 215, 255n25
Pinson, Jean-Claude, 253n11
Pollet, Jean-Daniel, 223
Ponge, Francis, 4–8, 10, 113–63, 179–80, 217–20, 222–3, 225n1
– L'Atelier contemporain, 131, 247n23; 'L'Atelier,' 137–8; 'Braque – Dessins,' 150, 250n56; 'Braque le réconciliateur,' 133, 249n38; 'Courte méditation réflexe aux fragments de miroir,' 154; 'Joca seria: Notes sur les sculptures d'Alberto Giacometti,' 131; 'Notes sur les Otages, peintures de Fautrier,' 111; 'L'Objet, c'est la poétique,' 133, 146, 153, 247n24
– Cahier de l'Herne: 'Je suis un suscitateur,' 119
– Comment une figue de paroles et pourquoi, 116–17, 135, 162, 251n66
– Douze petits écrits, 8, 115, 117–21, 124–5, 129–32, 138, 162, 245–6n9, 246n11; 'Compliment à l'industriel,' 123–4; 'Le Martyre du jour ou "Contre l'évidence prochaine,"' 127; 'Monologue de l'employé,' 121–3; 'Le Patient Ouvrier,' 127; 'Sur un sujet d'ennui,' 123; 'Trois poésies: I,' 123
– Entretiens avec Philippe Sollers, 140, 143–4, 162, 246nn11, 14, 248n28, 251n69
– La Fabrique du pré, 120, 134, 163, 245n6, 246n13
– Le Grand Recueil, 118
– Lyres, 120; 'Dimanche, ou l'artiste,' 128; 'Le Ministre,' 247n19
– Méthodes, 250n47; 'L'Homme à grands traits,' 247–8n25; 'Le

Monde,' 153–4; 'Le Murmure (condition et destin de l'artiste),' 152–3; 'My Creative Method,' 132, 154, 160; 'Pochades en prose,' 156–7; 'La Pratique de la littérature,' 145–6; 'La Seine,' 147–8; 'Tentative orale,' 133, 136, 153; 'Le Verre d'eau,' 141, 147

– *Le Parti pris des choses*, 6, 113–15, 117–20, 129–31, 138, 161–3, 234–5n5, 245–6n9, 246nn11, 14; 'Bords de mer,' 141; 'La Bougie,' 156; 'Le Cageot,' 133, 151, 158; 'De l'eau,' 147; 'Escargots,' 149–50, 161; 'La Fin de l'automne,' 140–1, 158; 'Le Gymnaste,' 156, 249n44; 'La Jeune Mère,' 137; 'Le Mollusque,' 162–3; 'Le Morceau de viande,' 137, 249n44; 'La Mousse,' 157, 160, 249n44; 'L'Orange,' 134–5, 147, 159; 'Le Pain,' 19, 137, 152, 158–9; 'Le Papillon,' 159–60; 'Les Plaisirs de la porte,' 136; 'Pluie,' 147, 155–7, 160; 'R.C. Seine n°,' 25, 118, 121, 123–5; 'Le Restaurant Lemeunier rue de la Chaussée-d'Antin,' 118, 121, 125–6; 'Rhum des fougères,' 136

– *Pièces*: 'L'Abricot,' 145; 'La Cheminée d'usine,' 249n44; 'La Pomme de terre,' 135

– *Pour un Malherbe*, 114–16, 134, 138–9, 146, 149, 152, 245n5, 248n27, 249n39

– *Proêmes*, 120; 'L'Avenir des paroles,' 129; 'Les Écuries d'Augias,' 129–30; 'La Forme du monde,' 132, 146–7; 'Introduction au "Galet,"' 139–40, 249n36; 'Notes premières de l'homme,' 243n1; 'Pas et le saut,' 8; 'Préface aux *Sapates*,' 151, 250–1n57; 'Témoignage,' 135–6

– *La Rage de l'expression*, 156, 162; 'Le Carnet du bois de pins,' 120, 138; 'La Guêpe,' 160–1; 'L'Oeillet,' 162

– *Le Savon*, 120, 142–4, 149

potatoes, 27, 135, 192, 200

Pound, Ezra, 235n7

Poussin, Nicolas, 210

Proust, Marcel, 194, 222, 250n48

Queneau, Raymond, 219

Réda, Jacques, 4, 6–7, 9–10, 164–216, 217–18, 220–3, 225n2; *vers mâché*, 177

– *Accidents de la circulation*, 9, 165–7, 171, 175, 179, 182, 190, 197–8, 208; 'Bords du treizième,' 172–3; 'Dans le dixième,' 175–6; 'Dans le huitième,' 169; 'Les Gris,' 181; 'Rue Serpollet,' 187–8

– *Beauté suburbaine*, 171, 202–3; 'Tôlerie peinture,' 200

– *Celle qui vient à pas légers*, 178, 214; 'L'Intermittent,' 209, 254n15; 'Langue maternelle,' 172

– *Châteaux des courants d'air*, 168, 171, 177–8, 188–90, 197, 199, 201–2, 206, 210; 'Au beau milieu,' 170; 'Au printemps,' 181–2; 'Au seuil de l'inconnu,' 206; 'By Night,' 205; 'Et avec ça?', 193; 'L'Été,' 207–8; 'Un jardin,' 214; 'Une lettre de Vaugirard,' 168, 206; 'Un passage,' 186, 196; 'XVe magique,' 207; 'Vers l'automne,' 214; 'Les Visiteurs du samedi soir', 198

– *Le Citadin*, 181; 'Automne,' 171; 'Bleuâtre? Jaunâtre?', 211

– *La Course*, 171, 178, 202, 210, 215; 'Le Chantier,' 196; 'Un Citadin,' 172, 186–7; 'La Course,' 177–8, 213; 'Un drame au Luxembourg,' 216; 'Éloge de la brique,' 214; 'Orage à Saint-Cloud,' 181; 'Un passage,' 183
– *La Liberté des rues*, 171, 179, 184, 189–90, 194, 214; '*Chutes répétées*,' 184; 'Grandes Expéditions,' 252n6; '*Paris spiral*,' 201
– *Le Lit de la reine*, 170
– *Recommandations aux promeneurs*: 'Éloge modéré de la lenteur,' 202; 'Lecture portative,' 253n8; 'Où, comment, quand, pourquoi?', 253n12
– *Retour au calme*, 178, 211
– *Les Ruines de Paris*, 6, 9, 165–6, 171–2, 178, 180, 182–4, 186, 188, 191–3, 195–201, 203–4, 207, 210–11, 213, 215, 254n20, 255n25; 'Aux environs,' 203; 'Du jour au lendemain,' 181; 'Je ne sais trop ce qu'elles penseront,' 185–6; 'Je rapporte...,' 224; 'On ne sait quoi d'introuvable,' 173; 'Le Pied furtif de l'hérétique,' 212, 215; 'Que le Nord transcendantal du poète,' 174–5
– *Le Sens de la marche*, 254n18; 'Bonjour, adieu,' 168
– 'Souvenirs de Cambridge,' 208
Rauschenberg, Robert, 221
Reverdy, Pierre, 79, 234–5n5
Richard, Jean-Pierre, 113, 243–4n2
Richter, Mario, 231n48
Rieu, Josiane, 244–5n3
Riffaterre, Michael, 113, 243–4n2, 244–5n3

Rimbaud, Arthur, 4–7, 10, 11–61, 85, 169, 179–80, 217–19, 221–3, 225nn1, 3, 245n6
– *Illuminations*, 5–6, 12–15, 26, 29, 33, 44, 45–61, 118, 222, 227n6, 232n57, 233n67; 'Angoisse,' 48; 'Après le déluge,' 53–4; 'Aube,' 52, 59, 227n3; 'À une raison,' 59; 'Barbare,' 57; 'Being Beauteous,' 46; 'Conte,' 54, 58–9; 'Départ,' 48–9, 54; 'Enfance,' 54, 56; 'Fleurs,' 53, 57; 'Jeunesse,' 56–7; 'Marine,' 53; 'Matinée d'ivresse,' 52, 56; 'Métropolitain,' 232–3n63; 'Mystique,' 58; 'Nocturne vulgaire,' 53, 56; 'Ouvriers,' 59, 233n65; 'Parade,' 57–9; 'Phrases,' 58; 'Les Ponts,' 45, 51, 59, 233n66; 'Promontoire,' 57; 'Royauté,' 54, 58; 'Scènes,' 58; 'Soir historique,' 58; 'Veillées,' 55, 58; 'Vies,' 48–9, 59; 'Ville,' 45, 50–1, 59, 121, 233n65; 'Villes I,' 57; 'Villes II,' 50–1, 59
– *lettres du voyant*, 11–12, 19–21, 40–1, 58, 232n62
– *Poésies*, 5–6, 13–14, 15–29, 48–51, 59–61; 'Accroupissements,' 28–9; 'À la musique,' 21, 228n26, 247n18; 'Les Assis,' 21, 24–5, 60; 'Au Cabaret-Vert,' 17–18, 32; 'Le Bateau ivre,' 13, 15, 21, 37, 45–8, 230n38, 232n62; 'Ce qu'on dit au poète à propos de fleurs,' 29, 50, 230n43; 'Les Éffarés,' 19, 228n23; 'L'Étoile a pleuré rose ...,' 52, 233n69; 'Les Étrennes des orphelins,' 22; 'Le Forgeron,' 16, 227n11, 229n32; 'Ma bohème,' 17–18, 32; 'La Maline,' 228n15; 'Oraison du soir,' 23; 'Les Pauvres à l'église,' 20; 'Les Poètes

de sept ans,' 16, 26–9, 230n39; 'Les Premières communions,' 20, 23, 229n29; 'Les Reparties de Nina,' 18, 229n34; 'Roman,' 16, 32; 'Sensation,' 13, 18–19, 26, 32, 60; 'Soleil et chair,' 18–19; 'Vénus Anadyomène,' 16, 21, 25, 50, 52, 60, 229n32, 229–30n37, 233n69; 'Voyelles,' 15, 21, 45–6, 53, 222, 232nn60, 61
– Une Saison en enfer, 5–6, 11–14, 16, 22, 26, 29–45, 48–50, 57–61, 221, 227n6, 231n47, 232nn54, 57; 'Adieu,' 33–4, 43; 'Délires: Alchimie du verbe,' 32–3, 35, 37, 39, 41, 44, 230–1n46; 'Délires: Vierge folle,' 38–9; 'L'Éclair,' 35, 38, 42; 'L'Impossible,' 42; 'Matin,' 35–6, 38, 43; 'Mauvais sang,' 30, 34–8, 41, 43–4; 'Nuit de l'enfer,' 33, 38–41; prologue, 33–4, 41
– Vers nouveaux, 'Bannières de mai,' 16; 'Bonne pensée du matin,' 230–1n46; 'Chanson de la plus haute tour,' 32, 230–1n46; 'Honte,' 27, 229–30n37; 'Larme,' 230–1n46
Robb, Graham, 5, 17, 225–6n1, 228n22, 230n41, 231n51, 232nn54, 62
Robbe-Grillet, Alain, 114, 236n17, 251n62
Robillard, Monic, 245n5
Ross, Kristin, 5, 225–6n1, 226–7n2, 227n12, 228nn17, 26, 230n43
Rothko, Mark, 222

Sacchi, Sergio, 232–3n63
Sacks-Galey, Pénélope, 234–5n5
Sartre, Jean-Paul, 113, 236n17, 243n1, 244–5n3

Scarry, Elaine, 158, 240n50, 250n50
Sedgwick, Eve Kosofsky, 241n57
Shakespeare, William, 59
Sheringham, Michael, 6, 168, 188, 208, 210, 212, 236n23, 238n39, 241n58, 253n12
Sherman, Cindy, 218
Simon, Claude, 222
Sollers, Philippe, 113, 118, 140, 143–4, 162, 243n1, 244–5n3, 248n28
Solnit, Rebecca, 253n12
Spada, Marcel, 134
Steiner, Wendy, 229n33, 233n71, 243n69
Stravinsky, Igor, 222
Supervielle, Jules, 252n3
surrealism, 25, 151, 222, 253n11; surrealist attitudes to the First World War, 82, 237n31

Theweleit, Klaus, 241n57
Thum, Reinhard H., 233n66
Tournadre, Claude, 240n55
Trotter, David, 229n35

Van Rogger Andreucci, Christine, 225n2
Varda, Agnès, 9, 194–5; Les Glaneurs et la glaneuse, 191–2
Verlaine, Paul, 39, 231n51
Villon, François, 101

war, representation of: in Apollinaire, 81–112
Warner, Marina, 242n63
Wing, Nathaniel, 31, 40, 42, 45, 225n3, 226–7n2, 232n56

Zola, Émile, 126, 247n22